COLONIAL PHANTOMS

D0747177

NATION OF NATIONS: IMMIGRANT HISTORY AS AMERICAN HISTORY

General Editor: Matthew Jacobson
Founding Editors: Matthew Jacobson and Werner Sollors

Colonial Phantoms

*Belonging and Refusal in the Dominican Americas,
from the 19th Century to the Present*

Dixa Ramírez

NEW YORK UNIVERSITY PRESS

New York

NEW YORK UNIVERSITY PRESS
New York
www.nyupress.org

© 2018 by New York University

References to Internet websites (URLs) were accurate at the time of writing. Neither the author nor New York University Press is responsible for URLs that may have expired or changed since the manuscript was prepared.

ISBN: 978-1-4798-5045-7 (hardback)
ISBN: 978-1-4798-6756-1 (paperback)

For Library of Congress Cataloging-in-Publication data, please contact the Library of Congress.

New York University Press books are printed on acid-free paper, and their binding materials are chosen for strength and durability. We strive to use environmentally responsible suppliers and materials to the greatest extent possible in publishing our books.

Manufactured in the United States of America

10 9 8 7 6 5 4 3 2 1

Also available as an ebook

CONTENTS

Introduction

At the Navel of the Americas

[T]he stranger [. . .] showed no colors [. . .]. It might have been but a deception of the vapors, but the longer the stranger was watched the more singular appeared her maneuvers. Erelong it seemed hard to decide whether she meant to come in or no—what she wanted, or what she was about.
—Herman Melville, "Benito Cereno" (1855)

The history of San Domingo was never completely written, and if it were, would never find a reader.
—J. Dennis Harris, *A Summer on the Borders of the Caribbean Sea* (1860)

In 1855, *Putnam's Monthly* published Herman Melville's novella "Benito Cereno" over three issues.[1] Melville based the story on the real-life account of a revolt on the *Tryal*, a slaving ship with Spanish-owned subjects from West Africa en route to Argentina. Melville's narrative develops from the perspective of Amasa Delano of Massachusetts, who spots a slaving ship from his seal hunting vessel off the coast of Chile. Delano sees that "the stranger [*San Dominick*], viewed through the glass, showed no colors," and, thus, did not reveal its provenance, ownership, or purpose.[2] From a better perspective, the ship then "appeared like a whitewashed monastery after a thunderstorm."[3] Closer still, it seems as if Delano has finally discerned what "the stranger" is about: "the true character of the vessel was plain—a Spanish merchantman of the first class, carrying negro slaves, amongst other valuable freight, from one colonial port to another."[4] And yet, Delano had not actually realized the "true character" of the ghostly ship, even after spending hours onboard the *San Dominick* asking its captain, the Spaniard Benito Cereno, his crew,

1

and some of the enslaved subjects what had caused the ship's stranding. The rest of the story unspools the many ways in which Delano's perception repeatedly fools him.

After several hours of growing confusion and dread, Delano suddenly realizes that the ship's cargo, black "slaves," had mutinied weeks earlier and were holding the (mostly white) crew hostage. The world order to which he had been accustomed had been turned on its head. He could not fathom that the enslaved subjects on the ship had mutinied and turned "the order of things" upside down. The terror humming beneath the story is that the *San Dominick*, named by Melville as a direct allusion to the Haitian Revolution, allegorizes the threat of slave insurrection and black self-governance.[5] Although "Benito Cereno" was written in 1855 and the real-life slave rebellion to which it referred took place in 1805, Melville set the novella in 1799, the middle point of the revolts and other myriad events now called the Haitian Revolution (1791–1804).

I start this book about Dominican cultural expression with "Benito Cereno" because it is an apt allegory for what generations of scholars have been unable to see: that anxieties about Haiti often applied equally to the entire island, Hispaniola, which in the early nineteenth century encompassed both Haiti and the eastern colony of Santo Domingo. The ghostly ship and the events onboard confused Delano because his world contained white masters and black slaves, and not black subjects holding whites captive while pretending to be enslaved. His worldview prevented him from "reading" or "perceiving" reality. Similarly, the Haitian Revolution augured over a century during which outsiders often did not care to differentiate between the two sides of the island, even beyond the twenty-two-year span (1822–1844) when the entire island was no longer under Haitian governance. Analyzing a variety of cultural expression by and about Dominicans from the late nineteenth century to the present, including literature, government documents, music, the visual arts, public monuments, film, and ephemeral and stage performance, *Colonial Phantoms* explores how Dominicans have negotiated the miscomprehension, miscategorization, and misperception—or what I call ghosting—of this territory.[6]

While my choice to open this book with the words of a canonical, white U.S. author may seem to undermine the project of centering Dominican cultural expression, I argue that it demonstrates how inequalities of power influence perception, and, as such, fields of knowledge. This book is about Dominicans' attempts to assert themselves in the face of a willingly amnesic and relentlessly self-assured U.S. imperialism, or what Anne McClintock calls "the administration of forgetting" in the process of "imperial ghosting."[7] Indeed, dominant Western discourses have ghosted Dominican history and culture despite its central place in the architecture of the Americas not only as the first Spanish colony in the hemisphere but also, alongside Haiti, as an exemplar of black self-rule. However, what Haiti came to represent in the Western imaginary overshadowed the other examples of free black subjectivity as they predominated for centuries on the eastern side of the island. In associating Santo Domingo/the Dominican Republic (hereafter called only the Dominican Republic, although this name officially applies only after 1844) with revolutionary Haiti, outsiders conflated what had been the toppling of the Plantation society par excellence with the majority mixed-race, free population that lived largely from cattle ranching and other forms of nonsurplus subsistence for centuries.[8]

I contend that the understudied Dominican example exists beyond the recognizable, and often oversimplified, visions of Haitian insurrection that inspired fear or hope in broader Western imaginaries. The free black and mixed-race negotiations of a slaveholding, impoverished, and scarcely populated society that developed in Dominican territory are too murky, compromised, and foggy to grab the kind of attention reserved for narratives of slaves toppling masters.[9] Looking at Dominican history and cultural expression across several centuries may leave us sympathetic to Delano's confusion while gazing at the *San Dominick*: "It seemed hard to decide whether [it] meant to come in or no—what [it] wanted, or what [it] was about."[10] The Dominican cultural expressions that I analyze in this book evince more tensions, silences, and loose threads than anything else. These loose threads signal what McClintock describes as "the ambivalent presence of ghosts," who "are fetishes of the in-between, marking places of irresolution" and who "embody the unsettling prospect that the past can be neither foreclosed nor redeemed."[11] According to Avery Gordon, "the ghostly haunt" points towards a something to be done. Gordon writes: "*Something is making an appearance to you that had been kept from view. It says, Do something about the wavering present the haunting is creating.*"[12]

Indeed, Dominicans from the nineteenth century to the present day have endeavored to make themselves legible—to "make an appearance"—within New World histories and narratives that have erased, misunderstood, or inserted them as inferior Others—"kept them from view." The "narratives of belonging" that I study throughout this book are Dominicans' attempts to be legible as citizen-subjects with access to political, economic, social, and cultural participation within national spaces (including the Dominican Republic, the U.S., Spain, and elsewhere) and transnational or supranational imaginaries and histories such as the African diaspora, Latin America, the Latinx U.S., and the Atlantic world. Equally important to being legible and visible have been Dominican strategies of refusal, that is, of refusing the terms necessary for their legibility in dominant histories and narratives. Discussions of blackness have most frequently conjured these refusals since Dominicans have emerged in early twenty-first-century African American and U.S. Latinx discourses as exemplars of "black denial."[13] The country is often seen as "the racial pariah of the Americas," to cite Raj Chetty.[14] This propensity signals the illegibility of the country's "strange" history within dominant Western discourses—including some African diaspora and Latinx discourses—because, in pathologizing Dominican ideas of race, these narratives do not consider that Dominican society beyond the capital city of Santo Domingo developed apart from, though in trade relations with, the Plantation system or what Ira Berlin calls a slave society (versus a society with slaves).[15] Scholars of Caribbean and North American slavery have made the important distinction between societies with slaves and slave societies or what I prefer to call the Plantation, after Antonio Benítez Rojo. The Dominican context is singular in that, while it was a society with enslaved subjects for centuries, it was also, and crucially, a society with a majority free black population that lived beyond the purview of any colonial oversight, whether urban or rural.[16] It should not be surprising, then, that distinct racial discourses would emerge from a slaveholding society structured in relationships not immediately legible to the novice imperial gaze, newly arrived to Dominican soil.

Through literature, music, and speech acts, island and diasporic Dominicans have expressed their dissatisfaction with how they have been described in dominant discourses. These Dominican cultural expressions of refusal are not necessarily emancipatory. As I mentioned, they are often deeply ambivalent, signaling the persistent interruptions and unfinished imperial and national projects augured on the territory. These expressions run the gamut from ultraconservative, anti-Haitian nationalist literature to present-day Afro-Latinx activism. For instance, the canonization and subsequent whitewashing of an Afro-descendant woman poet (chapters one and two), portrayals and self-expressions of nonwhite Dominican men (chapter three), diasporic Dominican musical performers (chapter four), and female Dominican sex workers catering to foreigners (chapter five) cannot easily be understood through common dichotomies between a ruling class status quo, on one end, and subaltern resistance, on the other. My engagements with these examples of expressive culture and socioeconomic realms have necessitated nuanced analyses that challenge the dominant discourses of race, gender, class, and sexuality in the Americas and the African diaspora.

This book's main goals are twofold. First, I seek to contextualize and analyze Dominicans' cultural expressions produced after the nation's founding in 1844 to the present. Dominicanist scholars have shown that many of these texts either critique or propagate nationalist discourses.[17] I extend their arguments by proposing that Dominican cultural expressions attempt to counteract the territory's ghosting within larger Western discourses, for better or worse. Second, I intervene at the level of knowledge production and analysis by disrupting some of the fields constructed to account for various modes of being in the Americas, which have not been able to discern, and, in some cases, have helped to obscure the kinds of free black subjectivity that emerged in the Dominican Republic. In so doing, *Colonial Phantoms* establishes a framework for placing Dominican expressive culture and historical formations at the forefront of a number of scholarly investigations of colonial modernity in the Americas, the African diaspora, geographic displacement (e.g., migration and exile), and international divisions of labor.[18]

Techniques of Ghosting

Techniques of ghosting, erasure, and silencing comprise some of the most powerful ways in which colonial, imperial, and nationalist entities wield their power.[19] My preference for the term "ghosting" instead of erasure, silencing, fragmentation, trauma, or even haunting requires thorough explanation. While these other terms apply to some of the specific examples I investigate in this book, "ghosting" encompasses most of the ideas I wish to convey. In his Nobel laureate speech, Derek Walcott named fragmentation as integral to Caribbean history and culture: "[T]he way that the Caribbean is still looked at, illegitimate, rootless, mongrelized. [. . .] No people. Fragments and echoes of real people, unoriginal and broken."[20] Literature and other forms of expressive culture, then, emerge as a "restoration of our shattered histories, our shards of vocabulary, our archipelago becoming a synonym for pieces broken off from the original continent."[21] While Dominican history and expressive culture can certainly be described as "fragmented," the term does not evoke some of the active elements of the process or set of processes that created such fragments in the first place. Moreover, evocative words such as "shards" and "pieces" exist as objects beyond the realm of time. My analyses in this book rest more on continuities and repetitions, which exist through time. One of the most important ways in which hauntings manifest themselves is through repetition, either "ritualistic" (McClintock) or "involuntary" (Gordon). As Diana Taylor contends, "[t]he ghost is, by definition, repetition."[22] Thus, the mark of haunting is evident in the Dominican Republic, which has seen repetitions and rehearsals of several national and imperial projects.

For its part, while the term "haunting" urges us to consider what is being haunted, "ghosting" also compels us to ask *who* is responsible for creating the ghosts. "Silencing" also motivates us to name the actor(s) behind the act, as Michel-Rolph Trouillot does in his influential *Silencing the Past: Power and the Production of History* (1995), but it can leave us with the sense that the act of silencing has produced inert historical gaps. Instead, "ghosting" implies that the acts of erasure that are part and parcel of colonial, imperial, and many nationalist projects have produced not so much actual silence as other unwieldy and recalcitrant presences. To cite Renée Bergland, ghosts "refuse to stay buried."[23] According to Avery Gordon, haunting "is an animated state in which a repressed or unresolved social violence is making itself known, sometimes very discretely, sometimes more obliquely."[24] *Colonial Phantoms* endeavors to show how the ghosts of Dominican erasure have tried to make themselves seen, heard, and recorded, as well as how Dominican subjects from the late nineteenth century to the present have engaged with them. Many of the cultural expressions that I discuss in this book suggest that acknowledgement of these ghosts opens us to the potential for redemption, healing, and, to cite McClintock, "the possibilities of alternative futures."[25]

It would be useful to outline the main ways in which the Dominican Republic has been ghosted within broader Western imaginaries:

1. Cultural producers (scholars, writers, journalists, cartographers, activists, and others) and policymakers, especially from Europe and the U.S., have ghosted how central the Dominican Republic was as a space where European and U.S. powers could rehearse their military, political, and economic imperialist projects.

2. Many Dominican nationalist cultural producers and policymakers, as well as cultural producers and policymakers from elsewhere, have ghosted the territory's historical and demographic singularity. The Dominican Republic had a diverse economy based mostly on cattle ranching, wood, and tobacco (reliant on trade with Plantation neighbor Saint-Domingue/Haiti) with a majority free black and mixed-race population. This economic and demographic reality started in the late sixteenth century and endured, arguably, into the twentieth century.

3. Cultural producers and policymakers from outside of the island (non-Haitians and non-Dominicans) persistently called the entire island Haiti for most of the nineteenth century even when only the Western third of the island had this name and government. This matters immensely because when Haiti was founded, much to the dismay of the world's ruling elite, especially those whose fortunes relied directly on slave labor, both sides of the island felt the cultural and material repercussions of the world's wrath.[26]

4. The ghosting of the Dominican Republic from dominant Western discourses, combined with at least a century of being associated (both accurately and inaccurately) with Haiti, means that categories of knowledge and disciplinary fields have been constructed and developed without considering its important example. This

led to present-day scholars of the nineteenth century, for instance, repeating earlier inaccuracies and silencings, and thereby perpetuating the ghosting of the Dominican Republic.[27]

5. Because association with Haiti would prevent Dominicans from garnering the world respect necessary for economic and political survival—within the dominant white supremacist world order—many in the ruling and intellectual classes were desperate to show that they were nothing like Haitians.[28] In so doing, these cultural producers also erased or, at least whitewashed, Dominican forms of black subjectivity. They also elided the ways in which many black and mixed-race subjects in the Dominican Republic partook in the set of events now called the Haitian Revolution on both sides of the island.

6. By the late twentieth century, what had been a unique territory within the Americas had become another "third world" island-nation providing cheap labor, sun, sex, and sand.[29] This occurred through the consolidation of the Dominican nation-state, the persistence of U.S. involvement in Dominican politics and economy, the reliance on foreign tourism as the main driver of the national economy, and neoliberal policies and trade agreements that restructured the relationship between the Dominican Republic and other national economies. This present-day commonplaceness obscures—but does not eradicate entirely—the strangeness of prior centuries.

While these six forms of ghosting are deeply intertwined, their unequal effects reflect the difference in global power between the Dominican Republic and Europe/the U.S. I focus mostly on ghosting at the level of knowledge production, while remaining aware that extreme violence (e.g., state-sponsored genocide) has also been a central technique of ghosting. However, various forms of knowledge production have had immense material repercussions on the people who have lived on this island. For instance, mid-nineteenth-century scientific racism as a form of knowledge production emanating mostly from the Western powers and white elites in other parts of the world influenced how foreign visitors categorized the Dominican population. It also informed several Dominican scholars who wrote about the degeneracy of the country's mixed-race and black populations. These visitors and scholars often had direct influence on policies that would affect the material circumstances, even the lives, of Dominicans.[30]

Persistent misnaming of either or both sides of the island in various fields of scholarship and over two centuries has compounded archival erasure or miscategorization. That is, non-Dominican and non-Haitian scholars writing about the island referred to either side accurately or mistakenly as San Domingue/San Domingo/Saint Domingue/Santo Domingo/Hayti/Haiti/Hispaniola/Española.[31] The western side of the island was first known as La Española/Hispaniola (alongside the rest of the island), Saint Domingue, and finally Haiti. The eastern side occasions more confusion; Hispaniola became Santo Domingo (also the name of the capital city), Spanish Haiti, and finally the Dominican Republic.[32]

The ghosting of the Dominican Republic from dominant Western discourses matters for several reasons. First, the vast diaspora of Dominicans in the U.S. and Europe, and the way that Dominican cultural expressions (e.g., *bachata* and *merengue*, the literature of Julia Alvarez and Junot Díaz) and labor (e.g., factory and domestic work, baseball) have made deep marks in the U.S. and European mainstream, behooves us to get to know the cultural background of an emigrant population that tends to maintain ties to the homeland.[33] Second, it matters because the history of the Dominican Republic for centuries contained whispers of a way of being in the Americas that to some extent evaded dominant socioeconomic and political structures. And finally, it matters because, in Trouillot's words, "[h]istorical silences [signal] archival power at its strongest, the power to define what is and what is not a serious object of research and, therefore, of mention."[34] Even revisionist histories and antioppression activist efforts, especially when issuing from the North American and European centers of global power, can constitute acts of "imperial ghosting."[35]

The term "navel" in this introduction's title serves as another allegory that clarifies this project. The navel sits at the center of the body. In this case, it symbolizes the geographic centrality of the island of Hispaniola within the hemisphere. Too, the navel represents a conceptual centrality and importance that nevertheless has been ghosted. The navel is the remnant of a once vital relationship, the umbilical cord that augured and fueled a history of the conquest and colonization of the Americas with all of its attendant violence. Celsa Albert Batista describes the colony of La Española or Hispaniola as the "center for the rehearsal of Spanish colonialism in America."[36] It was also the center for experiments in radical black freedom and self-governance as well as various forms of U.S. imperialism. That is, it is a symbol of the ghosted importance of this territory to the subsequent architecture of the Americas.

Because major fields of knowledge about the Americas have developed without revising their paradigms to allow for a conceptualization of the Dominican Republic, I have had to construct a reading practice that can discern the "lower frequencies," to cite Lisa Lowe, humming beneath nationalist, imperialist, and diasporic narratives, both popular and academic.[37] The texts I analyze not only "unearth that which the colonial experience buried and overlaid, bringing to light the hidden continuities it suppressed," to invoke Stuart Hall, but also "produce identity" in a "*re-telling* [rather than discovery] of the past."[38] Seen differently, Hall here distinguishes between a text as a filler of historical gaps and a text as the living ghost created by prior silencings. In the latter case, the text/ghost is an active presence with its own complicated vision of "what happened" and why it is speaking now.

Consider, for instance, the Dominican mythical figure of the *ciguapa*, a simultaneously alluring and terrifying creature whose feet face backwards. Ginetta Candelario argues that the ciguapa "is not a legend of Taíno origins that predates Spanish colonization of the island," as she is popularly understood.[39] The ciguapa was, instead, the invention of Francisco Javier Angulo Guridi (1816–1884), a nationalist Liberal "navigating the Dominican Republic's contradictory racial demographics, political economy, and geopolitics."[40] In this sense, the ciguapa as a figure of contradiction and ambivalence manages several ghostings, including the violent genocide of indigenous people on the island and the suppression of black freedom as it predominated in this territory. This interpretation of the ciguapa resembles Avery Gordon's reading of Beloved, the adult ghost who returns after being killed as a child in Toni Morrison's canonical novel.[41] Like Beloved, the ciguapa is "visible and demanding."[42] Unlike Beloved, however, the ciguapa emerges as a figure of obfuscation and distraction, rather than as a figure of "reckoning" who "makes those who have contact with her [. . .] confront an event in the past that loiters in the present."[43] I want to suggest that the act of invention for the purpose of denial and erasure does not produce vacancy or absence as much as it creates other contradictory, fleshy presences.

The Specter of Haiti

But if the revolution was significant for Haitians [. . .] to most foreigners it was primarily a lucky argument in a larger issue. [. . .] Haiti mattered to all of them, but only as a pretext to talk about something else.
—Michel-Rolph Trouillot, *Silencing the Past* (1995)

While the Haitian Revolution (1791–1804) inspired many subjects of African descent, the world's white elite recoiled in fear and horror.[44] Saint Domingue's colonizer, France, denied Haiti recognition until the new nation agreed to an exorbitant debt payment that crippled the Haitian economy. Western powers did their best to banish Haitian history, culture, religion, and people from world history, demonizing what remained.[45] In Gina Ulysse's words, "Haiti had to become colonialism's *bête noir* if the sanctity of whiteness were to remain unquestioned."[46] To be sure, as Sean X. Goudie writes, "an active silencing or disavowal of the Haitian Revolution in the archives has been at the heart of Western modernity, not the least in the nineteenth-century United States."[47] At a time when U.S. government officials and cultural producers consolidated the ideal of a white (male) citizenry, Haitian officials drafted a constitution that named its citizens as black.[48] According to Eric J. Sundquist, "Haiti came to seem the fearful precursor of black rebellion throughout the New World, becoming an entrenched part of master-class ideology in both Latin America and the United States."[49] This matters within the context of this book because the specter and fear of Haiti applied to the entire island, in terms both practical and theoretical. In a practical sense, texts about nineteenth-century Haiti/Saint Domingue/Santo Domingo are quite often about the entire island and even explicitly about the Dominican Republic—even when that latter name never surfaces. Its proximity to Haiti and its *oneness* with it from 1822 until 1844 meant that the fate of the eastern, formerly Spanish, territory was tied to Haiti's.

As Trouillot argues, the Haitian Revolution and the creation of a black state of Haiti made world leaders and others so anxious that it was unmentioned or excised during some of the most crucial moments in hemispheric history.[50] For instance, in 1819, U.S. president James Monroe ignored the existence of Haiti as a nation-state and, several years later, again made no mention of Haiti during his "articulation of the famous Monroe Doctrine asserting American primacy in the hemisphere," to cite Sara Fanning.[51] The subsequent Congress of Panama of 1826 systematically also excluded Haiti (the entire island at the time) at the insistence of the U.S. president, John Quincy Adams, and in the interest of slaveholders in his country. (Paradoxically, its absence from these moments of consolidation of U.S. imperial power did not protect Haiti from future U.S. aggression and involvement.) Haiti's weight as representing what the world's white ruling class most feared—black insurgency and self-autonomy—required a political and economic embargo. Thus, Haiti—the entire island for a crucial twenty-two years—underwent a systematic, sinister erasure, active and hostile, when the new nation-states of the hemisphere recognized each other.

Because of this global stance against Haiti, many nineteenth- and twentieth-century Dominican nationalists were eager to suppress Dominican connections to Haiti. In their efforts to convince foreign powers that Dominicans were nothing like Haitians, many Dominican officials rejected the ways in which many black and mixed-raced Dominicans had participated in slave revolts over the centuries, cheered for black insurrection in neighboring Saint Domingue, and welcomed Haitian governance over the whole island.[52] Mixed-raced categories in the Dominican racial spectrum emerged as part of a strategy of communicating to U.S. imperial officials in the nineteenth and early twentieth centuries that, while most Dominicans were not "white" in the way that the U.S. government described it (which at the time could also exclude Spaniards, for instance), they were also not "black" in the way that the Haitian constitution of 1805 proclaimed the country to be.[53] This book builds on and coexists with recent scholarly and activist attempts to undo some of the damage occasioned by anti-Haitian Dominican nationalism as refracted through anti-Haitian U.S. imperial desires.[54]

At the same time, the Dominican Republic helped U.S. leaders consider the language of free black subjectivity because it already existed there in a greater degree of autonomy and expanse than in the rest of the hemisphere. Pockets of black freedom, beyond maroonage, existed all over the Americas. However, what was unique to this territory is that this freedom from the surveillance of a white supremacist colonial and then national gaze was a predominant, if often suppressed, social element. During his time as U.S. president (1869–1877), Ulysses S. Grant pushed for annexation of the Dominican Republic: "The acquisition of San Domingo is an adherence to the 'Monroe doctrine'; [. . .] it is to make slavery insupportable in Cuba and Porto Rico [sic] at once, and ultimately so in Brazil."[55] Grant's case encompassed nothing less than a future-driven map of a slavery-free, U.S.-led hemispheric order. To Grant, the Dominican Republic would not only host the rehearsal of this project, but already contained the seeds of this future. Grant did not have to go through the trouble of figuring out how best to deal with recently freed black subjects; Dominican territory provided a glimpse of free black subjectivity. In seeing that the future did not lie in slave-holding societies such as Cuba, Puerto Rico, and Brazil, Grant looked to the island that showed what universal free black subjectivity and (male) citizenship looked like.

A Singular Colony

In order to understand the depth of what Dominican nationalists and European and U.S. political and cultural leaders ghosted, I must expand on the various forms of ghosting I outlined above. The Dominican Republic was the site of the first rehearsals of European empire in the hemisphere. There, Spanish colonists experienced their first successes— the first European city, the first sugar mills, the first enslaved indigenous and African subjects, and so on—and, from the colonists' perspectives, their first failures—the first indigenous rebellions, the first maroons (black and indigenous), the collapse of the first plantation economy in the Americas, and so on. Lynne Guitar argues that "[i]t was on Hispaniola that many of the patterns were formed that governed relations between African slaves and their new masters, patterns that spread to the other Spanish colonies across the Americas—patterns that included rebellion."[56] While many have learned about Spain's conquest of places like Mexico and Peru, few consider that Spain used the administrative knowledge and actual administrators they had rehearsed on Hispaniola to acquire better results elsewhere.[57] The vast corpus of information available about other Spanish colonies such as Mexico and even Cuba stemmed in great part from their wealth and the strength of colonial control. Scholarship about the Dominican Republic has often been based on the scant writings of confused outsiders or local elites isolated in a few main cities.

The centuries that followed Spanish neglect of Hispaniola are worth describing. What is now the Dominican Republic became a "forgotten" Spanish colony by the late sixteenth century, after its burgeoning sugar mill economy declined and the Spanish crown turned its attention to other islands and the mainland.[58] Unlike other Spanish colonies, a strong Spanish administrative presence had ceased to exist soon after the Spanish takeover of the island in the late fifteenth century. For hundreds of years, the territory became what Juan José Ponce-Vázquez calls a "de facto borderland," in which buccaneering and a contraband trade in hides flourished, racial mixture was more the norm than the exception, and slavery ended with the unification of the island under Haitian governance in 1822.[59] A society with a majority black and mixed-race rural population that was not centered on a Plantation system while reliant on one of the strongest Plantation societies the world ever saw—Saint-Domingue—rendered it unique among other slave-holding societies in the Americas. Analyses of race in the Dominican Republic that emphasize its strangeness, even absurdity, often adopt frameworks built to understand nations whose history and demographics differ markedly from the Dominican Republic.[60]

Demographic data evince the inapplicability of racial and other paradigms constructed to apply to places such as the U.S., Cuba, and Haiti. Eric Paul Roorda, Lauren Derby, and Raymundo González argue that "[o]ne distinctive feature of the Dominican Republic is that by the seventeenth century, freedpeople were more numerous than enslaved people, a feature some travelers noted with a degree of shock and dismay."[61] In 1791, the total population of the Spanish colony of Santo Domingo comprised 125,000 people, 12 percent of them enslaved.[62] The percentage of whites and nonwhites is generally unknown for this year. This gap in knowledge is noteworthy, since neighboring colonies recorded this information carefully.[63] A source from 1808 states that out of the total population of 50,089 on the eastern (Spanish) side of the island, 13,191 were white, 7,052 were black, and 29,992 were mixed race.[64] Sibylle Fischer states that "there were relatively few slaves before 1822 in Spanish Santo Domingo—15,000 out of a population of 120,000—and the economy did not depend on large-scale plantations."[65] In 1791, neighboring Saint Domingue (soon-to-be Haiti) had a population of 520,000 (four times the number of people in half the space of the territory of Santo Domingo), 86.9 percent of them enslaved. In Cuba in 1827, when the island was still far from independence and the abolition of slavery, the total population was 704,487 with a 40.7 percent enslaved population.[66] For the 1840s on the Dominican side of the island, David Dixon Porter, a U.S. Navy admiral, reported that "5,000 are white, 60,000 are quadroons, 60,000 are light-skinned mulattoes, 14,000 dark-skinned mulattoes, and 20,000 are of pure African descent."[67]

While any census data involving racial denomination is tenuous at best (e.g., how were degrees of racial mixture determined?), these numbers nevertheless reveal a few key points. First, the central government apparatus responsible for gathering population data was weaker in Dominican territory than in neighboring colonies. Second, distinguishing between the various racial classes and their attendant places in society was utterly important in places such as Saint Domingue and Cuba, where the Plantation predominated and which were French and Spanish colonial centers, respectively. Compared to these places, Santo Domingo was barely able to account who among the free people were white or not white for some of its colonial history. Pedro San Miguel corroborates that "unlike other Caribbean societies, in the Dominican Republic [...] a plantation economy that prevented the rise and existence of a peasantry did not exist."[68] The thorough racial mixture of the majority of the population, the low density (in 1681, for instance, the territory contained less than 10,000 people), the low number of large plantations, and the relatively low number of enslaved subjects vis-à-vis the rest of the population means that it should be a challenge to consider the Dominican case alongside places such as Cuba and Brazil.[69]

Although Plantation frameworks constructed to understand places such as Cuba and Jamaica do not apply neatly to the Dominican case, this territory was nonetheless a European slaveholding colony and, as such, a white supremacist and patriarchal hierarchy prevailed. Nonwhite subjects, enslaved and free, resisted in both small- and large-scale ways but, however frail the colonial system, white men were still considered superior in law and in practice.[70] In 1634, a free mixed-race woman had a party with her family and friends in Santo Domingo. One of the guests was a Spanish soldier who, reports Juan José Ponce Vázquez, "started to dismantle the decorations."[71] The hostess intervened, asking him to stop, and he asked her "whether she was crazy addressing him in such a manner and whether she thought she was talking to another *mulato* like herself."[72] The soldier also hit her on the head, creating a bloody wound. In 1680, colonial authorities "issued a summons" to a free *mulata*, Juana Maldonado, for having an affair with a white man of the upper class. This "caused a great deal of gossiping and scandal in this Republic" and Maldonado was ordered to move to another neighborhood and to cease contact with the upper-class man.[73] Authorities also "scolded" her for good measure. The unnamed white man of the upper class was neither reprimanded nor punished. These seventeenth-century examples remind us of the crucial gender, class, and sexual dimensions to the question of race as they emerged in this colony. While this society spurred the creation of various forms of black freedom, it was still governed, however loosely, by a patriarchal colonial regime. That is, although "a colorful assortment of saucy and insubordinate characters continued to move about and resist authority," the administrative and intellectual classes in power sought to curtail these recalcitrant behaviors.[74]

A form of the Plantation did arrive to the Dominican Republic in the late nineteenth century, following the abolition of slavery in the U.S., Cuba, and Puerto Rico.[75] At this time, foreign owners acquired permissions and sanctions to open large sugar plantations, especially in the southeast region.[76] There were long-term effects of the arrival of the most advanced form of the Plantation, including the imposition of a new form of land value that was the beginning of the end of the autonomous peasantry. Frank Moya Pons argues that "the plantation is [in the late twentieth-century] the dominant agricultural system in the Dominican Republic."[77] However, as Moya Pons also corroborates, "its appearance was not linked to the initial process of forming the Dominican nation."[78] In other words, the logic of the Plantation—which, according to Trevor Burnard and John Garrigus, "was the main driving force shaping most aspects of European colonization in the Atlantic World" in the seventeenth and eighteenth centuries—never superimposed itself over the whole of Dominican society as it did in other Caribbean colonies.[79]

Black Masterless Men in *El Monte*

La caza era una actividad de los hombres. (Hunting was a man's activity.)
—Raymundo González, "Ideología del progreso y campesinado en el siglo XIX" (1993)

I was struck by the free, frank, and manly way in which these men look and speak, evidently showing they feel their importance as freemen very different from the same class in Cuba.
—Samuel Hazard, *Santo Domingo: Past and Present, with a Glance at Hayti* (1873)

Some of the general characteristics of the Dominican society developed by former slaves, indigenous people, wayward white colonists, and their progeny include the subsistence farming of small sections in unfenced and shared land, the thoroughness of racial mixture, and the importance of free movement on horseback.[80] It is a history of nonwhite subjects' insubordination through, for instance, buccaneering—which Eric Paul Roorda, Lauren Derby, and Raymundo González, after Julius S. Scott, describe as a "contraband economy of black 'masterless men'"—and various other forms of resistance to colonial power and white supremacy.[81] In 1772, the governor attempted to reduce the number of free blacks and increase the number of whites in the colony. After reviewing the proposition, a prosecutor of the Council of the Indies agreed that the blacks, who were *derramados*, or spilled all over the island, constituted a significant threat to the colonial order.[82] At the same time, he considered the governor's plan to be a losing battle. A few years later, in 1784, Colonel Joaquín García was aghast at the behavior of free nonwhites on the island. He complains to colonial authorities that "[f]ree persons of color [...] travel across the colony with 'absolute confidence and impertinence' and confuse their identity with that of their white neighbors 'as if there were no more classes [dividing society] than free or slave.'"[83] As cited by Raymundo González, García recommends that the new laws of the Código Negro Carolino (the Black Code) of 1784 in Santo Domingo be applied not only to slaves but also—and *especially*—to free nonwhite subjects who comprised the real threat to the colonial order in this territory.[84]

The white elite subjects clamoring for the Spanish crown's attention yearned not only for a slaveholding society, which the colony was at the time, but also for a society organized by Plantation logic, in which nonwhites remained subservient to whites, especially in behavior. Spanish colonial laws supported this desire. Citing Dominican historian Carlos Larrazal Blanco, Franklin J. Franco writes, "although within the limitations of the time, most mulattos had no trouble in gaining their freedom [. . .] the ordinances regulating everyday social interactions in Hispaniola stipulated that 'blacks, mulattos, or terceroons shall be as submissive [and respectful] to every white person as if each one of them were his master.'"[85] Unlike other Spanish colonies, however, Santo Domingo's general impoverishment, combined with the lack of colonial infrastructure, prevented the ordinance's stringent enforcement.[86] Late eighteenth-century Martinican traveler, writer, and lawyer M. L. Moreau de Saint-Méry commented that in Santo Domingo, "prejudice with respect to colour, so powerful with other nations, among whom it fixes a bar between the whites, and the freed-people, and their descendants, is almost unknown in the Spanish part of Saint-Domingo."[87] The many laws preventing free nonwhites from parity with whites, observes Moreau de Saint-Méry, "are absolutely disregarded in the Spanish part."[88] After assuring readers that white elites "would turn with disgust from an alliance with the descendents of their slaves," he makes the almost offhand comment that "the major part of the Spanish colonists are a mixed-race: this an African feature, and sometimes more than one, often betrays; but [. . .] its frequency has silenced a prejudice that would otherwise be a troublesome remembrance."[89] To this white Martinican (French) member of the elite, the "white" Spanish subjects were only tenuously so; their bodies betray phenotypically their African ancestry. How could white elites enforce race hierarchies when their own nonwhiteness was an open secret?

As these examples demonstrate, black insurgency and autonomy, along with other ways of expressing the self that subverted Plantation logic, worried colonial administrators and white elites living on and visiting the eastern part of the island. The space in which this form of black freedom and autonomy proliferated was called *el monte*. Raymundo González describes el monte as "the site of thousands of dispersed and anonymous freed blacks and mulattos who were living in the mountains a life of autonomous subsistence in the wilderness."[90] Its archetypal subject, *el montero*, was a man who hunted wild pigs, goats, and cattle in a practice called *montería* (see Figure I.1).[91]

Assuming that this socioeconomic role and archetype was gendered masculine, what can be said of the women of el monte? The archives I have consulted reveal examples of recalcitrant free black and mixed-race women in the cities, as the two examples I relayed earlier demonstrate. Moreover, the colonial archive includes many examples of "mujeres de peso en la vida económica y social" (women with social and economic weight), as Frank Moya Pons writes, as well as "poor women who went to church and supported their families by working as servants,

Figure I.1. R. H. Beck, "Guides and Wild Pig Hunter [Montero]," Brewster and Sanford Expedition in the Dominican Republic, ca. 1916–1917. Image #236803. (Courtesy of the American Museum of Natural History Library, New York.)

seamstresses, food sellers, dessert makers, prostitutes or concubines."[92] But women living beyond the purview of the colonial administration, out in el monte, are almost entirely invisible in writings about montería.

Because of the degree to which the practice of montería and other forms of black autonomy in el monte rendered the territory singular among its Caribbean counterparts, it is difficult to avoid the potential conclusion that much of this singularity existed in the realm of men as it emerges in most writings about Dominican rurality. I wonder about women in el monte (and men who were not or could not be monteros) because gender, both embodied and rhetorical, is a crucial component of analysis. In *La parole des femmes* (1979), Maryse Condé suggests that Caribbean women's literature—and women's perspectives—can offer a more holistic understanding of Caribbean society: "[T]his female literature has social content that goes beyond the anecdotal nature of the author. It is situated at the heart of more general social concerns."[93] However, two challenges to this goal of centralizing women's cultural expressions present themselves in a study of el monte. First, the written archive genders this space of black freedom and autonomy as masculine. And second, for much of Dominican history, women (and men) in el monte had limited if nonexistent access to recording their thoughts and ideas for posterity.

That the central mode of living in el monte, montería, was "man's work" does not mean that women did not occupy central roles. Rather, women do not appear as distinctive from other Caribbean women in the sources I have consulted.[94] If anything, writes Celsa Albert Batista, colonial administrators considered "the [enslaved] African woman as a 'mechanism against insurgency'" and as a tool of domestication.[95] While my focus here is on freepeople and not on enslaved subjects, there is a discursive precedent in this territory that enslaved female subjects and black women in general represented a domesticating force. To colonial administrators, free black subjectivity was tied to the masculine endeavor of montería and other subsistence activities unprofitable to the colonial administration, and, as such, as an always subversive identity and performance. Samuel Hazard, a white journalist traveling with an official delegation sent by President Ulysses S. Grant to consider annexation of the Dominican Republic, records his surprise at the "manliness" of the men he encountered.[96] Part of the same official commission as Hazard, Frederick Douglass described the country as being "a place where the man can simply be a man regardless of his skin color. Where he can be free to think, and to lead."[97]

When nonelite women do appear in (male) foreigners' nineteenth-century narratives, the writers' heteronormative gaze circumscribes their accounts. Samuel Hazard's "sudden" encounter with rural Dominican women washing clothes in a river, for instance, paints an Eden-like scene of "forty or fifty women of various ages [. . .]. Some were entirely nude, some with only a waist-cloth, but all industriously washing away and chattering like parrots."[98] The traveling group's "astonished gaze" turned into outright voyeurism as they "stop[ped] to look."[99] J. Dennis Harris, an African American proponent of black separatism in the Caribbean, observed in 1860 that Dominican "women are frequently good-looking, but seldom spirited. The prevailing question seems to be, How low in the neck can their dresses be worn? and [sic] the answer is, Very low indeed!"[100] For their part, Dominican elite writers "disavowed black women as 'tristes extranjeras' (sad foreigners)," as Lorgia García-Peña maintains.[101] Conversely, argues García-Peña, "'the (white) woman' became the guardian of dominicanidad" as elite writers "whitened the nation-woman through Europeanized descriptions of feminine beauty."[102] These foreign and Dominican literary elite perspectives generally obscure, if not outright erase, a clear understanding of how women in el monte may or may not have subverted Caribbean models of free black subjectivity.

Some of the chapters in this book explore how the spirit of the montero emerges in late twentieth- and twenty-first-century quotidian and stage performances not only among Dominican men but also among Dominican women. As Lauren Derby argues, monteros became the model of masculinity that would evolve into the modern-day *tíguere*, a nonwhite, streetwise hustler and Dominican masculine archetype (chapter three). Thus, when Dominican women performers and writers adopt tíguere traits, they insert themselves into what had been a masculine genealogy for centuries, rejecting the single model of idealized white Dominican femininity (chapters two, four, and five).

Ghosting El Monte

The nineteenth-century urban bourgeoisie writing Dominican national identity into being feared the society and culture that predominated in el monte. Raymundo González emphasizes the extent to which el monte—and rumors about what happened there—made deep and long-lasting marks on what colonial administrators and other elites concentrated in the main cities and plantations thought.[103] According to Pedro L. San Miguel, this anxiety stretched into the national period: "Since the founding of the Republic, in 1844, the peasantry had constituted a social sector difficult to control by state organisms. For this reason, starting in the late nineteenth century, state efforts were largely routed to 'domesticate' the peasantry."[104] El monte as a racialized imaginary was an allegory for a backwardness that prevented progress and modernity. As a space that existed in reality, many nationalists turned to modernization in the form of agricultural and land reform, an extreme of which emerged in the many foreign-owned sugar plantations in the eastern region of the country starting in the late nineteenth century. Others focused on widespread education as the primary vehicle for modernity and nationalization, thus folding Dominican citizens into the national body. This "fanatical" attention to education and other forms of modernization were central elements of positivist, Liberal ideology that predominated in late nineteenth- and early twentieth-century Dominican writing.[105]

One crucial exception to this generalized attitude about modernization and progress in late nineteenth-century Dominican thought was Pedro Francisco Bonó, who wrote the novel *El Montero* (1856). Bonó's nationalism connected the montero subject to the territory's history of black freedom. What other intellectuals saw as rural backwardness, Bonó saw as the seeds of an inspiring future. In an 1887 letter to presidential candidate General Gregorio Luperón, Bonó describes the island of Santo Domingo as "the nucleus," "the model," and the "embodiment" of "the destinies that Providence is setting aside for the blacks and mulattoes in [the] Americas[s]."[106] Bonó not only acknowledges that the country was primarily black and "mulatto" but also that, alongside Haiti, it was representative of the mixed-race and black future of the Americas. Unlike Bonó, most intellectuals at this time adhered to an idea of modernity reliant on the ghosting of el monte.

Technological, agricultural, and educational progress, and the literature that propagated these values, started to fold more Dominicans into a centralized nation. However, only a small group of people, mainly literate men of the leading classes, could perform and embody the role of being standard-bearers of patriotism in practice and in the national imaginary. Roberto Cassá notes that in 1850 "the vast majority of the population lived in the countryside, where there were no educational institutions of any sort. But even in the scarce small cities, the general population remained illiterate."[107] While the 1874 constitution required schooling for all Dominicans, as Neici Zeller points out, "the budget for such a goal was only 3 percent of the government's total expenditures."[108] The intellectual elite in Santo Domingo and other major cities thus comprised what Angel Rama calls the *la cuidad letrada* (the lettered city), contrasting with the *cuidad real* (real city) that the rest of the population represented. The "real city," which was in fact mostly rural, was home to "the illiterate, indigenous or Afro-descendent majorities."[109] Pablo Mella maintains that some of the periodicals that dominated the cultural scene in the country served "as a synecdoche that pretended to represent discursively the Dominican Republic as a whole."[110] Though useful, the binary of "real" versus "lettered" city has its limits in a late nineteenth-century Dominican context. For instance, intellectual elites in the Dominican case were not always racially distinct from the subjects in the "real city," as this territory had had black and mixed-race political and cultural leaders since the colonial era.[111]

In ghosting el monte through and within these constructions of a "modern" imaginary, Dominican intellectuals also ghosted the African or black components of Dominican society and culture.[112] In part, this stems from the fact that "blackness" as a signifier had been relegated both to el monte and, after the Haitian Revolution, to Haiti. Indeed, to many ruling elites, especially those in favor of foreign annexation, Haiti represented a national threat that required intervention from more powerful nations, including the U.S. However, antiannexationist intellectuals, often followers of the "Blue" political faction, considered the U.S. as a threat to Dominican sovereignty and national identity.[113]

Despite ruling elites' and foreign scholars' propensity to see elites' writings as accurate reflections of the whole population, Dominican nationalist discourses themselves contain evidence of the singularity of the territory's history and society. For instance, it is remarkable that a Euro-centric, patriarchal elite considered an Afro-descendent woman, Salomé Ureña, the country's most important poet in the mid-to-late nineteenth century. This occurred in the midst of many proannexationist Domini-can officials' and intellectuals' attempts to render the population and its culture "whiter" to an interested U.S. gaze. Yet Ureña's blackness was entirely unremarked during her lifetime and her image was phenotypi-cally whitewashed in the many sculptures and paintings dedicated to her (chapters one and two). Another example of the contradictions evident in Dominican nationalism, the Dominican icon of montero masculin-ity, the tíguere, both resists white supremacist constraints and, at the same time, can perpetrate extreme forms of violence on noncompliant subjects (chapter three). These cases escape the frameworks of either triumphant resistance or abject failure, and, I argue, get to the heart of what is so strange and confusing about the Dominican case to many outsiders. Thus, dominant scholarly paradigms have not been able to account for Dominican modes of being in the hemisphere's history and therefore ignore, misunderstand, and perpetuate its ghosting.

The Dominican Nation-State and Geographic Displacement

Colonial Phantoms traces the long arc starting from the late nineteenth century, when Dominican territory remained singular in the ways I described above, to the present day, when the Dominican Republic is a "third world" nation among many in dominant developmental-ist thought. Smoothing out the prickly difference characterized by the autonomous, anonymous black subjects who proliferated in the most remote areas of the territory required strengthening the surveillance of both the nation-state and an increasingly powerful U.S. empire. The lat-ter had a direct influence on the territory through the terroristic U.S. military regime in the country from 1916–1924.[114] These changes, com-bined with the consolidation of a conservative Dominican nationalism during the Trujillo dictatorship (1930–1961) and after, especially under the governments of Joaquín Balaguer (1966–1978 and 1986–1996), trans-formed the Dominican population in significant ways. For instance, the majority of the population shifted from rural to urban. Frank Moya Pons writes that "for more than 400 years, and especially during the eighteenth and nineteenth centuries, rural customs predominated in Dominican society."[115] Still in 1920, in the midst of the U.S. occupation, 86 percent of the population lived in the countryside.[116] But, by 2010, 74.4 percent of the country's population lived in cities.[117] The vast emigration of Dominicans to places such as the U.S., Puerto Rico, Europe, and elsewhere also started in the 1960s. In 2010, the total population in the Dominican Republic stood at nearly 9.5 million, while the Dominican population in the U.S. alone was 1.5 million.[118] There are also sizable populations of Dominicans in Europe and other parts of the Americas.

Unsurprisingly, scholarship on the Dominican Republic outside of the island has emerged most keenly in relation to the issue of twentieth- and twenty-first-century migration.[119] Scholars have been particularly interested in how Dominican migrants influence the politics, the economy, and the culture of the homeland and the countries with significant Dominican populations. Some of the narratives I analyze demonstrate that the diasporic space is ambivalent in that it can echo and even surpass the nation's dominant racist and patriarchal ideologies or it can fuel dramatic reevaluations of nationalist narratives. Despite the diversity of viewpoints represented in the diaspora, as well as the racial, educational background, and gender of diasporic subjects, mainstream Dominican sources on the island often portray *dominicanos ausentes* (absent Dominicans) or *dominicanos en el exterior* (Dominicans in the exterior) as threats to national stability.

However, the long durée of this book gives me the opportunity to prove that conversations about *dominicanos en el exterior* emerge also in nineteenth-century writings. (Exile and migration were central concepts in prior centuries, but here I refer to the national period.) Cultural arbiters and government officials have considered emigration a problem to the cohesion of the Dominican nation-state since the middle of the nineteenth century (chapter one). Various forms of geographic displacement, especially exile and migration, have a long history in the Caribbean region and its letters. I group exile and migration under the single category of geographic displacement to emphasize that political (i.e., involuntary exile) and economic (i.e., voluntary migration) motivations to flee one's homeland are quite often inseparable from each other.[120] When I write about the geographic displacement of Dominican subjects, I write also of how their gender, race, and class embodiment and position emplace them differently within national, imperial, and diasporic imaginaries. In other words, I focus not so much on the fact of these waves of Dominican exiles and migrants as much as on the ways in which they have been *perceived* in these national and transnational contexts. Working-class and poor nonwhite Dominicans have also experienced the pain of exile or led transnational lives throughout the nation's history. However, because they represent the ghosted singular history of Dominican territory that developed outside of dominant hemispheric paradigms, nationalist Dominican literature and history do not celebrate these subjects.

While I am aware that terms such as "migrant," "exile," and "refugee" can help identify different motivations behind displacement, they can also obscure the larger structural forces at play, including imperial aggression and neoliberal policies. Some of these terms are raced and classed to such an extent that the only reason some exiles are not considered migrants is that they are educated, from the elite classes, and raced as white. In the nineteenth-century Dominican context I analyze, some so-called exiles did not have to leave the country because of political persecution—the standard definition of an exile. Moreover, so-called migrants are often fleeing an instability both economic and political, but their racial and class status may preclude them from the privilege of seeking asylum or even calling themselves exiles.[121]

With this in mind, geographic displacement as an idea and experience has had an enormous influence on the work of Caribbean writers and intellectuals who have defined their respective nations and the region as a whole.[122] According to Silvio Torres-Saillant, "Exile was and still is a constant element of the Caribbean experience."[123] The Dominican Republic is no exception to this regional characteristic. In spite of the recent claims by conservative nationalists that *los ausentes* are a threat to the stability of the nation, "[e]xile literature is often part of a nation-building project, despite its location outside of the geographic patria."[124] Many texts produced by diasporic Dominicans re-script national narratives, as I show especially in chapters two to five. However, going against some currents in the study of the Dominican and other Spanish Caribbean diasporas, I resist the impulse to see the diasporic space and the narratives it warrants as always emancipatory. Some of this scholarship overlooks the fact that many Dominicans who have never left the country have also been activists, scholars, artists, and writers resistant to conservative Dominican nationalism.[125]

In the nineteenth century, many elites escaped political persecution by living in what they called *destierro* or *exilio* (exile). This fact has resulted in the almost comical irony that many present-day Dominicans call for the cultural and political exclusion of diasporic Dominicans while conjuring the ghosts of nineteenth-century patriots who spent more time living in exile than in the homeland.[126] How, then, do we explain the dichotomy between present-day Dominican ideologues' veneration of some nineteenth- and early twentieth-century exiles as ideal patriots and simultaneous disavowal of current diaspora subjects? Throughout the Americas, the idea of a patriot is connected irrefutably with the creation of "modern" and "civilized" nation-states. Yet his image reflects the vestiges of European colonialism since these nation-states— with the partial exception of Haiti—inherited European racial and gender hierarchies of what modernity and civilization meant. *Colonial Phantoms* pinpoints the racialized, gendered, and class-based contours of ideal patriots who can continue to symbolize the nation even when geographically displaced. For instance, although the white, upper-class Juan Pablo Duarte, the Dominican founding father (1813–1876), spent the last thirty years of his life in exile, he continues to exemplify the nation's Eurocentric, patriarchal ideals. Nonwhite exemplars of Dominican patriotism, such as Francisco del Rosario Sánchez (1817–1861), undergo phenotypical whitening in commemorative imagery, tightening the knot that binds patriotism to whiteness.

When Dominicans migrate from the countryside to Dominican cities and when they emigrate from the Dominican Republic to other countries, they often carry traces of the country's singular history and its subsequent ghosting in embodied memories (chapters four and five).[127] The Dominican subjects that create and reside within the cultural texts I explore in this book re-create and engage with the ghosting of the territory's history and singularity ephemerally in gestures and speech and more lastingly through the written word. We may consider not only diasporic Dominican writers such as Junot Díaz and Julia Alvarez, who have transformed U.S. Latinx literature, but also musical artists such as Romeo Santos, a Bronx-born Dominican–Puerto Rican singer whose medium is *bachata*, a rural Dominican genre. In the summer of 2013, Santos performed two sold-out shows at Yankee Stadium, to an audience of 100,000, surpassing the ticket sales of Pink Floyd and only matched by the likes of Jay Z and Paul McCartney at this venue.[128]

However, migrant Dominicans also incorporate gestures, ephemeral acts, languages, and other cultural expressions of both mainstream and minority cultures in the "host" countries of which they become a part. As Michelle M. Wright warns: "While the passing down of knowledge from generation to generation is cherished by almost all collectivities, it does not operate as smoothly as most discourses describing it would prefer."[129] This nonlinear mish-mash is hardly a symptom of international migration; Dominicans on the island have been influenced by non-Dominican cultural expression for centuries. Nevertheless, as I endeavor to show throughout this book, Dominican nationalism, subaltern encounters with national and imperial powers, and Dominican narratives of blackness all engage with Dominicans' coloniality and refuse various forms of ghosting.

Many of the works of Firelei Báez, a Dominican-Haitian artist who grew up in Miami, instantiate the processes of unghosting that I argue has shaped various forms of Dominican cultural expression.[130] At least four of her artworks engage with the interplay between officialized forms of (Western) knowledge and, to cite Báez, the "often-inaccessible narratives dealing with histories outside of the global north."[131] These pieces—*Prescribed Seduction* (2012), *Blind Man's Bluff* (2012), *Man Without a Country (aka anthropophagist wading in the Artibonite River)* (2014–2015), and *Untitled (Memory Like Fire is Radiant and Immutable)* (2016)—incorporate pages ripped from deaccessioned library books. Báez collates the portraits, words, and visualized ideas of the apostles of the Western canon with women "sourced from revealing videos online [. . .]. These women perform publicly, but are unable to act as the central figure outside these videos because of cultural norms."[132] In *Man Without a Country* and *Untitled*, Báez adds colorful rogue limbs and dancing feminine figures to the mostly colorless library pages and maps. Several pages show small, almost imperceptible, nonwhite men wading in large bodies of water. Recalling the treacherous journeys of Caribbean migrants surrounded by water, one of the men holds a large, black plastic bag full of his belongings and another one is weighed down by two children on his back. Unlike the portraits of male scholars and government officials in the other pages, the waders' and the dancers' appearance in deaccessioned (i.e., worthless) books illuminate these subjects' subalternity and marginality.

On the other hand, the artistic inclusion of these subaltern figures onto these newly value-less pages prevents what Báez calls the "erasure" of "unsavory histories."[133] Indeed, these waders, dancers, migrants, and, in other pages of this piece, laborers give new life to and highlight the grotesque qualities of official histories. On one of the pages, Báez drew women dancing irreverently on top of a dour portrait of U.S. chemist James C. Booth (see Figure I.2). Red flame-like lines shoot out from Booth's head and eyes, turning him both devilish and carnivalesque. Other pages show the ghostly imprints of two photographs of Dominican dictator Rafael L. Trujillo and some of his officials, overshadowed by outlines of feminine, heeled bodies rendered in a botanical print.

On other pages, Báez obscures the portraits of "great men" with adornments both monstrous and beautiful, such as colorful dots of various sizes that resemble ink droppings. In *Untitled (Memory Like Fire is Radiant and Immutable)*, short, flowing hair strands cover three quarters of another portrait sitter's visage. Because hair does not usually grow on that part of a man's face, the result is both startling and comical. The serious countenance contrasts absurdly with the jellyfish-like waves of hair. He becomes a scholarly Chewbacca, a hapless prairie dog, or a Lucha Libre wrestler donning a furry mask (see Figure I.3). The hair strands reach backwards, suggesting a windy day that may at any moment obscure his vision. His eyes peek through temporary hair partitions. This specific man is Trujillo, a dictator who required veneration from his constituents on the pain of death. Báez's revision of his portrait disrupts the respect, gravitas, and hushed tones images such as these demand from the viewer, inviting mockery and revulsion. These mangled portraits are akin to a schoolchild's doodling, though certainly much more skillful and deliberate. As such, they repeat the almost sacrilegious act of not paying proper homage to either books or these outsized "great men" of history and knowledge. These acts of cheeky recalcitrance

Figure I.2. Firelei Báez, *Man Without a Country (aka anthropophagist wading in the Artibonite River* (detail), 2014/15. Gouache, ink, and chine-collé on 220 deaccessioned book pages, 9 x 21 feet. (Courtesy of the artist and Gallery Wendi Norris, San Francisco.)

Figure I.3. Firelei Báez, *Untitled (Memory Like Fire is Radiant and Immutable* (detail), 2016. Gouache, ink, and chine-collé on 28 deaccessioned book pages, 98 x 72 inches. (Courtesy of the artist and Gallery Wendi Norris, San Francisco.)

and refusal destroy the idealized visualities of imperial and patriarchal power through the creation of fragmented and irreverent images that invite the viewer to wonder: "What am I looking at?" Báez's work urges us to scrutinize Captain Delano's gaze and, in so doing, we render *him* the stranger.

The Chapters

Confirming the long-term transnationalism of Dominicans, the texts I analyze in this book were produced by and about Dominicans (and some non-Dominicans) either on the island or in the U.S., Europe, and other sites of the Dominican diaspora. The late twentieth century saw an important change in cultural demographics; the growth of the Dominican diaspora has accompanied an increase in access to information technologies, especially for Dominicans who migrate to the U.S., which has led to a democratization of who can record and share (not only produce) their cultural expressions. The book's shift from the written word in the nineteenth century to a great variety of cultural texts from the twentieth century to the present reflects this important shift.

The mid- to late nineteenth century, after the first republic (1844–1861) and a brief Spanish annexation (1861–1865), was a crucial period for the creation of a unified national culture. The herculean task of deciphering what it meant to be Dominican was always tied to either attracting or stalling imperial attention, depending on the political faction. Chapter one, "Untangling Dominican Patriotism: Exiled Men and Poet Muses Script the Gendered Nation," studies the conundrum that is Salomé Ureña (1850–1897), a nonwhite woman of the lettered elite who became the most celebrated poet in Dominican history. Studying poems, letters, speeches, and essays by Ureña and some of her contemporaries, I propose that Ureña's patriotic writings, and her never-mentioned blackness combined with her elite class status, allowed Dominicans of the intellectual and ruling elite to satisfy two intertwined impulses. The first was to construct a national identity that could explain Dominican difference from Haiti, and, as such, secure a seat at the (white supremacist) global table. The second, more subterranean or ghosted impulse, was a tacit acceptance that a nonwhite woman such as Ureña could only be considered "the muse of the nation" among an elite that valued whiteness because Dominican territory had a history of black freedom and leadership.

Chapter two, "Race, Gender, and Propriety in Dominican Commemoration," homes in on the gendered and raced contours of nationalist commemoration from the late nineteenth century to the present day, especially as it pertained to Ureña. I argue that the endurance of Ureña's legacy as the face of Dominican literature and education relied both on her phenotypical whitening in sculpture and painting and on the perpetuation of a selective reading or total elision of some of the subversive desires expressed in her work. The first half of the chapter focuses on which visual and rhetorical motifs remained and which changed so that Ureña could continue to be celebrated as a national icon well into the explicitly antiblack Trujillo and Balaguer regimes. Although Ureña's nonwhiteness was never mentioned either during or after her lifetime in the hundreds of pages dedicated to her life and work, her image was phenotypically whitened in commemoration, proving that her status as the nation's foremost poet coincided with the white supremacist impulses of the nation's elite. The second half of the chapter examines select writings by two twenty-first century feminist and diasporic Dominican women writers, Julia Alvarez and Sherezada (Chiqui) Vicioso, that resurrect an Ureña closer to the woman of "flesh and bone" and not the ghostly vestige she had become through commemoration. By the time that writers such as Alvarez and Vicioso create their versions of Ureña, feminist and critical race studies, the advancement of and greater variety of cultural dissemination technologies, the increase in Dominican literacy rates, and the astronomical growth of a diasporic Dominican community with a different vocabulary of race have all contributed to a moment when Alvarez's and Vicioso's recuperative acts are not only possible but could also compete with other dominant Dominican narratives.

Chapter three, "Following the Admiral: Reckonings with Great Men's History," examines how European colonialism, U.S. empire, and Dominican patriarchal nationalism intersected for over a century to create the Columbus Lighthouse Memorial in Santo Domingo. These entities, however, cannot account for subaltern subjects' relationships to monuments such as the Lighthouse and the history that they celebrate. To get at this "history from below," I analyze Junot Díaz's *The Brief Wondrous Life of Oscar Wao*, the Dominican-American film *La Soga*, and the controversy surrounding the 1985 murder of pop merengue icon Tony Seval in police custody. Juxtaposing these narratives, I contend that working-class island and diasporic Dominican men, most of them nonwhite, resist the persistent nationalist and imperialist violence that the Lighthouse celebrates through the performance of a distinctly Dominican hypermasculine performance known locally as *tigueraje*. While resistant to Eurocentric patriarchal history, these performances are nevertheless masculinist and, as such, prioritize the enactment of violence on noncompliant subjects, including women and queer subjects.

Chapter four, "Dominican Women's Refracted African Diasporas," engages the creative and antihegemonic apertures that become possible from a diasporic space and imaginary by analyzing the cultural expressions, including literature, music, and performance, of several diasporic Dominican women. I resist the teleology of blackness in which Dominican subjects do not know that they are "black" until they arrive in the U.S. The women artists I analyze stretch the boundaries of who is an ideal national (U.S. and Dominican) and diasporic (Dominican and African) subject. I juxtapose the various ways in which aforementioned writer Chiqui Vicioso and musical artists Amara la Negra and Maluca Mala perform what they view as their black identity, which prompts us to acknowledge the prismatic—and nonlinear—nature of the African diaspora.

Chapter five, "Working Women and the Neoliberal Gaze," focuses on several cultural texts about nonwhite Dominican women who work within economies created or strengthened by neoliberal policies. I focus especially on what Amalia Cabezas calls "economies of desire." By analyzing the photo series and personal account of a U.S. sex tourist, a short story by Dominican writer Aurora Arias, sex worker testimonies, and several recent films, I argue that the sites of sex labor and sex tourism reveal the extent to which post-1980s global market demands have folded Dominican society and culture into a dominant neoliberal global paradigm based on so-called free trade agreements. I demonstrate that the temporal and spatial logics of these neoliberal paradigms are reinstantiations of colonial world hierarchies, and that, as such, Dominican women working within these economies of desire negotiate centuries-old racist associations of nonwhite Caribbean women with hypersexuality or natural caretaking abilities, or both.

The brief "Conclusion: Searching for Monte Refusals," ponders how subaltern subjects, before the democratization of who can record and disseminate their worldview, refused or in some way manipulated the interpellating, imperial gaze.

Together, these chapters evince Dominican negotiations with various forms of ghosting from broader Western imaginaries. The texts I analyze show traces of the Dominican Republic's singular history as a territory in which the white colonial gaze could not entirely eradicate black freedom in el monte. The narratives that emerge from the clashes between colonial/national/imperial purviews and these ghosted forms of black self-rule manifest Dominicans' attempts to create inclusive (e.g., *afrolatinidad*) and exclusive (e.g., anti-Haitian Dominican national identity) forms of belonging, as well as their refusals to acquiesce to dominant racial narratives (e.g., the one-drop rule that determines blackness in dominant U.S. discourses).

1

Untangling Dominican Patriotism

Exiled Men and Poet Muses Script the Gendered Nation

The *patria* sings its siren song, luring the *pueblo* back to the
familiar, dominant, father-figure discourse.
—Raúl Coronado, *A World Not to Come* (2013)

Just a few days before Christmas 1878, the influential literary and cultural
society Amigos del País (Friends of the Country) held an event in honor
of one of the country's most renowned poets, Salomé Ureña.[1] Held at the
Public Library in Santo Domingo, which was "elegantly decorated" with
"flowers, paintings, lights" and tastefully catered, the event was attended
by some of the most important politicians, writers, and other notable
figures in the country.[2] In the words of Justo, a society columnist, these
important personalities, a crowd of approximately 80 women and 70
men, had gathered in order to "render the tribute of estimation and justice to the Dominican Avellaneda," a reference to one of Latin America's
foremost women poets, the Spanish Cuban Gertrúdis Gomez de Avellaneda (1814–1873), to whom Ureña was compared repeatedly.[3] Playing
"magnificent operas and delicious national waltzes," the orchestra added
to the atmosphere.[4] Several members of Amigos del País, including its
president at the time and Ureña's future husband, the nineteen-year-old
Francisco Henríquez y Carvajal, gave speeches in her honor. In Justo's
cheeky estimation, not all of the speakers were enthralling: "Penson
awarded us an extensive, very extensive, too extensive literary work"[5]
that almost ruined the evening until "a reading was given of *Oda a la
Patria* [Ode to the Homeland] by the eminent poetess Ureña."[6] Not only
had Ureña's verses provided succor to the many Dominican, and non-
Dominican, patriots yearning for a better, independent nation, but they
had also saved the evening. For her efforts and talent, the Amigos del

País gave Ureña a Medal of Honor, funded by members and by donations from the public at large.

Receiving the Medal of Honor consecrated Ureña as the most important voice in the Dominican Republic during a time when the country was beginning to narrate what it meant to be Dominican. A grasp of the gendered and raced contours of twenty-first-century Dominican nationalism requires a thorough analysis of these early moments of discursive consolidation among the ruling elite. This chapter turns to these moments when the Dominican cultural elite wrote and read the nation into being, focusing especially on the person who best fulfilled the needs of the era, the poet and educator Salomé Ureña. I unspool the knot of associations that tightened at this crucial late nineteenth-century moment after the Dominican Republic reinstated its independence from Spain after a brief annexation from 1861 until 1865; when U.S. annexation was a real possibility; "progress" was a buzzword; and intellectuals and politicians vied for what the official nationalist discourse should be. To some, the country should invite the Plantation economy, then collapsing in the surrounding region with the abolition of slavery (Cuba, 1886; Puerto Rico, 1873–1876; the United States, 1865). To others, education and advances in agricultural and medical technology were the solution. To a few leaders, the Dominican Republic and Haiti together were setting an example of black freedom. It was during this critical moment of both nationalist consolidation and the rise of the U.S. as a global imperial force that Salomé Ureña emerged as the "muse of the nation."

Ureña was born in 1850 in Santo Domingo and died of tuberculosis in 1897, having never left the country. Born into the urban bourgeois elite, her work as a poet and educator catapulted her to an unprecedented renown. After becoming the nation's foremost poet, she opened the first "normal"—that is, secular—institution of higher education for girls. It offered students the chance to study beyond primary school, and many of the young women who graduated from this institution went on to open their own schools around the country. Dominican scholars such as Ramonina Brea and Isis Duarte credit Ureña's educational efforts with "legitimizing middle- and upper-class women's infiltration into the labor force and the public sphere."[7] Despite her gender, Ureña succeeded in an era and a field in which the patriarchal standards that predominated in the governing elite should have excluded her.[8]

Studying poems, letters, speeches, and essays by Ureña and some of her contemporaries, I trace the complex but clearly gendered scripts of patriotic performance in which her readers partook.[9] Ureña's poems elicited a set of reactions and behaviors from her readers. The poems themselves did not *have* to elicit these behaviors, but, as I undertake to show in this chapter, they did so due to the developing and firming of gendered assumptions in Dominican nationalist discourse. Why did the Dominican lettered ruling class—composed mostly of men—viscerally need the patriotic poems of a nonwhite woman? This is the question I endeavor to answer. The strong desire for Ureña's poetry coexisted with many of these same men's generalized assumption that the ideal citizen subject was a man, if not actually a white man then at least a landowning, Europeanized man. The impossibility of answering this question with total conviction notwithstanding, I conclude that Ureña's embodiment of Dominican nonwhiteness combined with her status as a respectable woman allowed Dominicans of the intellectual and ruling elite to satisfy two intertwined impulses: (1) the desire to be a "civilized" (i.e., European) and "cultured" nation alongside the other nations in the Western hemisphere, and (2) a subconscious recognition that the Dominican territory differed markedly from the rest of this hemisphere. That is, Ureña's never-mentioned blackness combined with her elite class status wedded two driving impulses behind the burgeoning Dominican nationalism. The first was to construct a national identity that could explain Dominican difference from Haiti, and, as such, justify a seat at the global table. The second, more subterranean impulse was a tacit acceptance that a nonwhite woman such as Ureña could only be considered "the muse of the nation" among an elite that valued whiteness because Dominican territory had a history of black freedom and colonial neglect. This colonial neglect, as I described in the introduction, resulted in the haphazard policing of racial and color lines that had significantly shaped neighboring colonies such as Saint-Domingue and Cuba.

Race and gender are inseparable in this discussion. While Ureña's readers never mentioned her blackness during or directly after her lifetime, at least in writing, they obsessively discussed her gender. Her male readers were persistently surprised that Ureña was a woman, and they repeatedly gendered her patriotic poems as masculine—a positive trait—and her more "intimate" poems as feminine—a lesser trait.[10] Many of Ureña's readers called her the muse of the nation—rather than a poet whose muse was the nation, as was the case for male poets.[11] The prevailing ideology of nationalists such as Ureña and others like her combined a yearning for progress with an active construction of an appropriate national past. The pull of tradition was gendered as feminine and the modernizing impulse was considered masculine.[12] These binaries correlate with other semiotic categories so that tradition and *lo femenino* (the feminine) represent the (home)land and the hearth, while progress and *lo masculino* (the masculine) symbolize exile, movement, revolution, and modernity. In this case, tradition did not correlate with backwardness (the opposite of modernity), but with a domesticity that was a necessary, if lesser, corollary to modernity. That is, unlike the backwardness that el monte—the anonymous, autonomous, black, and often masculinized rurality—represented, this domestic femininity was not antithetical to progress. Ureña and her work could represent both poles comprising ideas of progress, rendering her an ideal vessel for the performance of late nineteenth-century patriotism.

The small but powerful elite of which Ureña was part created a long-lasting print culture that disseminated a nationalist vision. Ureña's husband, Francisco "Pancho" Henríquez y Carvajal (1859–1935), and her brother-in-law, Federico Henríquez y Carvajal (1848–1952), were crucial members of an influential Liberal, urban bourgeoisie. Both of these men became political and intellectual leaders. Francisco became the president of the country in 1916 before he was illegally ousted through the U.S. occupying forces, and both men had long been at the center of the most important intellectual debates of the era related to education, literature, medicine, and agriculture. Alongside Ureña and Eugenio María de Hostos, the Henríquez y Carvajal brothers helped increase the number of teachers in the country.[13]

These and other men and women of the positivist movement were also the publishers and editors of influential literary magazines. They read each other's work, published it, shared it, and wrote about it. The tremendous importance of literary periodicals at this historical juncture was such that one of Ureña's children, Max, recalls that one of his and his brother Pedro's favorite activities was compiling Dominican poetry and "publishing" a daily newspaper:

> But Pedro and I were not content to just compile verses taken from newspapers: we wanted to have our own newspapers. I launched into circulation in our home a weekly one-page manuscript [. . .]. I named it: *The Afternoon*. Naturally, I only printed one copy, which would circulate at home from person to person. [. . .] Pedro released another one-page periodical, also weekly, which he baptized: *La Patria*, and within it appeared reproductions of our poets accompanied by his comments, likely the earliest manifestation of his future talent as a critic and essayist.[14]

Certainly, the Henríquez Ureña household—headed by two parents of national stature—cannot be considered exemplary of Dominican families. Even before her marriage, Ureña's home was a literary salon of sorts, visited by intellectual elites from around the country and even other parts of the Hispanophone world. It became even more of a hub after she married an important patriotic actor and opened the Instituto de Señoritas in the family's first small house in the Colonial Zone of Santo Domingo.[15] Nevertheless, the point I wish to make is that reading, writing, and publishing was not a marginal component of the project of nation-building. The childhood game that Max describes illustrates how literary publications and newspapers were vehicles for writing the nation into being by the late 1880s and early 1890s.

Much of the literary print culture during Ureña's lifetime can be described as romanticist infused with a positivist political ideology that focused on progress and modernization.[16] Beyond the realm of literary discourse, positivist ideology prioritized "modern agricultural techniques, secular education, and political participation."[17] As Teresita Martínez Vergne writes regarding the late nineteenth- and early twentieth-century intellectual circles of which Ureña was part: "Progress, as they envisioned it, was the concerted effort of a political and intellectual elite, with regulated input from common people."[18] According to Michiel Baud: "Most Latin American elites tried to forge their nations in the name of el progreso, a concept that symbolized the desire for rapid modernization, but at the same time they feared, and sometimes resisted the destruction of 'traditional' society."[19] In the realm of literary and cultural discourse, fantasies of the future, as well as "memories" of a heroic past, drove positivist ideology as it emerged in some of the most representative literature of the era. This search for a foundational creation myth explains the surge in *indigenista* literature by writers such as José Joaquín Pérez, who wrote the collection of poems *Fantasías indíjenas* (1877), and Manuel de Jesús Galván, who wrote the immediately canonical historical novel *Enriquillo*.[20] Ureña was also part of this indigenista surge with her epic poem "Anacaona" (1880).[21]

Several scholars insist that indigenista works ghosted Dominicans' blackness by replacing it with the glory of the indigenous rebellions against the Spanish in the fifteenth and sixteenth centuries. Indeed, it has become pervasive that Dominican literature that does not mention Haiti proves anti-Haitianism. This scholarship on Dominican national identity contends that, on the one hand, indigenista discourse replaced Haiti with Spain as the Dominican nation's Other, and, on the other hand, it is "a form of Hispanicism."[22] Doris Sommer argues that Galván's *Enriquillo* "replac[es] rebellious blacks for peace-loving and long-extinct natives who become putative ancestors for today's 'Indian' masses in the Dominican Republic."[23] Sibylle Fischer proposes that Dominican *indigenismo* "displac[es] and suppress[es] any reference to revolutionary antislavery and a peripheral modernity within the core of the Dominican imaginary."[24] Lorgia García-Peña contends that these indigenista texts' "affirmative *diction*" that "Dominicans are Indians" "depends on the perpetuation of the negation" that "Dominicans are not black."[25] Maria Cristina Fumagalli concludes that "[t]he national anthem [. . .] refers to the country as 'Quisqueya' and to the Dominicans as 'Quisqueyanos' in line with the discourse of indigenism deployed in the Dominican Republic to deny the African presence on the territory."[26]

While I agree that Dominican *indigenismo* arose as a ghosting mechanism to erase the forms of free black subjectivity that had uniquely emerged throughout this territory, it must also be contextualized with literary and cultural trends in the region. Consider, for instance, that the name of Haiti also alludes to the indigenous past.[27] Anne Eller provides pan-Caribbean context to the indigenista literary surge:

Guarionex, the cacique hero of a number of the works, was from the island of Ayiti; he was used by Puerto Rican authors like Alejandro Tapia y Rivera (in *La Palma de Cacique*, 1852) and Eugenio María de Hostos (in *Bayoán*, 1863) to connect the Ayiti to Puerto Rican and Cuban figures. Favored rebels Guama and Hatuey, similarly, had Haitian-Dominican roots; during the Cuban independence fight of subsequent decades, the former was made analogous to Antonio Maceo and the latter to another famous Dominican migrant, Máximo Gómez.[28]

That is, several leading Puerto Rican intellectuals were inspired by Dominican indigenous history in the Puerto Rican and Cuban struggles against Spanish colonialism. That these efforts preceded Dominican *indigenismo* by at least a decade is also worthy of note. The Liberal Dominican elite were influenced deeply by intellectuals such as Eugenio María de Hostos—who helped Ureña and her husband open schools in Santo Domingo—and José Martí—who visited the Dominican Republic and met with Ureña's husband and brother-in-law. Considering how closely these intellectuals and writers worked together, it behooves us to consider the indigenista trend within this larger context of pan-Caribbean communication and shared allegories.

Moreover, the absence of any mention of Haiti or even blackness from Dominican indigenista works does not necessarily result from anxieties about Haiti. If anything, these works subconsciously, perhaps inadvertently, advocate for a unified island since the events of the conquest occurred well before the island's separation in the late seventeenth century. Scholars' critique of indigenista literature often relies on what goes unmentioned—blackness, black slavery, Haiti—but equally unmentioned in these indigenista works is that *taínos* struggled to protect the whole island from Spanish governance, not the Dominican Republic, which did not yet exist. Finally, when scholars critique Dominican indigenista literature, they often group Ureña with writers such as Galván without taking into account that these two authors' politics differed markedly. Galván was a staunch proannexationist and anti-Haitianist. Ureña believed in the idea of a sovereign nation and, while she certainly could not be described as a champion of "revolutionary antislavery," the only mention of Haiti in her writings is when her husband, other family members, and friends move there temporarily to live in exile.[29] That

Haiti emerged as a space of refuge for some in Ureña's cohort, while Galván and others were so aghast at the very idea of Haiti that they fled the island, is worthy of pause. Certainly, Ureña's indigenista poetry, as much as her other patriotic poetry, helped to ghost el monte and the autonomous, free blackness it had represented for centuries. However, in glossing over these differing relationships to and ideas about Haiti among these late nineteenth-century writers, we are in danger of enshrining anti-Haitianism as the heart of Dominican nationalism. In fact, Ureña's life and writings illustrate that burgeoning Dominican nationalism was deeply complicated. Grasping the variety of cultural expression that nationalist feeling occasioned requires that we pause on these ambivalences and contradictions.

The Woman Poet as Muse

While Ureña's audience knew that a woman had written the poems they loved, they maintained gendered, conceptual boundaries about which poems to exalt, what elements of her poetry deserved praise, and which words to use when expressing their admiration. The result is a nationalist script in which Ureña's patriotic poems were the "scriptive things," to borrow Robin Bernstein's concept, that incited certain "bodily behaviors" in Dominicans who wanted to express their love-of-nation to both limited audiences (e.g. through private letters) and to a larger reading public (e.g. through publication in literary venues).[30] Many cultural arbiters recorded and published for posterity their reactions to Ureña's patriotic poems. These responses are the scripts that helped codify how Dominican subjects embodied and expressed (i.e., performed) patriotism. Though these texts always commended Ureña's poetry—at times hyperbolically—they were not only celebratory. They also showed readers how Ureña's patriotic poems could help them perform patriotism, and the authors exhorted other Dominican subjects to also be inspired by Ureña's poems. These cultural arbiters wrote hundreds of pages that prompted readers to respond to Ureña's poems as scriptive pieces that could trigger patriotic actions and feelings. They did this by detailing their own reactions to her patriotic poems.

It is important at this juncture to understand who comprised Ureña's readership. More than likely, it included many women. For instance, there were more women than men present at her Medal of Honor ceremony in 1878.[31] This does not prove that all of these women had read her work, but we may surmise that at least some of them had. Though women read her poems, those who published essays and performed speeches about them were almost without exception men. A comprehensive anthology of writings about Ureña published in 1960 does not include a single essay or poem about Ureña written by a woman while she was still alive. Of the fifty or so selections in the anthology dedicated to panegyrics written upon and after her death, only eleven were penned by women, most of them Ureña's students. This offers fascinating proof of women's near invisibility in the public sphere of letters during Ureña's lifetime, as well as the extent to which Ureña's school helped to increase the number of women who wrote and spoke at public events. The sheer dearth of women who wrote and spoke in public during her lifetime highlights how incredible it was that Ureña could become such an important literary figure. Even more shocking is that she became *the* writer of her era and that her legacy endures to this day.

By the time she was awarded with the Medal of Honor for her poetry in 1878, she had emerged as one of the country's most important patriotic voices. Her poetry, which circulated widely in newspapers and other publications, called on her fellow Dominicans to rise up against the tyranny of those who wanted to annex the country to a foreign power and to work toward modernization. In 1874, some of her verses, including poems that had been published in Cuba, appeared in the anthology of Dominican poetry *Lira de Quisqueya*.[32] In 1880, her first anthology of poems was published. Of the thirty-four poems included, about a dozen deal with the nation's heroic and tragic history (e.g., "Colón" [Columbus, 1879] and "Anacaona" [1880]), its ruinous present state (e.g., "Ruinas" [Ruins, 1876]), and its potential glorious future (e.g., "La gloria del progreso" [The Glory of Progress, 1873] and "La fe en el porvenir" [Faith in the Future, 1878]). Several are dedicated to important Dominican literary and political figures (e.g., "Homenaje a Billini" [Homage to Billini, 1875] and "En la muerte Espaillat" [Upon the Death of Espaillant, 1878]). Most of the remaining verses explore more difficult-to-categorize themes, including mourning, melancholy, motherhood, the qualities of music, and sexual yearning for her husband.

Despite this great variety, it was her patriotic verses that led to her fame. "A la Patria" (1874), for instance, evokes some of the themes that patriotic Liberals of the time most celebrated. Her patriotic poems folded past and future as "tradition" and "progress" within their structure. Additionally, the conventional structure of the poems, which combined romanticist and positivist yearnings, obscured Ureña's subjectivity as a woman patriot, and many of her male readers could yearn for the nation unimpeded by the fact of her being a woman. One of the earliest anthologies of Dominican poetry, *Lira de Quisqueya* (1874), includes five poems named "A mi patria" or "Mi patria" by as many writers. This is not counting Ureña's own "A mi patria," as "A la Patria" was first titled, which is also in the anthology. While several critics argued that Ureña's verses to the *patria* reached a perfection unattained by other writers, I propose that patriotic verses had become so standard that they obscured Ureña as a distinct speaker of patriotic desire. In "A la Patria," she writes:

> Desgarra, Patria mía, el manto que vilmente,
> sobre tus hombros puso la bárbara crueldad;
> levanta ya del polvo la ensangrentada frente,
> y entona en himno santo de unión y libertad.[33]

> Tear off, my homeland, the cloak that
> barbaric cruelty placed over your shoulders;
> lift your bloodied forehead from the dust,
> and sing the saintly hymn of union and liberty.

The mostly unnamed desiring "I" in the poem is both Ureña herself and a generic Dominican patriot. The romanticist structure of the poem, in which a subject desires an object—"Patria mía" (a feminized patria)—obscured the desiring (female) subject-writer of the poem. Also conventional is the poem's gendering of the patria as a mother and Dominicans as her "*hijos*" (children or sons). As a woman poet who followed these conventions, Ureña subverted the paradigm that assumes a heterosexual male poet who desires the female patria by queering this patriotic desire. It was a potential space of subversion, however, that her male readers' persistently elided by placing themselves in the role of desiring "I" and displacing Ureña as a desired muse alongside the nation.

Ureña's adoption of the imperative verb tense in several of her patriotic poems also eased readers' performance of patriotism. In "A la Patria," the object of Ureña's admonitions is the personified, feminized patria herself. Several of her poems were written expressly for public events or institutions, and, as such, they addressed an audience directly. For instance, she wrote a poem in honor of society La Juventud (The Youth) called "La gloria del progreso" (The Glory of Progress, 1973). Scattered throughout the poem are words such as *contemplad* (contemplate) and *mirad* (look) in the imperative tense. The last two stanzas name her audience directly. She writes "¡Oh juventud, que de la Patria mía / eres honor y orgullo y esperanza!" (Oh youth, that in my Patria / you are honor and pride and hope!).[34] In another patriotic poem, "A los Dominicanos," which I discuss further later in this chapter, the imperative voice predominates. The first lines of the poem clarify the audience: "Los que del templo de la gloria / la Patria levantar a lo eminente" (Those who yearned to lift the Fatherland / into the eminent temple of glory).[35] Following these lines are several stanzas with directives such as "[v]olad a recibir el tierno abrazo / de la madre amorosa que os dio vida" ([f]ly to receive the tender embrace / of the mother who gave you life).[36] Several other patriotic poems more clearly evoke a desiring subject, an "I," who implores the patria into action. However, due to convention, the "I" could be any patriot, facilitating her male readers' entire identification with the desiring subject in these poems. "A mi Patria" (To My Patria, 1878), for instance, includes a desiring "I" in its very title. While the poem mentions what seem to be personal details, such as "tu inquieta brisa remeció mi cuna" (your restless breeze rocked my cradle), they lend themselves to a universalist reading.[37] To many of her readers, Ureña writes not of her own infancy, but that of any patriot. The universality of Ureña's patriotic poetry, which did not point either to her personal life or to her preference for a specific political party, became so prevalent a notion that over half a century later, the intellectual and politician Joaquín Balaguer described Ureña thusly:

> She was the first [poet] in Santo Domingo that had the sentiment of great poetry, the one who was truly great, because far from imprisoning herself

in the intimacy of a writer to gather only the echo of his or her own miseries, she rises up to dominate the entire spectacle of life and tends to make herself the interpreter of wider and simultaneously deeper areas of human sensibility.[38]

To Balaguer, the greatness of Ureña's verses stem from their distance to the personal, which she explored at length in her intimate poetry. These patriotic poems allowed men of her era and since to graft themselves into the position of desiring patriots, unimpeded by what were considered to be womanly feelings.

Within the set of gendered (classed and raced) binaries that informed how "scriptive things"/patriotic poems prompted Dominican subjects to perform patriotism, Ureña occupied a unique role as the woman who created them. Because they had the political and symbolic capacity to be full citizens of the nation-state as potential voters and elected leaders, Dominican men could best create the scripts that Ureña's poems inspired or prompted. But it was precisely the fact that she and her work were seen as the inspiration for scripting the nation, rather than as a scriptor of the nation herself, that elided Ureña's potential role as a Dominican patriot with complicated and ambivalent desires. The gendered set of binaries and assumptions of woman/land/tradition and man/citizen subject/progress explain the persistent slippage of Ureña from poet to muse that would have been unlikely in the case of a male poet.

Male poets who wrote of their yearning for the (feminized) homeland did not subvert gendered symbolic assumptions. That is, men who expressed their love of a (female) patria remained ensconced safely on their side of the binary. How did Ureña's readers reconcile these deeply entrenched assumptions with the fact that the poet who best expressed love-of-nation was a woman? The simplest answer to this question is that Ureña's readership often gendered Ureña's work as masculine, while insisting on her femininity. Six years after her death, the Puerto Rican poet Mariano Riera Palmer described Ureña as a "fecund and virile poetess."[39] Unlike another famed poet, schoolteacher, and national icon, the Chilean Gabriela Mistral (1889–1957), Ureña was never "described as being more masculine than feminine—or as ambiguous or simply 'queer.'"[40] What was queered, or at least curiously gendered, was her poetry. In a collection of the panegyrics dedicated to Ureña during her lifetime, upon her death, and decades later, two of the most frequent words used to describe her poetry are *viril* (virile) and *varonil* (manly).[41] Unsurprisingly, many critics exclaim surprise that she is a woman. After hearing one of her poems, the poet Angulo Guiridi reportedly shouts: "¡Es muy hombre esa mujer!" ("That woman makes a great man!")[42] Though one might compare Salomé Ureña's reception to that of her Puerto Rican contemporary, Lola Rodríguez de Tió, or Chilean Gabriela Mistral, it bears saying that it was Ureña's poetry, not Ureña herself, who was considered masculine.[43] Writing from Cuba in 1876, Nicolás Heredia makes the suggestive observation that Ureña "resembles a poet more than a poetess."[44] Regarding her poem "Gloria del progreso" (Glory of Progress), he esteems: "Do not search in it [the poem] the tenderness of a feminine sentiment that becomes *softer* the more it approaches poetry, no."[45] Heredia also describes her verses using words such as *severo* (severe), *grave* (grave), and *árida* (arid), which are all compliments. These masculinist descriptions rendered Ureña's literature an appropriate—if not ideal—vehicle through which men could perform patriotism. Indeed, *only* Ureña and her work could satisfy all of these seemingly inchoate desires for Dominican patriots.

As I show in the next chapter, it would not be until a late twentieth-century readership of diasporic feminist women that Ureña's intimate writings would be celebrated in the public sphere. These intimate works coincided with Ureña's emergence as a pioneer in women's education. In this era of her life, Ureña lived out the nuanced ways in which a literate woman patriot and educator could also remain utterly frustrated by certain elements of Liberal and positivist ideology.

Several of the men who read her patriotic poems saw Ureña as a *symbol* of the patria. Male poets during Ureña's era were never, to my knowledge, considered symbols of the patria, but rather patriots themselves. The reason for this is that, as I mentioned above, nationalist scripts tended to feminize the homeland. The homeland was both object (the land) and an eternal idea. When temporal, it represented tradition. In this scheme, men were agents and, as such, existed in time. Men could move geographically and temporally. They were not eternal. It is not surprising, then, that many of her male readers—the ones who published their reactions to her work—considered her both muse and symbol. These ideas become particularly evident when we study some of the contours around the word *patria*, which has no easy translation into English, for it means homeland, motherland, and fatherland. It is a feminine noun (*la* patria), but contains the Latin root for father (*pater*). "In this post-Independence era," writes Catharina Vallejo, "the concept of 'patria' is frequently personified with the concept of 'woman' [. . .] Generally [. . .] the personification of 'patria' falls back on the mother."[46] Like other feminized categories related to the nation, such as the land, "[l]a patria is always an abstract concept."[47] This contrasts with individual and distinct male subjects.

The gendered dichotomy between patriotic/masculine/important poetry and intimate/feminine/trivial poetry governed the estimations of most of her male readers. The exceptions to this tendency are in the minority. In a study of Ureña's poetry published in 1879, Ureña's future brother-in-law, Federico Henríquez y Carvajal, gives considerable weight to all of her work, including some of her so-called intimate or domestic works such as "Melancolía" (Melancholy) and "El ave y el nido" (The Bird and the Nest).[48] Two other critics who appreciate her intimate work on an equal or almost equal level as her patriotic verses are Federico Benigno Pérez and Rafael Deligne.[49] However, as influential as these men were, their estimations did not reflect the dominant propensities of the era.

In 1888, the writer Federico García Godoy deems Ureña's verses about parenting "una joya" (a jewel). However, "the chord that most vibrates in the golden lira of Mrs. Ureña de Henríquez is undoubtedly that of patriotism."[50] He continues: "Her muse did not descend to certain *trivialities*, nor does she allow herself to be led by the currents that always drag mediocre talents. Her poetry is *virile* and full of greatness, as if composed to the heat of the great ideas of regeneration and progress that the modern spirit continuously spreads to every corner of the globe."[51] García Godoy praises Ureña for maintaining a thematic emphasis on the grandiose ideas of modernity and progress, rather than on "trivialities"—a word with deridingly feminine connotations. He also pays Ureña the highest compliment of virility, alluding to masculine prowess and energy. He then connects this virility with "great ideas of regeneration and progress," a reminder of the assumption that "mobile" subjects are or should be masculine and "immobile" subjects are and should be feminine. Two months after Ureña's death, Luis A. Bermúdez complimented her thusly: "Salomé Ureña was a daring poet; within her bosom never fit all that sentimentality that makes some poetesses somewhat repugnant on certain occasions."[52]

Ureña's male readers were blinded to the ways in which her intimate poems, which portrayed Ureña's desires beyond patriotism, were vehicles to another set of performances. Her intimate poetry, as well as her private letters to her husband, modelled a subversive femininity unfamiliar to the lettered elite, more complicated than her readers could embrace or even discern, and distant from poetic conventions. Individual in their aim and subject, these poems were vehicles that scripted Ureña herself—the woman, poet, and patriot—into the national space. Several were dedicated to her husband as the man she loved and not necessarily in his capacity as a public servant. One of her most famed poems, "Mi Pedro," presages her son's ascent as one of Latin America's most important intellectuals. However, men such as Ureña's husband were not impressed with the vision of the nation that Ureña's intimate poetry and private letters explored. This vision was messy, contradictory, and uncertain, revealing desires alien to Liberal, positivist ideology.

Affective Releases of Patriotism

Many Dominican men, including those living in exile, considered reading Ureña's patriotic poetry an important component of practicing and performing patriotism. The archive of letters and published essays that were written about her poems illustrate this fact. Ureña's readers scripted their patriotic performances not only by reading her poetry—an act that could remain a secret—but also by sharing their emotional responses in writing. The act of reading, in which only a small minority of Dominicans could partake at the time, transformed the theoretical idea of "nation" into a performative patriotism. The transformation of reading from a private act between a subject and the written word to a public display of sentimentality took place on the pages of the era's literary magazines, in the classrooms filled with future leaders, and at literary events. Too, exiled readers' dramatic descriptions of their encounters with the verses portrayed them as true patriots whose love toward the nation only deepened with geographic distance.

The heterosexual coupling of a male citizen who yearns for a female homeland rendered safe the intense feelings that Ureña's poetry prompted from her male readers. Some of the most passionate demonstrations of positivist desires for nationalist progress and unification emerge in the letters that Ureña's husband, Henríquez y Carvajal, wrote to her. His earliest letters evince the common overlap, and even usurpation, of Ureña's personhood with her patriotic message. By the time they met, Ureña's poetry had brought her fame among Santo Domingo's literary and political circles, and even some renown abroad. Several non-Dominican literary societies made her an honorary member, including the Círculo Literario de Puerto Príncipe in Cuba and the Alegría of Coro, Venezuela.[53] Ureña's prominence meant that she moved within the small intellectual circles that included Henríquez y Carvajal, then president of the influential Amigos del País. Henríquez y Carvajal recalls his initial encounter with her on New Year's Day in 1879, just two weeks after the ceremony in which Amigos del País awarded Ureña the Medal of Honor:

> On June 10 of the year that has just ended, during a literary session that our society "Friends of the Country" celebrated as a Conference, I had the fortune to see you [. . .]. I did not know you personally, but I did through your work, which I had always admired, as I admired you that night with the poem that you read to those around you. My feelings of attraction to you that [your poetry] had inspired in me came to dominate me, placed me in a position to approach you, and, almost impudently, tell you a few words, without a doubt yearning to know if the words coming from your lips had the same sweetness as those in your poetry.[54]

These lines teem with the eroticism of meeting an author whose poetry had moved him emotionally and perhaps even sexually. They also show his conflation of Ureña with her poetry. When he writes that his "feelings of attraction to you that [your poetry] had inspired in me came to dominate me," he describes the immediate reaction that Ureña's poems instigate. This affective reaction is important enough to Henríquez y Carvajal, and perhaps within the larger culture of the era, to merit mention and to function as a way of wooing his intellectual "crush." The admiration he feels for Ureña as a poet comprises only one of the layers in the letter. Couched in the language of the humble intellectual admirer lurks his romantic desire, which "dominate" him and move him physically closer to her. As if in a trance, these feelings took hold of him and led him to "approach her." "Almost impudent" must have been the erotic desire that underpinned the magnetic attraction that pulled him toward Ureña. This excerpt exemplifies two of the elements crucial to the main claims I make in this chapter: Ureña's poetry is a scriptive thing that prompts a set of feelings and behaviors in the reader and the reader's sharing of this reaction.

Other parts of his letter express the connection between these elements and Henríquez y Carvajal's larger work as a positivist patriot. The main purpose, or pretense, of the correspondence is to offer his services as a teacher of mathematics and sciences, in which Ureña seeks instruction. Like other positivists, Henríquez y Carvajal believed in the importance of the hard sciences for the nation's overall improvement. Much of his youthful letter refers to bodies and body parts. In the citation above, he refers to the sweetness of her lips in a truly halfhearted—or perhaps cleverly purposeful—attempt to pretend that he is still alluding only to her poetry. He describes each of the subjects that will be offered in their tutorial relationship. For instance: "The laws of nature, according to which are operating in bodies phenomena that modify their properties or alter their intimate composition, are no less indispensable to learn."[55] The potential double entendres in this sentence need no further comment. Here, Henríquez y Carvajal weaves his feelings toward his wife-to-be with his fervent yearning for national progress through his improvement of Ureña's already great mind. Discernable also is his erotic patriotism, by which I mean the overt conflation between love of nation and erotic desire toward someone else. This is worthy of note because this desire enacts the heterosexual coupling that defines many nationalist narratives in which a male subject yearns for a female object or symbol (e.g., land, patria, tradition).

Published five months after this letter, an essay by Henríquez y Carvajal about Ureña further establishes her as both poet and potential muse of the Dominican people. Continuing the overlap between Ureña's poetry and her person, the essay intimates that both Ureña's message in her poetry and her eagerness to learn science should inspire Dominicans. Most of the essay argues that Ureña's patriotic verses provide a moral compass for all Dominicans, especially those who consider themselves patriots. He writes: "Inspire yourselves, politicians, with these compositions that the genius of our young poetess presents us. They contain lessons for all the sons of the patria, lessons full of an admirable morality, of a virtue fecund in good [ideas]. She reminds those at the peak of society of their duties with a voice that does not reveal a single fear; to those who are the hope of the country, she heartens them, gives them courage, traces for them a path [. . .]."[56] Henríquez y Carvajal shames young people who, unlike him, do not dedicate all their time to study: "Those who uselessly spend their time when they could excel in their studies should blush with embarrassment."[57] Ureña herself becomes an example worthy of imitating: "But you should all know that in order to write in a tone as exalted as hers it is necessary to invigorate thinking with the cultivation of the sciences and a deep literary erudition."[58] In imitating her, "young people of both sexes" could "restore the homeland from all of its evils."[59] He ends the essay by announcing proudly: "Yes, Miss Ureña studies ceaselessly and passionately the study of science. In this manner we can see how she climbs from point to point towards the apex from which tomorrow, in an even more exalted voice, she will speak to all the pueblos and they will all hear her."[60] Though he was only nineteen years old when he wrote these words, throughout Henríquez y Carvajal's life his faith in unrelenting self-improvement in the form of education, moral rectitude, and a dispassionate temperament remained consistent.

Years after they were first married, Henríquez y Carvajal's many extant letters from his time in Paris (1887–1891) reveal that he can only express any kind of erotic attraction to Ureña in correlation to her patriotic poetry. One letter written in Paris is an example of some feverish thoughts inspired by his wife's latest patriotic verses:

I have read and reread the cantos that your patriotic muse has produced with so much enthusiasm! The absence of the homeland and my constant thinking about her [the homeland]; in her future, both in her Glory and

in her present misfortunes, at times fill my spirit with suspense and produce profound commotions within me. *Being neither able to give form to
my thoughts in those moments, nor release to my excited sensibility, I turn
to you* and see that my thoughts are reflected in yours, and I am filled
with the same enthusiasm with which in my most tender years of youth I
admired and got close to you.[61]

Ureña's verses not only remind him of his initial admiration for and
attraction to her but they also inspire somewhat mysterious "profound
commotions" in his soul. Her poetry has the subtle but clear function
of uniting him to the national imaginary and allowing him to release
the sentimentality rendering him a patriot, even from a distance. This
affective release connects him to the erotic desire he feels for the nation
that underpins his desire for his wife. Henríquez y Carvajal, like several
other exiled subjects, relies on her verses—"I turn to you"—in order to
verify already existing feelings of love toward the distant homeland—
"and see that my thoughts are reflected in yours." These phrases make
evident that Ureña's patriotic poems mine feelings that seem dangerously close to becoming dormant in his patriot's soul. On February 26,
1888, he writes: "You know how enthusiastic I get with anything that you
write. Any memento of that sort would greatly encourage me."[62] In this
regard, Ureña's poetry is like a drug that fuels his enthusiasm to remain
in Paris completing his medical degree. In turn, he considers his study
under the most prominent French doctors for five years as his own gift
and sacrifice to his family.

Because the motif of a painful longing for the homeland defined
many of Ureña's patriotic poems, the number of tears shed was an appropriate way to measure the greatness of the verses. This was not an
uncommon response to Latin American literature in the nineteenth century. According to Ana Peluffo and Ignacio M. Sánchez Prado,

[t]he figure of the *sensitive man who is not ashamed to cry or to make visible his emotions* occupies an important space in the texts of [several Latin
American writers]. The flow of masculine tears in almost canonical texts
demonstrates that in the nineteenth century the feminized man was not
incompatible with civilizing projects and that masculine paradigms make
a quantitative leap from one century to the next.[63]

Men's tearful expressions of love of nation prompted by Ureña's patriotic poetry were not only acceptable among this lettered minority elite, but a desirable affection. An essay by Beatriz González Stephan about masculinity and nineteenth-century Latin American letters has the evocative title "Narrativas duras en tiempos blandos" (Hard Narratives in Soft Times), which reminds us of the general desire in the region for what was deemed "masculine"/hard literature through which male readers, the ones who mattered, could acceptably release their feelings.[64] Men's mournful expressions could garner more respect than women's, perhaps because misogynist discourse ensconces women within an always already emotional realm. These dichotomies endured beyond the nineteenth century. Comparing Ureña's poetry with that of her contemporary José Joaquín Pérez, Balaguer writes that while she has a "manly voice and a tearless pupil closed obstinately off to sorrows" ("voz varonil y la pupila sin lágrimas cerrada, con obstinación a los pesares"), Pérez's "pupils are full of tears, a voice bathed in weeping" ("la pupila llena de lágrimas, la voz bañada en llanto").[65] According to Balaguer, both have their merits, but it is worth wondering why Balaguer and most of her male readers during and after her lifetime considered Ureña's more intimate, less "manly," poetry as inferior.

That several male writers considered it worthy to express their tears in public is curious enough to explore further. We may consider the case of Francisco J. Machado, a Dominican exiled in Caracas, Venezuela, who found Ureña's poetry in a box of newspapers sent by a friend. He was already familiar with Ureña as a "distinguished poetess, glory of Dominican letters."[66] In an 1891 essay published over three issues in *El Lápiz*, a Santo Domingo literary publication, he recounts his feelings upon reading Ureña's work in remarkable detail:

> We read the verses; we reread them and we do not know how many times our eyes ran over these lines which awakened so many memories and said so many things to our soul![67]
>
> Reading them produced within us a *strange feeling*, an indefinable mix of *happiness and sadness*, one of those impressions that one cannot transcribe onto paper, and that our lips cannot repeat.
>
> We were pensive for a long time and the image of the patria, with all of its charms and attractions, arose in our mind.

> That [moment] was a true *ecstasy* in which we felt ourselves in the warm and balmy atmosphere of its breezes and we inhaled the scent of its flowers and, *overwhelmed*, we listened to the mysterious sounds that fill its jungles.
>
> We felt ourselves transported to Santo Domingo, to that beloved city where our eyes opened to the light and we ran serenely and happily during our childhood; where the house of our solitary parents stands who today weep over the absence of their children and where our grandparents sleep the sleep of the grave. [. . .]
>
> And [where] *we had fun, suffered and loved.*
>
> These verses produced within us all of this!
>
> Ah! one *rejoices* and *suffers* so much when through the passage of time and through absence we contemplated the image of that which we love, beautified by the light of our memories![68]

I cite this text at length because it provides a vivid picture of performing patriotism from exile. Later in the essay, Machado recalls another encounter with Ureña's poetry, this time in Puerto Rico: "We remember more than once suspending our reading to burst out exclamations of admiration and enthusiasm, and that also, why not admit it?, more than one furtive tear dampened our eyes."[69] Machado elaborates on the emotions that Ureña's verses unleashed. The sheer number of words evocative of this sentimental valence, which I italicized, underlines the centrality of the emotional response to Ureña's work. Even more peculiar to our present-day standards of literary critique is that Machado considered his reaction important enough to necessitate publication. What he describes in these passages alone is not unique, for many have remarked on the pleasures, and pleasurable pain, of reading. However, it is worth pausing on the fact that his emotional response precedes his more formalist analyses of several of Ureña's patriotic poems. By publishing them, Machado renders public these initially private behaviors prompted by Ureña's poems and he completes his script of a patriotic performance. This yearning for the homeland as instigated by Ureña's poetry transforms him into an exemplar of patriotism. Moreover, in publishing his feelings toward Ureña's verses, this exiled subject writes himself into a nationalist script that could potentially exclude him due to his absence from the national space.

Men in Exile

At this point, a small digression into the centrality of geographic displacement, including exile, in this nineteenth-century context is warranted. Living abroad was a common occurrence in the nineteenth century among the lettered elite. What many Dominicans in the mid- to late nineteenth century called *destierro* or *exilio* (exile) was prompted not only by political instabilities but also by a great variety of motivations, including some that may have been shared by nonelite migrants: the search for better medical treatment or environments, improvement of one's education or economic lot, or both, and so on. However, the violence and political instability of the Dominican Republic throughout the nineteenth century pushed many politically and culturally influential Dominican men into temporary and permanent exile.[70] For example, the political affiliations of Ureña's father, the lawyer and poet Nicolás Ureña, drove his frequent escape to other parts of the Caribbean. As was common, some of the most canonical texts were written from exile. In the Dominican case, texts such as Galván's aforementioned *Enriquillo* and Pedro Francisco Bonó's *El Montero* (1856) were written abroad. Though Ureña never lived abroad, a decision I discuss later in this chapter, others' exiles defined her life and work. That is, this most canonical of nationalist poets wove exiles into the fabric of the nation through her poetry and other writings.

The nineteenth-century *vaivén* (coming and going) of Dominicans in the upper classes emotionally affected both the traveler and those who remained at home. Writing from Haiti on his 38th birthday, Henríquez y Carvajal writes: "I am exiled from life itself."[71] Years earlier, while he lived in Paris, Ureña writes him that "it seems that exile lends wings to patriotic sentiment."[72] This comment refers to the inspiration that Henríquez y Carvajal's absence had prompted in both herself and her brother-in-law, Federico. Places that were otherwise unknown to Ureña became part of her everyday existence if only by association. On December 1, 1889, an anguished Ureña writes to her husband: "I live in Paris without having ever been there. Despite everything, I don't really want to go; I want you to come back, but I don't want to go there. Only in the case of an extreme necessity would I go there to meet you."[73] She came to know and exist in Paris in spirit through her husband's letters, leading to an emotional exile that did not require her physical absence from the homeland.

Several of Ureña's patriotic poems are either dedicated to exiled Dominicans or fold them inseparably into the nation. This overlapping emerges with such frequency in her most patriotic poems that one wonders if Ureña believed that exile rendered Dominicans more patriotic. Given that patriots fleeing political retribution in the homeland, including her father, surrounded her throughout her life, this is not a farfetched interpretation. In the aforementioned "A la Patria" (1874), Ureña reminds a personified, feminized patria of how she had seen her "hijos" (children or sons) suffering in exile: "Y luego los miraste proscritos, errabundos, / por playas extranjeras" ("And later you saw them exiled, wandering, / through foreign beaches). Another early poem, "Recuerdos a un proscrito" (Best Wishes to an Exile [1872]), records empathy for exiles and intimates a desire for them to return to the homeland. The title alone speaks to this all-encompassing reality. She writes:

> Así, aunque de otras playas jamás me vi en la arena
> ni de otros horizones las líneas contemplé,
> concibo del proscrito la abrumadora pena[74]

> In that way, though I never saw myself on the sands of other beaches
> nor did I contemplate the line of other horizons,
> I imagine the exiled person's overwhelming sadness

This excerpt elicits the degree to which exile pervaded Ureña's poetry and life, despite the fact that she never left her Dominican homeland. The poem continues with the entreaty "volver seguro debes a tus amantes lares, / al suelo bendecido que nunca te olvidó" (you must return to the place you love, / to the blessed earth that never forgot you).[75] "Recuerdos" describes a homeland-bound subject who not only remembers the exiled subject but yearns for him to return.

Ureña's poem "A los dominicanos" (1874) reinforces this perspective of exile. The poem's title interpellates the audience as "Dominicans." The context and content of the poem, however, clarifies that she is more specifically addressing those who fled in 1873 due to an attempt to overthrow Buenaventura Báez's government after his repeated attempts to annex the country to a foreign power. The Dominicanness of these exiles remains undoubted:

> Los que anheláis del templo de la gloria
> la Patria levantar a lo eminente;
> que supisteis luchar heroicamente
> por darle en los anales de la historia
> el renombre de un pueblo independiente,
>
> *venid y saludad la nueva aurora*
> que baña en luz la dilatada esfera;
> saludad la celeste mensajera
> que en nombre de la unión, que el libre adora,
> abre del bien la suspirada era.[76]

> Those who yearned to lift the Fatherland
> into the eminent temple of glory;
> who knew to fight heroically
> to give renown to an independent people
> in the annals of history,
>
> *come and greet the new dawn*
> that bathes in light the dilated sphere;
> greet the celestial messenger
> that, in the name of the union the liberated adore,
> opens for good the desired era.

The line "come and greet the new dawn" points to Ureña's Pied Piper-esque enticement of exiles to return home. The rest of the poem repeats this invocation: "volved a saludar en la llanura / de la Antilla preciada los palmares" ("return to greet in the plain / of the prized Antillean isle the palm groves").[77] Here, Ureña propels the narrative of the patria as mother, so common to nationalist discourses. The poem also suggests that peace *depends* on these exiled patriots: "reprimid de la guerra las pasiones / y revivan, al sol de la esperanza, / del patriota las dulces ilusiones" ("repress the passion from the war, / and relive, to the sun of hope, / the sweet illusions of the patriot").[78] In short, "A los dominicanos" voices the central significance of exiled subjects within the Dominican nation's intellectual, cultural, and political projects. As is clear from "A la Patria," "Recuerdos a un proscrito," and "A los dominicanos," Ureña's conception of the Dominican nation embraces exiles.

This brings us to the importance of class and gender in relation to exile, and, more specifically, *conceptions* of who these influential exiles were. When Ureña refers to exiles in these poems, her readers likely imagined men of the cultural and political elite such as her father. These men were and continue to be considered patriots whose exiles were motivated by the political machinations of which they were part. The discursive move to politicize these men and their time abroad has not extended to the peasant and working-class migrants or to the many nonwhite immigrants who entered the country in the late nineteenth century.[79]

Ureña's Complicated Desires

Though Ureña desired exiles to return and these expressions prompted affective releases in some of these people, two ideas that complicate present-day understandings about late-nineteenth-century Dominican patriotism, they are far from comprising the entire story. A much more complex narrative emerges when we consider Ureña's other desires. It was the dismissal of Ureña's other desires, her nonpatriotic or suprapatriotic desires, that helped solidify the gendering of Dominican nationalism as it developed in this era, despite the utter paradox that a woman was a central agent in its creation. These desires were so complicated that most of her readers, including her husband, were unable or unwilling to acknowledge them. They were most evident in the verses described as *intimista* (intimist), which, unlike the letters to her husband, were available to the reading public, especially after the publication of her 1880 anthology of poems. Though most male critics during her time and since deemed these poems inferior to her patriotic corpus, the present-day poet and scholar Chiqui Vicioso argues that "it is in her 'domestic' poetry where Salomé escapes the limitations of her classical education and the values of her time to express herself as she was: a woman with her anguish, her insecurities, her fears, her need for support and company, her nostalgia, her joys, her loves. As a human being."[80] Adding to Vicioso's estimation, I show that Ureña's intimate poetry and her letters to her husband chart an alternative relationship to the nation, which conflicted with and was elided by the dominant narratives and gendered binaries that I explored. To be more specific, the intimate poems and private letters educe the unheralded work that women and children did to aid in the project of "national progress." Further, these intimate writings reveal how a violent and unstable national space disturbs the fabric of quotidian life.

Though they were not meant for publication, Ureña's letters to her husband provide a window into her complex desires as both a patriot and a family woman. In them, she stakes a claim on alternative ways of performing patriotism. The problem is that her husband and other Liberal positivists dismissed these alternative scripts of patriotic desires. She does not relegate this alternative script solely to the realm of unpublished private letters, but elaborates on it in some of her published works as well. For instance, a poem dedicated to Henríquez y Carvajal titled "Tristezas" (Sorrows, 1888) comments on matters of national import through its "intimist" content. The poem quotes their first-born son, Francisco "Fran" or "Franc," who lamented his father's departure for Paris to study medicine: "Don't you remember, Mama? / The sun, how beautiful it was / when Papa was here!"[81] The poem evokes the simple sadness of a child who misses his father, an ambitious doctor, intellectual, and future politician who has to live in Paris to further his education. Confirming that at least some of her intimate poems reflected Ureña's and her children's desires, she writes in a letter to her husband: "I already knew that, by your side, [Francisco] would not miss me. [. . .] He loves you more than me; I'm convinced of this. You see, not even the sun looked beautiful to him because he missed you."[82] An initial reading of "Tristezas" inspired by the family's split across the Atlantic Ocean verifies a domestic and intimate aim. However, a closer reading exposes its portrayal of a homeland that not only misses the person in exile but that also looks different for those who remain. In this sense, this so-called intimate poem comments on matters that traditionally would concern men interested solely in the public, political sphere.

Other letters to her husband declare her anguish that Henríquez y Carvajal cannot or does not wish to understand that the national space

Ureña desires can accommodate the simple happiness of a united family. She pointedly rejects the merits given her by societies such as Amigos del País, which at the time of her award was headed by Henríquez y Carvajal, in a letter that she writes three years after her husband's departure for Paris:

> I don't want titles, I don't want anything that isn't you. No matter how grand are my good fortune and the pomp that are given me, I would give them all for not having suffered, for never having separated myself from the husband of my soul, of the very beloved father of my poor children. Do you remember when you told me that my aspirations were too scant? I desired a small home, a home without luxuries where I could live with you and my children without a care in the world, with your love and with plenty of virtue. I compare that life with the present one, and I see that I was right and you were mistaken.[83]

In her own expression of affective release, Ureña seems alarmed that what positivists want for the nation cannot provide her with a happy home. This renowned poet and educator would have rather been with her husband and children in a humble home than suffer through the absence of an ambitious husband, even if this sacrifice led to further intellectual glory or national progress. Her words suggest that national progress, the ultimate desire of men like her husband, was impossible when loved ones had to live abroad.

In Henríquez y Carvajal's unshaking adherence to positivist ideology, domestic happiness must be sacrificed to national progress. Though Ureña chastises herself for yearning for him instead of accepting their sacrifice to the nation, she also fills her letters with the regret and even utter desperation of having allowed him to go. Also about three years after his departure, when it becomes clear that he will not be soon returning to the homeland, she writes:

> What is this? My God! What is this? I can't go on, I don't have the strength to wait six more months; I feel myself dying when it is necessary for me to live for my children. What an immense misfortune overwhelms me! Our Franc was right: the sun is now so pale! How sad is everything that surrounds me! I would like to flee from myself; I would like to flee far away,

very far away where my thinking would not follow me; I would like to not think because that kills me. And I have no one in whom to confide my bitterness, because no one understands me. You alone would understand me; you alone have suffered, suffer what I suffer.

And I cannot tell you either, because that would kill you.[84]

This entire letter is filled with allusions to her own, Henríquez y Carvajal's, and her children's deaths in relation to her overwhelming suffering. These unsettling words elucidate an inkling of what it may have been like for a woman who has not seen her beloved husband for years and who spends much of this time consumed by fear of her children's succumbing to an illness. She continues, revealing her torment to an unyielding husband:

I would like to tell you how much I suffer; I would like to tell you that I cannot wait for you with tranquility, because my spirit is no longer strong enough to prolong its torment. I dreamt with the hope of seeing you within three or four months, and you kill me by telling me that the day we see each other is so distant that it is impossible to set a date. But, my God! I cannot live like this any longer; I am terrified, I am afraid of life, I am afraid of this loneliness in my heart![85]

It is tempting to diagnose Ureña with what we would now consider clinical depression, especially considering that she often spent many days cloistered at home. Without discarding this possibility, we can also contextualize Ureña's complicated desires within the confines of her era. For Ureña, national progress is impossible without personal and domestic contentment. Her plight as an educator, writer, wife, and caregiver were fused to such an extent that re-creating the standard binary between a public, rational political sphere and a private, emotional domestic sphere becomes a challenge.

Some of her letters reveal a more piquant attitude, reminding us of Ureña's multifaceted personality. In them are subtle critiques of Dominican nationalists' tendencies, including their Francophilia. In 1889, the couple had decided that the aforementioned first-born son, Fran, would move to Paris to be with his dad. Fran had always been a troublesome child, and had become more so after his father's departure. In a letter to his wife sometime after Fran's arrival, Henríquez y Carvajal complains about how much like a *"jibaro"* (peasant) he seemed. Ureña protests against such an assignation:

> In regards to your comment about Fran being like a peasant, I assure you that when you arrived in Paris you did not resemble the big man you are now [...]. It is certain that, unbeknownst to you, you had the air of one easily enthralled and distracted. And you wanted the poor little boy, torn from the warmth of his mother to be launched into a sea journey of more than twenty days, experiencing violent changes in the face of a world unknown to him, to remain unchangeable like a traveler consumed with all that he has seen and who is not impressed by new things. [...] *Don't pretend that he was an idiot here and that he has awakened in Paris.*[86]

When Ureña counters that what her husband interprets as stupidity is an understandable effect of the nearly monthlong ship voyage to Paris, she also argues against the notion that one's mere presence in Paris was civilizing. At the same time, she agreed with the urban bourgeoisie's association of the peasantry with backwardness. Although Ureña and her children enjoyed and considered crucial an education in French literature, this statement demonstrates that she resisted the Latin American intellectual elite's tendency to consider their own American countries mere regional outposts to the European metropolis.[87] In their minds, (high) culture emanated from Paris and trickled down and outwards toward Latin America, where it would reach only a chosen few. To these elites, culture worthy of appreciation and, at times, imitation did not emanate from the North American behemoth and most certainly not from the diverse masses, the "real city," with their African and indigenous cultural bases. Ureña's critique of her husband's Eurocentric assumption suggests that Ureña, though not outright rejecting it, did not so readily conform to that hegemonic assumption.

Indeed, Ureña was so unimpressed by the lights of Paris that she refused to go live with her husband. This is a striking decision not only because we have seen the anguish his absence caused but also because Paris in the late nineteenth century was a hub for Latin American intellectuals. Her reason for not leaving was the upkeep of her school, substantiating her investment in positivist progress and reminding us that her longing for a happy home coexisted with the zeal she shared with other positivist nationalists. In a letter written on June 29, 1889, Ureña writes: "Regarding my trip [to Paris] I will tell you that it is a very flattering idea but one that is difficult to realize. The impossible element is the Institute [for Girls]. Impossible, impossible, this place without me would collapse, and our work is the work of progress."[88] In another letter written in October of that same year, she warns Henríquez y Carvajal that she will never agree to leave the country: "Sometimes you've advanced the idea of choosing another patria for your family, if circumstances demand it. But I don't think that will ever happen; the future awaits us and we have to accomplish several tasks that will benefit the country."[89] Despite her agony at her husband's absence, Ureña did not budge from what she considered her duty to the nation as a whole, and its women more specifically. Perhaps she was aware that education was the realm in which women were most visible as agents of progress and not as symbols or muses.

Some of her letters to her husband do not reach the ideal femininity—that is, abnegation, domesticity, and propriety—that Ureña came to represent in twentieth-century commemoration. The letters to her husband during his years in Paris are rife not only with her agony but also with her strong will. When it seems that Henríquez y Carvajal is taking more classes in Paris than she deems necessary, lengthening his time away from the family, she writes to him: "Don't be stupid wanting to present yourself as a great scholar of the natural sciences."[90] Statements such as these challenge any simplistic estimations of Ureña's role as a wife and in relation to the couple's nationalist endeavors. Another example of Ureña's inner contradictions emerges in a statement regarding women's roles within the domestic sphere. Visiting the homes of two family friends, the famed José Dubeau and Emilio Prud'homme, whose wives dedicated their lives to homemaking, she doubts the advantage of having a household with two earning spouses.[91] The smooth running of these homes leaves her embarrassed at the memory of these friends' visits to the Henríquez Ureña household in the capital. Ureña writes her husband: "You always believed that with my work and your work we would be more well-off; and Dubeau and Prud'homme have shown us that when a hardworking woman dedicates herself to the running of the home, one lives better, because one saves more and the husband's work becomes more productive."[92] These statements and feelings coexist with Ureña's untiring efforts to help educate the nation's women. Twenty-first-century U.S. debates about whether or not women can "have it all" have a nineteenth-century Dominican corollary.

Unlike his wife, whose personal and professional desires often clashed, Henríquez y Carvajal's personal ideals correlated directly with his desires for the nation. The deeply complicated persona that emerges from Ureña's intimate writings is met with Henríquez y Carvajal's unwavering concern with national progress as evident in his missives to his wife and in some of his published work. While he frequently expresses a desire to return to his family and homeland, he reasons that the "empresa" (enterprise), as he often describes his medical study in Paris, requires his strength. In a letter written only a few months after his arrival in Paris, Henríquez y Carvajal concedes to his wife:

> Desire! I have no other than to return. I would gladly return, give up a career in medicine. But that is when I begin to reflect [on the matter . . .]. That is what weak spirits would decide, incapable of a magnum opus, unqualified to bear moral fatigue, *voluble in their desires* and in their intentions.[93]

The project of achieving his goal in Paris must stamp out his other desires, however strong these may be. Soon afterwards, he writes Ureña a curious letter in which he credits his studiousness with keeping him faithful:

> And nevertheless, you should be proud [. . .] to have a husband as faithful as me, that up to now lives in Paris completely isolated from contact with women.
>
> This notwithstanding is against nature, and instead of pleasing you, it should displease you. To believe in men's faithfulness is a false belief: they cannot be faithful because nature does not allow them to be. Because I don't know how to lie, I speak like this.
>
> Now then, how does one explain my conduct? Very simply: all the power in my soul is devoted to a single, unchanging end. The rest of nature is like deadened for now. During some moments of rest, I feel a bit excited; but then surge in my mind unspeakable ideas, indescribable

dreams, inconceivable desires, distant music, interior voices, pleasant hopes, in short, what has been very well captured by the French word *revêrie*.[94]

I cite this passage at length because it provides a window into how Henríquez y Carvajal expressed the disciplining of what he deemed men's natural (sexual) desires. He feels free to express these thoughts because he believes his wife to be free from *"necios celos"* (foolish jealousies) and, perhaps, to model for her the way to control her own passions.[95] He closes the above *"boberías"* (nonsense), as he calls these observations, by ordering Ureña to destroy the letter.[96] In other words, he wants to leave no trace of these complicated desires, an opinion that Ureña did not share, since she did not comply with her husband's command. The letters that remain for us to read do not give a clue as to when this occurred, but at some point during his five years, Henríquez y Carvajal "gave in" to these natural desires; he had an affair and a daughter with a Frenchwoman. It is unclear whether Ureña ever found out.[97]

His single-minded goal of attaining his medical degree in Paris is matched only by his concern with their children's education. One year after his departure for Paris, he writes Ureña: "I see with great satisfaction the progress of Pibin [Pedro], but at the same time I wish that I could see those of Fran traced. [. . .] You will give me a sense of [Fran's progress and instruction], noting what he has reached at each point. You will explain to me which kind of ideas grab his attention and whether his qualit[ies] as an observer weaken or improve."[98] Years later, Henríquez y Carvajal continues to be disappointed by his firstborn son, Fran. At fourteen years old, Fran does not have the discipline that his father expects. In a letter to Ureña dated December 1896, while she convalesced in Puerto Plata and during his political exile in Haiti, Henríquez y Carvajal reiterates his wish that their three sons acquire a doctorate in "the sciences, law, medicine," while hoping that "Camila [the fourth child and only daughter] will perhaps also attain a doctorate in letters or philosophy."[99] He believes that if his children would feel "all the moral energy" within him, they would "progress serenely towards their acquisition of victory."[100] As I noted above, the belief that rigorous education and a deep moral seriousness would lead to civilizing progress was at the heart of positivist ideology.

Henríquez y Carvajal's worldview led to his great frustration when faced with Ureña's yearning for both a peaceful, modern nation *and* a happy domestic life. Indeed, from the earliest days of his self-imposed exile in France, Henríquez y Carvajal urges Ureña to leave the house, implying that she spent many days shut up inside. Soon after his arrival in Paris, he writes: "Though I have advised you repeatedly to go outside and take the children for a walk, you don't do it. It is necessary that you do this and find a way to distract yourself. There is nothing worse than imprisoning yourself between four walls, because that is how continuous reflection sickens one's spirits."[101] A few months later, he reveals that he would rather Ureña remain silent than express her anguish in her letters, centered mostly on the fear of losing her children to an illness.[102] The complexity of his wife's tears spilled inconveniently over the confines of Henríquez y Carvajal's straightforward desire for individual and national progress at all costs.

Ureña's insistence on the validity of what men like her husband considered to be frivolous/domestic/feminine concerns looks very much like resistance. Her intimate writings, both private and published, evince nothing less than a competing claim about what should be considered important for Dominican subjects. It was likely that many other Dominicans, both men and women, shared Ureña's concerns, but only Ureña was a foundational nationalist figure who was able to record and publicize them to some extent. By publishing poems such as "Tristezas" and by writing against her husband in private letters, Ureña stakes a claim that "feminine" concerns are both reconcilable and integral to a patriotic Dominican subject. In so doing, she *scripted* an alternative subjectivity to the patriarchal, Eurocentric subjectivity of dominant ideals of patriotism. Considering, however, that the latter was hegemonic, her husband and other cultural arbiters elided Ureña's vision. In some ways, the Liberals who made up most of the intellectual elite of the era wanted to "have it both ways" when they insisted on the family home as the nucleus of the nation and as the heart of Dominicans' inculcation into dutiful citizenship, but trivialized or even vehemently opposed many of the concerns that emerged precisely from the so-called domestic, feminine sphere.

Ureña's intimate poems express desires that do not dovetail perfectly with nationalist projects. In fact, they overturn the masculinist scripts of the nation that I analyzed above. One of the most explicit, in all senses of the word, of Ureña's subversive demands emerges in the aptly titled poem "Amor y anhelo" (Love and Longing, 1879), which describes Ureña's sexual desire for an unnamed beloved. Because the year of its writing coincided with the year that Henríquez y Carvajal tutored Ureña in the sciences and was the year before they married, we can assume that it was about him. Despite the respectable air that marriage had lent Ureña by the time of the poem's publication in 1880, "proper" women like Ureña were not supposed to reveal their intimate, especially sexual, desires. Within the predominant literary and social standards of the era, it is inconceivable that any of her male readers would publicly discuss a poem such as "Amor y anhelo." Perhaps even more shocking is that Ureña wrote and published the poem at all:

> Quiero decirte que a tu mirada
> me siento débil estremecer,
> que me enajena tu voz amada
> que en tu sonrisa vivo extasiada,
> que tú dominas todo mi ser.[103]

> I want to tell you that before your gaze
> I feel a weak shiver,
> that your beloved voice maddens me
> that in your smile I live in ecstasy,
> that you dominate my whole being.

And later:

> Ven y tu mano del pecho amante
> calme amorosa las penas mil,
> ¡oh de mis ansias único objeto!
> Ven, que a ti sólo quiero en secreto
> contar mis sueños de amor febril.[104]

> Mas no, que nunca mi amante anhelo
> podré decirte libre de afán,
> gimiendo a solas, en desconsuelo

cual mis suspiros, en raudo vuelo,
mis ilusiones perdidas van.

Come and with your hand lovingly soothe
the thousand troubles from my chest,
Oh, sole object of my longing!
Come, that I want to secretly tell you
my dreams of feverish love.

But no, I could never tell you without eagerness
of my loving yearning,
moaning alone, with my disconsolate
sighs, in swift flight,
my lost illusions escape.

When Ureña wrote about her yearning for her husband or about her melancholy, she reminded her readers that she was, indeed, a woman with myriad desires just like her male counterparts. As Vallejo argues, in this and other intimate poems "the positions of lover and wife become equivalent and present a loving subject that includes both categories."[105] Words such as "shiver" and "feverish" point to Ureña's sexual desire and illustrate the extent to which the poem transcends gendered literary conventions. "Amor y anhelo" is striking considering that, in late nineteenth-century Dominican society, it was scandalous for respectable and respected women to comment on their desirous, moaning ("*gimiendo*") bodies.

Even when considering Ureña in other contexts, for example, she transcends the boundaries at the intersection of gender and nonwhiteness. Where would she fit within Puerto Rico's literary culture in the late nineteenth century, for instance? Eileen Suárez Findlay contends: "Incorporating pleasure into their conceptualization of sexuality was likely particularly unthinkable for the early feminists because female sexual desire was so closely associated among Puerto Rican elites with the allegedly bestial sensuality of poor black women. The vast majority of white, bourgeois feminists could not admit to such tainted feelings."[106] In the next chapter, I will discuss the issue of race and respectability in relation to Ureña, but for now it suffices to say that Ureña was part of the cultural elite, but she was not white, and, additionally, "got away with" writing poems such as "Amor y anhelo." I surmise that she "got away" with it because it was not a poem that would be performed or discussed in the public sphere; unlike most of her other verses, there was not a public event at which a poem describing a wife's sexual desire for, presumably, her soon-to-be husband would have been considered appropriate. Unlike graduations, the funerals of political leaders, and other events considered of public importance, the spaces for declaiming poems such as "Amor y anhelo" were scant or inexistent. Moreover, her status as one of the nation's most important poets, a position she already held by 1880, as well as her status as a married woman, protected her from criticism. On the other hand, the fact that these verses were added casually to a collection of otherwise "respectable" poetry still surprises.

While likely tame by our present-day sensibilities, "Amor y anhelo" must be considered in the context from which it emerged. We can contrast it with several poems published at the end of the nineteenth century, in which women emerge as objects of masculine analysis. While Ureña's intimate poetry collapses the binary between desired female object and male desiring subject, these poems concretize women's objectification through binary oppositions that render women either "good" or "evil." For instance, the poem "La mujer" (1893) by V.—likely a man— measures women in relation to the role of the subject and the extent of his desire: "As an unmarried woman, she is a problem; as a married woman, an effect; as a widow, a temptation; as a mother, an angel; as a lover, a luxury; as a mother-in-law, a demon[;] as a stepmother, an inferno."[107] (Though unlikely, there is a small possibility that the poem was written by a woman, which would complicate this interpretation.) In a poem of the same title published in the same year and signed "Ageno," women's value is measured in terms of their (white) beauty:

> For a woman to be beautiful she must have:
> Three white things: her skin, her teeth and her hands;
> three black things: her eyes, her eyebrows and her eyelashes;
> three long things: her height, her hair and her hands[108]

This poem suggests that women's primary value, according to this limited circle of intellectuals, was that of beauty and, furthermore, that this beauty was necessarily white. I include these examples primarily to showcase the extent of Ureña's transgression when she expresses sexual desire while also being a nonwhite woman.

Ureña's intimate poems demonstrate the remarkable contrast between the melancholia of male patriots yearning for the homeland who seek succor in a woman poet's verses and the melancholia of a woman patriot whose yearnings for her husband find little to no relief. As I mentioned above, the intimate poems that best expressed these wants did not receive the same level of adulation in the press as her patriotic verses.[109] One would hope the object of the heated desire evident in "Amor y anhelo" would respond in kind, but, by the time Henríquez y Carvajal wrote to his wife from Paris, the passion that he had felt for her toward the end of his adolescence had cooled. While he remained one of her most important readers, he had a single-minded desire for her patriotic poetry, and not verses on other topics or her feelings in general. As I discussed, when apart from the family, Henríquez y Carvajal sought news on the education of his children, the running of the school, and anything else related to the struggles for national progress. He beseeched Ureña to write more patriotic verses, whose creation had slowed especially after the opening of her school. Discussing the eighteenth-century U.S., Elizabeth Dillon argues that "men's participation in the public sphere is dependent upon an array of support services that are located outside the political sphere in the realm of necessity—a realm designated as prepolitical, and, in the fiction of liberalism, populated primarily by women, and, as I will argue, people of color."[110] The same could be said of this late nineteenth-century Dominican context, where even exemplary women such as Ureña who were respected by her male peers in the public sphere were often relegated to an inferior and "prepolitical" realm. Ureña's romantic distress could not compete in the public arena with the pain of male exiles who yearn for the homeland, a pain alleviated by Ureña's poetry in an exchange that one could consider part of her "support services."

* * *

My focus in this chapter has been to prove that the dominant ideologies guiding elite literary circles during Ureña's lifetime prevented them from seeing her writings as the evocations of a citizen-subject who both yearns for her country's progress and for her family to be united. It is fascinating to consider the following paradox: while Liberal nationalists often considered the family unit to be the nucleus of the national body, the work of nationalist progress often meant that heads of households— always male in these frameworks—had to leave the nucleus of the family. Thus, while nationalists sought to unify the populace in a coherent national whole, the family, which was supposed to represent the whole nation, was often in rupture. Even if she was unaware of this paradox, Ureña persistently expressed this distance between ideal and reality. She did so subtly in her underappreciated intimate poetry and quite explicitly in her letters to her relentlessly positivist husband. Ureña's desires as she expressed them in her writings function as imperfect reminders of how the Liberal tenets of the era did not encompass the needs and wants of a diverse population. They are imperfect because Ureña was nevertheless part of an intellectual elite that had a more central role in the running and writing of the nation than most Dominicans, both men and women. Moreover, they are imperfect because Ureña's writings also evinced her strong investment in positivist endeavors. Among them were numerous missives to local and national political representatives to ensure not only that her school for girls remained open but also that funding would be secured for girls who wanted an education but could not afford their own schooling.[111] Ureña desired a unified family as well as a financially viable vehicle through which girls and women could acceptably enter the public sphere. As Zeller observes, the new generation of women educated under Ureña, and Ureña herself, "were pioneers in exploring a sphere that was not always restricted to the maintenance of the family unit."[112]

The numerous tensions that Ureña evoked are not only gendered but also raced, since Ureña's mixed-race body clashed with the idealized figure of the proper, white Dominican woman. As I will show in the next chapter, the persistence of her phenotypical whitewashing in commemoration prove that Ureña's body—and complicated desires— reminded Dominicans of el monte, that physical and imaginary space beyond the world of letters. That is, Ureña's body and body of work reveal how the intellectual elite, including Ureña herself, tried to ghost the singularity of Dominican history and especially its nonwhite rural majority. Ureña's writings combined with her nonwhite female personhood instantiated the distance between the ideal nation and the reality. Commemorative efforts starting immediately after her death, and consolidating during the Trujillo dictatorship, sought to ghost these tensions.

2

Race, Gender, and Propriety in Dominican Commemoration

> Women of African descent, particularly those unwilling or unable to "whiten" themselves through dress and behavior, were believed to be inherently disreputable.
> —Eileen Suárez Findlay, *Imposing Decency* (1999)

"National letters are in mourning." Such are the first words of Salomé Ureña's March 1897 obituary.[1] Surrounded by her family in her mother's home in the Colonial Zone of Santo Domingo, Ureña succumbed to the tuberculosis she had suffered for years. The streets flooded with mourners. A funeral procession of her many friends, many of them political leaders, and dozens of her students paid tribute to this exemplary woman. Many spoke in her honor, citing her verses and her pedagogy. The famed Puerto Rican intellectual and Ureña's close friend, Eugenio María de Hostos, mourned from Chile.[2]

For months, the nation's literary publications dedicated sections, even entire issues, to her life's work. *El Cable*, one of the country's most important cultural publications, which was based in the city of San Pedro de Macorís, published an "Extraordinary Issue" commemorating the poet. The cover inaugurated the phenotypical transformation of Ureña in commemoration. Far from fading into obscurity through the next century, Ureña's likeness adorns many cultural and educational institutions bearing her name around the country. Busts, statues, and other images memorializing Ureña preside over plazas, schoolyards, and walls throughout the Dominican Republic. At least four of them are scattered within the three square miles of the neighborhood in which she lived in the heart of the old city. Considering the ubiquity of her image, the original daguerreotype of Ureña can only elicit surprise; it shows a woman whose African ancestry would be obvious to most Dominicans in a way that the image on the cover of *El Cable* or the dozens of other versions

Figure 2.1. Daguerreotype of Salomé Ureña taken by photographer Julio Pou. (Courtesy of the Archivo del Instituto de Literatura y Lingüística in Havana, Cuba.)

of Ureña is not (see Figure 2.1). This rare image sits inside a box at an archive in Havana, because Ureña's family moved to Cuba after her death. Its location has ensured that Ureña's real visage, or at least the one on the original daguerreotype, would be relegated to near oblivion for most of her compatriots.

In this chapter I argue that the endurance of Ureña's legacy as the face of Dominican literature and education relied both on her phenotypical whitening and on the perpetuation of a selective reading or total elision of some of the strongest desires expressed in her work. As I proposed in the previous chapter, the use of masculinist literary standards to interpret Ureña's work led to the omission or dismissal of those poems that did not directly express patriotic ideals. These masculinist readings prevailed for most of the twentieth century as Ureña's place at the center of nationalist literature became further entrenched. As I also intimated, the perfection of Ureña's poetry as a vehicle of patriotic performance relied on an elision not only of her complexly gendered relationship to the nation but also of her inconvenient nonwhiteness. Indeed, one of the most evocative silencings around Ureña is the fact that she was not a white woman and would not have been considered as such even in the nebulous racial structure of late nineteenth-century Dominican society.

What I, alongside other Dominicans, interpret as evidence of Ureña's blackness becomes clearer in contrast to each successive retouched version of the poet. For instance, in the revised versions, Ureña's glossy, straight strands call attention to the tamed curls in the original daguerreotype. In the Dominican Republic, when a person is otherwise racially ambiguous, hair texture provides one of the most defining clues.[3] The importance of hair texture in the taxonomy of racial hierarchies has a long history on this territory. An eighteenth-century white cattle-rancher complains that "those who pretended to hide their racial origin did so through the use of 'newly introduced wigs,' through which could be hidden 'the natural hair that would testify the quality of the provenance of the men [who used them].'"[4] Alongside other markers, phenotypical and otherwise, hair texture helps determine whether or not a person can enjoy the treatment accorded to those who look and perform a certain way within the Dominican body politic. Artists painting or sculpting Ureña have either followed already retouched images or taken certain liberties with her portrayal. These liberties have shifted her away from phenotypical signs of blackness.

Just as evocative are the details that remain across revisions: the cross, the serious countenance, the high collar, the earrings, the brushed-back hair, and the pose. In other words, while her phenotypical features shift with each version, the visible attributes cloaking her in feminine propriety endure. Her demure, Victorian-era clothing signals her seriousness as a woman and person as well as her high standing in society. As in other (post)colonial, former slaveholding societies, clothing mattered immensely, especially when worn by nonwhite subjects. Just on this territory, for instance, the vestments of blacks and "mulattos" had been subject to debate among colonial administrators and the Spanish crown for centuries.[5] That Ureña's clothing did not change, while traits such as hair texture and eye color did, invites pause. What physical attributes, natural or as added adornment, fit within increasingly consolidating ideas of what an ideal object of nationalist veneration should look like?

By homing in on the contextually determined optics of race, the first half of this chapter focuses on what had to remain and what had to change in order for Ureña to be celebrated as a national icon well after her death. I trace her commemoration in sculpture, imagery, and biography to argue that Ureña's canonization in the late nineteenth and throughout most of the twentieth century entailed her phenotypical whitening as well as a simultaneous overemphasis on the aspects of her work and life that buoyed the idea of Ureña as a respectable—that is, asexual, religious, and motherly—woman. Ureña's status as a beacon of Dominican letters through a century that saw the rise of institutionalized antiblackness during the U.S. occupation (1916–1924), the Trujillo dictatorship (1930–1961), and beyond required ideological and aesthetic labor.[6] That is, her cultural prominence was far from natural or self-evident, especially because she was a nonwhite woman. However, it is significant that it was Ureña, and not some of her contemporaries, such as José Joaquín Pérez, author of the important *Fantasías indígenas* (1877), and Manuel de Jesús Galván, author of the canonical *Enriquillo* (1882), who crowds the national landscape as an icon of Dominican letters and education. Perhaps it is this tension between who is supposed to be the ideal patriot—a white man—and the reality of a mixed-race population that has rendered Ureña a compelling national symbol. As a mother and educator, she seemed to seamlessly blend two strands of nationalist thought: domestic nurturing and progress. Moreover, as I discussed in chapter one, to many of her readers she was both muse and poet.

In the second section of this chapter, I examine select writings by two twenty-first century feminist and diasporic Dominican women writers, Julia Alvarez and Chiqui Vicioso, primarily the works that re-envision Ureña's place within the Dominican national script. Discussing Julia Alvarez's novel about Ureña, Anna Brickhouse uses a curiously apt word: resurrect. She writes: "Alvarez resurrects Salomé—edited, disembodied, and whitened for posterity by her husband and family, critically dismissed by her son and generations of literary scholars writing after modernism—and envisions her at the center of an alternative, reshaped tradition through the story surrounding [her daughter] Camila and told by Salomé herself."[7] Ureña's rise to prominence during her lifetime and her commemoration beyond required various forms of ghosting. Through her invocation of "resurrection," Brickhouse underlines the kind of work necessary to unearth what had been buried or ghosted in the process of creating a national literary icon.

Alvarez, in tandem with Vicioso, indeed excavates an Ureña fitting for an early twenty-first-century reading public—Dominicans and non-Dominicans—ready for an Afro-descended woman poet of subversive verses. Their texts overturn conventional notions of who can read and write themselves into the nation by centralizing Ureña's desires as a woman and as a nonwhite subject and, as such, they subvert the affective, gendered, and raced script of the nation as it developed in the late nineteenth century and solidified throughout the twentieth, especially during and after the Trujillo regime (1930–1961). Alvarez's and Vicioso's fictional reconsiderations of Ureña's roles as a poet and educator, as well as wife and mother, transform the nationalist scripts based on patriarchal patriotism into narratives of belonging in which women and nonwhite subjects can be legible as full subjects. Their works are "radical revision[s] of the *conceptual bases* of literary criticism," writes Vicioso, "and examination[s] of the theoretical presumptions about reading and writing, which have been based on masculine literary experiences."[8]

By the time that Alvarez and Vicioso created their versions of Ureña, which, though fictional, recuperated the Ureña lost in the process of canonization, the world had changed significantly. Feminist and race theories, the advancement of and greater variety of cultural dissemination technologies, the increase in Dominican literacy rates, the astronomical growth of a diasporic Dominican community with a different vocabulary of race had all contributed to a moment when Alvarez's and Vicioso's recuperative acts were not only possible but could also compete with other dominant narratives. Both writers have significant experiences living as part of the Dominican diaspora in the U.S., which they credit with having provided a new lens through which to view Dominican nationalism.[9]

Though I focus on Ureña, other national heroes, including those known to have African ancestry, have also been whitened in commemoration. Moreover, that a powerful group of intellectual leaders starting in the late nineteenth century chose "blond-haired, blue eyed" Juan Pablo Duarte as founding father, commemorated in countless spaces and moments, cements the tie between white masculinity and heroic patriotism.[10] As I warned earlier, however, these official commemorative acts do not represent the beliefs of the majority of Dominicans. Only with the consolidation of a nation-state that could reach all Dominicans through formal education, adequate roads, police and military structures, and other modes would the belief that Duarte was the nation's founding father become generalized.[11] Even so, scholars and other public intellectuals have tried to chip away at Duarte's myth.[12]

Thus, the issue of whitewashing nonwhite national icons and ghosting the blackness of Dominican history and society extends well beyond the example of Ureña. However, I chose this woman poet in part because of the ubiquity of her image as well as the several tensions her case presents. In the 1870s, Ureña's talent as a poet, as well as her placement in a cash-poor family of Santo Domingo's cultural elite, secured her entry into some of the most influential cultural and political circles of the era. While I point out that Ureña would have likely been "read" as having black ancestry by her contemporaries, it went unwritten, perhaps even unsaid. My concern here lies with cultural arbiters' need to tweak Ureña's phenotype in certain ways. In the crevices of this transformation lies a tension in Dominican conceptions of race. On the one hand, the country's first national poet, chosen by a group of elite Dominicans, was a nonwhite woman; on the other hand, her commemoration during her lifetime and well into the twentieth century relied on phenotypical and biographical distortions.

Visualizing Ureña

If we consider Ureña within a hemispheric context of other slaveholding, colonial societies, her status as a nonwhite woman should have excluded her from the many honors she received. In the racial hierarchies that buttressed all colonial systems in the Americas, black and mixed-race women's bodies overdetermined their existence. That is, they were prized or denigrated for their bodies' labor and sexuality—often one and the same—and certainly not for their intellectual capacities. As we know, the unequal binary between mind and body had emerged as an Enlightenment sine qua non. That a racist colonial economy tied black and mixed-race women, enslaved and otherwise, inexorably to their bodies helped ensure their placement at the bottom of a racial hierarchy in which white (propertied) men symbolized the highest intellectual capacity. While the colonial apparatus had spotty control over Dominican territory through the centuries, the ruling elite had always sided with these European ideals. As Silvio Torres-Saillant, Ginetta Candelario, Anne Eller, and others have argued, outside pressures to show whether or not the Dominican Republic was like Haiti helped compound Dominican elites' "silence on race."[13] This active ghosting of Dominican blackness explains why Ureña's blackness was never mentioned. It does not explain, however, why this nonwhite woman would not only become her generation's most celebrated poet but also representative of national letters beyond her lifetime and especially during an explicitly antiblack dictatorship. That the Dominican elite catapulted Ureña to intellectual fame, never mentioned her race in writing, and then oversaw her subsequent whitewashing in commemorative imagery point to Dominican nationalists' unresolved tensions around who was worthy of national veneration. On the one hand, it was the blond, inconveniently absent Duarte who had lived in Venezuelan exile for over thirty years; on the other, it was the staunchly present nonwhite Ureña, who, as I discussed in the previous chapter, refused to leave the country.

In the larger context of the Spanish-speaking Caribbean and Latin America, few other women reached critical acclaim in the nineteenth-century, postindependence era when these young nations or soon-to-be nations were grappling with how race and gender would inform national identity. Most of these women, including Gertrudis Gómez de Avellaneda (1814–1873) in Cuba and Ana Roqué de Duprey (1853–1933) in Puerto Rico, were ensconced securely within the white elite. In contrast, Ureña became her country's first national poet in 1878, before any man or white woman—an extraordinary rarity in this geographical and historical context. While the mixed-race Puerto Rican Julia de Burgos (1914–1953) is currently celebrated as a national icon, she was not Puerto Rico's first national poet. Moreover, it is crucial to emphasize that Burgos lived in the twentieth century, after the abolition of slavery in the entire hemisphere, whereas Ureña began writing poetry when several places in the Americas, including Puerto Rico, Cuba, and Brazil, had not yet abolished slavery.[14] Stretching the boundaries to include men but maintaining the important historical specificity in which many nations in the Americas upheld the institution of slavery, we find the Brazilian Joaquim Maria Machado de Assis (1839–1908), a mixed-race man who, like Ureña, represented the apex of his country's letters. Nevertheless, that Dominicans—alongside Haitians—had lived in a nonslaveholding society for decades by the end of the nineteenth century fomented questions and tensions around race, class, and national identity that could not emerge in slaveholding Cuba, Puerto Rico, and Brazil.

Writing about Ureña for a collection of critical biographies of Afro-descendent Latin American women, Fernando Valerio-Holguín writes that she "would have never imagined that her biography would be published in a book about Afro-Caribbean or Afro-Dominican women."[15] It is difficult to decipher when people started to notice or mention Ureña's African descent. It may be that she was always understood to be a nonwhite member of Santo Domingo's elite and that there had been no need to qualify her racially. Going against the current in several U.S. approaches to Dominican racial identity, I would not categorize the overlooking of her nonwhiteness as a sign of Ureña's or her contemporaries' "black denial," but rather as proof of the complicated ways in which blackness operates and has operated in the Dominican Republic. Unquestionably, Ureña was a patriot and the object of her veneration was a mixed-race nation in which, because of her class status, she did not have to suffer the reminders of the oppression that many black Dominicans—and the vast rural majority—experienced.

Having spent a childhood in Santo Domingo and adolescence and adulthood in the United States—in both majority nonwhite and majority white situations—I am at the nexus of several, often competing, discourses of blackness. I recognize that what Dominicans perceive as blackness or whiteness may not coincide with non-Dominicans' interpretations. Although local, relational, national, and other contexts determine how subjects define blackness, it is useful to summarize what definitions of blackness are most appropriate to my analysis of Ureña's commemoration. In the Dominican Republic, phenotype has often determined a person's race. Ginetta Candelario summarizes the main differences between Dominican and U.S. conceptions of race:

> [D]espite the fact that the Dominican nation (in both senses of the word—state and folk) developed, and continues to operate, within and under European and European-diaspora colonization, Dominicans seem historically and contemporarily to reject hypo-descent as a racial paradigm and racial categorization as black, both in the Dominican Republic and in the United States. That is, for Dominicans, racial categories are occupied by individuals based on their given appearance, not by entire families based on descent.[16]

For instance, in his anti-Haitianist text *La isla al revés* (1983), the conservative intellectual and politician Joaquín Balaguer includes what he deems to be photographic evidence of the untarnished whiteness of the peasantry in the country's central Cibao region.[17] To many other eyes, however, some of his visual evidence supports precisely the opposite thesis—that, in fact, these Cibao subjects had some black ancestry. In many cases, visual evidence of blackness or whiteness is highly unstable and subjective.

The difference in how racial optics tend to operate in the United States is evident in Shawn Michelle Smith's discussion of W. E. B. Du Bois's American Negro Exhibit at the Paris Exposition of 1900. The exhibit included 363 "images of people and places" gathered by Du Bois.[18] Smith writes: "Du Bois's portraits of *white-looking African Americans* contest a racial taxonomy of identifiable (because visible) difference, and in so doing they highlight a closeness that troubles the imagined autonomy of a white viewer."[19] The phrase "white-looking African Americans" is nonsensical in a Dominican context. However, the phrase has salience in a place where "by the end of the nineteenth century several states had laws that deemed one thirty-second African or African American ancestry the key that distinguished 'black' from 'white,' a distinction so narrow as to make explicit the invisibility of 'blackness' and 'whiteness' as racial categories."[20] Legal demarcations that policed racial categories to such a high degree did not exist in the Dominican Republic, especially after the final abolition of slavery in 1822. Indeed, it would be surprising if a majority white space such as the U.S. and a majority mixed-race space such as the Dominican Republic shared the same racial demarcations. To Balaguer, looking white meant being white, while to Du Bois, and according to U.S. law, looking white did not preclude one's belonging within the African American community. Both cases highlight the absurdity of race as identifiable difference while acknowledging that they continue to matter in both societies.

On the other hand, this demarcation is not as simple as it seems at first glance. For instance, in 1932 Du Bois eulogizes Charles Chesnutt, the white-looking African American writer, thusly: "Chesnutt was of that group of white folk who because of a more or less remote Negro ancestor identified himself voluntarily with the darker group, studied them, expressed them, defended them, and yet never forgot the absurdity of this artificial position and always refused to admit its logic or its ethical sanction."[21] In calling Chesnutt "white folk," and not a "white-looking African American," Du Bois contradicts the stakes of his earlier project.

Phenotype is far from being the only determining factor. The optics of race is further complicated by class, language, and group context. Writing about racial passing in the U.S., Allyson Hobbs maintains that "[l]ooking white is, in many ways, contingent on doing white. Racially ambiguous slaves drew on highly sophisticated understandings of racial, gender, and social norms to enact whiteness; by doing so, they successfully passed to freedom."[22] Moreover, in her study on Dominican blackness, Kimberly E. Simmons finds it useful to compare twentieth- and twenty-first-century Dominican racial denominations, such as *trigueño* and *indio*, that are akin to African American "intra-group colorization practice" of using words such as light-, brown-, and dark-skinned or even *redbone* and *high yellow*.[23] In a remarkable obituary, Langston Hughes considers Dominican playboy Porfirio Rubirosa vis-à-vis U.S. concepts of blackness:

> He must have possessed the same sort of personality attraction for women as does our Congressman from Harlem Adam Clayton Powell, who, although Negro, is several shades lighter than was Rubirosa. Mulatto Latins, in

their own Caribbean or South American lands, are not classed as Negro in the U.S.A. sense of the term, especially if their tongue is Spanish.[24]

Rubirosa's racially ambiguous features and Latin American provenance allowed him to travel in white spaces in the U.S. and Europe in a way that, according to Hughes, many light-skinned African Americans could not. This kind of racial fluidity, combined with the in-group phenotypical terms used in the African American community, complicates the notion that U.S. concepts of blackness can be described entirely by the so-called one drop rule. Just as twenty-first century Dominican concepts of blackness have started to shift with the return visits of diasporic Dominicans with their "new" ways of looking at race, literally and figuratively, discussions about blackness and racial mixture have come to the forefront with the election of the first black *and* mixed-race U.S. president.[25] Though pervasive, phenotype is not the only way in which Dominicans ascribe race. Sociologist Wendy Roth's interviews with Dominicans demonstrated that the level of formal education also influences how subjects assign racial status.[26] In general, however, Dominican ideas of blackness differ markedly from those in the U.S. in great part because of the legal and long-term terroristic policing of whiteness in the U.S. case and the demographic reality that most Dominicans are racially mixed.[27]

When it comes to Ureña, the fact of her racial ambiguity becomes central to an understanding of her "whitening" in imagery. For instance, her husband, Francisco Henríquez y Carvajal, was likely also of mixed race, but his amply photographed visage captured the straight locks, light skin, and facial features that rendered him a "white" Dominican. The only photograph of Ureña, however, is blurry and faded enough that there was some room for interpretation. Its placement in Cuba further obscures the impact this daguerreotype may have had throughout the twentieth century in her homeland.

Some of the major trends in Dominican visual arts in the late nineteenth and early twentieth centuries reflected Eurocentric neoclassical and romanticist aesthetics.[28] Within the relatively new technology of daguerreotypes, Dominican photographers took certain "painterly" liberties. They retouched and repainted photographs "to achieve the beauty of the photographed subject."[29] One such practitioner was Ureña's photographer, Julio Pou, though his photograph of Ureña does not reveal signs of obvious retouching.[30]

I have not yet found the artist, or commissioner, who first distanced Ureña's looks from those evident in the original daguerreotype. It is likely that the earliest version of a re-envisioned Ureña is in the May 31, 1897 edition of *El Cable*, a San Pedro de Macorís periodical (see Figure 2.2), mentioned in the opening of this chapter. The entire issue is dedicated to honoring her after her death two months earlier. Emilio Rodríguez Demorizi writes that the issue included a "Semblanza" (Semblance) of the poet, adding no other details.[31] The image itself closely resembles the daguerreotype image of Ureña, but with the somewhat straight hair

Figure 2.2. Salomé Ureña on the cover of a special issue of *El Cable* after her death, ca. 1897. (Courtesy of the Archivo General de la Nación in Santo Domingo, Dominican Republic.)

and facial features that most Dominicans would consider more European (or, perhaps, more *taíno*). Another early version, resembling or copying this 1897 image, appears in the September 23, 1916, issue of the magazine *Renacimiento*. Though the image includes the artist's signature, it is too faded to decipher. An early version of the portrait that most daringly distances Ureña from the daguerreotype is a 1922 oil painting by Oscar Marín Bonetti.[32] Though the painting loosely resembles the original daguerreotype in pose, clothing, and demeanor, it nonetheless makes the changes consonant with whitewashing as evident in Ureña's facial features, skin color, and hair texture. Much remains unclear about these images, including how and why those who knew her in life permitted these "semblances."

The early twentieth century, during and after the U.S. occupation (1916–1924), as well as the years of the Trujillo regime (1930–1961), witnessed the consolidation—perhaps perversion—of some of the nationalist rhetoric that had emerged in the late nineteenth century. In the years between Ureña's death and the U.S. occupation, the elite circles to which Ureña and her family belonged coalesced their power in Santo Domingo and other major cities, as the work of Teresita Martínez Vergne, April Mayes, and Neici Zeller demonstrates. We may consider, for instance, that Francisco Henríquez y Carvajal, Ureña's husband, was voted Dominican president in 1916 before the U.S. ousted him. As I discussed in the previous chapter, this urban bourgeois elite had started the seemingly insurmountable project of "civilizing" el monte. U.S. occupying forces, not surprisingly, also held the dominant worldview that considered a noncapitalist subsistence rural society composed of mostly nonwhite subjects to be anathema to modernity and progress. As such, these years of U.S. control sought the modernization and unification of the nation-state through infrastructural changes such as roads that opened previously secluded areas of the country to major cities, as well as through the crushing of those who did not fit these ideals of modernity and resisted the imperial presence in any way.[33]

According to Lauren Derby, after this long military occupation, many Dominican intellectuals desired a strong, perhaps "masculine," nationalist rhetoric that would strengthen and unite the country as a sovereign nation-state. Trujillo emerges, then, as a patriarch strong enough to resist the imperial force that "emasculated" the entire population.[34] By the start of the Trujillo dictatorship, Ureña's canonization and commemoration were already in full swing, but leading intellectuals during the dictatorship further elevated certain figures into a pantheon of national heroes.[35] The regime finally completed the project of nationalist consolidation in great part because those who did not agree with Trujillo's ideas were disappeared, killed, jailed, or forced into exile. As a copious body of work on Trujillo has shown, and as I will discuss in the next chapter, part of what made Trujillo an object of fear, awe, and respect was how all-encompassing he was. Whereas in earlier centuries and into the early twentieth century, rural subjects could live in relative or complete autonomy and anonymity, Trujillo entered the homes of all of his constituents both literally with his person and figuratively through his government officials and spies. The anonymity and autonomy that had plagued urban intellectuals for decades and colonial administrators in prior centuries all but disappeared. According to scholars such as Pedro San Miguel and Richard Turits, Trujillo and his intellectuals incorporated these rural subjects into a newly strengthened national body. Belonging to this nation required absorbing and repeating nationalist ideology as espoused by Trujillo's intellectuals and reproduced in educational institutions and other government offices and spaces. These intellectuals, namely Joaquín Balaguer, Manuel Arturo Peña Batlle, and Emilio Rodríguez Demorizi, consecrated a Dominican nationalism based on enmity with Haiti as well as the hagiographic celebration of patriots such as Juan Pablo Duarte. Part of this project was also to perpetuate the ghosting of "impossible patriots" from the national imaginary, to invoke Sara Johnson's work on the Dominican-born mixed-race slave who joins Jean-Jacques Dessalines' Haitian army in 1805.[36] Among those worthy of canonization and veneration remained Salomé Ureña.[37]

At the height of the Trujillo era, in 1942, Spanish exile and sculptor Manolo Pascual founded the Escuela Nacional de Bellas Artes and, among his many sculptures, made one of Salomé Ureña in 1945.[38] The work, completed so soon after the founding of this important school, highlights the connection between conservative nationalist commemoration, the institutionalization of the arts, and the canonization of Ureña as a national icon. The bronze sculpture, as with the many busts of the poet, seems to be based on the retouched image and not on the original daguerreotype (see Figure 2.3). Another image of Ureña from this time is

Figure 2.3. Manolo Pascual, *Salomé Ureña de Henríquez*. Bronze, 1945. (Courtesy of the Museo Bellapart in Santo Domingo, Dominican Republic.)

a commemorative button that dates from 1950, the year of the centenary celebration of her birthday, which sits in the same box as the daguerreotype at the Instituto de Literatura y Lingüística in Cuba (see Figure 2.4). Though closely resembling the original daguerreotype, this image also phenotypically "whitens" her facial features and hair texture. More recently, a drawing with unclear provenance floats around the Internet and appears in print commemorative fare that shows Ureña as a blue-eyed, white-presenting woman whose verisimilitude to the "original," once again, replicates the original markers of gendered respectability in pose, demeanor, and vestments. It is significant, for instance, that, out of the many versions of the Ureña that one may find in a Google Image search, the version that was chosen for a 2009 article about the poet in honor of her birthday in the nation's leading newspaper, the *Listín Diario*, features

Figure 2.4. Commemorative button of Salomé Ureña on the centenary of her birth, ca. 1950. (Courtesy of the Archivo del Instituto de Literatura y Lingüística in Havana, Cuba.)

a pale Ureña with light blue-gray eyes, straight dark brown hair, and facial features commonly associated with whiteness.

In erasing the traces that in the Dominican Republic denote African ancestry, the artists and sculptors charged with prolonging her legacy conform to a raced nationalist imaginary in which women who "look black" cannot be commemorated. Simultaneous to this continual whitening has emerged a recuperation of sorts. In 2011, a short article in *Listín Diario* is accompanied by a drawing of the poet that most resembles the original daguerreotype. The article was penned by Rafael García Romero, who had written a short novel based on the letters between Ureña and her husband.[39] Directly below the drawing, the website's designer included a hyperlinked image of García Romero's novel, leading to a larger image of the novel's cover. On the surface, the function of this link is to inform readers of the existence of the novel. Below the surface,

Figure 2.5. The cover of the first edition of Rafael García Romero's novel about Ureña, *Ruinas*. Subsequent editions did not use this image.

however, there is a marked juxtaposition between the image that accompanies the article and the image on the cover of the novel, which portrays Ureña in her palest incarnation (see Figure 2.5).

García Romero's article opens with another doubling of Ureña: "In the morning she looks like another woman when her hair is not yet gathered in a bun and her hair falls darkly, with some gray strands, thick and tightly curled."[40] These words elucidate a duality between Ureña in her most "natural" state after waking up in the morning and Ureña as presented to the outside world. As I mentioned earlier, in the Dominican context, hair texture is as important as skin color (at times more so) in phenotypical denominations of race. García Romero's description of Ureña's hair as *crespo* (tightly curled or kinky)—and not *rizado* (curly)—therefore, cannot be seen as a simple aside, but as a clear demonstration of his stance when it comes to Ureña's "race." This physical description of her hair alongside more poetic and subjective statements such as her "serene forehead" and her "ochre and distant gaze" is what the artist rendering seeks to emulate. The end result is the depiction that most closely resembles the daguerreotype. Without a doubt, García Romero saw an image of the original daguerreotype for no other circulated versions of Ureña show the key sign that has been erased most vigorously in commemoration: her tight curls. The drawing includes the caption: "Photo described in the text and that summarizes the image of the mother, poetess and teacher Salomé Ureña."[41] Unlike the captions accompanying other images of Ureña, this one defends its choice to show the poet in this manner. Perhaps it was necessary to a readership that is not used to seeing Ureña portrayed as such. It is telling that the whitewashed versions of Ureña require no explanation.

As with most of the imagery of Ureña, it is difficult to identify the artists behind the portrayals in either online newspaper articles or the cover of *Ruinas*. Despite the wide phenotypical expanse between the two images, the signs of proper femininity remain intact. Indeed, the article aims to highlight her role as a mother and not as a poet. Its subtitle decrees: "When we educate, let us appreciate the legacy of Salomé Ureña through her best work: her dedication and consistency in her children's education."[42] This discourse around Ureña's maternal propriety emerged during her lifetime and grew louder as the twentieth century wore on.

"No Better Example of Feminine Abnegation": Gender and Propriety in Ureña's Life and Work

Ureña's phenotypical whitening intersected with, relied on, and ran parallel to a biographical focus on her propriety as a woman and mother.[43]

During Ureña's lifetime, social norms within the upper classes dictated that women be judged within a prescribed set of standards that precluded the idea of a desirous and patriotic woman poet. As Dominican writer Angela Hernández argues, "When judging feminine creations, [cultural] critique has echoed stereotypical, belittling, even caricaturesque, references."[44] She provides the example of the aforementioned nineteenth-century poet Manuela Aybar, whom several male critics described as "incredibly ugly" and as "an old maid."[45] As recently as 1997, Pedro Mir, who was named poet laureate in 1984, found it relevant to describe Ureña as a "skinny little woman, who was even a little ugly" during a speech *celebrating* the great poet on the centenary commemoration of her death.[46] Comments such as Mir's illustrate the misogynist prejudices of the country's cultural overseers and posthumously "puts her in her place," so to speak, qualifying his likely admiration for her work. Their standards ensured that Ureña's work and legacy supported a gendered idea of what kind of literature would be useful/public/masculine to nationalist projects and what kind of literature was trivial/private/feminine.

Her "intimate" corpus of writing, combined with the letters she wrote to her husband, complicate glossy understandings of this icon. Continuing the previous chapter's engagement with gendered literary hierarchies, and extending the work of scholars such as Chiqui Vicioso, Daisy Cocco de Filippis, and Catharina Vallejo, I argue that many intellectuals' discomfort with Ureña's complicated desires continued, perhaps intensified, throughout the twentieth century. Moreover, Dominican literature during Ureña's era and afterwards equated feminine propriety with whiteness; as in other parts of the Americas, white women were considered more chaste, more beautiful, worthier of masculine protection, and more valuable as marriage partners than nonwhite women. When nonwhite women emerge in Dominican literature in the late nineteenth century and the early twentieth, "the quality of goodness, innocence and fragility attributed to the white woman are absent," argues Cocco de Filippis.[47] As a nonwhite woman who was nonetheless part of the capital's cultural elite and whose works had garnered the highest critical acclaim, Ureña already complicated several of these ideals. Values expressed in literature do not necessarily reflect reality, and the Dominican case is no exception. Nevertheless, Ureña's visual whitening, combined with the reshaping of her work and life, was part and parcel of bringing Ureña closer to these raced and gendered nationalist ideals.

Discussions of propriety or respectability, race, gender, and class are not new in African diaspora, Caribbean, and African American studies. For well over a century, intellectuals and activists have argued for the ways in which black subjects' racial uplift counted on performing propriety to contest racist notions of black subjects as hypersexual, indolent, and unintelligent. As Mimi Sheller argues:

> [I]n taking up positions as "free subjects" freed men and women at times had to (indeed wanted to) perform normative scripts of sexual citizenship such as the "good mother," the "respectable woman," or the "father of a family," which had the effect of delimiting freedom to particular embodied forms. [. . .] Even (or especially) in emancipation, then, the body, sexuality, and sexual orientation remained contested terrains for the elaboration of freedom.[48]

However, it is somewhat precarious to apply this wealth of scholarship to a woman who, as I mentioned above, never used racial terms for herself, her family, or those in her social class, at least in writing.

The only racial or ethnic terms I have found are in reference to foreigners and domestics under her employ, pointing to the interconnections between class, race, and nationality in this Dominican context. For instance, she describes her daughter's caretaker, Regina, as "*una jóven negra*" (a young black woman) and another domestic worker as "*una criada inglesa*" (an English maid).[49] As in other parts of the Americas, working-class subjects were more susceptible to racialized interpellation, violence, and oppression than mixed-race or black subjects of the elite classes. April Mayes argues that, in the Dominican Republic of the late nineteenth century, "[p]olicing the boundaries of honourable womanhood assisted the process" of "elite and aspiring women's entrance into the public domain."[50] According to this logic of propriety, Ureña's celebration and then commemoration relied at least partly on the concomitant policing not only of her own sexuality and phenotypically whitened image but also that of working-class and poor women whose lack of cultural capital racialized them as black.

Despite her elite status, the letters between her and her husband teem with economic worries and, importantly, she fought to secure funding so that girls from poor to middle-class families could enroll at her school.[51] Even when we take into account that she did not describe herself as black or as mixed race, Ureña was still part of a world order that protected white women or women who approached what were considered the performative signs of whiteness. This propriety was a double-edged sword, for it also prevented her from being seen as a woman with complex desires.

During the Trujillo era, Silveria R. de Rodríguez Demorizi published a biography of the poet, *Salomé Ureña de Henríquez*, which depicts Ureña as a model of ideal femininity and patriotism.[52] Though written by Rodríguez Demorizi, Ureña's son Pedro presides over the text. The author concedes that she took advantage of "Dr. Pedro Henríquez Ureña's manuscript notes, as well as verbal news that he communicated to us in Cambridge, Massachusetts in 1941."[53] The biography's fixation on propriety echoes Henríquez Ureña's exclusion of the poem "Amor y anhelo" in his 1920 reissue of the 1880 anthology of his mother's poems.

The biography opens by establishing Ureña as part of two old, though impoverished, families. Rodríguez Demorizi states that all ancestors on record had been Dominican, with the exception of one from the Canary Islands, highlighting Ureña's genealogical Dominicanness and, concomitantly, her non-Haitianness. As became tragically evident during the 1937 massacre, the Trujillo government violently wrought anti-Haitianism as state-sanctioned dogma by the year of the book's publication in 1944. Moreover, Rodríguez Demorizi writes that Ureña had come from a long line of lettered folks, which is no small feat in what had been a mostly illiterate society. Too, she evokes the sense that a genteel grandeur surrounded Ureña. For instance, she notes that Ureña was born in her maternal grandmother's house in a neighborhood full of *"buenas familias"* (good families).[54] The seemingly innocuous descriptor of "good families" encodes raced and classed notions of propriety. Despite this ancestry, Ureña and her husband struggled economically. While he studied medicine in Paris, they worried constantly about finances and keeping the household and Ureña's school afloat. These details add texture to Rodríguez Demorizi's glossy genealogy.

Even a glance at the section headings that organize the book demonstrates that one of the biography's main concerns is highlighting Ureña's propriety: Antecedents, Birth and Religiosity, Poetic Vocation, Patriotism, Salomé at Home, Femininity, At the School, Death.[55] The two out of eight sections of the book dedicated to domesticity and femininity are consonant with the values of decorous femininity. In the "Salomé at Home" section, Rodríguez Demorizi assures the reader that "Salomé did not forgo her duties as a mother for those of education."[56] Before her relatively late marriage at age 29, Rodríguez Demorizi writes that, as a single woman, Ureña rarely left the confines of her home, except to go to church.[57] These details suggest an impeccable reputation and hint at Ureña's virginity before marriage.

However, the personal letters between Ureña and her husband reveal a greater complexity. For instance, in 1888, she admits that she had not been to church in five years and nine months and had forgotten how to kneel for long periods of time.[58] "Salomé Ureña was unable to annihilate the [ideal of the] 'domestic angel,'" notes Angela Hernández, "but she mocked it occasionally."[59] While some of the letters support the vision of Ureña as a recluse, she was not driven by her concern for propriety. Although we can never know truly why Ureña preferred to remain indoors, the letters between her and her husband highlight that she was *"profundamente melancólica"* (profoundly melancholic).[60] Rodríguez Demorizi obscures or is not aware of this when she attributes Ureña's reclusive nature to the poet's valorization of domesticity.

Further establishing Ureña as a paragon of upright Dominican womanhood, the "Femininity" section of the biography starts with the simple statement that "Salomé Ureña was extremely feminine."[61] The shortest section in the book, its role is to placate any doubts, to my knowledge nonexistent, of what was considered to be, by her contemporaries, Ureña's commendable femininity.[62] Rodríguez Demorizi clarifies that, while Ureña was praised for writing "virile" verses, these dubious compliments do "not refer to hateful manly airs, to bastardly masculine manifestations in her verses, but instead to the majesty of her inspiration; she was manly also in her greatness of action, but always feminine in her attitude. That woman was never manly in her attitude, she was so extremely feminine."[63] In Rodríguez Demorizi's estimation, Ureña was feminine because she acted in a certain way. Citing a speech by Ureña's close collaborator Eugenio María de Hostos, she notes that Ureña always had "a delicate sentiment, a hidden complacent smile, noble encouragements."[64] These attributes correlate with traditional ideals of quiet, unassuming femininity. Finally, the last sentence of the "Femininity" section sums up the dominant, Trujillo-sanctioned stance toward women in the mid-twentieth century: "Had she not been feminine, she would have been deserving of praise in one sense, but not in the most sacred one, because not even the greatest glory is worth sacrificing a woman's femininity."[65] The connotation here is that Ureña's poetic accomplishments are not alone worthy of praise, and that it is her ability to be a poet as well as a dutiful mother and wife that render her a model for Dominican women. "No other regime has exalted and promoted women as mothers, wives, and homemakers" as much as the Trujillo regime, write Ramonina Brea and Isis Duarte.[66] Given this, Rodríguez Demorizi's emphasis on Ureña's status as a wife and mother entrenches Ureña within these mid-twentieth-century values. In this manner, Rodríguez Demorizi's biography, along with the phenotypical whitewashing of her image already evident by the time of the book's publication in 1944, repackaged Ureña as a female national icon worthy of her status. However, the rise of feminist critique combined with the exponential growth of the Dominican diaspora overseas—far too large to deny that it includes other people besides men of the elite classes—was beginning to create the potential for a new kind of reading practice based on Ureña's writings.

"Of Flesh and Bone": Chiqui Vicioso's Diasporic Intervention

My search through the Ureña archive led me Chiqui Vicioso, one of the most important Dominican scholars, activists, and poets. Her 2001 play *Salomé U.: Cartas a una ausencia* (Salomé U.: Letters to an Absence) foregrounds Ureña's complicated intertwining of domestic happiness and nationalist zeal.[67] The play is based on Ureña's love poems, the family's epistolary, and another play by Dominican dramatist Germana Quintano.[68] A single actress plays both Ureña and a present-day writer who discovers the more complicated Ureña, adopting one character per scene. As Vicioso describes the play in the introduction to the published script, "The most important thing is to underline that this monologue's connecting thread is the absence of a loved one, seen and felt through the lens of two women writers separated by a century."[69] The decision to cast one actress to play two characters emphasizes the unity of the two women, despite the wide historical gap. The monologue in Ureña's scenes blends inner thoughts related to the government, her husband, and her children; fragments from the correspondence between husband and wife; and excerpts of her poetic work. The monologue of the twenty-first-century woman writer focuses on the frustration of having to write an essay on the canonical, patriotic Ureña most familiar to Dominicans, as well as the absence of her husband, Ernesto, who has neither returned home nor returned her calls.

Vicioso became fascinated by the woman *"de carne y hueso"* (of flesh and bone) after reading Ureña's less venerated, personal poems, a transformation that the fictional twenty-first-century writer in *Salomé U.* also undergoes. Vicioso's encounters with the original daguerreotype inspired her to refute Ureña's phenotypical whitening and the publication of Ureña's family epistolary galvanized her to complicate the antiseptic, canonical Ureña. "This revalorization of women's 'domestic' poetry, and, as such, their poetry as a whole, as men's works have always been analyzed," Vicioso explains, "would become one of the central themes in feminine literary critique almost one hundred years after Ureña's birth."[70] The play disrupts the image of an almost mythical Ureña.

Through its structure and content, *Salomé U.* upturns the reading practices described in the previous chapter, which relied on the erasure of nonmasculinist subjectivities. Tired of the endless patriotic cantos, the present-day author in the play finally reaches the poem "Quejas" (Complaints) in Ureña's anthology and says: "¡BINGO!"[71] As a woman who awaited a phone call from an absent beloved, she had found the Ureña to whom she could relate. The stage directions after citing from the poem state: "In this scene the writer internalizes the sensibility in Salomé's poem and the transference is completed, that is, the poem becomes HER poem and to have initially devastating consequences."[72] The present-day author shouts the name of her beloved, "¡Ernesto!," which the stage directions describe as the overlap between the contemporary author with Ureña and Ureña's husband, Francisco Henríquez y Carvajal, with Ernesto. Finding solace in the melancholic Ureña, not the patriotic muse, the twenty-first-century woman writer can finally finish her assignment. The play suggests that the loves that Ureña experiences beyond love-of-nation are just as worthy of contemplation. Moments such as these capture the ways in which the play restructures how female subjects read and write themselves out of masculinist scripts, creating their own.

Vicioso was inspired especially by the letters between Ureña and her husband. As I discussed in chapter one, most persistent are his reprimands of Ureña's melancholia as inconsistent with positivist values, paralleling her readership's disregard for Ureña's intimate and domestic poems. Both Vicioso's play and Julia Alvarez's novel *In the Name of Salomé* (2000),[73] which I discuss below, do the work of "making up for" Henríquez y Carvajal's and other male readers' dismissals by featuring the mutual echoing of women's voices. Through their woman-centric echoes, Vicioso's and Alvarez's texts suggest that Ureña's entire body of work has found appreciative readers.

Salomé U. restructures the hierarchical and masculinist scripts that Ureña's male readers constructed into a set of woman-centric echoes that can be described as *dialogic, intersubjective,* and *omnivocal.* These terms all invoke the notion of inclusive dialogue as a form of relating to others, rather than hierarchical, vertical, and paternalistic relationships. Michelle M. Wright defines the term "intersubjectivity" as one reflecting "not a simple merging of two into one (the synthesis in an ideal dialectic revolution) but the conflated coexistence of two subjects, defined by, through, and against one another."[74] Unlike the male readers I discussed in chapter one, who often consumed Ureña's patriotic yearning as their own, the play's structure instantiates an indirect but equal "exchange" between two writing subjects. Wright cites Mae Gwendolyn Henderson's concept of an "'omnivocal' subjectivity" that allows for difference, and which provides the framework for a diaspora subjectivity removed from the nationalisms that render certain subjects, such as subversive females, illegible.[75]

This diasporic, dialogic subjectivity grounds the reading practice that emerges in Vicioso's play. As part of this reading practice, the play also blurs the demarcation between patriotic and intimate concerns, and, as such, the public and private realms. Since many of Ureña's intimate poems dwell on the absent beloved who must return in order for national unification to take place, they illustrate the interrelatedness between domestic/private and political/public desires. As I mentioned, the poem that transforms the twenty-first-century writer's opinion of

Ureña is "Quejas" (Complaints), which dwells on Henríquez y Carvajal's absence and on the feelings of rejection it prompts:

> Te vas, y el alma dejas
> sumida en amargura, solitaria,
> y mis ardientes quejas,
> y la tímida voz de mi plegaria,
> indiferente y frío
> desoyes ¡ay! para tormento mío.[76]

> You depart, and leave the soul
> submerged in bitterness, solitary,
> and my ardent complaints,
> and the timid voice of my supplication,
> indifferent and cold
> you ignore, oh! to my torment.

This poem reveals that absence—*"te vas"* (you depart)—correlates with the image of a lover deaf—*"desoyes"* (ignore)—to the narrator's demands and desires. There is an obvious allusion to Henríquez y Carvajal's physical absence from the home(land), as was his habit, but there is also a subtle, and perhaps unintentional, reference to his dismissal of Ureña's intimate poems.

In prioritizing Salomé's concerns as a wife and lover, *Salomé U.* implies that what happens in a domestic setting and in women's minds is just as important as the government's machinations.[77] It questions the dichotomy between public and private, and between political and intimate, a blurring that conjures the legacy of feminist theory.[78] Brea and Duarte confirm that, in the Dominican context, women's subordination manifests itself through several routes: "their supposed inferiority, their confinement to the private and domestic sphere, exaltation of motherhood, control over their bodies through its exaltation as object of human reproduction or as an object of pleasure."[79] More generally, Ana Peluffo and Ignacio M. Sánchez Prado posit that "[o]ne of the strategies of Latin American feminist critique [. . .] consisted of demonstrating that the construction of the feminine subject of the republic as private, domestic and sentimental was a discourse that was more desired [by nationalists] than real."[80] Vicioso's play evinces the extent to which "private, domestic, and sentimental" concerns were real but also inseparable from public, political, and emotionally arid ones.

The present-day writer in *Salomé U.* ponders: "And later they say that love has nothing to do with politics. Forget that! When a woman is in love she could even live in Haiti and believe that everything will turn out well, that the country has hope." Besides disclosing stereotypical ideas about Haiti, the contemporary writer makes a direct connection between Salomé's yearning for her husband with a desire for a peaceful patria.[81] In *Salomé U.*, the peaceful nation is the object of desire not only for Salomé but also for men intimately involved in national politics like her father and, later, her husband. Salomé recalls:

> When I was a little girl, I thought that *patria* must be a very
>   beautiful woman for my father to risk himself so much and
>   abandon us for her.
> When I was older, I noticed that it was not just my father.
> In the East, the *patria* had driven Santana mad.
> In the South, in the blink of an eye, she had Báez.
> In the Cibao region, persistent and firm, she got Luperón.
> All of them fighting each other in the name of the *patria*.[82]

In this excerpt, the patria adopts the role of the seductive woman for whom important men in Dominican history risked their lives and, ironically, provoked their lengthy absences from the domestic space of the hearth and the homeland. Vicioso's rendering of the patria as a seductive woman calls attention to the gendered binaries I discussed in chapter one, in which the male citizen-subject desired a feminized land, thereby excluding the possibility of women as citizen-subjects from the nationalist script. In highlighting this gendering, Vicioso denatural-izes its hetero-patriarchal logic. By emphasizing, instead, the dialogical, transhistorical connection between two women writers, both as profes-sional women and as unhappy lovers, Vicioso rewrites the script through which women can write and read themselves into national belonging with diasporic feminist tools.

"The Great Silence from Which These Two Women Emerge": Julia Alvarez's *In the Name of Salomé*

I now turn to another diasporic feminist rewriting of national scripts—Julia Alvarez's biographical novel of Salomé Ureña and her daughter Camila Henríquez Ureña, *In the Name of Salomé*.[83] Alvarez is one of the most celebrated Latina writers in the United States. Though she was born into a white Dominican elite, Alvarez's fiction, poetry, and essays explore her newfound identity as a Hispanophone ethnic minority in the U.S.[84] I argue that Alvarez's diasporic experience as an ethnic minority, combined with her personal and intellectual connection to Vicioso, fueled the production of a fictional Ureña biography that unsettles the whitewashed legacy of the poet.

Like Vicioso's *Salomé U.*, the structure of *In the Name of Salomé* evokes Ureña's transhistorical reach in both form and content. The chapters move interchangeably between Salomé's and her daughter Camila's lives.[85] They also move backwards in time with Camila and forward with Salomé, showcasing the mother's and daughter's temporal meeting at the end of the novel as Salomé nears death. The chapters' titles are borrowed from the titles of some of Ureña's most famous poems, appropriately fitting the life experiences described in each chapter. Each chapter has two versions, one for Salomé's life and the other for Camila's. For instance, chapter "Uno" is entitled "El ave y el nido" (Bird and Nest) for a young Salomé and chapter "One" is called "Light" for an adult Camila returning to Cuba to work for the Revolution. The last chapter, "Ocho," is entitled "Luz" (Light), referring to Salome's giving birth to Camila, and "Eight" is called "Bird and Nest," referring to Camila's earliest memories as a little girl trying to process her mother's death. When referring to Camila the title "Light" alludes to her intellectual "enlightenment," whereas when referring to Salomé "Luz" refers to *dar a luz* (literally, "to give to light"), which means "to give birth." That the titles translated into English are dedicated to Camila points to the latter's long-term life in the United States. That this novel about the first Dominican poet of national import was written in English also points to Alvarez's own life in the diaspora.

As in Vicioso's play, a twentieth- or twenty-first-century woman's reading of Ureña forms the core of the novel's structure. The novel's transgenerational conversation between women across the distance of time replaces male readers' silencing of a woman's complicated desires. In Alvarez's fictional rendition, Salomé continues to exist to a daughter who values her mother's written voice wherever it emerges. Camila reads and memorizes Salomé's letters and poems when the latter needs her mother's wisdom. The prologue describes Camila giving up her position at Vassar College, where she had been a professor of Spanish, and moving to a postrevolutionary Cuba. This initial moment in the novel makes apparent the mentorship that her mother's writing had provided to Camila and that she may no longer need: "She is taking only her suitcase and the trunk of her mother's papers and poems carried down just now by the school grounds crew to the waiting car. To think that only a few months ago, she was consulting those poems for signs!"[86] Camila's intellectual and personal communion with her mother as facilitated through writing replicates the encounter that the contemporary writer in Vicioso's play has with Ureña's nonpatriotic poetry.

Echoing Ureña's *quejas* (complaints) in the poem titled as such and in some of her letters to her husband, the Salomé of Alvarez's novel remains tormented by her husband's inability to consider all of her wants.[87] After writing a poem that expresses her anguish when her husband Francisco "Pancho" travels around the nation for work, he states that "you must not squander away your talent by singing in a minor key [. . .] You must think of your future as the bard of the nation. We want the songs of la patria, we need anthems to lead us out of the morass of our past and into the glorious destiny as the Athens of the Americas."[88] Salomé responds, "I am a woman as well as a poet," which emphasizes the holistic way in which Alvarez reads Ureña's work.[89] Salomé further narrates: "With the last few poems, I had begun writing in a voice that came from deep inside me. It was not a public voice. It was my own voice expressing my secret desires that Pancho was dismissing."[90] This statement encapsulates Alvarez's awareness of the masculinist literary standards that have shaped Ureña's legacy, confirming that the novel is partly a feminist intervention preoccupied with the valorization of what were considered "trivial" feminine concerns by the cultural status quo.

Alvarez alludes to this idea in her novel every time that Pancho reminds Salomé that domestic contentment must be sacrificed in their efforts to improve the patria. She dreads having to endure Pancho's lengthy absences as secretary to the Dominican president at the time,

Fernando Arturo Meriño. In the face of Salomé's erotic distress, Pancho remains coolly positivist:

> He was holding me in that absent way of his. Already he was far away, sitting on that veranda in a small village talking to local leaders about the glorious future of la patria. [. . .] My eyes felt puffy and my nose was running. For the hundredth time I wished for one of those pretty faces that soften men's hearts. "Salomé, our patria is just barely standing again on its shaky legs. We have to roll up our sleeves [. . .] and work hard, side by side, to bring about that future we both dream about."[91]

The word *patria* in this and the previous examples from Vicioso's *Salomé U.* connotes two conflicting ideas; restoring the patria is not only what Salomé herself desires as palpable in her patriotic poetry but it is also the object of her husband's more passionate love. Salomé compares what she sees as her lack of beauty with the siren call of the patria. In the novel, Pancho's dismissal of Salomé's melancholy and its concomittant personal poetry shapes their marriage. He claims that "[p]ositivists all over the world were fighting a peaceful evolutionary battle to replace the dark cloud of unreason and violence and religion with reason and progress and science."[92] However, as Salomé wonders, "does a person in love ever listen to reason?"[93] The relevant point here is not to admonish the real-life Henríquez y Carvajal as an unloving, scientifically and not poetically minded husband, but to see him as representative of the values that would come to dominate Dominican intellectualism in the early twentieth century.

Moreover, Alvarez's critique of Pancho's desire for national progress and not for his wife gestures toward more than his less-than-ideal behavior as a husband; the novel ruptures the gendered symbolisms in nationalist discourses in which heterosexual coupling and the formation of a nuclear family is the ideal. Unlike traditional Latin American nationalist texts, or "foundational fictions," in Doris Sommer's coinage, in which "marriage [. . .] is the core metaphor for political coalitions," Alvarez's fictional biography of Ureña points precisely to the failure of marriage as a conciliatory institution that can fix political turmoil.[94] In many nationalist Latin American novels, marriage triumphs over political strife and represents the unification of previously discordant sectors of the nation. However, Alvarez portrays the many ways in which marriage brings strife to women such as Salomé Ureña. The psychological consequences of Salomé's husband's absence, infidelity, and indifference are the elements that prompt Alvarez to produce literature that builds on this motif of the failure of marriage, and, concomitantly, the failure of a patriarchal family and national structure to fulfill its promise of protection and unification.[95] The novel also breaks from the ideal of the home-bound family unit as expressed in many "foundational" Latin American novels; the scattering of the Henríquez Ureña family throughout the hemisphere, escaping imperial control and dictatorship, demonstrates that the reality for many displaced Dominicans and their loved ones was distant from the ideal. That Ureña constantly wrote about and to the many exiled people in her life, and that her children would live and die in exile, means that Alvarez's novel respects this reality. In doing so, she constructs an alternative vision of love-of-nation—for Salomé and her daughter Camila are shown to love their country (or countries)—that forges connections across geographic displacements and across time through women's mutual echoing.[96]

Indeed, both the novel's and the play's woman-centric echoes emerge in their very production since Vicioso encouraged Alvarez to write *In the Name of Salomé*. The novel's "Acknowledgements" section thanks "Chiqui Vicioso, who five years ago [. . .] sat me down in her apartamento in Santo Domingo and loaned me her copy of the just-published *Epistolario* of the Henríquez Ureña family, and a copy of the poems of S. Ureña, and like some bossy musa said, 'Your next book, Julia!'"[97] Here, the muse is a demanding woman writer and activist who inspires Alvarez to read the words of and re-create the world of a "flesh and bone" Salomé Ureña. Further, *In the Name of Salomé* is dedicated to "Quisqueyanas valientes" (brave Dominican women), invoking the national anthem that begins with the words "Quisqueyanos valientes" (brave Dominicans or Dominican men). This dialogic conversation or chain denotes women listening to and reading other women in stark contrast to the masculinist silences and silencings of what were deemed to be apolitical and inconsequential concerns.

Both Alvarez's novel and Vicioso's play reject the notion that the nation stands on the shoulders of patriarchs by elaborating, instead, on the woman-centric chains of thought binding women's voices from the earliest days of the nation to the present. They reject a national structure in which"[t]he arbiter of this nationalist/naturalist ethic," writes Homi Bhabha, "is the bearer of a peculiar, visible invisibility (some call it the phallus)—the familial patriarch."[98] The echoes of women's voices or writing shape these texts' forms. As in the previous chapter, the act of reading and the feelings associated with it dominate both texts. Unlike the previous chapter's exiled subjects' performance of patriotism, however, these late twentieth- and early twenty-first-century readings of Ureña generate dialogue between women writers across the distance of time.

The theoretical consequences of this shift are enormous. In the late nineteenth century, the national script allowed exiled men to maintain their legibility within the nation by reading Ureña's patriotic poetry and simultaneously ghosting her and other non-ideal Dominicans', especially women's, desires. Vicioso's and Alvarez's twenty-first-century reconfigurations transform the relationship between author/speaker and reader/listener to a collaborative one among women. As such, they reshape the basis for who is legible in these scripts or narratives of belonging.

These feminist recoveries of historical and literary figures as they emerged especially in the late twentieth- and early twenty-first century have not replaced masculinist literary culture. Both narratives coexist uneasily in a public sphere that allows more room for previously marginalized voices than it did during Ureña's lifetime. In 1985, Dominican writer Carmen Imbert Brugal published the essay "The Manly Intellectual Woman," which decries the masculinism predominant in literary culture:

> Intellectual gatherings celebrate the varona [manly woman] who is willing to sing the praises of her lord. But were the same woman to dare to sing the praises of her own vagina she would be marginalized and plunged into the chaos caused by ugly rumor. Were she to sing in celebration of her body, she would be assailed by the participants, and rumors about her frigidity, lesbianism or possible nymphomania would have their day.

Imbert Brugal then wonders what is to be done with the perpetual exclusion of women in the anthologies, events, and institutions of import. She concludes that "we can write our own history, to make the product of our creation lasting, which on occasion comes out of a dramatic process, with frustrating consequences."[99]

Who Is the "Real" Ureña?

On a scorching day in June 2014, I stepped into the cool corridors of the Centro de Excelencia Salomé Ureña, formerly the Instituto de Señoritas Salomé Ureña, in Santo Domingo's Colonial Zone. With its two stories of classrooms, the current campus accommodates the school's coed student population, marking the distance between the present day and the late nineteenth century when Salomé Ureña presided over the first graduating class of six young women. My mission during those quiet hours of repose after the noontime meal was to find any last details about Ureña that I might have missed after my years of research. Though I did not find a dusty box full of letters and mementos, as I had fantasized, I did have an illuminating conversation with one of the schoolteachers. As she led me to the school's decorative centerpieces—a golden bust of the poet in the central hall and a fresco on the ceiling—she asked if I knew that Ureña had been a melancholic person. As I nodded in assent, she remarked: "Did you know that she looked more like me than she does in those images?" and she pointed to her dark brown arm to signal what she meant.[100] I mentioned that I was in the process of acquiring a clear image of the original daguerreotype of Ureña. When we arrived at the circular hallway with Ureña's golden bust, I noted that the Ureña it portrayed, as well as the Ureña of the painting on the spherical ceiling, looked like the many images of Ureña that I had already seen. Nevertheless, the schoolteacher was able to reconcile the idea that Ureña had not been a white woman with the whitewashed images she saw every day at work. Similarly, sociologists and ethnographers have pointed out that many Dominicans recognize that when they use the word *indio*—a practice instituted during the Trujillo regime—they are aware that they are not indigenous in the same way as other subjects in the Americas and they are also aware that they have African ancestry. That Ureña's family and friends seemed to accept whitewashed drawings and paintings of the poet points to this tendency. The coexistence of what seem to be contradictory ideas and images confounds non-Dominicans, but it is crucial to accept these tensions as Dominicans and non-Dominicans work against antiblack discourses.

Alvarez's *In the Name of Salomé* delves into the potentially confounding approach to the visuality of race among Dominicans. These tensions emerge in the several moments when the fictional Salomé experiences her nonwhiteness vis-à-vis the white-presenting elite that surrounds her. After her future brother-in-law, Federico, compliments her poems, an embarrassed Salomé thinks: "He was not seeing me, Salomé, of the funny nose and big ears with hunger in her eyes and Africa in her skin and hair."[101] In this single phrase, the novel encapsulates the sense that the white elite approached Ureña with a kind of racial "blindness" that prevented them from seeing her blackness, and, as such, allowed for their respect. In another crucial moment of the novel, two characters reckon with the legacy of this blindness or silencing as they encounter one version of Salomé's whitening. After Salomé's death, her young daughter Camila sees an

> oil portrait her father recently commissioned by an artist in London. [...]
> Her aunt [Salomé's sister Ramona] is looking at the portrait and shaking her head. "That's not what your mother looked like. [...] Your mother was much darker, for one thing."
> "As dark as me?" Camila wants to know. [...]
> Her aunt hesitates. "Darker. Pedro's color, with the same features."[102]

Alvarez connects the "real" Salomé to her son, the aforementioned Pedro, the darkest complexioned of the Henríquez Ureña children. This is the same Pedro who, in reality, wrote of the family's European and indigenous—and not African—ancestry.[103] Alvarez's fictional moments, however, unearth Ureña's obscured African ancestry and connect it to the larger forces of canonization.

* * *

In this chapter, I discussed the canonization of Ureña as a desexualized, whitewashed, and maternal object of veneration before and during the Trujillo era, as well as her subsequent "resurrection" through the work of two feminist diasporic Dominican women writers. Considering the persistence of the elite white man as the ideal patriot in the conservative nationalist imaginary, the Ureña that Vicioso and Alvarez—and myself—unearth is far from being a perfect symbol of ideal patriotism. The variety of materials I consider throughout the chapter together evince different elements of Ureña's work and life, perhaps different Ureñas entirely. Yet, it is her image and name, and not that of the other male canonical writers, that decorate Dominican schoolyards. I propose that the distance between the ideals upheld by nationalist scripts and the complicated reality of Dominican history and society

Figure 2.6. Anonymous graffiti of Salomé Ureña (denominated by her marriage name, Henríquez) on the wall of a building in Calle Meriño of the Colonial Zone, ca. 2014. (Author's image.)

ensured Ureña's rise, for she and her legacy embody the tensions and contradictions inherent to the construction of nationalist identity. That a nonwhite woman would become the first "national poet" is a reminder of the uniqueness of Dominican history. As a colony then nation, the territory hosted for centuries a large percentage of free mixed-race and black subjects. Moreover, slavery was abolished in the early nineteenth century with Haiti's unification of the island at a time when much of the hemisphere relied on slave-supported Plantation economies. Despite this unique history, a conservative, Eurocentric elite persistently strove against any signs that would align Dominicans with what Haiti represented around the world—rebellious, unapologetic blackness. The world had punished Haiti's assertion of freedom, one that formerly enslaved subjects had not been given but taken for themselves. In their efforts to distance the Dominican nation from its neighbor, Dominican elites relented to the increasing influence of the northern imperial power, an uneven relationship that ensured that white supremacist ideology would continue to fold itself into state-sanctioned dogma. We must see Ureña's celebration and subsequent whitewashing within this context.

For all of these reasons, perhaps the most compelling image of Ureña is a ghostly graffiti of the poet marking the wall of a nondescript building in the Colonial Zone (see Figure 2.6). Unlike the simple lines that take shape as a dress and the always-present cross, her head is blurred, shaded, and obscured entirely not only by the deteriorating wall but also by the artist. Unlike the photographers, sculptors, and painters mentioned throughout this chapter, the graffiti artist has made no attempt to produce an accurate likeness.

3

Following the Admiral

Reckonings with Great Men's History

Columbia
[. . .].
You're terribly involved in world assignations
And everybody knows it.
You've slept with all the big powers
In military uniforms,
And you've taken the sweet life
Of all the little brown fellows
In loincloths and cotton trousers.
—Langston Hughes, "Columbia" (1933)

The guarded secret is buried alive by forms of obfuscation
and denial. [. . .] The crypt becomes part of the landscape.
—Anne McClintock, "Imperial Ghosting and National
Tragedy" (2014)

In the spring of 2015, popular *dembow* artist Enmanuel "El Alfa" Herrera was arrested for insulting the three men recognized as the Dominican founding fathers in a video uploaded to YouTube.[1] Filmed at the capital's Plaza de la Bandera (Flag Plaza), the video shows El Alfa pointing to the Dominican flags, turning to the camera, and saying, "¡Duarte Sanche' y Mella, mamaguevo!" (Duarte, Sanchez, y Mella, cocksucker!) Because of the Dominican proclivity to drop the "s" at the end of certain words, it is unclear if he meant the insult in the plural or the singular, which might have clarified its object. Despite this uncertainty, Judge John Henry Reynoso issued a warrant for El Alfa's arrest on behalf of the Ministerio Público. Several constituencies raised a furor over El Alfa's disrespect for the founding fathers. The president of El Instituto Duartiano (Duarte

Institute), César Romero, asked for a boycott of the artist and the destruction of his albums.[2] *El Caribe*, one of the country's most important newspapers, affirmed that it had "censored" El Alfa's insults because "the founding fathers and the emblematic plaza demand respect."[3] Just a few days after his arrest, El Alfa's punishment was made public; he was to clean the Plaza de la Bandera and to sing the national anthem for two hours over the course of fifteen consecutive days. Another element of the punishment was to hand out educational pamphlets about the founding fathers at stoplights throughout Santo Domingo.[4] In his subsequent apology via press release, El Alfa proclaimed: "I apologize to my fans and to the Dominican people because they are the *patria*, it was never my intention to offend them, nor the hero martyrs of my country [. . .]. I said [the slur] because people were speculating that I stayed in the United States to get [immigration] documents when in reality I was working. I was happy to be back in my homeland and I made this video clarifying to many people that what was being said was not true."[5] Interviewed after the completion of his second day of punishment at the Plaza de las Banderas, El Alfa states: "I'm totally fine with the decision taken."[6]

The case of El Alfa serves as a perfect starting point for a discussion about several shifts in post-Trujillo Dominican society: the population becoming mostly urban for the first time in the territory's history; the fall of subsistence agriculture alongside the rise of un- or underemployment; the massive emigrations to other countries especially after the U.S. government loosened restrictions through the Immigration and Naturalization Act of 1965; and the imposition of international trade agreements such as the CAFTA-DR (Dominican Republic–Central American Free Trade). Within this context of questionable national sovereignty, the policing of Dominican citizens' behavior toward commemorative objects signals the desperate—but no less dangerous—attempts to protect conservative ideas of nationalist identity. El Alfa's arrest and subsequent punishment reflect a justice system and government that does not tolerate free speech and that insists on the performance of an uncritical and blind defense of a specific form of patriotism. Moreover, El Alfa's shaming over having had to live temporarily in the U.S. to make ends meet reveals the discomfiting reality of many working-class Dominicans, many of whom live in perpetual transmigrancy.[7] This kind of transnational existence involves uncertainty more than the unfettered possibility often imagined by celebrants of globalization.[8] El Alfa's case also evinces the struggle between official nationalist history and the resistance of subaltern voices. On one side stand the three white or whitened founding patriarchs. On the other side stands El Alfa, the racialized, criminalized, and transmigrant "urban music" performer who reminds the status quo of the always threatening "monte" society.

As I mentioned in earlier chapters, the power of the nation-state strengthened throughout the twentieth century, especially during the Trujillo dictatorship (1930–1961) and during the ultraconservative and repressive Joaquín Balaguer presidencies that followed (1966–1978 and 1986–1996). National unification became possible once the central state could account for all of its subjects, thereby eradicating the autonomous, anonymous monte that had predominated throughout the territory for centuries. El Alfa was able to record and disseminate his defiant act because he had access to a new form of information technology, YouTube; unwittingly, however, the YouTube video became the prime piece of evidence in a case against his "lewd" patriotism or antipatriotism, depending on the intent of his act. At the moment that "the archive" includes voices such as El Alfa's—a nonwhite, working-class, and transmigrant Dominican man with a tenuous hold on a steady income—it immediately becomes a site of surveillance and prompt discipline. Such is the materialist and pervasive power of official national history in perpetrating the active silencing of alternative interpretations of national belonging. El Alfa is relatively fortunate; in other contexts, he could be among the hundreds, if not thousands, of Dominicans who were disappeared and murdered during the Trujillo regime and into the present for their anti–status quo speech acts.

By analyzing various works of prose fiction, film, as well as a grandiose public monument, in this chapter I contend that certain performances of Dominican masculinity are small-scale individual negotiations with large-scale, systemic patriarchal patriotism at both the national and imperial levels. However, I also illustrate that these negotiations of island and diasporic Dominican hypermasculinity themselves often invoke and repeat masculinist violence. To expose national and imperial history as it has been constructed and imposed from above, I analyze the fascinating story behind the Columbus Lighthouse Memorial in Santo

Domingo. The monument itself celebrates conservative Dominican na-tionalism, but its fraught construction uncovers Dominican national-ists' long-term ambivalence toward their inferior position in relation to imperial powers such as Spain and the U.S. In many ways, the feverish celebrations of Columbus in the late nineteenth century restructured U.S. relations with the Dominican Republic. In particular, Dominican officials and intellectual elites' own fixations with Columbus, and their unique role as being in the city he and his family founded, shaped a new discourse with the U.S., replacing or at least placating some of the anxi-eties over Dominican connections to Haiti.

The importance of the Columbus Lighthouse project to cultural lead-ers of both the Dominican Republic and the U.S. confirmed that both countries tied their fates to the spirit of Columbus, an identification be-tween ideal citizenship and white masculinity. In both cases, this patri-archal and Eurocentric vision of ideal patriotism excluded women and most nonwhite men. Moreover, Dominicans involved in the Lighthouse project leveraged the relationship that Columbus had with this territory to secure participation in global discussions about modernity and prog-ress. Paradoxically, doing so required the disinterring of ancient bones and resurrecting a centuries-old spirit.

While the Lighthouse serves as a totemic celebration of Columbus's spirit, Junot Díaz's *The Brief Wondrous Life of Oscar Wao* (2007) and the Dominican-American film *La Soga* (2009), written by its lead actor, Manny Pérez, reveal the deeply violent maintenance required in sup-porting this history from above.[9] Crucially, both texts also uncover working-class Dominican and diasporic Dominican men's uncomfort-able positions as men empowered by their masculinity but marginal-ized by their race and class within hemispheric hierarchies. Indeed, both texts also intimate that participating in the maintenance of patriarchal nationalist and imperial status quo has been one of their only vehicles for socioeconomic mobility. On the other hand, they also unspool the suffocating pressure of performative masculinity and the repercussions of compliance as well as the inability or refusal to conform.

The Specter of Columbus and the Rise of U.S. Imperialism

This monument will be like the light of a terrible shooting
star with millenarian ambition, a star that has disappeared
but that still shines strangely under the low nocturnal sky of
the Caribbean sea.
—Edgardo Rodríguez Juliá, *Caribeños* (2002)

This lighthouse is the symbol of the man who has revolution-
ized history more than anyone else since Jesus Christ, and
once they get over their orgy of criticisms, everyone will love it.
—Peter Morales Troncoso (1992)

What is it about Columbus that leads writers to paroxysms of hyperbole?[10] A pamphlet dedicated to the 1893 World's Columbian Exposition,
otherwise known as the Chicago World's Fair, renders breathless homage to the sailor:

> In the inauguration of the World's Columbian Exposition and the carry-
> ing through of the project, honor was done to one man. No other event in
> the history of the universe has ever transpired where such gigantic prepa-
> rations were made, occupying several years of time, engaging for months
> the attention of the brightest minds of the nation, causing the expendi-
> ture of millions and millions of dollars, bringing to one central point all
> of the civilized nations of the earth, all in the honor of one name. *The
> spirit of Christopher Columbus* can rightfully stand with majestic dignity
> before all other spirits, while they bow in obeisance, for none who have
> passed away have ever received such homage. Nor among the living can
> there be found any one name to which such adulation will ever be paid.
> In this, the name of Christopher Columbus stands alone.[11]

This kind of exalting discourse around the sailor was common in the
late nineteenth-century era of "colonofilia" (Columbusphilia), to borrow Christopher Schmidt-Nowara's term.[12] The Chicago World's Fair
was just one of the many celebrations of Columbus pivoting around
Eurocentric, patriarchal understandings of U.S. subjectivity in the late
nineteenth century. Columbus's legacy had become a vehicle through

which Italians and Irish Catholics could assimilate into ideal U.S. national belonging. Fraternal organizations such as the Irish American Knights of Columbus, founded in 1881, and the Italian American Sons of Columbus Legion, founded in 1896, celebrated members' appropriate American whiteness.[13] Michel-Rolph Trouillot argues that "the final measure of Chicago's success [in the World's Fair of 1893] is the extent to which it naturalized Columbus," and "this more American Columbus was also a whiter Columbus."[14] Rolena Adorno identifies Washington Irving's nineteenth-century biographies of the Admiral as an even earlier moment of Columbus's incorporation as a U.S. icon, representative of enterprising individualism.[15] As I will demonstrate later in this chapter, the ways in which celebrations of Columbus eased white immigrants' incorporation into the U.S. body politic in the nineteenth century simply do not extend to most Dominican immigrants, who are often racialized as black, arriving in the U.S. a century later.[16]

Columbus also came to symbolize Eurocentric visions of national identity in the Dominican Republic. Frederick A. Ober, commissioner to the West Indies for the 1893 Chicago World's Fair or World's Columbian Exposition, reports that President Ulises "Lilís" Heureaux sought to secure a U.S. loan in exchange for a Dominican exhibit at the Fair.[17] An added bonus, reports an incredulous Ober, was that the exhibit would include "the most sacred remains of Don Christopher Columbus."[18] Ober excerpts at length the official memo from the Dominican Ministerio de Fomento y Obras Públicas (Ministry of Development and Public Works) regarding the offer. In exchange for Dominican participation in the World's Fair, including the alleged remains, "it will be necessary for the Dominican government to effect a loan, in the United States, of one hundred thousand dollars [$100,000], in gold, interest on the same to be at six (6) percent; and the principal to be refunded at the rate of ten thousand dollars ($10,000) annually."[19] Moreover, if Ober as commissioner could secure the loan, "he may reserve the sum of twenty thousand ($20,000) for the construction of a Government building at Chicago, said building to be an exact reproduction of the old castle in this Capital [of Santo Domingo], known as the 'Homenage.'"[20] Ober's recounting of his interactions with Heureaux and other Dominican officials remains vaguely mocking throughout but especially in his dictation of Heureaux's thick Dominican accent: "Now, Mistair Commissionaire, it ees not ze honaire zat we want, but ze loan."[21] Despite this conde-scending amusement, Ober signed the memo "in the presence of the late President Heureaux, who looked smilingly on, nodding his approval."

"This precious document," as Ober describes it, evinces a small na-tion's attempt to stake a claim on its place in hemispheric affairs. Aware of the worldwide fever around the quadricentennial celebrations of Columbus's arrival to the so-called New World, Dominican officials as-tutely surmised that Columbus's historical connection to this country, and his physical remains specifically, were a valuable bargaining chip. That the memo also demanded a special building replicating a palace in Santo Domingo is more than an appeal to be recognized by this imperial power. The building would be physical manifestation of the Dominican Republic in U.S. territory; a symbolic inclusion in world affairs to follow decades of misrecognition or outright exclusion; and a sense that the Dominican Republic had been instrumental to a U.S. imaginary and, as such, had a right to mark a U.S. city's skyline.[22]

In the late nineteenth century, the urban elite that codified Domini-can nationalism sought to enshrine the legacy of the sailor. Skipping over the previous three centuries of Spanish disregard, these national-ists returned to the conquest as it reminded them and the rest of the world that Santo Domingo was the founding site of European "civili-zation" in the hemisphere. When Salomé Ureña penned the poem "A la patria" (1874) she crowned the Dominican Republic the "reina del mundo de Colón" (queen of Columbus's world), alluding to the entire hemisphere.[23] A few years later, she wrote the exalting "Colón" (1879), commemorating the finding of his alleged remains in Santo Domingo's Primada de América Cathedral. When construction of the Lighthouse was finished in Santo Domingo in 1992, Columbus's legacy symbolized a conservative Dominican government's celebration of colonialism and the pride of being the first colony in the Americas. This adherence to the values that Columbus has come to represent brought the Dominican Republic closer to Eurocentric, patriarchal ideals of the nation-state.

Indeed, the continuing idealization of Christopher Columbus was central to the conservative historical narratives that became official-ized especially through the intellectual and political work of Joaquín Balaguer. To officials like Balaguer, who spearheaded the completion of the Lighthouse over a century after the initial inception of the idea, official commemorations of Columbus in the Dominican Republic would perhaps remind an uninterested world that this small country deserved a place in the Western imaginary. Balaguer recognizes Columbus as a "world-historical individual" who helped uncover and propel history toward what G. W. F. Hegel calls a World Spirit.[24] The completion of the Lighthouse, then, could remind the world that Columbus had exalted this island's beauty and founded a city there before anywhere else.

While Balaguer put money, effort, and power behind enshrining Columbus's name and legacy at the head of official, masculinist history, he could not prevent how the Dominican population and the rest of the world would react to the construction of the Lighthouse. Columbus's legacy, and his spirit, was unwieldy in great part because it was not alone: it had to contend with the ghosts of el monte. The cultural practices, gestures, stories, and music of the vast majority of Dominicans who migrated from the countryside to the urban centers throughout the twentieth century, and then migrated to the United States, Europe, and so on, emerge as phantasmagorical expressions that persistently knock against the walls of official history.

Although countless statues, streets, cities, institutes, and other commemorative objects around the world bear Columbus's name, few memorials so well replicate the hyperbole that surrounds him as the Columbus Lighthouse Memorial (see Figure 3.1).

Balaguer ensured the completion of the Columbus Lighthouse Memorial in time for the 1992 quincentennial celebrations of Columbus's stumble into the New World. Before I analyze further the larger significance of the memorial, I delve into the long and fascinating history behind its construction and some of the controversy that surrounded it in 1992. Dominican historian Antonio Del Monte y Tejada conceived of the idea of a Columbus lighthouse in 1852.[25] Impetus to build it came in 1877 when Columbus's alleged remains were exhumed in Santo Domingo. After this discovery, the Liberal Dominican nationalists of the Sociedad de Amigos del País, the same group who awarded Salomé Ureña, organized a fund to build a Columbus memorial in which to house the recently found remains.[26] In 1879 and 1880, the Dominican government tried and failed to build a monument.[27] Though not a lighthouse, "an elaborate marble mausoleum was erected [. . .] in time for the quadricentenary celebration in Santo Domingo's cathedral."[28]

Figure 3.1. Aerial view of the Columbus Lighthouse in Santo Domingo. (Courtesy of Otto Piron.)

By the late nineteenth century, political and mass media discourses in the U.S. infantilized places such as the Dominican Republic as wayward children in need of instruction and also feminized them as helpless maidens in need of rescue.[29] What had originally been a Dominican project became a U.S.-led pan-American project, signaling the shifting world order.[30] In 1923, the Pan-American Union, predecessor to the Organization of American States (OAS), "started planning the construction in Santo Domingo of a commemorative lighthouse dedicated to Christopher Columbus' legacy."[31] According to Robert Alexander González, "The history of U.S. imperialism is intertwined with the building of the Columbian memorial."[32] González further maintains that the architectural aims of the project reflected "an Old World–New World dichotomy," while the competition process "mirrored U.S.–Latin American relations."[33] U.S. desires to consolidate its imperial power in the hemisphere meant that it had a stake in cultural representations of official hemispheric history. The celebration of the project in the U.S. media in the early twentieth century fits this narrative. A *New York Times* article grandiosely decreed: "May the beacon, flashing north and south symbolize the clearer light of understanding between the two continents, and help to dispel the mistrust which has too often in the past darkened pan-American relations."[34]

In 1927, the Dominican Republic promised funds and land for the project.[35] Architectural design competitions, organized by U.S. architect Albert Kelsey, were finally held in 1929 and, two years later, the committee chose a design by Manchester-educated architect Joseph Lea Gleave.[36] Detailing his various inspirations, Gleave described his design as "an Aztec serpent or a human body lying prostate," as well as "reminiscent of aeroplanes, ships, motor cars."[37] These descriptions evoke the sense that the Lighthouse was supposed to represent both progress and technological innovation as well as to render tribute to what was considered the indigenous past. Impediments to its construction abounded, including World War II, Lea Gleave's death in 1965, and Trujillo's inability to share the spotlight; in 1955, the dictator organized an expensive, international fair in his honor rather than Columbus's. Under Balaguer's presidency and with Dominican architect Teófilo Carbonell's modifications, construction began finally in 1986. The Lighthouse was finished in time for the quincentennial celebrations of Columbus's "discovery" of the New World in 1992, fulfilling Balaguer's dream.

The result was met with humorous contempt from various corners of the world. Visitors report on the monument's "surreal scale" and resemblance to a catacomb.[38] Puerto Rican writer Edgardo Rodríguez Juliá describes it as "massive, oppressively monumental."[39] He also adopts sinister words such as "funereal temple," "sepulcher," and "ultratomb," as he tries to "appreciate its ungraceful posture."[40] "The Columbus Lighthouse [. . .] is a horizontal structure, like a recumbent beast, designed to throw its light vertically, upward," decrees a *New Yorker* article, continuing that "[i]t has the look of a concrete pyramid with one long extended arm: a humped, dinosaur look; an anonymous, inert grayness."[41] An article in the *Nation* states that "[f]rom the ground level it doesn't look like a cross, or like a lighthouse, or like anything, for that matter."[42]

To the world, the Lighthouse in Santo Domingo seemed like another sign of the country's backwardness rather than the culmination of a project that U.S. officials had earlier considered of high importance. After all, a U.S.-led commission had chosen the winning design. Against

Balaguer's intentions, the monument rendered Santo Domingo conspic-
uous in its failure to attract the international praise he had expected.
The widespread disapproval among Dominicans, combined with the
worldwide protests against the quincentennial celebrations, rendered
the Lighthouse and its octogenarian creator a global punchline. The fact
that "the country was ill-equipped economically to afford such a gaudy
and expensive (multi-million dollar) display of commemoration" upset
many Dominicans.[43] Indeed, of all the "world leaders invited, only the
Pope saw fit to attend the opening of this monumental embarrassment,
which the rest of Latin America studiously ignored."[44] The humiliating
reality was that such ostentatious displays of Columbian celebration
were no longer acceptable, especially at the site that inaugurated Native American genocide.[45] Ironically, while government officials from
around the hemisphere turned their backs on the Lighthouse, many of
them continued to celebrate an official Columbus Day—as in the case of
the U.S.—and to support persistent economic and political disenfranchisement of their countries' indigenous and black populations. Perhaps
it was the Lighthouse's exorbitant, monumental tone rather than its Eurocentric, colonialist message that jarred the sneering invitees.

Cementing the sense that the construction of the Lighthouse satisfied
only the interests of a conservative elite was the removal of poor residen-
tial housing at the construction site. Like many tourist spots around the
world, the surrounding low-income area was placed out-of-view from
tourists: "Surrounding the Faro is a tall stone wall that blocks poor barrio residents from crossing the Faro's grounds [. . .]. This wall, built
to hide the realities of Dominican poverty from the visiting dignitary
or tourist, is known by everyone as the Muro de la Verguenza, or the
Wall of Shame."[46] Even former Balaguer supporters wanted the blind
octogenarian out of office and many people began calling the project
"Faro a Balaguer."[47] Apparently, "[t]he only others who supported the
Faro's construction were those who had a stake in celebrating Columbus: Spaniards, Italians, and upper-class Dominicans who identified
with the European roots of their culture."[48] In fact, Balaguer's behavior
regarding the Lighthouse broke many of the ties that he had for decades
established with the Dominican people. While people's confidence in
Balaguer as a patriarch stemmed from his adherence to the crucial duties of gift-giving and patronage, as Christian Krohn-Hansen asserts, his

behavior regarding the Lighthouse, seen by many as taking resources from the people rather than giving, changed some of his previous followers' attitudes toward him.[49]

Rumors recorded in Dominican and U.S. mass media around the construction of the Lighthouse portray Balaguer's greed for power as tempting a malevolent higher power to sweep down in punishment. For instance, reports "prophesied that Balaguer would die on the day of the Columbus quincentennial."[50] Many saw the death of Balaguer's sister Emma just days before the inaugural event as evidence of the curse of Columbus.[51] Rodríguez Juliá remarks that this chatter rendered the monument "a sort of macabre joke stemming from a dark, merengue-esque curse. [. . .] The fukú persists."[52] Even *The New York Times* mentions *fukú*, or curse, in an article about the Balaguer administration's failure to attract many international dignitaries to the quincentennial celebrations: "To many supporters and opponents of the lighthouse alike, that Mr. Balaguer's long-cherished project should be so bitterly opposed is not surprising given a longstanding and widely held belief, known as fucú, or curse, that anything bearing the name of Columbus will bring enduring trouble."[53] Rodríguez Juliá details two earlier examples of a so-called Columbus curse or "fucú a El Almirante."[54] In 1937, four Dominican-Cuban airplanes were flown to promote the "grandiose idea" of the Columbus Lighthouse. The event, however, did not go according to plan since, depending on the source, either one or three of the planes crashed.[55] Like so much of the discourse around the Lighthouse, it is difficult to sort fact from rumor. A few years later, a beauty contest was held in Santo Domingo to celebrate Columbus's first trip to the Americas. However, one of the worst earthquakes of the century interrupted the coronation.[56] During the late twentieth-century construction of the memorial, Dominicans were incredulous that despite the "hunger in the countryside" and the "misery in the slums on the edges of the capital [. . .] Balaguer continued in Olympian indifference, unperturbed, deaf to dissent" to build the structure.[57]

I interpret some of the international mockery aimed at Balaguer and the Lighthouse as stemming from a disgust with the project's anachronistic celebration of a turn-of-the-twentieth-century ideology. In the Dominican Republic, the monument's representation of history, visible from miles away and for generations to come, triggered a deep discomfort and distrust among many people. Columbus's legacy is, at its very root, an affirmation and celebration of a violent patriarchal and Eurocentric hierarchy that requires work to maintain. The Dominican Lighthouse Memorial displaced an entire neighborhood and cost millions of public funds that had multiple better uses. Student groups, displaced residents, and others protested against the construction of the monument, leading to a violent police response in which at least two protestors were killed.[58] This strenuous hyperbolic work, combined with the monstrous size and expense of the site, elucidates the power behind its evocation of an enduring social-racial New World order in which certain lives, stories, and histories simply matter less. In this world order, one of the few avenues for socioeconomic progress available to non-white Dominican men is helping to support these violent patriarchal structures through enactments of hypermasculinity in both official and off-the-record positions.

The Spirit of Columbus, or the Fukú of the Admiral in *Oscar Wao*

I believe that Trujillo must be killed again in the Dominican people's imaginary of power. He must be killed again, and, how does one kill Trujillo again, well, by empowering a democracy that does not justify him.
—José Miguel Soto Jiménez (2011)

Complex personhood means that even those who haunt our dominant institutions and their systems of value are haunted too by things they sometimes have names for and sometimes do not.
—Avery Gordon, *Ghostly Matters* (1997)

While the Columbus Lighthouse perpetuated an official Dominican history that excluded and alienated a majority of Dominicans, the controversy surrounding the findings of Columbus's alleged remains in Santo Domingo in 1877 reveals also Dominicans' surprising insouciance in the face of Spanish power and the legacy of colonialism.[59] The "discovery" of these remains in the Cathedral must be seen in the context of the War of Restoration that had just reestablished Dominican sovereignty after annexation to Spain from 1861 until 1865. The Dominican Republic had been annexed to Spain in 1861, a decision so unpopular with the population that a war broke out that finally restored the independence of the Republic in 1865. Thus, when Dominican authorities claimed vociferously that Columbus's remains were in Santo Domingo and had not been transported to the Spanish colony of Cuba in 1796, they performed a peculiarly anti-Spanish Hispanophilia. As Schmidt-Nowara recounts, this claim infuriated Spanish authorities. Dominicans (and the Italian priest who announced the finding) not only had the gall to claim Columbus's remains but also to criticize Spain for its negligence of Columbus's legacy. Spanish authorities spared no resource and expertise to counteract Dominicans' claims, including sending a report detailing their contestation of the claims to several nations in the Americas and Europe but pointedly not to the Dominican Republic.[60] A century later, during a visit to the country in 1976, the Spanish monarchs refused to be photographed by the altar with the infamous remains, despite the entreaties of the Dominican diplomatic corps. Their refusal of the cheeky requests was not surprising, "because they understood that it could be interpreted as an affirmation of [the remains'] legitimacy."[61] Although objects sent by countries around the world—including Japanese samurai armor—are prominently displayed in the Lighthouse museum, its primary aim is to celebrate Santo Domingo's story of origin as the Ciudad Primada de América.[62] Though the actions taken by Dominican authorities throughout the century starting with the finding of the remains and culminating with construction of the Lighthouse reflect a deeply entrenched colonofilia, I am struck by a Dominican disinterest in complying with colonial ideas of Spanish superiority. When considering that authorities stood firm in their conviction that the remains were in Santo Domingo in 1877, requested outrageously that the Spanish sovereigns pose next to the controversial remains in 1976, and finally built a monstrous edifice to house these remains in 1992, what emerges is a remarkably anti-imperialist colonofilia.

These individual and collective performances of recalcitrance notwithstanding, the Lighthouse invokes a long-standing Caribbean tradition to consider Columbus's arrival as the start of a male-centric history. In a noteworthy coincidence, two important scholars released their Caribbean histories in the same year with the same title, though in two different languages: Eric Williams's *From Columbus to Castro* (1970) and Juan Bosch's *De Cristóbal Colón a Fidel Castro* (1970). To these eminent scholars (or, perhaps, their editors), Caribbean history starts and ends with two, larger-than-life male figures. "The history of Dominican literature starts with the name of Columbus," writes Balaguer in *Colón: Precursor literario* (Columbus: Literary Precursor; 1974), "who left us, in his maritime diary and letters, the first descriptions of the island's nature and who knew how to feel and express the charms of the national landscape like none other and to still transmit a poetic and at times exceedingly literary vision."[63] In Balaguer's vision, Columbus's words bring the very existence of the island into being. That is, Columbus is the fount of this "new" world.

Junot Díaz's *The Brief Wondrous Life of Oscar Wao* also starts with Columbus's arrival but explodes it immediately. The novel not only quells persistently the celebration around 1492, but it also remixes the pseudohagiographies of the region's "great men." An immigrant novel, sci-fi tale, and bildungsroman, to name a few genres it instantiates, *Oscar Wao* focuses on the tragicomic life of Oscar de León Cabral, a Dominican American nerd who struggles to find a girlfriend and who is killed by a police captain before he can reconstruct his family's history. Narrated mostly by Yunior, Oscar's bully and sometime friend, the novel is also the history of the catastrophic fate of the erstwhile upper-class Cabrals, who are Oscar's maternal ancestors. Like Columbus and other world-historical men, Oscar's name entitles the novel while his legacy endures through Yunior's pen. Unlike these heroes of history, however, Oscar does not have the power to remap the world. Rather than a teleological retelling of Caribbean or even Dominican history, the novel's narration is nonlinear and multivocal. More directly, it testifies to the violence of these major historical actors. In so doing, it critiques the authoritarian leadership of men like Trujillo and Balaguer, who repeat the "spirit of Columbus," and, as such, reinscribe the wounds of the Spanish conquest on an already traumatized region.

In this sense, the Lighthouse as it emerges in the novel is a "concrete example of the interplay between inequalities in the historical process and inequalities in the historical narrative."[64] Though mocked by a global audience and physically distant from the rest of Santo Domingo, the Lighthouse looms metaphorically over a disenfranchised Dominican citizenry. There are only a few references to the Lighthouse in *Oscar Wao*. However, they reinforce its role as a totem to official history. The Lighthouse appears in a photograph that Oscar's sister finds after the protagonist's murder: "In the pictures Lola brought home are [. . .] shots of Oscar at the Columbus lighthouse, where half of Villa Duarte used to stand."[65] For Oscar, the Lighthouse was simply a point on the tourist map of Santo Domingo. Within the narrative, however, it stands as the ghostly remains of a diaspora subject who is murdered before he can construct his family's and, concomitantly, his nation's history. The Lighthouse recalls not only Oscar's ghost but also that of the poor neighborhood that it superseded. Thus, Díaz's Lighthouse—despite its physical enormity—fails to usurp entirely the fragmented history of the Dominican people with its celebration of teleological progress. If anything, the novel's references to the Lighthouse question this kind of linear history. After Oscar is kidnapped and led to his own beating in a sugarcane field, he notices the darkness around him: "Nighttime in Santo Domingo. A blackout, of course. Even the Lighthouse out for the night."[66] This alludes to the fact that the Lighthouse's illuminating capacity comes at the cost of many city residents' household electricity. The most basic modern conveniences are secondary to the whim of a man—Balaguer—whose idea of progress is the entombing of Columbus.

The history that the Lighthouse celebrates signals the Cabral family's inability to write its own story. The exorbitant power and vociferousness of men like Trujillo and Balaguer silenced, in many cases violently, most Dominicans' versions of history. Both Trujillo and Balaguer were known to bend the will of history to aggrandize themselves. For Trujillo, this included the incarceration or murder of anyone whose ideas did not fit into his grand narrative as well as the carte blanche remapping of the country in his image: streets and plazas were named after his favorite (legitimate) children and the 500-year-old capital was renamed Ciudad Trujillo. Self-promotion for Balaguer meant protecting the reputation he had achieved as a conservative intellectual during the Trujillo regime by churning out anti-Haitian, Eurocentric narratives of the island. Crucially, Balaguer's policies also led to wide-scale economic disenfranchisement, forcing many Dominicans to emigrate to places such as the United States during his years in office.

Though the Lighthouse celebrates Columbus's "discovery" of the Americas and the evangelization of the region, in popular discourses and in *Oscar Wao* it more malevolently harnesses the power of what Yunior calls "Fukú americanus."[67] While Salomé Ureña crowns Hispaniola as the "queen of Columbus' world" and other nationalists invoke Columbus as the start of a glorious history, *Oscar Wao* describes the island as "ground zero" for hemispheric calamity. The novel's first words invoke the name of Columbus, the Admiral:

> They say it came from Africa, carried in the screams of the enslaved; that it was the death bane of the Tainos, uttered just as one world perished and another began; that it was a demon cracked open in the Antilles. Fukú americanus, or more colloquially the Curse and the Doom of the New World. Also called the fukú of the Admiral because the Admiral was both its midwife and one of its great European victims; despite "discovering" the New World the Admiral died miserable and syphilitic, hearing (dique) divine voices. In Santo Domingo, the Land He Loved Best [. . .] the Admirals' very name has become synonymous with both kinds of fukú, little and large; to say his name aloud or even to hear it is to invite calamity on the heads of you and yours.[68]

With these opening words, Díaz intertwines the events in the novel with the terrors of the conquest and its "midwife," Columbus. Fukú, as mentioned earlier, quite simply means curse—but with very specific culturally bound semantics. Citing Dominican folklorist R. Emilio Jiménez, Lauren Derby describes it as an "evil charge passed through bodily extensions such as clothing, house, touch, or even the uttering of one's name."[69] "Columbus" is one such name, which explains the literary and cultural preference for monikers such as "the Admiral." Jiménez further explains that people often take precautions against fukú's potential destruction, such as avoiding contact with the object, animal, or person who is said to have a fukú.[70] The scholar Antonio Olliz Boyd argues that fukú is the "transcendent force" and "metaphysical expression" of the spirituality of the enslaved African "transformed from its African image to accommodate the conditions of a new geographical and social environment."[71] Too, Olliz Boyd connects the word to *fufu*, *fufú*, and *juju*, which are used in other parts of the Americas and also reference African and African diasporic spirituality.[72]

Yunior's narration frequently alludes to fukú, connecting it to supernatural power. He explains, "It was believed, even in educated circles, that anyone who plotted against Trujillo would incur a fukú most powerful, down to the seventh generation and beyond. [. . .] Which explains why everyone who tried to assassinate him always got done, why those dudes who finally did buck him down all died so horrifically."[73] Yunior can only describe Cabral family's transgenerational punishment as a curse placed upon it by a malevolent, powerful spirit and its stand-in, Trujillo. Abelard Cabral, Oscar's maternal grandfather, was a wealthy doctor who "possessed one of the most remarkable minds in the country."[74] However, "[t]he Reign of Trujillo was not the best time to be a lover of Ideas, not the best time to be engaging in parlor debate [. . .] but Abelard was nothing if not meticulous. Never allowed contemporary politics (i.e. Trujillo) to be bandied about."[75] Despite Abelard's vigilance, one of his adolescent daughters is too beautiful to go unnoticed; when Abelard refuses to bring her to a party to be presented to Trujillo, he is sent to prison. Consequently, Abelard's wife, Socorro, commits suicide soon after the birth of her third and final daughter, Belicia, while the other two daughters are dead within three years.[76] A torture called La Corona (The Crown) renders Abelard a "vegetable," neither dead nor alive.[77] The extended family sells Belicia into servitude in the desert of Azua until a distant relative named La Inca rescues her.[78] Later, as a young woman, Belicia would endure a tragedy in the sugarcane fields that would lead to her emigration to the United States where she has two children, Oscar and Lola. Yunior, the narrator, believes that the Cabral family's near-extinction results from a curse placed on them by Trujillo. As he puts it, "when he [Trujillo] couldn't snatch her [Abelard's daughter], out of spite he put a fukú on the family's ass," cementing the dictator's all-encompassing power.[79]

Moreover, "many people actually believed that Trujillo had supernatural powers! It was whispered that he did not sleep, did not sweat, that he could see, smell, feel events hundreds of miles away, that he was protected by the most evil fukú on the Island."[80] Fukú or not, no one could escape Trujillo during his regime because the way he enacted his power would not allow it; Trujillo's ruling style required the participation of the entire citizenry in the drama of the Dominican state. For instance, invitations to regime events could not be declined, which explains Abelard's imprisonment after refusing to bring his daughter to a Trujillo party. Guests at these events had to conform to a strict protocol that included panegyrics. These theatrical declarations of the speaker's love of and loyalty to Trujillo became the standard conversational register.[81] Just seven years after Trujillo had risen to power, a Trujillo intellectual wrote the following words to describe him:

> Only average men leading average lives conform to the rules of general mediocrity. Mediocre men adapt themselves to universal standards; the great men of history are those who tower over the masses. [. . .] On two occasions, leaving behind his astonished aides and at grave risk of his life, he penetrated alone into an enemy guerrilla encampment. His personal magnetism and his power of persuasion won the day without need of using any weapons. The guerrillas laid down their arms.[82]

Books published during the regime seem to all be dedicated to him. A 1933 book about Columbus by a Dominican author states: "To the honorable President of the Dominican Republic, General Don Rafael Leonidas Trujillo Molina, promoter of the Commemorative Columbus Lighthouse."[83] That the book was published in Buenos Aires just three years after Trujillo had taken over the country did not prevent the author from ensuring he rendered proper tribute. Two decades later, after Trujillo had amassed several honorary titles, a book of photographs of the Dominican Republic by Dutch Francis Stopelman opens with the following dedication: "Dedicated to the Supreme Commander Doctor Rafael Leonidas Trujillo Molina. / Benefactor of the Homeland and Father of the New Homeland. / This book is nothing but a very incomplete reflection of the great works realized by him, and of the incomparable beauty of the hospitable Dominican Republic."[84] Trujillo was not even the president in the year this book was published; his second son Radhamés held the courtesy title.

The hyperbolic forced adulation "charged" Trujillo's persona and name with significance and recalls the exalted praise heaped onto Columbus.[85] A writer for the newspaper *La Nación* states: "Men are not indispensable. But Trujillo is irreplaceable. For Trujillo is not a man. He is [...] a cosmic force [...] Those who try to compare him to his ordinary contemporaries are mistaken. He belongs to [...] the category of those born to a special destiny."[86] When conversations even in one's home were subject to eavesdropping and denunciation by an undercover neighbor or housekeeper, Trujillo's seeming omnipresence added to the perception and reality of his exorbitant power.[87]

The events surrounding Trujillo's assassination further evince the almost omnipotent aura that surrounded the dictator by the end of his regime. The attempted coup d'état after his assassination in 1961 failed in great part because of the insistence of key conspirators that they see Trujillo's corpse before carrying out any subsequent steps. The atmosphere of mistrust among government officials and common citizens bred by Trujillo's regime is evident in the plotters' extreme caution. At the crucial moment, the assassins, some of whom had held high posts in the government, simply could not trust their fellow plotters' words that Trujillo was truly dead. Hence, the macabre proof in the shape of Trujillo's bullet-riddled body stuffed into the trunk of a car was evidence of a power impossible to eradicate through a single night's events, even if these had led to the dictator's physical death.[88]

The interconnections between power, magic, and masculinity in Dominican lore, from Columbus to Balaguer, glue together the narrative strands in *Oscar Wao*. Although the standard anecdote in texts about Dominican magic is that of the scorned woman seeking to bring an indifferent lover into her arms, the religious history of the country leaves room for the masculinization of magic.[89] Because there were few priests in the impoverished Spanish colony of Santo Domingo—by 1809, only about a dozen priests remained—compared with the heavy presence of Catholicism in places like Mexico and Peru, the Spanish crown and the Catholic Church exerted little control over how people used spiritual practices to understand their world.[90] Popular, scholarly, and literary discourses about the supernatural and the usage of so-called black magic reveal that both men and women were considered potential sorcerers.[91] That Dominicans did not consider magic exclusively feminine allows for a discursive precedent in their interpretations of Trujillo's and Balaguer's power as resulting from magical negotiations.

Indeed, in the literature and imagery of Trujillo, the tyrant's grotesque desires render him demonic, gendering magic as a masculine longing for money and power. For instance, *Oscar Wao* establishes that both Trujillo and Columbus have a similar relationship to occult power: "But in those elder days, fukú had it good; it even had a hypeman of sorts, a high priest, you could say. Our then dictator-for-life Rafael Leónidas Trujillo Molina. No one knows whether Trujillo was the Curse's servant or its master, its agent or its principal, but it was clear he and it had an understanding, that them two was *tight*."[92] Moreover, Trujillo's main moniker was, and continues to be, *el chivo* or the goat. For centuries, the goat has not only symbolized a creature who delights in luxury and wealth but also a demon-like, pagan figure and sometimes even Satan.[93]

Derby reports that it was rumored that Trujillo had the help of a *muchachito*, which translates into "little boy," but that likely refers to a *baká*.[94] A baká is "a malevolent spirit that surrounds and protects the property of its owner under the appearance of an animal."[95] Furthermore, "the one who buys a baká is not always aware of the nature of the deal, and the brujo [witch doctor] who is in charge of its preparation can fool his patient."[96] Many descriptions of a baká identify it as a "[l]arge animal, usually black, of the dog family" and with "eyes [that] glow like fiery coals at night."[97] They are also described as "imaginary hybrid beasts that steal farm animals, harvests, and cash through shape-shifting. Created by sorcerers, bacás are spirit creatures that enable people to become dogs, cats, pigs, and goats and also to amass wealth."[98] Anecdotes about buying a baká tend to contain the moral that neither power nor wealth is ever worth the loss of life, dignity, family, and friends that the purchase often requires. For instance, ethnographer Carlos Estaban Deive recounts the story of a man in the province of Eliás Piña whose sixteen-year-old son died suddenly because the father had promised him to a baká.[99]

As with other manifestations of the occult, bakás are not always clearly instruments of evil. In *Oscar Wao*, Belicia's encounter with an otherworldly, mongoose-like creature is either fortuitous in that she survives a near-death experience, or catastrophic, in that her life following the event is filled with hardship: "So as Beli was flitting in and out of life, there appeared at her side a creature that would have been an amiable mongoose if not for its golden lion eyes and the absolute black of its pelt. This one was quite large for its species and placed its intelligent little paws on her chest and stared down at her."[100] The creature persuades Belicia to fight for her life: "*You have to rise now or you'll never have the son or the daughter*."[101] In this moment of potential doom amid the cane fields, an omniscient creature pulls Beli from certain death. The discourse surrounding bakás in Dominican popular culture and in texts like *Oscar Wao* suggests that they are otherworldly manifestations of historical trauma.[102] The Mongoose[103] comes to stand as the "wound that cries out, that addresses us in the attempt to tell us of a reality or truth that is not otherwise available."[104] Throughout the novel, the Mongoose appears in moments that echo earlier violent events in places as historically "charged" as sugarcane fields. It appears, for example in the description of Oscar's dream after his first beating in the cane fields. The Mongoose demands to know: "More or less?"[105] Perhaps what it wants to know is whether or not Oscar will relent in his suicidal mission to court his romantic obsession, Ybón, who was a sex worker and the girlfriend of a police chief. However, the question remains vague, implying that the voice of this traumatic wound is ambivalent, neither good nor evil, rejecting what Maja Horn calls the Manichean impulses of the Trujillo regime.[106] If the Mongoose is the clue that trauma still determines the fate of colonial subjects, including the characters in *Oscar Wao*, then Trujillo and Balaguer are both victims of its violence and the figures who can provoke the eruption of these wounds.

Despite the ambivalence of the otherworldly, the tales reveal that harnessing the power of the occult for selfish desires results in larger social devastation, chaos, and loss. The notion of a vampiric entity that feeds on living things is common to colonized or economically dependent societies, though there are important contextual nuances that determine how, when, and where these creatures manifest themselves. This is the spillage that results from the inadequacy of official explanations of extreme socioeconomic inequality.[107] Haitian-American writer Edwidge Danticat shares her own experience of hearing rumors of organ harvesting, one that shows how the powerful "other" can reach demon-like proportions:

As a child growing up in Haiti at the time, I heard [. . .] stories of children being kidnapped so their organs could be harvested and used to save rich sick children in America, an idea that frightened me so much that I sometimes could not sleep.[108]

For Danticat and other poor Haitian children, fear took the horrific form of death for the benefit of the imperial power to the north. It cannot be surprising that a power that is so feared is transformed into a monster, and it applies not only to entire countries but also to individuals, such as Trujillo.

Tigueraje as Historical Echo in *Oscar Wao* and *La Soga*

After ascending through a U.S.-created police force, Trujillo schemed and plotted his way into the Dominican presidency in 1930. Trujillo's brand of masculinity humiliated a traditional social elite unable to accept a mixed-race man as a leader and he retaliated against his social exclusion by sleeping with as many of his upper-class officials' wives and daughters as he desired. Trujillo's countless (often coerced) mistresses, attention to immaculately pressed and tailored garments, displays of military medals, and sustained self-promotion as the nation's paterfamilias exemplified an unparalleled commitment to the idea of the tíguere. As Lipe Collado's classic *El tíguere dominicano* states and other scholars corroborate, the tíguere is a Dominican archetype, "a trickster who rises from poverty to a position of wealth and power, often through illicit means" and "the mythic paragon of barrio masculinity who gains power—riches, women, control over others—apparently from nothing."[109] The wife of a foreign minister on assignment in Santo Domingo "knew of [Trujillo's] humble background [. . .] and she met his parents, noting that 'both of them were quite dark in color.'"[110] Eric Paul Roorda concludes that, "[e]ven so, she found that his personal style nearly neutralized his questionable social and racial status."[111] In this sense, "clothes came very close to making the man," according to Roorda, but Derby historicizes Trujillo's attention to fashion and comportment as rooted in tigueraje. She argues, moreover, that "Trujillo officialized [tigueraje] by bringing it into the corridors of power," which "forced a reluctant respect on the part of Dominicans."[112]

I now turn to Dominican men's quotidian performances of this particular kind of hypermasculinity referred to as tigueraje, whose definition I provide below. In my discussion of tigueraje, I follow Judith Butler's definition of gender as "performative in the sense that the essence or identity that they [acts, gestures, and desires] otherwise purport to express are fabrications manufactured and sustained through corporeal signs and other discursive means."[113] I argue that performances of tigueraje as they emerge in many Dominican and Dominican-American texts are small-scale signs of Dominican subjects' struggle against *and* alongside the large-scale instantiations of colonial history manifested in the forms of Trujillo, Balaguer, and the Lighthouse. That is, tigueraje instantiates gendered modes of individual power that can be in line with colonial and patriarchal oppression or assert subversive, anticolonial subjectivity, or both.

The tíguere's historical precedents have mostly emblematized resistance to colonial power. Among the tíguere's historical predecessors were figures such as "the Creole of the sixteenth, the freed slave of the seventeenth, and the mulatto of the eighteenth—all figures of difference that threatened the social hierarchy through their status as strangers who had more latitude for movement in the social order than everyone else."[114] These subjects' wiliness, however, could manifest itself in individualistic, rather than systemic, subversions. One need only think of the maroons who made deals with colonial administrations to capture enslaved subjects who ran away in order to protect their own enclaves or the nonwhite privateers working in the slave trade.[115] Many of these predecessors to tigueraje, broadly speaking, "provide more evidence that transcolonial endeavors were often no more emancipatory than the imperial and national powers that gave birth to and succeeded them."[116] Trujillo embodies well this contradictory status; while his rise to power subverted the Dominican "old guard" elite, his regime consolidated antidemocratic, patriarchal power. Tígueres embody not ideal, legitimate masculinity exemplified by the founding fathers in official history, but, rather, an excessive masculinity that, in some instantiations, gained a certain mass approval after the *trujillato*. Carlos Decena considers tigueraje to be on a continuum with *locura* (madness) or the performative excess that men embodying "legitimate" masculinity eschew.[117] As the *ur-tíguere*, Trujillo's class-racial transgression and excess is part of what set him apart from other Latin American and Caribbean dictators.[118]

I press on the point that part of the tíguere's excess stems from his nonwhite status, for only white men could embody legitimate masculinity in the Dominican colonial and national order.[119] During the colonial era, white men or convincingly white men could attain official forms of power. However, because of colonial Santo Domingo's unique situation as a colony composed greatly of a mixed race and free population "everyone had a potential claim to whiteness" and "the free mulatto in the Dominican Republic became a locus of fear and revulsion representing the antithesis of the civilized colonial order."[120] Indeed, tigueraje was and is a vehicle for class-racial mobility. Lipe Collado contends that "to name someone 'a Tíguere' is to assume that he was not one of those white guys in high social positions."[121] However, that Collado's preface-writer denominates Columbus as the first "tíguere blanco" does not expunge the fact that the Admiral is also a genealogical precursor to more "legitimate"—white, elite—patriarchal figures.[122] Not surprisingly, Trujillo's embodiment of iconic "mulatto" masculinity did not lead to "black consciousness." Indeed, his government and intellectual apparatus helped consolidate the nation-state with an antiblackness connected to anti-Haitian ideology. Despite the rebellious roots of the term, Trujillo's tigueraje evinces the replacement of "one phallus for another," to cite Maja Horn after Doris Sommer, and not a dismantling of the patriarchal coloniality of power evident in men as disparate as Columbus and Trujillo. Indeed, the tíguere is a persistently masculine figure who may subvert race and class, but who must maintain his manly status.

Many men, especially those like Oscar, cannot measure up. *Oscar Wao* captures both the humorous and alienating extent to which the hypermasculinity of the tíguere becomes synonymous with Dominicanness itself. Krohn-Hansen argues that "notions of masculinity among Dominicans have played, and continue to play, a central part in the everyday production of political legitimacy—inside and outside the political parties, and the state."[123] *Oscar Wao* portrays characters that struggle not only with patriarchal structures of power in the form of men such as Balaguer and his henchman, *el capitán*, the man who kills Oscar, but also the oppressive pressure of performative masculinity. For instance, though not all tígueres are handsome, impeccable grooming and sartorial style are central components of many forms of tigueraje.[124] Many Díaz readers complain that his female characters are always beautiful bombshells. Though this is certainly accurate, one must admit that Díaz's fiction also includes numerous examples of masculine beauty.

Unlike overweight, clumsy, and sweet-tempered Oscar, the capitán who ends up murdering him is described as "[o]ne of those tall, arrogant, acerbically handsome niggers that most of the planet feels inferior to."[125] Standards of masculine beauty are so important that they save Oscar the first time el capitán beats him. According to Yunior, it is fortunate that Oscar did not look like his "pana [chum], Pedro, the Dominican Superman, or like my boy Benny, who was a model," but, instead, "was a homely slob."[126] For el capitán, Oscar's lack of beauty places him too low on the hierarchy of masculinity to even merit his death, at least initially. Belicia's boyfriend in her youth, Dionisio, was "[h]andsome in that louche potbellied mid-forties Hollywood producer sort of way."[127] And, of course, Yunior's muscular physique and ease with women stands in opposition to Oscar's large, clumsy body.

The narrative's odes to the capitán's, Benny's, Dionisio's, and Yunior's handsomeness resemble mainstream Dominican and international societal odes to Dominican masculine beauty as personified most emblematically by Porfirio Rubirosa (1909–1965). Rubirosa married several well-known women, including Trujillo's daughter Flor de Oro, Barbara Hutton, and Doris Duke, and he is rumored to have bedded almost every famous woman of the era. Rubirosa's charisma, charm, beauty, and style were so powerful that he remained one of Trujillo's most trusted confidantes even after divorcing Flor de Oro.[128] There are FBI files dedicated to him and his exploits because, after all, he was an ambassador for Trujillo. References to his phallus, including in Truman Capote's last novel, apparently numbered in the hundreds, recalling racist obsessions with black sexuality.[129] The power that tígueres like Rubirosa had over women also evoked the "Latin lover" archetype.

When people encounter Oscar, they cannot align this history of Dominican masculinity and sexual prowess with him. The combination of Oscar's personality, looks, and class-racial status preclude him from embodying either tigueraje or legitimate, white masculinity. By high school, Oscar had become the "neighborhood parigüayo [since he had] none of the Higher Powers of your typical Dominican male, couldn't have pulled a girl if his life depended on it."[130] Collado defines the parigüayo is a man who "lacks the minimum conditions to escape any difficult situation successfully" and "who always assumes that he will lose and who constantly pities himself."[131] Indeed, his inability to conform to a

Dominican ideal of hypermasculinity makes others doubt the authenticity of his Dominicanness: "Our hero was not one of those Dominican cats everybody's always going on about—he wasn't no home-run hitter or a fly bachatero, not a playboy with a million hots on his jock. And except for one period early in his life, dude never had much luck with the females (how *very* un-Dominican of him)."[132] Moreover: "Anywhere else his triple-zero batting average with the ladies might have passed without comment, but this is a Dominican kid we're talking about, in a Dominican family: dude was supposed to have Atomic Level G, was supposed to be pulling in the bitches with both hands."[133] Oscar's main problem is that he cannot perform ideal masculine Dominicanness, not that he cannot perform mainstream U.S. subjectivity. He does not search for acceptance within a white U.S. mainstream so much as within his diverse community in urban New Jersey. This community demands that Oscar conform to an idealized model of Latino masculinity. That Dominican hypermasculinity emerges as the dominant form of masculinity in *Oscar Wao* and other works by Díaz parallels the ubiquity in the U.S. media and popular culture of the hypermasculine figures of the baseball player, the drug dealer, and, recently, a more sensitive incarnation through crooning *bachateros* such as Romeo Santos whom I mentioned in the introduction.[134] Oscar's lack of masculine prowess is precisely what challenges his feelings of belonging; not only is he a diasporic Dominican—an identity that already implies a tenuous relationship to the homeland—but he is also a diasporic Dominican who does not fit the strict, gendered parameters of Dominicanness. In this case, the diasporic space extends and exaggerates the gendered ideals of the nation.[135]

In *Oscar Wao*, those who do not conform to Dominican gender norms are violently punished. To be a proper Dominican woman is to guard one's virginity until marriage, to be obedient to one's elders, and to physically embody femininity by taking up less space and exuding a soft grace (e.g., primly crossing the legs at the ankles when sitting). Crucially, a proper Dominican woman remains at home, at school, or in church. Both Belicia and Lola, Oscar's older sister, fall short of these ideals. An adolescent Belicia lusts after a schoolmate who belongs to a white elite family. After she loses her virginity with him in a school closet, she is expelled from the prestigious school. This consequence shatters La

Inca's hopes that Belicia would regain the socioeconomic status of her deceased parents. The loss of her virginity and her dismissal from the school cement Belicia's failure as a "proper" young lady, already a challenge considering her dark skin and working-class status. Lola ignites an intergenerational war with her mother when she shaves her head, discarding a crucial bond to her white ancestry in the form of long, flowing hair. Belicia starts psychologically abusing Lola by calling her "ugly," cementing the connection between beauty, whiteness, and femininity.[136]

As a Dominican boy, Oscar is victim to his mother's and his community's violence against those who do not conform to gender expectations. Unlike Dominican women, a Dominican man's realm is outdoors, in the "streets." To Belicia's distress, Oscar's love of reading keeps him inside. Fighting against his natural inclination, she would force him out to play: "Pa' 'fuera! his mother roared. And out he would go, like a boy condemned [. . .] Please, I want to stay, he would beg his mother, but she shoved him out—You ain't a woman to be staying in the house."[137] A similar moment of masculine instruction occurs in the film *La Soga*, which expresses the performative vigilance and instruction required to achieve ideal models of upright, nonexcessive masculinity. The film's protagonist Luis Valerio, played by Manny Pérez, seeks to avenge his father's murder by a transmigrant Dominican drug dealer visiting Santiago. In the meantime, Luis works as the henchman/assassin of General Colón, whose raison d'être is to incarcerate or kill criminal returning deportees. Toward the end of the film, Luis discovers that the deportees can pay off Colón to save their lives.

A country butcher's son, Luis is expected to learn his father's trade. The problem is that Luis becomes attached emotionally to the pigs that are meant for slaughter. Echoing the gendered bullying that Oscar undergoes in *Oscar Wao*, Luis's father and cousin Tavo tease him by calling him *maricón* (faggot). Through their homophobic slurs, Luis's father and cousin inculcate Luis into appropriate Dominican masculinity. This moment is akin to the testimonies of Carlos Decena's queer Dominican male informants, in which masculinity emerged "as a straightjacket, an apparatus of collective surveillance and regulation of what is supposed to be a male body."[138] When Luis finally acquiesces to perform his familial duty, his father responds: "My son, you are a very sensitive boy. And we don't have the means to be sensitive all the time."[139] In his father's eyes, Luis's hesitation to kill an animal evinces not only a worrisome effeminacy but also unsustainable *lujo* (luxury). Hardworking men of the Cibao, the country's "heartland," such as Luis's father, must confront violence head on. If this quality does not come naturally, it must be learned. Luis discovers that the best way to lessen the pig's suffering and to maintain the integrity of its blood is to stab it through the heart. After witnessing his father's murder, Luis proves his mettle as an appropriate Dominican *varón* (man) by stabbing the man that he and Colón later kill in jail by injecting a deadly serum into the man's heart.

La Soga pits the masculinity that his father teaches Luis to embody against the "excess" of tigueraje, which by the 1980s had become most closely embodied by so-called Dominicanyork *cadenús*. These were men who fashioned themselves in what Dominicans considered the garb of black Americans, an unacceptable kind of Americanness: thick gold chains, "doo-rags," cornrows or dreads, sports jerseys, and expensive cars with blaring music. *La Soga* follows suit with this association of signifiers through its consistent racialization of deportees as embodying a non-Dominican blackness that is antithetical to respectable and acceptable Dominicanness (see Figure 3.2).[140] Luis's *chacabanas* (i.e., guayaberas) and Colón's military uniform, as well as both characters' lighter skin and straighter hair, racializes them as "whiter" within a Dominican racial and masculine hierarchy (see Figure 3.3). Their whiteness and self-fashioning brings them closer to embodying ideal patriarchal patriotism. Like the term Dominicanyork, argues Jesse Hoffnung-Garskof, the term *cadenú* connoted a "new kind of Dominican, soiled by life in

Figure 3.2. Criminal Dominicanyorks in *La Soga*.

Figure 3.3. Luis Valerio, General Colón, and FBI agent Simon Burr (from left to right) in *La Soga*.

the United States. Both also came to express the danger that the corrosion of Dominican identity in New York might seep back across the border."[141] However, as Hoffnung-Garskof further contends, the class-racial anxieties around this criminalized figure preexisted the explosion of emigration to the U.S. Indeed, they echo and intersect with the anxieties focused on the tíguere discussed above. In the Dominican media of the late twentieth century, the tíguere became coterminous with the Dominicanyork cadenú in that the criminality that the tíguere had always symbolized began to correlate directly with the criminality that many Dominican media outlets ascribed to diasporic and transmigrant Dominicans.[142]

After the exponential growth of the Dominican diaspora after 1965, but especially in the 1980s and '90s, the criminalized so-called Dominicanyorks stood on one side and the kind of tígueres made acceptable and official by men like Trujillo and Rubirosa stood on the other side. Among the latter, we can include the protagonist, Luis, in his *chacabanas*, and his boss, General Colón, in his military uniform. They embody the swagger of the homegrown tíguere, who contrasts with the Dominicanyork cadenús' representation of a foreign, black criminality. Both kinds of tígueres, however, do the bidding of U.S. authorities personified by FBI agent Simon Burr. Burr and Colón would receive cash payment from Dominican deportees in exchange for their lives. Unlike Colón, who is brought to justice for his corruption at the end of the film, Burr remains unpunished. Burr ignores Colón's desperate phone calls after the latter is caught. The message of the film in this sense is clear: U.S. power is omnipresent and unpunishable.

Although the film's villains are General Colón and agent Burr, it is difficult to ignore the racialization of the migrant deportees as black. (This racialization is an inverse of Salomé Ureña's and the founding fathers' whitewashing.) In an early scene, Luis and two other henchmen chase an unarmed, dark-skinned man, Fellito Polanco, through a Santiago slum. Contrasting with the three henchmen, who wear stylish sunglasses and travel in an expensive truck, Fellito runs on foot wearing tattered, filthy clothing (see Figure 3.4). The chase ends when the three men surround Fellito at a dusty clearing that serves as the center of the slum. The entire neighborhood, including many children, witness the impromptu execution. After telling a few jokes at Fellito's expense and shooting his foot, Luis shoots him in the chest as his screaming mother watches helplessly. The shooting of Fellito's foot displays Luis's sadistic undercurrent and demonstrates that, to a certain extent, he revels in his power and forgets his father's childhood lesson to lessen his victim's suffering. Fellito's dirty clothing, as well as his presence in the slum, suggests that he did not have the funds necessary to pay off Colón and save his life. At this point in the film, Luis remains unaware of Colón's corruption. The assassins display the corpse on the back of a truck with a cardboard sign on his chest that interpellates him as a "*Vende-droga*" (Drug dealer), a warning to anyone who views the macabre display.[143]

Figure 3.4. Luis Valerio, Fellito Polanco, and Luis's cousin Tavo (from left to right) in *La Soga*.

Too, the film taps into a long history of Santiago's symbolic representation of Dominican whiteness within which Fellito exemplifies a foreign, criminal blackness. Analyzing an image of Olivorio Mateo, an Afro-religious leader killed by U.S. occupying forces in 1922, Lorgia García-Peña writes: "Olivorio's performative diction of black masculinity placed him in direct confrontation with the powerful allegiance of the Hispanophile elite and the US empire."[144] Fellito Polanco emerges in the film as a similarly unincorporable black subject from the perspective of the criminal, yet sanctioned, white or light-skinned Dominican police force and the U.S. agent controlling the whole operation. Before Luis kills Fellito, one of the other henchmen reads the official accusations against him: "Fellito Polanco is a wanted man. Killed an FBI agent in New York. A criminal, a deportee, a junkie, and a drug dealer. Not only does he sell drugs, but he sells them here, in Santiago!"[145] Of relevance here is the emphasis on Fellito's audacity to corrupt Santiago, the capital of the Cibao, with drugs. The location of this corruption is critical since the idea of a white peasantry in the Cibao was at the heart of twentieth-century nationalist literature. Crucially, this peasantry differed from the resistant peasantry of el monte that emerged in the seventeenth century, as I discussed in the introduction. In the idealized version that emerged in the twentieth century, peasants were white hardworking tillers of the land who provided the nation with the fruits of their labor. Indeed, the white rural peasant in this nationalist imaginary ghosts the anxiety-inducing black and mixed-race peasants who, to invoke Raymundo González, lived anonymously and autonomously. According to Pedro L. San Miguel, this white peasant "became the prototypical habitant of the Hispanophone Antilles."[146] While this idealization of the white peasant emerged also in neighboring Cuba and Puerto Rico, it was on Dominican territory that a recalcitrant nonwhite free population, living removed from colonial and national purview, predominated for centuries.

Texts such as Ramón Emilio Jiménez's *Al amor del bohío (tradiciones y costumbres dominicanas)* and Balaguer's influential *La isla al revés* uphold the Cibao as having preserved this ideal of Dominicanness.[147] The valley is surrounded by a mountain range that, in Balaguer's perspective, protected Dominicans from Haitian incursion. These texts erased the many examples in which nonwhite Dominicans in this region resisted the logic of the Plantation as represented by local, nationalist, and imperial power. Moreover, they codified the idea of "[b]lack revolt and revolutionary events [. . .] with blacks from 'afuera,'" in the words of Sara Johnson.[148] As I have mentioned throughout, Dominican nationalism ghosted the free black subjectivity that had predominated in the territory in part by associating "blackness" with foreignness. To cite Rubén Silié, "the black [subject . . .] and, even more, his culture cease to be creole [native to this territory], both going back to being considered African."[149] That which became authentically Dominican (autochthonous to the territory), continues Silié, is a culture associated with whiteness and Hispanicity, however accurate or not that may be.

In this way, La Soga traffics in racialized tropes through which waged or "aboveboard" labor and business ownership are respectable and, as such, "whiter" or acceptably Dominican, while labor traditionally considered to be done by non-Dominicans (e.g., sugar cane cutter) and "black market" labor (e.g., drug trafficking) are nonrespectable and, as such, represent a foreign blackness (e.g., Haitian, Anglophone West Indian, or African American). The "good" tíguere fashions himself in a style considered local and traditional, while the Dominicanyork cadenú or "bad" tíguere fashions himself in what is considered to be the style of a foreign blackness. The first either masquerades as or is the law, while the second, when not outright illegal, is interpellated as illegal because it is stereotyped as a foreign blackness that is incompatible with Dominicanness. As scholars such as Sylvia Wynter and Maria Elena Martínez corroborate, from the earliest days of Spanish colonialism, de jure and de facto laws have defined the black subject as someone who is neither native to the Americas nor has any rights to/within the land.[150] Nationalist projects throughout the Americas hardly strayed from colonial hierarchies of race.[151] Indeed, most portraits of blackness throughout Spanish-speaking Latin America demonstrate that subjects considered black are often assumed to be foreign. For instance, Afro-Argentines are assumed to be from Uruguay or Brazil, Afro–Puerto Ricans are assumed to be Dominican, Afro-Mexicans must have Cuban ancestry, and so on.[152] In the Dominican case, the fact that the majority of the population has visible (i.e., phenotypical) black ancestry means that the foreignness of blackness common to the Americas instantiates somewhat differently. Unassimilable blackness is rendered foreign through racialized tropes of labor and a set of equivalences whereby both the "Haitian" field laborer (who is often Dominican), for instance, and the Dominicanyork drug dealer, in another instance, are both associated with the "illegality" of undocumented subjects, not only with the "illegality" of their labor. Torres-Saillant proposes that "[t]o speak as a dominican-york presupposes the recognition of an intrinsic marginality. It implies an acknowledgment of one's voice of alterity."[153] This alterity is generalized so that, although stereotype of the undocumented Dominican drug dealer as a foreign body arose first in the U.S., his criminalization extends into Dominican mass media stereotypes.

Thus, *La Soga*'s concern for an uncorrupted Santiago replicates a conservative Dominican racialized social order and suggests that black men such as Fellito Polanco remain unincorporated national subjects both in the U.S. and in the Dominican Republic. Perversely, a corrupt transnational alliance directs the men most concerned with "purging" Santiago of criminality. Though *La Soga* indicts the antidemocratic leadership of men such as Colón, as well as the U.S. officials who support it, it also replicates the exclusion of certain, usually black, Dominican subjects who do not belong and can never be ideal citizens. The blackness that men like Fellito embody is repudiated in both Dominican and U.S. contexts. Light-skinned, appropriately masculine men such as the police captain in *Oscar Wao* and Luis in the film, on the other hand, embody a new kind of ideal Dominican patriarchal patriotism.

Both *Oscar Wao* and *La Soga* evoke the inescapability of the post-Trujillo nation's patriarchal legacy, even in the diaspora. Like other diasporic or transnational narratives, or both, these texts betray the sense that for many migrants "the trauma of diaspora is not 'merely' the loss of a homeland [. . .] but, more chillingly, the awareness that home and all its assaults [follow] the fleeing subject into the clean, empty space of escape."[154] While *La Soga* ends with a smiling Luis behind the butcher counter of a New York City supermarket, an unconvincingly optimistic scene, most of the film revolves around Luis's chasing of men who cannot escape General Colón's and Simon Burr's corruption, whether in New York or in Santiago. In the novel, Oscar returns to his native Dominican Republic in order to research and write his family's history. If Oscar's inability to perform Dominicanness in the diaspora stems from his failure to perform hypermasculinity, in the homeland his diasporic status also renders him an outsider. When he visits Santo Domingo, he tries to ignore "that whisper that all long-term immigrants carry inside themselves, the whisper that says *You do not belong*."[155] On the other hand, his murder at the hands of an authoritarian leader's henchman renders his Dominicanness unquestionable, since even he—a citizen of the United States—must come to grips with the aftershocks of the island's violent history.

"El capitán," the jealous boyfriend who murders Oscar, is the masculine antithesis of the novel's hapless antihero. The capitán's exorbitant masculinity manifests itself in his violence. Moreover, he exemplifies how appropriate masculinity beholden to rightful patriarchs, such as Balaguer, eases socioeconomic mobility: "The Twelve Years [of Balaguer's rule from 1966 to 1978] were good times for men like [el capitán]. In 1974 he held a woman's head underwater until she died (she'd tried to organize some peasants for land rights in San Juan); in 1977 he played mazel-tov on a fifteen-year old boy's throat with the heel of his Florsheim (another Communist troublemaker, good fucking riddance)."[156] Sadistic duties such as these allowed many men during the Trujillo and Balaguer eras to rise up in the ranks. So many Dominicans became these men's victims or knew their victims that a collective fascination with some of these tortures remains, a mode of reckoning with this historical trauma. A footnote in *Oscar Wao* describes the head of Trujillo's secret police, Johnny Abbes García, as "[a]n enthusiast of Chinese torture techniques, Abbes was rumored to have in his employ a dwarf who would crush prisoners' testicles between his teeth."[157]

Not surprisingly, women tend to be more vulnerable to unfettered patriarchal power, as exemplified by the horrific violence that Belicia endures before her escape to the U.S. As an independent and beautiful young woman in Santo Domingo, Belicia meets Dionisio, alias the Gangster, "a flunky for the Trujillato, and not a minor one."[158] His success was indebted to a sharp business acumen and loyalty to Trujillo:

> The Gangster's devotion did not go unrewarded. By the mid-forties the Gangster was no longer simply a well-paid operator; he was becoming an alguien—in photos he appears in the company of the regime's three witchkings: Johnny Abbes, Joaquín Balaguer, and Felix Bernardino [. . .]. In the forties the Gangster was in his prime; he

traveled the entire length of the Americas, from Rosario to Nueva York, in pimpdaddy style, staying at the best hotels, banging the hottest broads [. . .], dining in four-star restaurants, confabbing with arch-criminals the world over.[159]

Dionisio's loyalty both to Trujillo and to a brand of violent Dominican hypermasculinity paves the way for his socioeconomic prosperity. In other words, he is a perfect tíguere. Belicia's and Dionisio's passionate affair results in Belicia's pregnancy. Her refusal to get an abortion enrages him. After all, he is married to one of Trujillo's sisters, an "important item he'd failed to reveal."[160] Belicia narrowly escapes being killed by Dionisio's wife's minions at first, but, just like her son decades later, her obstinacy, optimism, and foolish love invites catastrophe. She gets into a car she thinks belongs to the Gangster but which, in fact, holds the men who will beat her until they believe her to be dead. It is a miracle that she survives for

> [t]hey beat her like she was a slave. Like she was a dog. Let me pass over the actual violence and report instead on the damage inflicted: her clavicle, chicken-boned; her right humerus, a triple fracture [. . .]; five ribs, broken; left kidney, bruised; liver, bruised; right lung, collapsed; front teeth, blow out. About 167 points of damage in total [. . .]. Was there time for a rape or two? I suspect there was.[161]

Only La Inca's prayers and a visa to the U.S. save Belicia's life. That a similar event led to Oscar's violent death also proves that the oppressive forces that caused the disintegration of the Cabral family, starting with Abelard's imprisonment, persist. Dionisio and the capitán, as representatives of Trujillo and Balaguer, respectively, emerge in the novel as masculinist manifestations of the trauma haunting Oscar's and countless other Dominican families, that is, the spirit of Columbus or fukú of the Admiral.[162]

In both *Oscar Wao* and *La Soga*, the U.S. emerges both as a site of potential liberation and as the shadowy power behind much of the oppression and violence on the island and in immigrant U.S. communities. The U.S. passport, for instance, is both empowering and useless, demonstrating that the privilege of double citizenship comes with limitations for racialized and non-ideally gendered subjects. Oscar's mother, Belicia, escapes certain death by fleeing to the U.S., away from the Gangster and his furious wife. However, a U.S. citizen like Oscar must grapple continually with a Dominican legacy of patriarchal violence, which Columbus augured and whose apex Trujillo and Balaguer represented. Sadly, Oscar's attempts to defend himself during the first encounter with the capitán by proclaiming, "I'm an American citizen," do not keep the angry police officer and his sidekicks from beating him to his near death.[163] In fact, the capitán replies, "I'm an American citizen too. I was naturalized in the city of Buffalo, in the state of New York."[164] This simple, and humorous, exchange indicates that Oscar's U.S. citizenship offers little protection if he cannot defend himself physically "like a man." More significantly, it shows that having a U.S. passport cannot secure protection from the homeland's violence, trauma, and masculinist standards.

Toward the end of *La Soga*, a Dominican representative of the U.S. consulate hands Luis a U.S. passport with a new identity, an escape. But for the most part the film portrays the U.S. as an ambivalent space for Dominican migrants or exiles. Most of the few scenes in *La Soga* that take place in the U.S. are centered on criminal activity and violence. The exception comes in the last scene of the film, which shows the predominantly Dominican space of Washington Heights in an entirely new light, literally. Unlike the earlier scenes in the U.S., which are shot in gray and blue tones, this final scene displays a sunny, optimistic cityscape. Put differently, the earlier U.S. scenes portray migration to the U.S. as *una lucha* (a struggle) against the cold, the bleakness, the unfriendliness, and the crime, alluding to a cultural tradition that emerged in the late twentieth century, especially in popular music, describing migration as a difficult process.[165] The last scene, however, shows the U.S. as a land of possibility and opportunity. The difference in how these scenes are shot may seem irrelevant, but they demonstrate a shift in what the U.S. represents in the film. Luis and his paramour, Jenny, wake up in a sunny apartment. With Jenny's playful urging, Luis departs for his job as a supermarket butcher. In the last shot, Luis stands behind the butcher counter and transforms a thoughtful countenance into a smile. The scene suggests that Luis and Jenny are safe, an unconvincing illusion since the film opens with the public execution of a deportee who cannot escape the claws of a corrupt

FBI agent. Moreover, although Luis embodies an ideal of Dominican masculinity, he must escape to the U.S. to save his life. This outcome casts doubt on the notion that adherence to gendered and raced ideals secure a successful integration into either nation. Finally, Luis's new neighbors in the diaspora may very well include the family members of his and Colón's victims. Despite the size of the Dominican diaspora around the world, there is an intimacy and closeness instantiated by the fact that Junot Díaz and Manny Pérez are cousins.

* * *

In this chapter, I analyzed the architectural apogee of and two cultural reckonings with the legacy of the conquest. I argued that Columbus's legacy reemerges not only in the countless celebrations and monuments in his honor but also in texts in which subjects struggle to comprehend and survive the exorbitant power of male leaders such as Trujillo and Balaguer. Both *Oscar Wao* and *La Soga* showcase how Dominican subjects, especially men, struggle against or support the unrelenting violence necessary to maintain Eurocentric, patriarchal conceptions in both national contexts and the wider neocolonial context of U.S.-Dominican relations. Dominican popular discourses around these modern-day echoes and repetitions of Columbus's legacy—that is, the legacy of layered colonialisms—adopt the language of the supernatural, infusing the larger Dominican public's sense that money and political power remain in the hands of a few. Part of the enduring struggle against this power from above is the dissemination of diverse stories that counteract the power of official history, a task improved by an increased access to a wider array of communication technologies in the last few decades. However, the gendered and raced socioeconomic hierarchies established during the colonial period endure even in this much-celebrated "globalized" world. While more Dominicans can make public their dissent, neoliberal restructuring of what was supposed to be a democratic government after Trujillo has fueled massive geographic displacement, both within the country and internationally, as well as the continued political and economic disenfranchisement of Dominicans who do not conform to race and gender ideals.

Coda: Masculinist Hauntings

On October 24, 1985, popular merengue performer Tony Seval was brutally tortured and murdered under police custody in Santo Domingo.[166] Two days earlier, police had arrested him on false charges of drug possession. His band Tony Seval y Los Gitanos, formed just a little over a year earlier, had reached great acclaim with their catchy merengue songs and the outrageous outfits the band members donned on their weekly gig on the *Show del Mediodía* (Noontime Show). This show united the *pueblo* in a performance of Dominicanness, for the noon hour was when even working Dominicans returned home to eat the most important meal of the day. In the early 1980s, it was common for merengue groups to acquire a signature "look," and Seval worked with his neighborhood tailor to ensure Los Gitanos would stand out from the fray. My father, José Ramírez Valdez, who was Los Gitanos's pianist, recalls not only the namesake gypsy costumes but also those clearly meant for comic relief, including a costume of pajama sets and nightcaps made out of women's stockings.[167] People who met Seval always described him as charismatic; my father remembers him as *jocoso* (playful), constantly joking around. Combining this charm with his brilliance as a musician, the astuteness necessary to stand out from the fray, his attention to garments, and his socio-geographic move from his hometown of La Romana to fame in the capital, Seval had all the elements of the kind of tigueraje capable of catapulting someone to folk fame.

The band never got the chance to perform in their pajama costume, for Seval was arrested right after their Tuesday rehearsal on the week it was to debut. Though the murder happened two days later, my father remembers being told the very next day that Seval was dead. I can only imagine the disbelief and shock, for Seval was a beloved member of his community and, increasingly, of the entire nation. His arrest alone must have been surprising, but his murder was so exorbitant, so unbelievable that it quickly became a national symbol of military and political abuse. Thousands of Dominicans all over the country mourned and protested his death by lighting candles they placed outside their homes in what is often described as a "spontaneous" act that lasted for days.[168]

The climate of fear was so intense that my mother and father had to sneak back home using back alleyways after Seval's funeral. My father remarks that he and his bandmates had been too afraid to meet to talk about what happened. After all, they had witnessed Seval's arrest since it occurred at the end of the band's weekly rehearsal. The indignation of the *pueblo* at Seval's savage murder in prison was so great that the president at the time, Jorge Blanco, accompanied by Chief of the Military Manuel Antonio Cuervo Gómez, had to make a televised statement. No one believed the official version, which stated that Seval had gotten into a fight with other prisoners. Seval's corpse, full of stab wounds, including on the soles of his feet and in his armpits, told a story of horrific torture. My father recounts that other prisoners had heard his screams. Though the official narrative also accused Seval of being *endrogado* (on drugs), an autopsy revealed that Seval had no traces of drugs or alcohol in his system. Unlike many other musicians of the early 1980s, my father confirms that Seval did not use drugs.

At least two, at times intertwining, versions of the reasons behind Seval's arrest and murder have emerged.[169] The most widely known is that Seval had been having an affair with a military or police officer's girlfriend. To several people, this would explain Seval's hyperbolic torture, a sign of a "crime of passion." The second version emerges in a 2013 television interview with Seval's widow, Josefina Camarena, finally unafraid to tell her story. According to Camarena, Seval had come home a few days prior to his capture telling her that he had seen "algo que es problemático" (something that was problematic) involving high-ranking officials.[170] Camarena recalls that Seval told her that he had gone to pick up a young woman he had been seeing: "You know how those girls are with musicians."[171] She assures the viewer that this did not bother her, "because he fulfilled his role as a husband and as a father, you see? And as a son, too."[172] She continues:

And then he told me that he went into [Chief of the Military] Mr. Cuervo Gómez's house and they were unloading a van. He went into that house to get the girl, and a guard, who noted his presence, asked Mr. Cuervo Gómez who was this man who was there. And when Mr. Cuervo Gómez went there, he [Seval] told him who he was. Then the mother of the young woman [that Seval had gone to pick up] told him [Cuervo Gómez] that [Seval] was the girl's fiancé and in that moment was when the problem started. Well, I see a car [. . .] and five men get out, one

with a [baseball] bat, another gets out with [. . .] one of those things
that you hit a horse with [. . .] and the others have [fire]arms.[173]

This is the tumult of the arrest that my father had not seen, but had
heard, while he was still packing up his keyboard after the rehearsal.
Once Camarena learned that Seval had been detained, she went to the
police precinct, which was crowded with people demanding that Seval
be released. During the interview Camarena fought back tears as she
remembered how beloved Seval was by the community. She had been
told that he would be released the next day, but when she went to pick
him up, she learned that Seval had been killed.

My father notes that both versions of what had led to Seval's murder
are compatible. It is possible, for instance, that Seval was romantically
involved with a high-ranking official's girlfriend and had also seen this
official doing something illicit. In any case, the public knew that the official version of the story *no cuadabra* (did not add up) and his murder
revealed the depth of military and police impunity. Considering that this
occurred neither during the Trujillo dictatorship nor during Balaguer's
governments highlights my claim that Seval's murder stemmed from an
entrenched, generational, and systemic masculinist violence. The root
cause was not a single man, but an entire social-political structure. Indeed, in 1984, under Jorge Blanco's government, the aforementioned
General Cuervo Gómez had ordered a military intervention against national protests of the government's handling of the economy. Dozens of
civilians were killed in this intervention.

One of Los Gitanos's biggest hits was the song "El muerto" (The Dead
Man), for which the band made a playful music video. In the early 1980s,
it was quite rare for Dominican artists to dedicate resources to making a
music video, a fairly new way of disseminating music. After his murder,
Seval's humorous portrayal of a ghost stalking a beautiful woman in the
video seemed to foreshadow his death. Dressed in fashionable clothes
evoking an early 1980s Michael Jackson, Seval/the dead man haunts the
woman. At one point she takes recourse at the local precinct, where, of
course, police can do nothing to help her. Seval stands behind the policeman on duty, who does not see *el muerto*. On the wall behind both
of them is a painting of the map of the island. The policeman laughs at
the woman while making a gesture with his hand demonstrating that he

believes her to be insane. "El muerto" also laughs at her. The video ends in a plot twist: the woman drags *el muerto* into the bedroom because, apparently, she cannot get enough of him sexually.

Many Dominicans interpreted Seval's portrayal of a ghost as foreshadowing the tragedy that befell him. However, I consider the video and song "El muerto" to have a triple interpretation, because "the dead man" is both victim and torturer. First, the video portends Seval's untimely death. Second, the video and the lyrics can also stand for the voices of the disappeared who reemerge continually to haunt the present. The song's catchy chorus warns: "It is not in your best interest to be haunted by a ghost, because I'm going to scare you, because I'm going to push you, because I'm going to pull you, because I'm going to scratch you."[174] "El muerto" and the *pueblo*'s reaction to Seval's murder evoke the traumatic "wound that cries out," in Cathy Caruth's words, as the repetitive and deafening roar of patriarchal history tries to silence it.[175] After all, the "disappeared," like Seval, Oscar, and the victims of Luis Valerio, General Colón, and Agent Burr, do not, in fact, disappear; official historical narratives cannot do away with the memories of the populace. Though Seval enacted the gendered charm and violence of the tíguere, he was ultimately the victim of another instantiation of the structural violent patriarchal forces I have discussed throughout this chapter. However, Trujillo's, Balaguer's, and Blanco's official versions cannot erase the stories that emerge in innocuous conversations, even in the diasporic New York City space where my father recalled Seval's murder.

Finally, "El Muerto" is a disturbing portrayal of a man stalking a woman relentlessly, confirming that playful performances of tigueraje often rely on violence against women and nonideally masculine subjects. In one scene, a group of men point and laugh at the woman because she is frightened by the *el muerto*/Seval as he follows her. Since they cannot see him, the bystanders conclude that she is *una loca* (a crazy woman). Seval and the video's directors almost certainly did not intend for the video to be interpreted through a feminist lens, as I have done here. We may recall as well that Oscar is not only a sad *parigüayo* (loser), but also, from another perspective, an obsessed stalker of several uninterested women. If anything, these three intertwined readings of tigueraje demonstrate that "life is complicated," to cite Avery Gordon.[176] This is especially the case when it comes to ghosts and hauntings.

4

Dominican Women's Refracted African Diasporas

In the summer of 2014, *HuffPost Live* dedicated a nearly thirty-minute segment to the issue of Dominican blackness entitled "Black in the Dominican Republic: Denying Blackness."[1] It featured three professors based in the U.S., Silvio Torres-Saillant, Lauren Derby, and Kimberly E. Simmons, who parsed the generalization that Dominicans deny their blackness. Two students with Dominican ancestry living in the U.S., Christopher Pimentel and Biany Pérez, also shared their thoughts on race. Describing her experience as a Dominican Afro-Latina, Pérez recalls: "I learned that I was black from my experience [in the South Bronx]. I grew up in a predominantly African American and Puerto Rican neighborhood. At the time, in the early '90s, there were no Dominicans where I was living except us, so I learned early on that my skin color and my hair were markers of my blackness." She admits that she could not "opt out" of blackness, because she did not look like a "stereotypical Latina," and realized that "over time, [she] found a lot of solidarity with African Americans and darker skinned Latinos who really had similar experiences with [her]." In contrast, Pimentel says quite simply, "I do not identify as black." Asked to clarify further, he expands: "Dominicans in general, we do have African ancestry. We do admit it [. . .]. The thing is, we do not identify as how Americans seem to construe things as either white or black. That whole one drop rule does not operate in the Dominican Republic." He insists on a narrative in which can he accept his African ancestry alongside his European and indigenous ancestries.

Torres-Saillant situates both of these stances thusly:

In the United States, where the racial politics operate in a certain way, it is even unsafe for you to try to exist outside of the confines of that racial regime. So you have to, in a sense take, sides. You may find yourself in a situation of having to adopt North American racial codes. But that is different, that is a contextual thing. That is different from actually declaring that Dominicans have less racial proficiency than other African descended populations. The fact is that there is no society that has endured colonialism [. . .] and black slavery that can actually say that it is free of black issues.

Both Derby and Simmons also contextualize blackness, indicating that U.S. subjects often cannot register Dominican expressions of blackness.[2] The students' personal experiences demonstrate at least two ways in which Dominican subjects living in the U.S. negotiate blackness. In Pérez's case, growing up isolated from other Dominicans and surrounded by people who could not quite accept the concept of *afrolatinidad* or Black Latino-ness pushed her to embrace an enunciated blackness (i.e., a blackness that calls itself as such). That is, her persistent interpellation as black by those around her prompted this identification. It is unclear whether or not Pimentel has encountered such interpellation, but, when asked by host Marc Lamont Hill if he would reject his blackness to a cop who would not care to delineate between black (or African American) and Dominican, he continues to push against the interpellation.

I open with this *HuffPost Live* segment because it perfectly frames the discussion that follows. As Torres-Saillant states above, despite the diversity of narratives of blackness (and, concomitantly, whiteness) around the world, the U.S. prompts Dominicans to consider where they stand vis-à-vis its dominant narrative of blackness. Making room for both Pérez's and Pimentel's definitions of blackness, I push against the teleology or progress narrative in which Dominican—and other nonwhite immigrant subjects—attain black consciousness in the U.S. Within this paradigm, Afro-descendent immigrants who do not enunciate their blackness through U.S. dominant vocabularies of blackness and race have not reached black consciousness.

In this chapter, I explore some of the ways in which diasporic Dominicans engage with, adopt, or refuse predominant definitions of blackness. More specifically, I examine the writings and performances of diasporic Dominican women, both U.S.- and Dominican-born, who evince various intersections between the Dominican and African diasporas.[3] Because dominant Dominican ideas of blackness—to which many Dominicans ascribe—are generally discordant with dominant U.S. ideas of blackness, these engagements highlight the prismatic nature of the African diaspora. Through analyses of these women's cultural texts, I show the extent to which diaspora—in the Dominican and African senses—does not and cannot signify a single, linear trajectory, experience, or aesthetic.

My analysis of Dominican expressions and performances of African diasporic identity emphasize multiplicity, refraction, and inversion. I follow Stuart Hall's vision of identity "as a 'production,' which is never complete, always in process, and always constituted within, not outside, representation."[4] Hall's ideas about the African diaspora have been invaluable to my analyses of how Dominicans fit within, reject, stretch, and conform to its boundaries. In particular, I am inspired by Hall's description of this and "all enforced diasporas" as "the experience of dispersal and fragmentation."[5] I also build on black diasporic feminist theory, which, in Samantha Pinto's words, "coalesce[s] through contradiction rather than recovery, difference rather than consensus."[6] Equally influential has been the work of Caribbean scholars such as Édouard Glissant who emphasize nonteleological terms such as rhizome and routes to understand the region's history and culture. In Glissant's definition, the "rhizome [is] an enmeshed root system, a network spreading either in the ground or in the air, with no predatory rootstock taking over permanently."[7] Whatever we call it, this antiteleological, nonlinear approach radically shifts the dominant conversation about Dominican blackness, especially in North America.

Because all of the women artists I study are in some way resistant to the white supremacist and patriarchal ideologies that govern dominant paradigms throughout the hemisphere, I have located improper behavior as the primary vehicle in which they invert or refuse the gendered, classed, and raced scripts expected from Dominican women. I analyze Dominican writer Chiqui Vicioso's attempts to resist her mother's and grandmother's disciplining of her body in looks and behavior in order to render her a proper (i.e., "white" and domestic) woman. I also analyze what she calls her "discovery" of her blackness in the U.S. through her "experiences with the 'bichromatic model' of US racism or anti-racist struggle," to cite Raj Chetty after Louis Chude-Sokei.[8]

After a brief discussion of improper behavior as a slippery but powerful resistant act, I turn to two Dominican musical artists starting with Amara la Negra (née Diana Danelys De los Santos). Born and raised in Miami, Amara's resistant impropriety emerges from her message of Afro-Latina affirmation combined with a joyful celebration of her sexualized body. That is, she embraces what is persistently exoticized, if not outright denigrated, in the Spanish-language Miami, Latinx, and Latin American entertainment scene in which she operates.[9] Finally, the New York–born and raised musical artist Maluca Mala (née Natalie Yepez) also negotiates her intersectionalities as Dominican, Afro-Latina, and New Yorker, never acceding to a driving impulse in the U.S. for people to pick a single identity category. In Maluca's case, I focus more on her appropriation of Dominican tigueraje through performances of some of its central tenets, including hustling, taking up space in the street, attention to style and garments, and irreverence, while maintaining her femme identity.[10] Because I have shown that tigueraje is rooted in masculine black insouciance, Maluca's appropriation of it comprises yet another refraction of the African diaspora.

Together, these diasporic subjects (in the sense of the Dominican and the African diaspora) evince the complicated contours and loose threads at the various intersections between diasporic Dominicanness and African diasporic identities. They demonstrate that the African diaspora, trans-Americanity, and Dominicanness together map out rhizomically and not in a linear manner.[11] To put it differently, I seek to push for a conceptualization of blackness that prioritizes space and time, or "spacetime" to borrow Michelle M. Wright's coinage, and that eschews a propensity to measure Dominican proximity or distance to a U.S.-centric black consciousness. In Wright's conceptualization, blackness is a question of "when and where" rather than "what," which expands our legibility of how a great variety of subjects throughout the Americas relate to their African ancestry.[12] A focus on spacetime exposes various registers of blackness, both enunciated and otherwise.

Chiqui Vicioso's Diasporic Intervention

[D]iaspora frameworks bring the historical category of race to bear on the logic of the nation.
—Michelle Stephens, "What Is This *Black* in the Black Diaspora?" (2015)

In this section, I analyze Vicioso's personal essay, "Dominicanyorkness: A Metropolitan Discovery of the Triangle" to show the extent to which the "when and where" is crucial to a study of blackness throughout the African diaspora.[13] I argue that, just as growing up isolated from other Afro-Latinx subjects fueled Biany Pérez's enunciated blackness, Vicioso's experience of studying and living in the United States during the civil rights movement shaped her shift in racial perspective and vocabulary. When I interviewed Vicioso in 2009, she credited her education at Brooklyn College under Marxist scholar Hobart A. Spalding, as well as her readings of non-Hispanophone Caribbean thinkers Frantz Fanon, Marcus Garvey, and C. L. R. James, with giving her a new perspective from which to consider Dominican identity. Her communion with various students from "the islands" beyond Puerto Rico and Cuba were also part of her education.

During our interview, she described her encounter with immigration officials upon arrival to the U.S., who asked her the meaning of *india clara* (light Indian), a racial denomination on her Dominican passport:

[I]t was the first time I realized [. . .] the craziness of Dominican culture regarding colors because here you cannot even call yourself a mulatto. I'm supposed to be white, and, you know, you are white [pointing to me], even though you are a *mulatto* woman, but then they have indio claro, indio oscuro, indio canela if you are so black as [the deceased longtime presidential candidate José Francisco] Peña Gómez, because they don't want to call anybody a negro [. . .] That is an insult.

Here, Vicioso rejects the Trujillo-era decision to include the category *indio* (Indian) in identity documents such as the *cédula*, an I.D. card that all citizens must carry, issued for the first time during the U.S. occupation of 1916–1924.[14] It would not be until 2011 when the category of "indio" was removed from the *cédula*.[15] Dominicans continue to use the word in quotidian speech. Much has been written about the adoption of the word *indio* as a phenotypical marker of the racial mixture of *blanco* and *negro*.[16] Many have interpreted Dominican usage of "indio" to disavow blackness.[17] For instance, Wendy Roth writes that, for Dominicans and Puerto Ricans, "[r]acial terms may serve as euphemisms, to avoid negative associations; the terms *indio* and *trigueño*, for example, are often used to avoid describing someone as negro."[18] Others have put more weight on the terms' description of a phenotype (medium-brown skin color and straight black hair) and acquiescence to mixed black and white (and some indigenous) ancestry.[19]

Without refuting the above interpretations, I consider the term "indio" as a ghosting mechanism. The descriptor of "india/o" as it has been used in the Dominican Republic for a century has been a way to both manage and perpetuate two large-scale ghostings. In one sense, it marks the almost total decimation of the *taíno* population of the island. In another sense, it marks the ghosting of Dominican blackness from official nationalist discourse especially from the early twentieth century.[20] While most writings about tropes of blackness and indigeneity in the Dominican Republic use terms such as "displacement," "erasure," and "denial" to describe the latter process, it is also fruitful to see it as a technique that manages the various ghostings at play. To say one is *indio* instead of *negro* or even *mulatto* is an utterance more complicated than mere black denial; it contains "the memory of otherwise forgotten substitutions—those that were rejected and, even more invisibly, those that have succeeded," to cite Joseph Roach.[21] To describe oneself as *indio* in the Dominican Republic is an acquiescence—often necessary, especially for those in the most precarious socioeconomic positions—to an official nationalist narrative of origin. But it also contains whispers of those centuries of "forgotten substitutions," most notably the "substitution" of *taíno* labor with African labor in the sixteenth century and, starting in the late nineteenth century, the discursive substitution of nonwhite insurgency and black self-autonomy with the idea of Dominican whiteness *in relation to* Haiti.

Despite the existence of spaces and practices that complicate dominant U.S. ideas about indigeneity and blackness, especially among indigenous and so-called "tri-racial" communities in the eastern coast of the U.S., the term *india/o* as it is used in daily speech and in official documents in the Dominican Republic is illegible in the U.S. The documentation of indigeneity and how it emerges in official documents in the Dominican Republic differs significantly from the U.S. for a myriad of reasons too complex to enumerate here. However, it is worth considering how blackness has refracted differently onto indigeneity in these two nation-states. Official indigenous status in the U.S. almost always precluded blackness at the same time that it included whiteness.[22] A consideration of how indigeneity and blackness have not been officially allowed to intersect in the U.S. and Native American nations highlights the constructedness of racial categories in the U.S. as much as in the Dominican Republic. That is, indictments of Dominican perspectives of race, and how and why they were constructed, rarely point the critical gaze in the other direction, toward the constructions and the boundaries of indigeneity, whiteness, and blackness in the U.S. I consider at least some of the discomfort around Dominicans' usage of the term *india/o* as stemming from the illegibility of many African Americans' indigeneity. It is an illegibility and nonrecognition that concretized itself through the denial of the documents meant to prove indigenous status in the U.S. and within Native American nations. These ghostings of indigeneity and blackness, and how they served the purpose of rendering certain kinds of identities legible to official governing bodies and nations while submerging other identities in enforced oblivion, instantiate themselves in starkly divergent ways in the Dominican Republic and in the United States.

Thus, the illegibility of Vicioso's Dominican denomination as "light Indian" has as much to do with U.S. racial constructions as with Dominican ones. Living in the U.S. occasioned Vicioso's reevaluation of dominant Dominican understandings of race within an African diasporic context. Her essay "Dominicanyorkness" describes her resistance as a young girl to her mother's and grandmother's admonitions to follow Eurocentric Dominican beauty ideals and patriarchal expectations of proper feminine behavior. The essay juxtaposes her childhood in the Dominican Republic, where her mother implored her to straighten her hair and her grandmother prevented her from playing outdoors, with her black nationalist and pan-Africanist education in the U.S. as a young adult. As she echoed during our interview, this education induced her to embrace that previously rejected part of herself—her African ancestry.[23] In the end, she feels more "at home" in the African diaspora than in the Dominican nationalist space and, I surmise, a white mainstream U.S. space.

The essay describes a childhood marked by attempts to assert herself outside the racialized and gendered parameters that would render her legible within the nationalist Dominican scripts that I described in earlier chapters. During an argument, a young Vicioso interjects her mother's attempts to police the boundaries of racialized femininity:

"Can you imagine yourself white and with Juan's green eyes? And Antonia, with Luis's blue eyes and blond curls? It would've been a knockout!"
"But, mother!"
"No buts! If you want to go to that party, you must have your hair straightened. [. . .] To have taken after your father! It's not that I didn't love him just as he was, don't get me wrong, but the boys should have taken after him, and you and Antonia, after me."[24]

Most striking about this passage is the clear delineation of ideal femininity as white; there is more discursive room for Dominican masculinity to be associated with blackness, as I discussed in previous chapters.

Proper Dominican femininity is not only codified through phenotypical whiteness or white signifiers but also through actions such as remaining indoors, within the domestic realm.[25] We may recall, for instance, Silveria R. de Rodríguez Demorizi's approval of Salomé Ureña's preference for remaining indoors as well as Belicia's distress that her son Oscar avoids playing outside in *The Brief Wondrous Life of Oscar Wao*. Unfortunately for her grandmother, the young Vicioso preferred the outdoors, leading to another intergenerational struggle:

"Grandma, let me go to Canaima!"
"That's not for girls! [. . .] Who did you take after, such a tomboy?"[26]

Here, Canaima, a small river in Vicioso's hometown of Santiago, represents the masculinized space of the outdoors forbidden to respectable young Dominican women after a certain age.[27] Domestic containment combined with the adoption of phenotypical signifiers of whiteness—such as straight hair—were the parameters within which Vicioso had to fit in order to be legible as a citizen-subject within the dominant narrative of the nation. The restrictions around Vicioso's mixed-race, female body parallel Salomé Ureña's, but the former's staunch refusal to accept them is distinctly that of a feminist, diasporic subject. This is not to say that only diasporic subjects have the possibility of rebelling. Indeed, Vicioso's essay demonstrates that her resistant behavior started as a child in the homeland. Rather, I propose that it was her diasporic education during the U.S. civil rights era that facilitated this process for her.

As these examples evince, her mother's and grandmother's policing of behavior sought to curtail Vicioso's potential slippage into what, according to Eurocentric nationalist discourses, was an embodied blackness and savagery. In these discourses, blackness is also connected to both the untamed monte and the urban "streets." In this manner, Vicioso's maternal figures attempted to prevent her from embodying a black femininity that represented a reviled element of Dominican society. This racist connection between blackness and impropriety (or lewdness, anti-respectability, and hypersexuality) spans Western discourses around the world. Writing about a nineteenth-century and early twentieth-century U.S. context, Evelyn Brooks Higginbotham writes: "Black womanhood and white womanhood were represented with diametrically opposed sexualities."[28] As a response, "[African American] Baptist women's emphasis on respectable behavior contested the plethora of negative stereotypes by introducing alternate images of black women."[29] Sharing these concerns but writing about the Jamaican context, Belinda Edmonson argues that

> [s]ince respectable middle class black women could not create physical differences between themselves and working class women—to the nonblack observer, though, black was simply black—it became imperative to create notable and distinct differences in habit, speech, and style. This essentially political need to establish difference is, I believe, at the root of modern anxiety about black women's performances in the public sphere, an anxiety that requires "decorous spectacles" of black womanhood as its antidote.[30]

While I have shown that the Dominican socio-racial context differed markedly from places such as the U.S. and Jamaica, especially in relation to socio-racial status, I have also maintained that it shares with these societies an idealization of whatever signs and behaviors represent whiteness. That is, while its status as a non-Plantation society shaped discourses of blackness differently than these places, white supremacist ideals dominated discourses during the colonial and, in many cases, the national eras. Antiblack rhetoric became explicit especially during and after the Trujillo regime, which is the world that Vicioso inhabits. As a middle-class, mixed-race woman, Vicioso's social status was somewhat precarious and her maternal figures' admonitions must be considered in this larger historical and social context.

About halfway through the essay, Vicioso shifts away from her experience growing up on the island to her experience as a Dominican immigrant residing in the U.S. and "discovering" that she is a subject of the African diaspora. Writing about an earlier version of "Dominicanyorkness," Daisy Cocco de Filippis writes:

> For Dominican writers in the U.S., the admission of a shared African heritage as well as the understanding of their position as marginalized members of North American society, has brought about another level of consciousness to be shared with other Dominicans who in the past have accepted anti-Haitian sentiment in the island. As a member of the diaspora, as well as the Dominican community of writers, Vicioso offers a more inclusive approach.[31]

Vicioso describes how the growth of her African diasporic education provided "evidenc[e] of the underlying racism, transmitted from generation to generation, that exists in the Dominican Republic."[32] Learning about these pan-Africanist intellectuals and leaders during the civil rights movement furnished Vicioso with "a political language from which to articulate [her] experience of racialization, oppression, disenfranchisement, and silencing—a process that allow[ed her] to build alliances with other oppressed communities around the world," to cite García-Peña.[33] These diasporic tools helped Vicioso to discover the Eurocentric nationalist patriarchal roots of the intergenerational struggle that shaped her childhood in the Dominican homeland.

The African diasporic intersubjectivity that Vicioso attains in the U.S., which she describes as the "journey of 'buts' to consciousness," contrasts with the aforementioned intergenerational struggle she experienced as a young girl with her mother/grandmother. While the latter relationship is didactic and patriarchal (a rejection of the person she already is), the former is dialogical and offers the possibility of a self-conceptualization that goes beyond the constraints of patriarchal patriotism.[34] Put differently, Vicioso's transformation moves from an intergenerational dispute—a push for a linear progression in which the daughter repeats the mother's and grandmother's way of embodying Dominicanness and femininity—to a dialogical, omnivocal, and intersubjective way of relating to and learning from others. We may recall from chapter two that these concepts emerge in Vicioso's play *Salomé U.*, which also highlights horizontal relationships over the vertical, hierarchical relationships enforced through nationalism. According to Michelle Wright, the concept of black feminist diasporas frames and foments these kinds of relationships precisely because they resist the patriarchal and hierarchical dicta of nationalism. However, as Wright and other diaspora scholars argue, a diasporic perspective alone does not preclude hierarchical and patriarchal ways of relating to and organizing our world. Maja Horn ends her book *Masculinity after Trujillo: The Politics of Gender in Dominican Literature* (2014) with a caution against the ways in which diasporas "often get marshaled, even by well-meaning critics, not to unsettle an exclusionary U.S. American identity but rather to consolidate and bolster it."[35] In *Impossible Desires: Queer Diasporas and South Asian Public Cultures* (2005), Gayatri Gopinath concedes that "the concept of diaspora may not be as resistant or contestatory to the forces of nationalism or globalization as it may first appear."[36] It thus becomes necessary to qualify "diaspora" with terms such as "queer" and "feminist."

Although in "Dominicanyorkness" her intersubjective relationships are primarily with esteemed male scholars and activists of the African diaspora, Vicioso clearly considers race and gender to be inseparable identity categories. Vicioso's experience of race in Dominican and U.S. societies is inextricable from her lived experience in a female, nonwhite body. Nevertheless, her critique of nationalism is launched against Dominican nationalism and not, for instance, against black nationalism, which relies on similar patriarchal tenets as those of the Dominican nation-state. In "Dominicanyorkness," the U.S. becomes the space of diasporic possibility in great part because her "spacetime" is New York City during the civil rights movement. The U.S. Vicioso writes about is certainly not anywhere/anytime U.S., but rather one of the most important place-moments within dominant narratives of U.S. blackness. Moreover, against this spacetime of diasporic possibility, Vicioso describes the Dominican homeland entirely through its dominant Eurocentric patriarchal nationalism, despite the fact that dominant U.S. nationalism can be described similarly.

Time and place continue to be important in the next section when it comes to the question of blackness. After my brief detour into the possibilities of inversion and refusal available through impropriety, which emerge more subtly in Vicioso's recollection of her refusal to perform as a proper (i.e., more phenotypically white and domestic) girl, I delve into the work of two diasporic Dominican musical artists. I contend that their work evinces how Dominican identity as it shifts between various nationalist and diasporic imaginaries—if not actual geographic spaces—presents a prime case of African diasporic refraction and inversion.

Refusal and Inversion in Performances of Impropriety

In all of the cases I analyze in this chapter, improper behavior becomes a performative stance against or, at least, in tension with the status quo, whether Dominican nationalism or the patriarchal and white supremacist leanings of dominant U.S. Latinx culture. Focusing on how impropriety manifests in different places and at different times of the Dominican and African diaspora in the U.S. and the African diaspora in the Dominican Republic also illuminates the imbrications between gender, race, and class. The public discourse around improper and lewd behavior and its threat to the status quo is as prevalent in the Dominican Republic as it is in other contexts, including other former colonies and among minority groups in the U.S.[37] As I discussed in chapter two, the gendered, raced, and classed performance of propriety has been an important vehicle of socioeconomic mobility for Dominican women. As the (gendered, raced, and classed) script of the Dominican nation solidified in the late nineteenth century, it became clear that women who seemed white, feminine, maternal, and upper class garnered wider social respect than other women.

Inverting and refusing these expectations, the performers I discuss below are empowered through "bottoms-up" performances of Dominican and Afro-Latinx pride. Their embrace of lewdness pointedly subverts the paradigms in which black women, and Afro-Latinas, have a precarious hold on citizenship in either the U.S. or the Dominican Republic. At times, their performances and public personas seem to ask: Why should I act proper/prim/chaste/domestic when dominant social forces and discourses always already conflate black women and their bodies with abjection, hypersexuality, dirt, madness, and being unworthy of civic protection and veneration? While their work implies this inquiry, it is never as existential or nihilistic as the question suggests. Rather, Amara's and Maluca's performances are joyful and exuberant celebrations of various forms of Afro-Latina femininity, sexuality, and creativity. Invoking Carolyn Cooper, Mimi Sheller describes "bottoms up" as a "tongue-in-cheek yet serious call [. . .] that reminds us of the 'pubic' that is the root of the word 'public' and of the 'sexualised representation of the potent female bottom in contemporary Jamaican dancehall culture'—these nether-regions are not spoken of in polite/political society."[38] These bottoms-up performances, which emphasize the playful, the "dirty," the "crazy," the sexual, and the best-left-hidden, are powerful ways of resisting the pressures of gendered respectability or propriety in a variety of contexts, including Dominican, Caribbean, African diasporic, and U.S. Latinx contexts.[39]

Amara: La Negra

Given the politics of voyeurism and fetishism that frequently accompany the representation of black bodies, can a resistive praxis emanate from the spectacle of women masqueraders gyrating in full view of television cameras?
—Natasha Barnes, "Body Talk" (2000)

The scene is a familiar one.[40] Exasperated passengers endure a traffic jam in Santo Domingo's Colonial Zone. However, something extraordinary breaks the tedium of this quotidian scene. A dark-skinned woman with a large Afro, spandex "Daisy Dukes," and midriff-bearing top exits her vehicle and, with two other similarly attired women, snakes her way through the cars to the samba beat and announces: "Soy Amara la Negra. Los chicos me caen atrás. No sé si será mi pelo o mi forma de bailar" ("I am Amara la Negra. Guys come after me. I don't know if it's my hair or the way I dance.") (see Figure 4.1). She and her two fellow street provocateurs then turn around and begin "twerking," or "wining" as it is known in some parts of the Anglophone Caribbean, to the song's catchy main lyric: "Ayy." The camera zooms into Amara's and the other women's twerking bottoms, and captures the male figures' visual consumption.

Figure 4.1. Still from Amara la Negra's music video "Ayy."

Amara's performances both on- and offstage induce us to consider the fragmented nature of her embodiment of black diasporic feminine sexuality. Amara's stage and video performances, in which she often unironically, yet playfully, embraces her black female body, prompt questions about what is subversive, especially in light of her investment in propriety in interviews. I consider this tension indicative of the limits of the focus on resistance and even subversion, and the usefulness of terms such as refusal and inversion.[41] If we only consider her body-hugging outfits, sexually suggestive lyrics—one of her singles is called "Quítate la ropa" (Take Off Your Clothes)—and twerking, Amara clearly seems to reject the expectation that all nonwhite, Caribbean women must strive toward chaste, decorous feminine behavior. On the other hand, Amara la Negra's public persona also conforms to norms of propriety in that she always smiles, speaks in a mainstream-friendly standard Spanish in filmed interviews, and frequently alludes to her love of God and respect for her mother. Amara's respectable persona combined with her twerking bottom complicates "the narrative of black experience which takes as its poles exploitation and respectability, or exploitation and resistance, as the clear and opposing options for reading these public histories," to cite Samantha Pinto.[42] Moreover, Amara's complexity as a Dominican diasporic and African diasporic performer evinces multiple refractions of the African diaspora. Her embrace of her blackness and simultaneous embodiment of a hypersexuality that runs counter to the demure decorum that other black women have felt that they have to enact in order to acquire respect ensures that we consider some of the many tensions evident in Dominican refractions of blackness.

Amara's chosen moniker embraces the figure that has most embodied lewdness in the Americas: the "negress." Her work and body navigate a white-centric, Spanish-speaking status quo in the Miami Latinx mainstream. Anyone watching U.S. Spanish-language networks Telemundo or Univisión would see that the Latinx and Latin American celebrities on their screens are often light-skinned mestizos/as or white. In fact, one would be hard pressed to find black or indigenous faces. Despite the popularity of many black Latinx musical artists and sports stars, many of them Dominican, the sight of a black Latina remains relatively rare. Amara's emplacement in the Miami musical mainstream, as well as the mainstreams of the Dominican Republic and Puerto Rico, informs how she engages with her blackness.

Amara's unwavering celebration of her overlapping Afro-Latina and Dominican identities demonstrates that these identities must themselves be considered contextually. Amara's self-fashioning as a proud black woman and as Dominican subverts dominant paradigms within a Miami-based U.S. Latinx and Dominican context. Several of her Instagram posts centralize her emphasis on the "and" in her intersectional identity as black *and* Latina *and* Dominican. For instance, in January 2016, Amara uploaded a picture on her Instagram account that portrays her almost hyperbolic performance of Dominicanness (see Figure 4.2). The Dominican flag features prominently in the picture. The architectural style of the buildings behind her show that she is likely somewhere in the northeast U.S., while her placement in relation to these buildings indicates that she is on a parade float or on a stage at a block party. Moreover, her caption proclaims "Sangre Dominicana!" (Dominican blood!). The most interesting element of this Internet vignette, however, emerges in her choice of hashtag—#AfroLatina—because it demonstrates that her Dominican national pride is inseparable from her black Latinx identity. Amara's choice to hashtag her "AfroLatina" identity and not her Dominican identity indicates her choice to connect, in this one instance, with other Afro-Latinxs whether Dominican or otherwise. This

amaralanegraaln   4h

♥ ○ ↱   ○ ○ ○

♥ 1,694 likes

amaralanegraaln Sangre Dominicana!
#AfroLatina

Figure 4.2. A screenshot of Amara la Negra's Instagram post from
January 2016.

Instagram post is not only an example of Amara's investment in raising
awareness for and celebrating *afrolatinidad*, but also the importance of
social media and other new media venues and genres in twenty-first-
century cultural archives. In this image, Amara drapes her Dominicanness in the form of the flag over her proudly black female and feminine
body. This simple move challenges the nationalist erasure or submersion

of enunciated blackness or blackness that calls itself as such. In another post, a stylized image of Amara with the superimposed hashtag #Latina, her caption states, "Orgullosamente Soy #Latina / Im [sic] proud to be #Latina." This simple message of a dark-skinned black woman subverts mainstream Latin/o American and white mainstream U.S. paradigms in which Latinas/os, in the words of Afro-Cuban American actress Gina Torres, "look Italian."[43] It is important to note that, despite her dark skin, Amara has the relative class, language, and citizenship mobility that, for instance, an under- or undocumented dark-skinned Dominican woman of Haitian ancestry does not have.[44] Amara, and Maluca as I will discuss below, have access to a performance of insouciance and irreverence that is only possible with access to various kinds of mobility. We may recall from the previous chapter the punishment that even El Alfa endured for his discordant act of patriotism. His citizenship status—Dominican and not U.S.—combined with the fact that his primary audience is in the Dominican Republic limits his ability to "play with" performances of Dominican patriotism.

Despite this caveat, Amara, who performs frequently in the Dominican Republic, thrives in the uncomfortable grey area that is *afrolatinidad*. In fact, there is nothing unclear or strange about *afrolatinidad*, but within dominant U.S. discourses of *latinidad*, including those perpetuated within the Latinx community and media outlets, it remains an anomaly. Increased awareness about Afro-Latinxs means that fewer people are confused about it. Nonetheless, much work remains to be done. For instance, when Tony Andrades, a Dominican reporter for Univisión's news magazine show *Primer Impacto*, asks Amara how people respond to her "look," he is referring entirely to her Afro, overlooking the fact that this is simply how her hair grows out of her head. Her response demonstrates the extent to which embracing her natural hair is considered anathema to feminine beauty or simply to the social norm and differentiates her from mainstream Dominican, Latinx and Latin American standards of beauty.[45] Indeed, she tells Andrades, who himself reads as black in the U.S., that people have asked her if she is on her way to a Halloween party, if she has been electrocuted, or if she stuck her head out of an airplane window.

Amara's unapologetic celebration of her tightly coiled hair is also rare in the Dominican Republic, though less so in the last few years. In an episode of the Dominican talk show *Mujeres al Borde*, Amara talks about antiblack discrimination especially as it pertains to beauty. After describing her physical and emotional suffering when getting her hair chemically straightened, she states:

> [U]nfortunately [. . . many people] think that, for a black woman [pauses while looking at the camera defiantly], because I am a black woman, for a black woman to be pretty she has to have straight hair. She has to have hair down to her knees. This is a lie! By nature we are not like that.[46]

Without commenting on Amara's heartfelt remarks, the white Dominican talk show host, Ingrid Gómez, stands up and pulls Amara's hair without asking for permission. She does this in order to prove to her daughter, an Amara fan, that her Afro is real. Due to her consummate professionalism and extreme patience, Amara laughs, but it is clear that Gómez re-creates precisely the kind of objectification of black women that renders them ripe for touching, violating, or consuming in some way. Women like the host Ingrid Gómez do not expect to be manhandled in this manner.

This incident reminds us of the violence that lurks beneath even the most lighthearted conversations when it comes to black women and their bodies. While the natural hair movement has made significant inroads in the Dominican Republic, women and girls persistently run up against the disciplining antiblack boundaries of their societies.[47] In the summer of 2016, Afro-Dominican natural hair activist Carolina Contreras, more commonly known as Miss Rizos (Miss Curls), recounted the story of a newly natural teen girl to her significant number of social media followers. The girl had visited the Miss Rizos hair salon, which caters exclusively to women who do not chemically straighten their hair or who want to make the transition, to cut off her chemically straightened hair. The girl had reached out to Contreras in tears, because her private school wanted to expulse her. The girl's mother told Contreras that the school considered natural hair styles, such as certain braids and Afros, to be the "'new trend' of tígueras and locas."[48] From the school officials' perspective, proper young women must straighten their hair if they were not already born with it. Similar stories abound about black women having to spend hours disciplining their hair into styles that are difficult to achieve—hours that women with straight or non-tightly curled hair, and men with short hair, can use for different purposes—in the U.S. and elsewhere.[49] Afro-descended women's hair, when it is tightly curled, remains a site of hypersurveillance that requires women both to acquiesce to certain beauty standards and norms as well as to spend hours precisely on accomplishing this task. The school's immediate association of hair that is allowed to grow a certain way with "tigueraje" and madness, and the willingness of officials to prevent one of their students from completing her school education because they cannot accept her natural hair texture, reminds us of how far many societies are from releasing the fetters of the racial hierarchies consolidated centuries earlier. This is especially the case when it concerns black women's bodies, whose "iconography," according to Daphne Brooks, "remains the central ur-text of alienation in transatlantic culture."[50] The appropriation of tigueraje by Maluca, whom I discuss in the next section, must be seen in this larger global context.

Maluca: La Tíguera

Yo soy la Mala, sí, yo soy ma' dura. Pelo malo, pelo suelto
como una bruja. Me llaman Loca pero así te gusta.
I am the Bad One, yes, I'm harder. Bad hair, hair out like a
witch. They call me Crazy but you like it like that.
—Maluca Mala, "Mala" (2016)

Unlike Amara, who performs propriety in general, but whose embrace of her phenotypical blackness and twerking renders her "lewd" within a hemispheric paradigm that sees black women as undeserving of the same respect as white women, Maluca would proudly embrace the term of impropriety to describe her performances.[51] For instance, on Dominican Independence Day in 2011 at the downtown N.Y.C. venue S.O.B., Maluca exuberantly screams into the microphone: "Yo soy Maluca, la mala, la fea, la bruja, la sucia!" ("I am Maluca, the bad one, the ugly one, the witch, the dirty one!")[52] Her cri de coeur connects her Dominicanness—espoused through the celebration of Dominican independence—with her embrace of the behavior that proper Dominican women should eschew. Maluca's performance name itself exemplifies her tongue-in-cheek, ludic "badassness": Maluca means "crazy" and Mala means "bad." Some of her song titles further evince the discordant and resistant identities her music showcases, "El Tigueraso," "Lola (Ging Danga)," and "Mala."[53]

In these ways, Maluca's oeuvre leans into a rejection of idealized codes of feminine behavior. Her vehicle for this refusal is a mixture of the musical and performance cultures of both her multiethnic N.Y.C. upbringing, including the Dominicanyork space of Washington Heights, and the Dominican Republic. Maluca cites artists as homegrown as the Bronx Nuyoricans ESG and as far-flung as Mexican *cumbia* and Dutch electronic music as important inspirations to her work.[54] Despite this diversity, her greatest influence, at least when measured by the number of times it comes up during interviews, is the music and culture of her parents' homeland, the Dominican Republic, and its diaspora. Her music also homes in on the icons that subvert dominant paradigms of gender, race, and sexuality within all of these cultural spaces. Among them are those subjects she calls "Lolas," whom she describes as

> the characters in the underground who society deems as [. . .] non-compliant [. . .] It's not gender-specific. It represents the hustle [. . .] Lolas don't cook. We eat take out. Cause we're too busy hustling. We're too busy inspiring people, looking fly, making shit happen [. . .] We inspire fashion. We inspire music. We inspire art, and what's hip, and what's fly. Beyoncé and her girls, they rule the world, but the Lolas, we rule the underground.[55]

Her song "Lola (Ging Danga)" celebrates Lolas and was inspired by a woman she knew as a child who stripped in order to "better her life." As evident above, the basic definition of a "Lola" is a subject who has to hustle to make ends meet and to move up the socioeconomic ladder. In other words, he/she is a *tíguera*. I write "tíguera" only and not also tíguere because her definition of a Lola avoids the hypermasculine connotation of tigueraje while retaining the hustle, playfulness, and style central to it. While tígueres conform to masculine ideals of being out in the street and in the public sphere, tígueras or Lolas represent impropriety in any traditional sense of Dominican femininity.

According to Maluca Mala, Lolas preside over the underground, which Petra R. Rivera-Rideau argues "connotes a space that exists outside of the 'mainstream,'" "[a]s something that is spatially 'below,'" and, thus, can be thought of "as the foundation for the things that exist above it."[56] Rivera-Rideau's definition of "underground" offers a reminder of Sheller's invocation of the term "bottoms up" as that which is underneath and beneath polite society. In this context, we may consider Lolas' sphere as one that subverts the dictates of status quo Dominican and U.S. nationalisms, dominant ideas about *latinidad* as disconnected from blackness, and U.S.-centered blackness.[57] As a regendered appropriation of tigueraje, Lolas/tígueras instantiate yet another refraction of the African diaspora. In Maluca Mala's theorization of Lolas emerges also the crucial point that dominant mainstream culture absorbs the "surplus" value of *sucias*.[58] As theorized by Deborah R. Vargas, the analytic of *lo sucio* (that which is dirty) is "first, lewd, obscene, offensive hypersexual undisciplined bodies; second, darkened, suspect citizens perpetually untrustworthy, impure, and nonloyal to the state; and third, diseased 'cultures of poverty' subjects overdetermined to fail to arrive to normative womanhood and manhood."[59] The creative work and energy of these "lewd bodies," "suspect citizens," and "diseased subjects" such as Lolas, tígueras, and *sucias* do not always remain surplus but are, in fact, rendered more respectable or more marketable, or both, a task often accomplished through a performance of this previously surplus act by a suitably white performer.[60]

In other interviews and features, Maluca states that hustling (i.e., tigueraje) requires creativity and intelligence. One of the best examples of Maluca's creatively expressed financial need occurs in the first episode of her aforementioned web series. In this episode, "Fly on a Budget," she applies for food stamps while wearing a stylish furry Russian-style Cossack hat. The contradiction of this marketable, stylish body that needs government aid to be fed becomes particularly stark when clips of Maluca strutting down a fashion runway are juxtaposed with her paying with a food stamp card at the supermarket. The popular rap song "Ghetto Superstar" by Pras playing in the background is the proverbial cherry on top. Being "fly on a budget" is a central element of being a tíguera. Being fashionable in spite of poverty has deep roots in black

Atlantic culture. Punk and hip-hop required the usage of salvaged items, the mix of "high" and "low" fashion, trash used as musical instruments, and burnt-out empty buildings as concert venues.[61] Gina Ulysse argues that "[h]aving a sense of style and fashion is very important in the Caribbean, especially because the performance of gendered identities is based upon and understood in the context of representation."[62] In this manner, Maluca's webisode unfolds one of the many intersections between Dominican tigueraje as performed by Maluca and a black Atlantic hip-hop aesthetic. Though both strains—tigueraje, as I discussed in chapter three, and hip-hop—emerge partly as performative and embodied responses to curtailments to socioeconomic mobility and survival, they nevertheless reflect the intersecting rhizomic routes of African diasporic creativity.

When she was interviewed for a short NBC Universo documentary called *Black and Latino* alongside other Afro-Latinx celebrities, Maluca continued to place her Dominicanness center stage. She expresses frustration at being misrecognized: "When I did move out the Dominican neighborhood [at thirteen years old] a lot of people at that time didn't even know where, like, the Dominican Republic is. Either I was like Puerto Rican or black or mixed and I was always like, 'I'm Dominican! Argh!'" That she considers blackness and being mixed race as separate, for instance, evinces the importance of localization. To many Latinxs, the term "black" refers specifically to African Americans and not to other subjects with black ancestry. Further, had Maluca been born and raised in other parts of the U.S., the distinctions between Puerto Rican and Dominican, for instance, would have ceased to matter in the same way. In this sense, we cannot underestimate the extent to which the local informs ethnic and racial terms.[63] As the number of self-described Dominicans increases in the United States, along with their prominence in the mass media and popular culture, the possibilities of misrecognition will likely decrease.

Yet another refraction of the African diaspora emerges in Maluca's first released song and music video, "El Tigeraso," which was inspired by "'mambo violento' or 'mambo from la calle' [. . .] a sped-up merengue."[64] Though this video and song is purportedly an homage to "el tíguere," I propose that this video—along with much of Maluca's body of work and performativity—is really an homage to *la tíguera* or Lola, the

"*mamasita* del block."[65] The first images from the video show a quintessential Dominican sight/site: the hair salon.[66] Several clients drying
their roller sets under hood dryers bop their feet to the beat of the song.
The hairdresser sets Maluca's hair into large rollers as she also dances
along to a bare percussive beat and the opening lyrics: "Yo tengo todo,
papi. Yo tengo todo, papi" ("I have everything, papi. I have everything,
papi"). The playfulness of the video, and of the artist herself, becomes
particularly evident when Maluca leaves the salon wearing the rollers.
The *means* of attaining the smooth, yet voluminous, look that makes the
"Dominican blow out" famous in the black and curly hair community
becomes the *end goal* in the video. Perhaps Maluca also good-naturedly
mocks the fact that many Dominican women on the island have been
known to sport their damp hair in rollers because the electricity has
gone out in one of the daily blackouts that people in poor neighbor-
hoods endure. Perhaps a visit to their barrio's salon was cut short by a
blackout, as some of these homegrown small businesses simply cannot
afford the kind of powerful generator that could support a hood dryer
and the hairline-scorching, kink-destroying heat of the blow dryer. In
this manner, the first few seconds of the video are an ode to the routine
performances of working-class Dominican femininity. Ginetta Candelario
argues that "[t]he Dominican salon acts as a socializing agent. [. . .] At the
salon, girls and women learn to transform their bodies [. . .] into socially
valued, culturally specific, and race-determining displays of femininity."[67]
Candelario's research at a Dominican salon shows that "the extensive technology, time, and effort employed to make hair 'loose and manageable'
must not show."[68] What do we make of a scene in which the final "look" is
not the flowing, silky hair resulting from a Dominican roller set and blow
out, but, instead, the roller set.

I consider Maluca's ode to Dominican women's self-fashioning as an
act of disidentification, to borrow José Muñoz's definition of the concept.[69] She neither wholeheartedly embraces Dominican women's hair-
straightening practices—rooted in the racist notion that black hair is
"bad"—nor rejects the practice of going to the *salón* by, for instance,
wearing her hair in its natural curls. Instead, she stops the process mid-
way, her embrace of the rollers a complicated embodiment of both African diasporic and diasporic Dominican subjectivity. In this manner,
she escapes the binary in which a black woman's body is always either

in radical contestation or in submissive agreement. Maluca refuses the dichotomy between, on the one hand, falling prey to Eurocentric standards of beauty, and, on the other, embracing her African roots. She refuses having to choose as so many other Afro-Latinxs have been induced to. As with Amara, Maluca's performances do not offer easy-to-categorize failures or successes along a single teleology of blackness. In this sense, Maluca's performance and embodiment of *afrolatinidad* escape the parameters of a common stance in U.S. academic and popular media discourses that place the Dominican Republic within a "not yet" stage of temporality that will ideally end with the "correct" embodiment and performance of blackness. The hair straightening practices that, in at least one perspective, evince Dominicans' black denial become, instead, the space of creative possibility.[70] These salon scenes also unwittingly nod to another point of African diasporic intersection between the African American and Dominican routes, for the hair salon is also a keenly African American site and cultural referent.

Beyond its being a tongue-in-cheek act of African diasporic disidentification, roller sets and the Dominican hair salon as a site have often signified Dominicanness in the diaspora. We may consider the centrality of "rolos" in the work of Dominican designer-artist M. Tony Peralta. In 2005, the Washington Heights–born artist created the Peralta Project, through which he sells objects that display his artwork, including posters, coffee mugs, and refrigerator magnets. One of his artworks, *Doña con Rolos*, based on a photograph by Iñaki Vinaixa, shows a woman wearing large rollers on her hair. This acrylic on canvas piece is part of a series called *Complejo* (A Complex/A Hang Up) that includes other images of what Peralta described in a *New York Times* interview as "the backwards mentality in regards to race" and "self-hate."[71] Despite his critique of dominant Dominican views about race, and "rolos" as a symbol of black negation, his commercial work tells a slightly different story. In the Peralta Project website, one can purchase from his collection of *Rolos & Icons Posters*, a series of playful images of female pan-Latina and Latin American and feminist icons wearing rolos.[72] Among them are Frida Kahlo, Celia Cruz, Selena, Wonder Woman (as played by Lynda Carter, an actress with Mexican ancestry), and even the Latina cartoon icon Dora the Explorer. The rolo here emerges not so much as a symbol of self-hatred or of a "hang up" with one's own blackness, but as an exuberant and joyful celebration of what Peralta seems to acknowledge as a quint-essentially Dominican act of self-fashioning. That these non-Dominican icons are shown to wear the rolos constitutes an act of boundary stretching, of Dominicanizing *latinidad* and even mainstream U.S. icons.

Returning to Maluca's video, though the large rollers in her hair are enough to call attention to her body in the upper Manhattan streets, Maluca's clothing adds to the spectacle. She dons red sequined "booty" shorts, sheer stockings with a red seam running along the back of her legs, red heels, a bustier, and bright red lipstick (see Figure 4.3). She saunters down the sidewalk until she kicks off her heels in favor of *chancletas* (flip-flops) that aid her ride on a bicycle. Traveling from the salon to her apartment building involves circumventing the kind of street harassment in the form of "catcalls" that many women have to negotiate in New York and Dominican streets. Right before she reaches her building, several men of various ages surround Maluca, lasciviously gazing at her. However, this threatening image is rendered humorous since the actors themselves look quite amused by the situation and by their exaggerated performance of a lip-licking "urban" masculinity. The camera moves

Figure 4.3. Still from Maluca Mala's music video "El Tigeraso."

from man to man, replicating Maluca's own gaze as she pivots around, wearing an increasingly disgusted and comical expression on her face. She escapes the circle with the paradoxical words, "Ay no no no no no. Me mata el novio" (My boyfriend would kill me). The exhortation that she cannot acquiesce to these catcallers' desires because her "boyfriend would kill her" is a fascinating lie. After all, she is hardly tempted by these men, as her look of undisguised disgust demonstrates. However, the statement illuminates her precarious position and lack of control in this circumstance, for she assumes that these men would only allow her to escape with proof that another man controls her body.

I interpret the video for "El Tigeraso" as inverting Tony Seval y Los Gitanos's music video for "El Muerto." As I discussed in the previous chapter, "El Muerto" features a ghost relentlessly stalking a woman. In this video, the camera captures Maluca's stealth navigations through the masculine spaces of the Upper Manhattan streets as she persistently rejects various forms of the masculine gaze and gendered aggression. We may also consider "El Tigeraso" as an inversion of another video of a woman who saunters down the street occupying space: Amara's "Ayy." Unlike Amara's desire to attract the male gaze in her song and video, Maluca rejects the undesired male gaze while the camera revels in gazing on examples of desirable masculinity. While we never know where Amara's desire lies beyond the desire to be visually appreciated and consumed, Maluca and her video leave little doubt as to who is a desirable man and who is not. Because traditional (i.e., masculine) tigueraje also involves the act of (visual) consumption of and prowess with women, Maluca's and the video's clear visual consumption of handsome, presumably Dominican men inverts the gendered relationship between gazed and gazer. The object of desire in the video is the "Tigeraso" himself, an archetype portrayed by several insouciant men at the start and toward the end.

Despite what seems to be Maluca's total appropriation of tigueraje and frank return of the gaze, she reaches the limits of her inversion when she escapes the threatening circle of undesirable male gazers by claiming that her boyfriend would kill her. The reason behind her hypothetical boyfriend's wrath remains unspoken. "My boyfriend would kill me [if I desire you in return]." Or perhaps "My boyfriend would kill me [if I even let you look at me for too long]." Most likely, it truly does not matter, for men have killed women for both reasons. Even Maluca's comical, irreverent, and empowered performance of female and feminine tigue-raje runs into the persistent threat of gendered and raced violence, an issue I discuss more concretely in the next chapter. Women who seem to transcend any traditional patriarchal and racialized boundaries prompt the eruption of misogynist and patriarchal rage.[73]

The last scene in "El Tigueraso" takes place at a party where Maluca dons another outrageous outfit with beer cans as rollers and gold-colored *shower* slides with athletic socks, a look that was popular among young black and Latino men in early 2000s N.Y.C.[74] Among the partygoers is a young, female accordionist, a seemingly incongruous sight, since it directly references the *merengue típico* prevalent in rural, low-income areas of the Dominican Republic and which this song samples. Contrasting with the bouncing joy of the dancing revelers is a figure sitting in the corner. Like a Don assessing his territory—for el tíguere "tiene la calle on lock" (has the street on lock) as the song affirms—the handsome man with a tear tattoo on his face coolly regards the festivities. His masculine seriousness is undercut by his contemplative petting of a small blow-up tiger sitting on his lap. The contrast is, like the rest of the video, comical. In this manner, the video and song both render homage and mock Dominicanyork street culture. This is also evident with her mid-video outfit change, which involves not a removal of the rollers, as a Dominican woman often removes her *túbi* (hair wrap) or rollers right before an event, but a change from plastic rollers to beer can rollers.

The comical elements of the video add to both the song's and the video's celebration of performative Dominicanness in N.Y.C., home to the largest diasporic Dominican community. Indeed, the video, like the moment at S.O.B.'s that I mentioned earlier, accords Maluca Mala's quotidian and stage performances an exuberance that is inextricable from her diasporic Dominicanness. The Washington Heights landscape is dotted with Dominican flags. One of the first images the viewer sees is of the Dominican flag itself, taped to the hair salon's front glass window. A hair salon in the Dominican cities of Santo Domingo or Santiago has no need to display the flag, but the signifier carries symbolic weight in a diasporic space. The video debuts Maluca as embedded into a clichéd-yet-real Dominicanyork landscape. As Maluca saunters down the sidewalk, we see glimpses of various men's hands performing tasks that have come to signify diaspora Dominicanness, for better or for worse: a man counting dollar bills on the street corner, a man scattering dominos on a table atop a Dominican flag, a man playing the *tambora* (the drum used in merengue), a man shaking *maracas*, a man with a small accordion, and finally several men of various ages staring directly at the camera with what is meant to be an alluring tigueraje.

In many ways, Maluca's larger work speaks to a desire not only for artistic recognition that would ideally also pay her bills but also for the ability to embody Dominicanness. Maluca's work, like Amara's, constantly evokes a Dominicanness that may or may not exist in reality. Maluca's is not a desire to "return," for she was born in the U.S., but a desire for Dominicanness that is contingent more on its signifiers and its creative potential. For instance, in the aforementioned second episode of her web series, a large Dominican flag is held up on S.O.B.'s stage while Maluca's voicemail message to her mother plays in voiceover: "Hey, *mami*. We got emotional when I played the Dominican national anthem at the end. It was just nice to see a roomful of Dominicans who are progressive and who are trying to, you know, push the envelope and do something different and unique and embrace what I'm doing, too."[75] In this moment, she stretches explicitly the conservative boundaries of Dominicanness in which the kinds of embodiments showcased in this episode—self-proclaimed loud, creative women; openly gay men; Dominicanyorks—can be proudly Dominican. But that she does so from a nightclub in downtown N.Y.C. as a woman who was born and raised in N.Y.C. also reminds us of the complicated nature of national and African diasporic identity. Her U.S. citizenship status accords her a level of security that many do not have.

* * *

In this chapter, I analyzed the writings, music, performances, and self-fashioning of diasporic Dominican women who together evince various intersections of African and Dominican diasporas. Though they take different routes, I argued that these women create vehicles through which non-ideal Dominicans—diasporic, working class, and black—can read, write, and perform themselves into Dominican and U.S. national spaces and diasporic imaginaries. Focusing on the intersection between improper femininity and blackness in diasporic Dominican women's writings or performances allowed me to highlight the prismatic nature of the African diaspora.

5

Working Women and the Neoliberal Gaze

Why didn't you tell your mother that I wasn't the cleaning
lady? Do I *look* Dominican to you?
—Mindy Lahiri, *The Mindy Project*

Connections between Dominicans and tourists are made
easily, and there is no stigma. Sex is just another local commodity, one that the Dominicans take much less seriously
than their clients, who ply them with cash and trinkets.
—Stephen Holden, "Review: Sand Dollars," *New York Times*

Just as the masculine stereotype of the Dominicanyork drug dealer arose
in the late twentieth-century, Dominican women "caretakers" became
another set of associations in Dominican and U.S. popular culture in the
early twenty-first-century in the imaginaries of "first world" nations.[1]
Following Barbara Ehrenreich and Arlie Hochschild, caretaking or
"women's work" encompasses the work of "nannies, maids, and sometimes sex workers."[2] References to Dominican women caretakers have
ascended as shorthand in films, television shows, and books not only in
first world spaces but also, as was the case with the masculine stereotype, in the Dominican Republic.[3] The epigraphs above aptly frame the
discussion that follows. They tie a racialized colonial imaginary to mainstream U.S. perspectives on Dominicans in relation to sex, gender, and
labor. I cite, for instance, an episode of the television comedy *The Mindy
Project*, which aired in September 2014. The success of this joke relies on
the assumption that a mainstream U.S. audience can connect Dominican women to domestic work. The other quote is from a *New York Times*
review of the Dominican film *Dólares de arena* (Sand Dollars, 2015). The
reviewer's assessment of the film slips into a centuries-old global imaginary in which nonwhite natives befuddle emotionally complex white
foreigners.

This chapter focuses on cultural representations of a transnational "economy of desire," to cite Amalia Cabezas, which has become an important vehicle of socioeconomic mobility for working-class Dominican women.[4] Focusing on cultural representations of these women confirms that Dominican society has fully entered a dominant political-economic global paradigm often described simply as neoliberalism. The fact that related stereotypes and clichés are applied to Dominican women as much as to nonwhite women from other parts of the world signals the depth of the Dominican Republic's embroilment with dominant global economic capitalist networks and their concomitant imaginaries starting in the late twentieth century. This stands in marked contrast to prior centuries when the Dominican Republic was a unique colony with a majority black and mixed-race free population and then a nonslaveholding, black-led nation-state. In the late twentieth century, the rise of neoliberal economic restructuring at both national and transnational levels finally folded working-class and other nonelite Dominicans into a larger, unequal global economy. Currently, Dominican women mesh with other nonwhite "third world" subjects performing manual, caretaking, and service-focused labor. Whatever singularity predominated in the Dominican Republic for centuries has generally ceased to exist, only remaining in some of the residues and ghosts I explored in previous chapters.

I focus on Dominican female sex workers as a case study to support my broader argument about how global demands aided by neoliberal free trade policies accommodate centuries-old colonial fantasies. In these fantasies, so-called *mulatas* in the Caribbean and throughout Latin America represent natural sensuality and sexuality to be enjoyed by people, especially white men, from wealthier countries.[5] Amy Kaplan's term "libidinal maps" is useful here. Although she applies the term to "fantasies of unlimited expansion" in historical romances in the late nineteenth-century U.S, it also evokes the pervasive association between certain racial groups (especially as concentrated in certain parts of the world) and certain forms of labor.[6] Aníbal Quijano argues that "race and the division of labor remained structurally linked and mutually reinforcing, in spite of the fact that neither of them were necessarily dependent on the other in order to exist or change."[7] In this chapter, I explore the association between nonwhite women, especially but not exclusively mixed-race "mulatto" women, and sexual and caretaking labor.

As I have argued throughout this book, for centuries the Dominican territory did not follow the developmental trajectory of its neighbors. Despite this history, global economic restructurings as controlled and led by the wealthiest nations in the world succeeded in turning the Dominican Republic into yet another source of certain kinds of labor. This shift occurred after U.S. economic intervention in the late nineteenth century and consolidated in the late twentieth century, especially through the increased reliance on foreign tourism. In this neoliberal restructuring of global markets, a savvy foreign consumer-citizenry demands that Dominican and other nonwhite women from the "third world" fulfill racist visions of compliance, hypersexuality, and maternal instinct.[8] Moreover, the foreign tourism industry profits from an acceptance of a new colonial history in which the Dominican Republic resembles its Cuban or even Jamaican neighbors. Tourism relies on visions of a tropical colonial history and caricatures of blackness as they emerged especially in Plantation societies. For this reason, I adopt scholarship and theories created to understand circumstances in other Caribbean spaces that now resemble the Dominican Republic.

The transnational economy of desire I discuss may appear at first glance to be based on reciprocal and equal wants. On one side stand consumer-citizens with relatively high geographic mobility, including sex tourists.[9] On the other side stand those with low to no geographic and socioeconomic mobility, such as Dominican sex workers and other working-class women. Transactions or relationships between the two sides seem equal, reciprocal, and complimentary. And, in many ways, they are. However, even celebratory cultural representations of these transactions and relationships display their unevenness and the colonial roots of global socioeconomic and geographic mobility. Through close analyses of several texts, I consider Dominican women's stealth maneuverings within a neoliberal transnational economy of desire in which their success relies on fulfilling first world demands. Without overlooking these women's negotiations and the material improvement that some of them achieve, I argue that the rising demand for Dominican women's caretaking labor in the neoliberal era extends associations set during and through Atlantic chattel slavery and colonialism.

I analyze cultural texts that exemplify the range of interactions in a Dominican-based economy of desire.[10] A consideration of Europe, especially Spain, as an important site of Dominican immigration and as the initial source of colonial fantasies stretches the Americanist frame of the rest of this book. To clarify further, while most of my book's analysis remains invested in hemispheric American frameworks, Europe is discursively crucial to this chapter because current global systems are rooted in European colonialism.[11] As I discussed in previous chapters, it would not be until the late nineteenth century that the U.S. consolidated its control and power over the hemisphere. This control was hardly made anew; it was deeply entrenched in European colonialist imaginaries and paradigms.

My analyses of varied cultural expressions develop my claim that the present-day transnational economy of desire involving Dominican women has colonial underpinnings. In the first section, I provide a necessary overview of the global economic-political frame as it has developed starting in the late twentieth century and its relation to the Dominican context. In the second section, I analyze a U.S. photographer's and sex tourist's photo essay of Dominican sex workers, the testimonies of Dominican sex workers, and a short story by a Dominican writer featuring a sexual encounter between a foreign man and a young Dominican sex worker. In the third section, I focus on two films that develop immigrant Dominican women's agency, however limited, within a transnational economy of desire in Spain. The final section brings together my concerns throughout the chapter as I examine a Dominican-directed film featuring the same-sex relationship between an older white European woman and a much younger Afro-Dominican woman, as well as some musings on the emplacement of the Dominican actress who plays the protagonist within a twenty-first-century global economy.

Colonial Paradigm, Neoliberal Gloss

The government does not take it upon itself to create a new source of employment that would favor rural women, nor does it create laws that would protect the dignity of women and that would overpower misogyny.
—MODEMU (Coalition of United Women)

Despite their variety, all of the texts I analyze in this chapter explore some facet of the transnational economies of desire concomitant with a consolidation of what Carla Freeman terms the "global assembly line," in which "[t]hird world countries have increasingly become central producers of commodity goods and parts in labor intensive industries, and management and research, the white-color strata of industrial interests, have increasingly become the preserve of 'core' or industrialized nations."[12] Freeman distinguishes this global order from earlier ones in which "'third world' territories have long been the source of raw materials and the powerful 'first world' 'mother countries' have represented the privileged realm of industrialization and consumption."[13] While this distinction works well within discussions of the production of material goods, the distinction is not as marked when we consider the issue of sex and caretaking as a commodity. When looking at these kinds of commodities, the perpetuation of a colonial global structure that bolstered and was then bolstered by racist ideas about nonwhite women's sexualities is striking.[14]

Transnational policies often described as neoliberal have unevenly revamped most of the world. According to the World Bank, the "Dominican Republic (DR) has enjoyed one of the strongest growth rates in Latin America and the Caribbean over the past 25 years."[15] Despite this general growth, poverty remains high (in the double digits) and "access to public services remains unequal and is of generally low quality, particularly for people living in poverty."[16] Indeed, IMF researchers admitted in 2016 that "[i]nstead of delivering growth, some neoliberal policies have increased inequality, in turn jeopardizing durable expansion."[17] Although the Dominican economy is varied, free-trade zones protected by the CAFTA-DR (Dominican Republic–Central American Free Trade) Agreement has eased foreign companies' access to cheaper labor and lower taxes and has "unlock[ed] opportunities for well-paying work as goods flow across borders."[18] According to this logic, the items manufactured in these "well-paying" jobs in places such as the Dominican Republic have free rein to travel, while no such concessions are made for people. The unrestricted access accorded to international businesses simultaneously curtails the right to a living wage and the possibility of socioeconomic movement for working-class subjects and those lacking official documents from the nation-state. It is not "sufficient," according to Saskia Sassen, "simply to assert that globalization has brought with it a declining significance of the state in economic regulation."[19]

Instead, she continues, the "state is the strategic institution for the legislative changes and innovations necessary for economic globalization as we know it today."[20] What seems, from one perspective, to be a profitable and fair opening up of national borders is, from another perspective, the increasing control of borders, the increased demand for citizenship and migration documentation, and the decreased access to and funding for public institutions that in the past eased socioeconomic mobility.[21] I consider this era's global economic-political structure to be a new accommodation to a colonial global structure. In turn, these colonial structures, as Lisa Lowe demonstrates, had already been reconfigured through liberal "processes through which 'the human' is 'freed' by liberal forms, while other subjects, practices, and geographies are placed at a distance from 'the human.'"[22] This distance between quintessential human subject and those who remain "at a distance" becomes crucial in present-day emphases on humanitarian and philanthropic acts, which, as I will show, connect seamlessly with neoliberal faith in free trade and citizenship through consumerism.

Connected to these global economic shifts and continuities is what Sassen calls the "feminization of wage labor," which she describes as the "incorporation of Third World women into wage employment on a scale that can be seen as representing a new phase in the history of women."[23] Women take on this work both in their homelands and in the countries to which they migrate.[24] In the latter case, businesses and individuals profit from undocumented or underdocumented migrant women's precarious circumstances, resulting in rampant wage theft, blackmail, and other kinds of abuse.[25] Despite the unprecedented nature of some of these late twentieth- and early twenty-first-century changes in global migration and economic patterns, racist colonial assumptions and associations drive some of this global demand for the labor of women from previously colonized, majority nonwhite, nations of the world.[26]

Most, but not all, of the accounts I analyze in this chapter revolve around Dominican sex workers.[27] Some of the sex work as it is practiced by Dominican sex workers catering to foreigners so closely resembles more socially accepted forms of dating that the term "sex work" is insufficient. This might include spending time with clients at the beach, bars, and other sites. Indeed, sex tourists may choose a person with whom to spend their entire vacation. This murkiness has prompted me to adopt the term "transnational economies of desire" to unite the accounts explored in this chapter, borrowing Amalia Cabeza's term "economies of desire." The term emphasizes the inequalities in mobility that circumscribe the possibilities of sex workers and their clients. It also helps prevent reaching conclusions about what is impossible to know: the extent to which romantic love—the current ideal within mainstream U.S. and other societies—is involved. Moreover, the ideal of equal partnership presumes equal freedom of choice, an assumption difficult to make in the transnational context I analyze.[28]

Starting in the late twentieth century, many Dominican people joined the global work force by working in relatively lucrative jobs in free-trade zones, the tourist sector, and within the transnational economy of desire I have been discussing. International businesses profit from the tax exemptions promised through free-trade agreements and from the inexpensive, nonunionized labor that economically and politically vulnerable women often offer.[29] The economic reliance on export manufacturing and the decline in agriculture after the Trujillo dictatorship led to a rise in male unemployment and underemployment within informal economies.[30] This rise is coterminous with "conditions that have promoted the formation of a supply of migrant women in third world countries,"[31] conditions that partly stem from "the prevalence of women in export manufacturing and the high incidence of manufacturing jobs among women in countries where this type of production is prominent."[32] The types of production most frequently outsourced are in "electronics, garments, textiles, toys, and footwear [. . .] that is, industries that have traditionally employed women."[33]

Within this global economy, I analyze representations of an economy of desire rather than other kinds of labor exchanges because of the centrality of sexual desire and heterosexual coupling to nationalist narratives. It is worthwhile to recall my arguments in earlier chapters about Dominican women's symbolic roles within the national body. The dominant conservative Dominican nationalist desire for women to remain in the home(land), behave in a "proper" manner, and use their sexuality for reproduction of future citizens runs counter to global economic demands for hypersexual *mulatas*, *negras*, and hot-tempered Latinas. Here, it suffices to say that Dominican sex workers who cater to tourists or operate within first-world spaces illuminate the tension between nationalist demands and the demands of imperial powers controlling the world economy. Sex workers and other women operating within transnational economies of desire and, as such, folded into a global neoliberal paradigm subvert Dominican conservative nationalists' expectations of Dominican women while realizing the neocolonial fantasies of sex tourists and other first-world consumer-citizens. In this sense, they remind Dominican subjects of the extent to which places like the Dominican Republic and its people have not escaped the "Western," that is, European and North American, colonialist imaginary. Nationalist paradigms, in which, according to Mary Louise Pratt, women's value is "specifically attached to (and implicitly conditional on) their reproductive capacity," become problematic in light of the fact that national and transnational economies worldwide have relied on racialized women's labor in the late twentieth and twenty-first centuries.[34] The result is a fundamental tension between the transnational demand for women as participants in the labor market, on the one hand, and a national framework that celebrates as it obscures the unpaid domestic labor of wives and mothers, on the other. In this contradictory situation, "third world" women are both asked to be traditional mothers by their homeland's cultural and political ideologies and to financially support their dependents from a distance through necessary remittances or in the homeland by, for instance, working for foreign-owned corporations or within ostracized industries like sex tourism.[35]

Prostitution, rape, and other terms connoting unequal sexual exchanges are often used to describe oppressive colonial and national relationships. Women (and men) who partake in economies of desire both represent and disrupt some of these ideas.[36] Denise Brennan contends that "sex tourism [. . .] is also a focal point of people's fears of change and cultural transformation. Thus, sex workers become the symbol of a 'prostituted' country, while they generate significant resources for business owners and investors, as well as for their families and boyfriends."[37] Dominican female sex workers' liminality within an imagined and real national-transnational nexus, as well as the general association of sex worker with "the street," render them ideal sites of overdetermined anxiety. (As I mentioned in earlier chapters, the "street" is a masculine space in the Dominican national imaginary.) This anxiety functions to support these women workers' perpetual disenfranchisement within both national and transnational political-economic spaces, and a continual disavowal of the ways in which both rely on their labor.[38]

The naturalization of Dominican women's hypersexuality or caretaking abilities that render them ideal laborers in this transnational economy blends with a postslavery and (post)colonial notion that these women's labor is paid and therefore fair. Ethnographers report sex tourists' remarks that they are helping sex workers support their families. Similarly, triumphant articles in the mainstream press extol the virtues of certain labor sites, including factories, that provide what resemble living wages. These articles overlook the nagging question of why certain kinds of labor become persistently available in certain parts of the world. In the summer of 2010, the Global Business section of the *New York Times* published "Factory Defies Sweatshop Label, but Can It Thrive?" The image atop the article shows Joseph Bozich, the white U.S. chief executive officer of Knights Apparel, embracing Mireya Pérez, a Dominican worker and union leader. A Dominican man stands by a table in the background, busy with work. The article quotes one of the factory's workers, Santa Castillo, as saying, "We never had the opportunity to make wages like this before [. . .]. I feel blessed." Described alternatively as "the world's most unusual garment factory," "a high-minded experiment," and "a risky proposition," Knights Apparel emerges in the article as a noble, but highly volatile, enterprise. Paying "nearly three and a half times the prevailing minimum wage, [in 2010] $147 a month in [the Dominican Republic's] free trade zones," Knights Apparel would indeed be a "godsend," as Castillo describes it, for the Dominicans employed there. While I celebrate the ways in which work at this factory has improved the material reality of its Dominican employees, as well as the important role of Pérez as union leader, the article takes for granted a world order in which the livelihoods of hundreds of Dominicans depend on the individual benevolence of a white U.S. man. More striking is that, within the business world, a $500 per month wage is considered so generous that the article's readership would need to be convinced of its viability. We may consider this article in light of Aníbal Quijano's argument that "the lower wages 'inferior races' receive in the present capitalist centers for the same work as done by whites cannot be explained as detached from the racist social classification of the world's population—in other words, as detached from the global capitalist coloniality of power."[39] This

New York Times article is just one within a genre of similar articles and enterprises, exemplifying the philanthropic tinge of these transnational markets.[40] Lisa Lowe usefully defines "liberalism as a project that includes at once both the universal promises of rights, emancipation, wage labor, and free trade, as well as the global divisions and asymmetries on which the liberal tradition depends, and according to which such liberties are reserved for some and wholly denied to others."[41] Rather than contradictory, the impulses behind free trade and some philanthropically flavored business practices perpetuate the global paradigms set by colonialism and consolidated through liberalism.

Twenty-First-Century Colonial Imaginaries

[E]ven those who live in the most dire circumstances possess a complex and often contradictory humanity and subjectivity that is never adequately glimpsed by viewing them as victims or, on the other hand, as superhuman agents.
—Avery Gordon, *Ghostly Matters* (2008)

With the first woman I met in Sosúa, I tried only to photograph. No sex. This was not a reflection of hesitation rooted in principle—I didn't find her attractive. But she had a service to sell, and she sold and sold hard. I paid for sex and she allowed me to photograph her.
—Peter Schafer, "Diary of a Sex Tourist" (2015)

I start this section with what may perhaps be the most straightforward example of the colonial underpinnings of present-day global sex tourist networks.[42] The sex tourist in question, U.S. photographer Peter Brian Schafer, would likely be surprised at this characterization, since he considers himself to be different from other sex tourists. Schafer insists that his photo project, *Whores and Madonnas*, "contrasts quite a lot to other photo essays on prostitutes, which typically place the viewer as a voyeur to a degraded yet exotic existence, with depictions that harden rather than challenge prejudice and stigma."[43] Moreover, he believes that his photos show sex workers to be "[d]isarmingly ordinary [. . . neither] madonna [n]or whore."[44] Schafer insists on his goal of portraying Dominican sex workers with dignity, providing a nuanced narrative of what drives some Dominican women to pursue sex work in Sosúa and elsewhere. This includes a desire for socioeconomic mobility and even freedom from some of the constraints of "the strictures of family life and hometowns."[45] Despite his attempts and intentions, I argue that his photographs of sex workers combined with his description of his own relationship to his subjects exemplify fully the neocolonial paradigms that make sex tourist–sex worker encounters possible. Schafer's work is especially appropriate to this chapter for two reasons. First, he is one of the few sex tourists who has both written about and produced art in relation to sex work. Second, in his attempts to portray himself as a responsible global citizen, Schafer's work and narrative reveal the inequalities of mobility and access to consumer goods.

The main way in which Schafer's photographs and explanations fall within colonial paradigms is his disembodied intellectualization of his sexual desire for Dominican sex workers alongside his photographs' emphasis on their bodies. Following Mimi Sheller's work on other Caribbean contexts, my analysis of his photo project and his descriptions of it attempts to "offer a critique of the universal 'disembodied' (white male) subject who animates Western philosophies of freedom through the disavowal and abjection of grotesquely 'embodied' others (women and racialized others)."[46] Unlike the bodies of the women he photographs, Schafer's body is nowhere to be seen. Instead, as readers and viewers of his interviews, essays, and photographs, we become privy to his intellectual approach to the topic. His body, however, is implicated, for he repeatedly admits that he "became their client," but it remains absent, merely implied.[47]

Schafer's essay, "Diary of a Sex Tourist," was published in *Vantage*, an online photography magazine. The date of publication, August 2015, coincided with the debates around Amnesty International's call to legalize sex work worldwide. It opens with the simple declaration: "I had never thought of myself as a sex tourist." Schafer sees himself as a photographer "embarking on a project about prostitution."[48] Denise Brennan's ethnography *What's Love Got to Do with It: Transnational Desires and Sex Tourism in the Dominican Republic* (2004) had inspired him to photograph nonc__clichéd portrayals of Sosúan sex workers' motivations and desires. That Schafer would cite a work of ethnography should come as no surprise. Although Brennan's nuanced and responsible scholarship does not repeat the Otherizing narrative of countless other ethnographies, the field as a whole cannot be divorced from its colonial, Eurocentric underpinnings.[49] Anthropology, ethnographic and travel photography, entire schools of painting (e.g., the work of Paul Gauguin), the language of "tropical" and other forms of tourism in the "global south," among other discourses, have shaped immeasurably how many subjects of the world see themselves and each other. The "cash and trinkets" detail in the *New York Times* review cited in the epigraph to this chapter, for instance, quite clearly issues from the language of European colonial representatives reporting to the crown, and, much later, descriptions of "primitives" by anthropologists who could not escape their Eurocentric worldview. Schafer's declaration that he was inspired by a work of ethnography must be considered within this larger context.

Beyond this ethnographic inspiration, Schaefer also "understood" that he had to become a sex tourist "in order to do the photo project [he] wanted to do" while he packs for the trip.[50] At first, it remains unclear what prompted this decision, for he had not yet arrived at his site. The next few sentences clarify what motivated this shift in perspective:

> To be frank, I looked forward with some excitement to the prospect of having sex with Dominican prostitutes. It had been a while since I had sex by the time I flew down to the DR, a fact likely connected to my choice of photo project. My only prior experience with a prostitute was many years earlier, in Amsterdam. I recall that she, like most of the women I met in Sosúa, was from Santo Domingo.[51]

In this statement becomes apparent the equivalence or association between sex and prostitutes, and then between prostitutes and Dominican women. His desire to have sex realized his desire to document Sosúan sex workers. That is, his interest in capturing the lives of Dominican sex workers exceeded the intellectual constraints of the ethnographic scholarship that he claims as his inspiration. In admitting that he enjoyed having sex with Dominican sex workers, we become aware of his desiring body (though he never photographs it) and confirm that what is supposed to be the objective, ethnographic eye is far from it.

"Diary of a Sex Tourist" also suggests that not only does Schafer desire to have sex with Dominican sex workers but he also desires to be seen as a nonexploitative consumer. In this sense, he believes in the power of consumer choice as an act of humanitarian global citizenship. While he argues against the victimization of sex workers in polemics against legalization, he is equally invested in arguing against the vilification of their clients. He writes: "Men who patronize sex workers are invariably portrayed as abusive and demeaning in order to fit that narrative. And I have no doubt that many are. But caricatures only get you so far in developing sound policy."[52] He insists on his difference from these "villains" by describing what sex workers think of him, or at least what they said they think of him. For instance, he recalls one instance when the woman he calls his friend in the photo essay tells him "You respect me." In another instance, she tells him that "she can be herself with [him]."[53] My point is not to cast doubt either on Schafer's or his friend's sincerity in those moments, but rather to underscore his need to include them in the essay. Though Schafer's photographic essay is not sentimental, the narrative surrounding his motives borrows from sentimentalist narratives of yore, in which his "honorable feeling 'humanizes' him, as the narrator and reader [or, in this case, the viewer] are likewise humanized by their benevolent and sentimental identification with him."[54] Lisa Lowe uses the latter words to describe the sentimentality of Aphra Behn's *Oroonoko*, a seventeenth-century work of fiction, but Schafer's project echoes some of these impulses.

Through his photographs, Schafer hopes to intervene in mainstream portrayals of sex workers as either hapless victims with no power or as predatory seductresses. He hopes to show them as fully knowledgeable workers in charge of themselves and their financial well-being. Indeed, several of his photographs show some of the women in their lives beyond sex work with their children or undertaking mundane tasks, such as shopping for clothes, highlighting that sex work, like other forms of labor, is not an all-encompassing identity. These women occupy roles in their daily lives as mothers, daughters, and friends. He respects several of the women's refusal to be photographed "with any frontal nudity with their faces" and even "sent them pictures [he] took, asked for their feedback and they were either pleased or didn't seem to care one way or another."[55]

However, the extent to which some of these images actually portray lives "beyond sex work" remains unclear for two reasons. First, as I have mentioned, sex work does not always entail sex but time together, including time spent on the minutiae of daily life. Second, and crucially, Schafer paid sex workers to take photographs of them, prompting the question of whether or not he is documenting their nonlaboring lives. Schafer recalls that "[i]t took a while for one [woman] in particular to stop posing every time I took the camera out, but after a while I finally achieved that sought after state for photographers of being completely ignored."[56] Without doubting that this state of being ignored is an ideal one for a photographer who seeks to document reality, this statement highlights a crucial dichotomy between sex worker and sex tourist that mimics some of the colonial hierarchies I described above: the former consumable visibility and the latter's omnipresent invisible gaze. It is, of course, the imperial gaze. As a photographer, it is also the desirous male gaze.[57] However much Schafer wants to believe that he is a conscientious consumer, as both photographer and sex tourist he replicates and embodies—through his disembodied lens—the role of first world subject who wants to capture the racialized and feminine third world object. That is, even with what Schafer considers high-minded intentions and armed with a scholarly ethnographic framework with which to dress his wants, Schafer's photographs and narrative evince the deeply entrenched way that colonial restructurings of the world inform certain desires.

What his photographs do show, however, are Dominican women's naked bodies, faceless bodies in seductive underwear, women in distress, women gossiping with each other, enjoying a meal, and so on. Some images show sex workers in various stages of undress in private bedrooms. Some of them sleep. Some are awake. A few are enveloped in shadow and others in sunlight. Another series of photographs show one of the women in utter despair, crying on the floor, and "devastated by the news that her daughter was abducted from her parents' house by her daughter's father."[58] Another one shows the same woman on a bus, looking away from the camera and outside the window, "traveling to retrieve her daughter."[59] The question becomes: What does this image offer the viewer? We see the sex worker naked at work and during what must have been moments of distress. Was the woman who had potentially lost her daughter being paid to be photographed? Was she at work during what must have been a painful ordeal?

With one or two exceptions, all of the images show the women looking away from the camera, busy with other tasks, such as looking at their cell phone. In capturing Dominican sex workers' going about their daily lives, Schafer also achieves precisely what he did not want to: he becomes a voyeur and implicates the viewers of his photographs in this act of voyeurism. Work by scholars such as Malek Alloula, Laura Wexler, and Suzanne Schneider turn their own scholarly gaze onto the (white) photographer in his or her desire to capture some sort of "authentic" Otherness.[60] Their analyses of the desires lurking beneath what are supposed to be objective or benevolent endeavors (or both) uncover photographers' own perversities. They bare (white or imperial) photographers' unquestionable sense of their own full humanity and their complicity in fomenting a discourse of the nonwhite photographed subjects' questionable or lesser humanity. Many nonwhite subjects have frustrated photographers' relentless attempts to photograph "authentic Otherness," however. Overcoming these challenges would then become part of the photographers' pleasure. Alloula writes of the (European) photographer's frustration in the face of Algerian women's various veils:

> Turned back upon himself, upon his own impotence in the situation, the photographer undergoes an *initial experience of disappointment and rejection*. Draped in a veil that cloaks her to her ankles, the Algerian woman discourages the *scopic desire* (the voyeurism) of the photographer. She is the concrete negation of this desire and thus brings to the photographer confirmation of a triple rejection: the rejection of his desire, of the practice of his "art," and of his place in a milieu that is not his own.[61]

While Dominican women do not wear veils, Alloula's words are nonetheless useful when considering Schafer's photographs and his narrative about them because Alloula is describing a colonial relationship that is gendered and racialized. The gazer is a white man from the so-called first world or colonial power and the object of the gaze is a nonwhite woman from the so-called third world or (neo)colony. Suggested by his announcement that he has reached the ultimate goal for photographers of being ignored by the photographed subject is his unveiling of what he sees as the last layer obscuring sex workers' "reality," the last frontier. Schafer's global consumer citizenship allows him to photograph Dominican sex workers at their most intimate, not only in their physical nakedness but also, at times, in their emotional nakedness.

No matter how much he intends to avoid replicating an exploitative relationship between photographer and photographed, first-world and third-world subject, sex worker and client, Schafer's camera replicates the gaze of a mobile subject who has the privilege of remaining disembodied, faceless, and rational. Both Schafer and Pete Brook, *Vantage*'s opinions editor, carefully exclude the sex workers' names in the *Vantage* article, but a visit to Schafer's own website—hyperlinked in the *Vantage* piece—includes several women's first names. Because of Sosúa's smallness, it would be easy to locate the women he photographs. In contrast to the women's hypervisibility, there is no photograph of Schafer on his website or any other readily available website at the time of writing.[62] Implied in this willing invisibility is the sense that Schafer need not be photographed and documented; within a global order deeply shaped by colonialism and Enlightenment ideas of humanity, Schafer provides little to no ethnographic interest.

Schafer's interest in photographing—and then publishing—the emotional pain of a Dominican sex worker must be considered separately from sex workers' own testimonies of lives often filled with painful ordeals. Notwithstanding all the caveats involved in the testimonial genre, the self-told life stories of Dominican former or current sex workers complicate Schafer's images, captions, and essays. In marked contrast to Schafer's narrative, the testimonies in *Rien mis labios . . . llora mi alma*, published by the sex worker rights' organization MODEMU (Movimiento de Mujeres Unidas/Movement of United Women), demonstrate repeatedly that taking on some form of sex work is rarely about "opportunity." Instead, the testimonies are rife with extraordinary physical and psychological violence as perpetrated by family members, partners, acquaintances, clients, and other work associates. The violence is most clearly evident in the accounts of rape and physical abuse, but it also pervades in another form: the violence of having few options. The violence of a child with little to no opportunity to get a formal education. The subtle violence undergirding the lack of options available to many women beyond spheres in which they are particularly vulnerable to sexual harassment, rape, and other forms of abuse, including sex work and housekeeping. And, of course, the violence of being diminished as a "proper" woman in society. These accounts do not victimize these sex workers or former sex workers. On the contrary, they testify to the open-eyed, difficult choice-making necessary to make a living from sex work. However, they are far from the kind of free-trade celebration touted by Schafer. These testimonies describe lives of constant hustling to make ends meet and to acquire some economic stability—and growth—for themselves and their families.

Moreover, the joy and sexuality that many foreign clients consider natural to these "sensual mulatas" and "hot-blooded Latin women" is a perpetual performance that can be not only laborious but also psychologically damaging. Roxana, who had been a sex worker in the Netherlands, returns to the island with what seemed to be the signs of trauma and depression.[63] In the Netherlands, she had been threatened by Dominican pimps, whom she believed could find her back in the Dominican Republic, and often had to perform as a dominant for masochistic clients, an act that she found particularly difficult. Moreover, sex workers in long-term relationships with a client must perform an affection that is rarely felt. Indeed, the introduction to *Rien mis labios . . . llora mi alma* emphasizes that "sex work is our selves, selling our affection, our image, in and outside of our work."[64] Total victimizations of sex workers as having life histories of abuse tend to erase their humanity because they do not account for the stealth negotiations they make. It also does not account for the fact that sex work itself is complicated. On the other hand, some celebrations of sex work tend to the other extreme of ignoring the pernicious inequalities between many sex workers and their clients and the rampant violence to which many of them are vulnerable.

The MODEMU book of testimonies opens with an introduction that explains the organization's stance on the role of sex work and sex workers in Dominican society in both practical and discursive senses. Like the testimonies that follow, the introduction is less optimistic about the idea that sex work can be seen as an avenue for women's socioeconomic growth (the organization focuses on women sex workers). It is not that the organization denies that sex work might provide workers with economic stability. However, unlike Schafer's and other clients' perspectives, the narrative focuses less on the optimistic language of opportunity and more on the sobering realities that sex workers face. The introduction suggests that there is very little room for celebration when sex workers endure the most basic challenges to their human rights. It also insists on the misogyny behind a society that both supports men's desire for sex workers and denigrates sex workers themselves.

This societal misogyny does not preclude women who do not consider themselves sex workers from its pernicious effects. Indeed, the introduction refutes the idea that some women who receive gifts and money from men for sexual and other caretaking labor are sex workers while others are wives, girlfriends, and other more acceptable roles. The writers indict the misogynist (patriarchal) society in which women's bodies have a specific kind of cash value. The ultimate problem is *"alimentar el machismo"* (feeding machismo): "We understand that anyone who exchanges sex for money or object is a sex worker [female] and that women who are having sex for free with more than one partner are also sex workers because that feeds misogyny, which damages us as well as men."[65] Moreover, they argue that "many people believe that sex work is only a woman in a bar or cabaret and they do not realize that they are also part of a web. For example, sleeping with your professor to pass the class or sleeping with an old man so that he pays for your university, that is prostitution. Other women who work in companies prostitute themselves in exchange for their employment."[66] By folding other examples of instances and jobs under the umbrella of sex work, the writers emphasize sex work as part of a social network in which women are almost always in a role of subjugation to patriarchal (sexual) desires. They note that sex work pervades all aspects of Dominican society, including and perhaps especially tourism:

> Another thing is that there are a lot of tourists in this country and the first thing they are presented with is a woman on the beach, very sensual, in a thong. The image of a woman in a thong is used to sell any item in the country, not knowing that it promotes prostitution. Therefore, as soon as the tourist arrives, [he] knows that there are beaches with very pretty women.[67]

Here, the writers argue that generalized hypersexualization of women's bodies within capitalism directly feeds the demand for sex work.

Moreover, by pointing out the various industries that profit from sex workers—the beauty industry, the hotel industry, corrupt governing bodies, and so on—they illuminate the impossibility of considering sex workers separately from the larger social context. Considering the framework uncovered by these MODEMU writers, Schafer's act of rendering himself as invisible as possible from his portrayals of sex workers, as if they exist in a vacuum, emerges as an absurdity and a violence unto itself.

The question of what attracts men like Schafer to visit the Dominican Republic to consume sex became a central concern in the Dominican press. One of the country's most important journalists, Nuria Piera, aired an investigation on the matter.[68] Piera and her producers found an advertisement online for a hotel in Boca Chica, a tourist beach town about thirty minutes away from the international airport in Santo Domingo, offering packages that include time (and presumably sex) with local women. The advertisement includes pictures of the sex workers for potential clients to choose. Upon arrival at the airport, the hotel website advises, customers should walk up to a police officer to get directions to the hotel. Though the Canadian owners of the hotel were not present at the site, Piera and her crew descend on the hotel and confront on camera several of the Dominican men who work there. Piera clarifies that, while prostitution in the country is legal, pimping is illegal, and, as such, the hotel's actions could be prosecuted. Throughout the report, Piera remains alarmed at how advertisements such as these portray the entire country: "The way that the country is portrayed on the website is shocking. It emphasizes that prostitution is not penalized and that this type of vacation is completely legal."[69] Her concern lies with the codification of an entire country as a source of sex, an association with undeniable colonial underpinnings.[70]

Interviews with Julio Llibre, president of the Association of Hotels and Tourism, and Napoleón de la Cruz, director of press for the Ministry of Tourism, reveal similar anxieties. De la Cruz affirms that the nation's official tourism office does not support sex tourism. Llibre offers an insightful perspective on the situation:

Many of the foreigners who visit the Dominican Republic sometimes have expectations regarding Caribbean women that she is an easy woman, that she is a woman who is even more high-spirited than many European women and this means that there is often the attraction to brothels or places where one could easily find [. . .] this kind of contact.[71]

Llibre's comment shines a light on how sex tourists' desires skew visions of an entire country, even region. Their desires prompt them to seek specific experiences and, as such, are self-fulfilling prophecies. A sex tourist who first encounters the Dominican Republic through a webpage advertising a sex tourism package and then vacations accordingly could only have a limited perspective. Nevertheless, several ethnographers' interviews with sex tourists confirm the ease with which many of them conflate the behavior of sex workers—who are being paid precisely to behave a certain way—with the psyche and culture of an entire nation. They report on many sex tourists' belief that "sex is more 'natural' in Third World countries, that prostitution is not really prostitution but a 'way of life,' that 'They' are 'at it' all of the time."[72] As is evident in the epigraph from the *New York Times* review of *Dólares de arena* that opened this chapter, this racist colonial scaffolding of a present-day transnational economy of desire is pervasive.

The question of how information technologies of the late twentieth- and early twenty-first century confirm these ideas and ease the realization of "first world" desires emerges also in Aurora Arias's short story "Novia del Atlántico" (Girlfriend of the Atlantic). Arias is a Dominican writer who rose to critical acclaim in the 1980s with her poetry and short stories. "Novia" was published in a short story collection, *Emoticons* (2007), which explores how Dominican men and women on the island and in the diaspora from all socioeconomic backgrounds face socalled globalization. "Novia" captures the conflicting, but often resolved, desires of Schafer-like foreign men who see themselves as virtuous. "Novia" unravels the inequality between those who can experience the mobile possibilities of globalization and those who cannot.[73] The main character in "Novia" is James Gatto, a foreigner who travels to various Caribbean countries in order to escape the drabness of his life at home, presumably a wealthy North American or European country. Strictly speaking, Gatto is not a tourist, but his foreignness and mobility accords him the descriptor of expat, rather than migrant or exile.

"Novia" follows Gatto as he looks for work as a night manager at a Canadian-owned "adult resort" catering mainly to men from the U.S., Canada, and Europe. Most of the story describes the atmosphere at the resort's bar and the exchanges between the clients and the sex workers both from Gatto's perspective and through the lens of a sarcastic and critical narrator. By the narrative's end, Gatto cannot help but give way to his sexual desire for Jennifer, a young, drugged Dominican sex worker. (Gatto does not drug her.) While Gatto had been compelled to reject her in the first place because, in his view, Jennifer "[i]s just a prostitute. A whore," he ends up having sex with her out of a sense of benevolent moral duty.[74] The last few lines of the story capture this moment where Gatto's ideas about himself in relation to the sex worker become clear: "Jennifer, girlfriend of the Atlantic, victim of underdevelopment, I want to be your hero, I, James Gatto, will save you. Gatto touches her breasts."[75] Men like Schafer and Gatto move in this world carrying a sense that they must enact a "classic 'rescue fantasy' of Western masculinity—one fixated on saving third world women from the excesses of their own cultures," as Rosa Linda Fregoso writes in her discussion of the salacious reporting around the Juárez, Mexico feminicide.[76]

The notion that free trade increases everyone's options, not just those from powerful countries, is contested not only by nation-based immigration policies that curtail certain subjects' mobility but also by the conceptual confinement of employment opportunities within an older colonial order. While ethnographers have documented Dominican women workers benefiting from increased access to information technologies, the unevenness of socioeconomic and geographic mobility within transnational economies of desire is striking. That is, the international communication possibilities that the Internet provides rarely result in material improvements in the form of visas, marriage certificates, and cash. Brennan argues that "it does not matter what consumption possibilities the media depict and how much individuals fantasize about them: living out fantasies means having access to required resources, particularly the right passport. Otherwise, citizenship trumps transnational desires every time."[77] What seems to proponents of the free market to be the fair exchange between two consenting adults is mired in the uneven liberatory potential of this market. According to

Néstor García Canclini, "With the imposition of a neoliberal conception of globalization, according to which rights are necessarily unequal, the novelties of modernity now appear to the majority only as
objects of consumption, and for many as little more than a show to be
watched."[78] Simply put, people are embedded differently within these
transnational economies. Unfettered celebrations of globalization do
not take into account, or perhaps take for granted, that only some people have access to unrestricted geographic mobility. Not all passports
are created equal.

In earlier centuries, a vast proportion of the Dominican population
lived a subsistence lifestyle both apart from and because of these unequal global exchanges. As I discussed in the introduction, this way of
life developed throughout the Dominican territory in great part because
the Spanish crown moved its administrative attention and control to
other colonies. I mention this not to romanticize these earlier moments,
for it was also a time of other great inequalities, injustices, and little to no
socioeconomic mobility, but to point out a simple fact: few, if any, spaces
remain outside of dominant neoliberal paradigms that inform both nationalism and imperialism. When the narrator of "Novia" describes
the scene on the dance floor earlier that night as "money, decadence,
sexual frustration, and impunity on one side; youth, misery, hunger
on the other," we see that little has changed in the differences of power
between colonizer or first world subject and colonized or third world
subject.[79] Sex workers at the adult resort choose their clients, which is
described as a kind of role-play in which the predator sizes up her prey:
"'Damn, papi, you look so good, you hound!' [. . .] Just one full-voiced
yell without fear, conscious of her power."[80] Yet, "Novia" also seems to
ask, how much agency do these women have if the main reason that they
are led to sex work is the lack of options for poor Dominicans who lack
substantial formal education? Dominicans, like subjects from other nations constrained by and bound to unequal free trade agreements, must
enter and move through the neoliberal paradigm if they hope to thrive.
We may consider the language of "escaping the grid" that undergirds the
movement of usually white subjects from wealthy nations to third-world
spaces. In traveling to places like the Dominican Republic, subjects like
Gatto seek a reprieve from the fast-paced lifestyle expected of successful citizen-subjects in wealthy nations. Their foreign (more powerful)

citizenship, relatively higher purchasing power, and quite often their whiteness allow them to move unencumbered through these usually tropical climes in great contrast with the working-class Dominicans who have to hustle and who, if they are enjoying a slow pace, do so due to lack of work.

In this manner, globalization in "Novia" emerges as a gap between global access to the mass media portrayals of imagined transnational possibilities and real material access to these possibilities. Arjun Appadurai remarks that, in great part because of the mass media, "[m]ost persons in more parts of the world consider a wider set of possible lives than they ever did before,"[81] which he sees as an opportunity for the world's poor to become aware of "the ironic compromise between what they could imagine and what social life will permit."[82] "Novia" reveals the differences in access to transnational possibilities between the clients and the sex workers. At the bar, while Myriam Hernández's popular love song "El hombre que yo amo" (The Man That I Love) is playing, one of the sex workers "sitting at the bar smokes, drinks, and sings, watching, teary-eyed, a soap opera on the TV placed behind the bartenders."[83] Since the Latin American *telenovelas* broadcast in the Dominican Republic often focus on a Cinderella-like figure whose beauty and benevolence allow her to win the heart of a wealthy man and thus to escape poverty, we can deduce that the tearful telenovela viewer is able to contrast her situation with the one on the screen while also mentally escaping her immediate surroundings. In her case, transnational "mediascapes," to borrow Appadurai's term, allow her to imagine a world different from her own, while also providing her with the imaginative possibility of escaping or improving her socioeconomic conditions. After all, sometimes the clients "fall in love and take some of these unhappy women to live with them in their countries."[84] However, for the majority of them, this is not the case, nor is it without its risks, as I show later in this chapter.

The narrative voice in "Novia" estranges the reader both from a taken-for-granted ideology of globalization and from the brothel space as normalized in Latin American literature.[85] Sex workers' imagined goals contrast with their clients' interactions with new media. The story alludes to an Internet-based "message board of the World Sex Archives," on which former clients post information about the best places in the world to find cheap sex labor. They also post pictures in which one may see a

> little Dominican girl with illiteracy and malnutrition written on her face with my penis in her mouth and her eyes vacant from taking so much cocaine, how pretty she is and how much she enjoys what she does. Look for her, she's easy to find on the web, look at her face, hers; not mine, which I erased to prevent being recognized, in case the girl is a minor.[86]

This detailed description encapsulates the difference of power between the Dominican sex worker, who may or may not be underage, and a man who is able to blur his own face and who can choose his level of participation with ease. He has the power to protect himself from social and legal repercussions, while she is probably unaware that her face and body are available for the world to see on the Internet. The sheer violence of posting this picture online, not to mention his part in the exchange, undermines significantly the cheerful declarations of a transnational world community connected through faster modes of communication and mass media. In the case of the potential and former clients who visit the online World Sex Archives, the possibilities of going to a *paraíso de carne* (meat paradise) are very real, as the example of Peter Schafer proves.[87] In "Novia," transnational information networks function very differently for the sex worker watching the telenovela than for those posting and researching on the website. For the latter, mediascapes enable the realization of fantasies, while for the former, they serve as a reminder of the gap between the haves and the have-nots or, at best, as fueling a dream of escape or political action. Schafer's celebration of his sexual/artistic transactions with Dominican sex workers does not take this gap into account. Without overlooking or diminishing the negotiations and self-determining decisions that sex workers make, I seek rather to emphasize the frames that delineate these encounters.

Dominican Women and Economies of Desire in Spain

Dominican women's active engagements within a transnational economy of desire and as migrants emerge more centrally in the Spanish films *Princesas* (Princesses, 2005) by Fernando León de Aranoa and

Flores de otro mundo (Flowers from Another World, 1999) by Icíar Bol-laín. Despite their important differences, both of these films capture the "enormous gender difference among Dominican transmigrants in Spain, with women representing the immense majority of the migrant population."[88] Indeed, "[i]n the early years of migration to Spain, over 85% of the migrants were women, three-quarters of which worked in domestic service. The Dominican migration chain to Spain was initiated by women who migrated independently as economic providers. Family reunification later increased the absolute number and relative prevalence of Dominican men."[89] This stands in marked contrast with Dominican migrations to the U.S. and other places in which both men and women migrate in fairly even numbers.[90] According to several surveys cited by Domingo Lilón and Juleyka J. Lantigua, "The majority of Dominicans in Spain come from rural areas of the Dominican Republic and have a very low educational level, which also explains why most of them are employed in domestic services."[91] I would add that an advanced educa-tion has little value when the educated immigrant is undocumented. The lack of legal documentation in many of these cases (at least at first) further restricts Dominican women to domestic and sex work.[92] In order to migrate to Spain, many Dominican migrants are required to sell their land or homes to pay the high fees "demanded by the networks of smugglers."[93] That, in addition to the fear of deportation, is a hurdle that many of these migrants have to endure before looking for work in Spain.[94] Hence, in many, if not most, of these cases, these women and their families undergo great personal and economic sacrifices and risks in order to improve their standards of living, access to education, and, in these senses, enfranchisement as global citizens who are able to partake in at least some of the benefits of the transnational economy.

Princesas focuses on two sex workers in Madrid: Cayetana, the *madrileña* (inhabitant of Madrid) with a middle-class background who is trying to save enough money to get a breast augmentation, and Zulema, a Dominican immigrant sending money to support her son back in the Dominican Republic. Other Spanish sex workers accuse Zulema and other immigrant sex workers of stealing their clientele by selling services at lower prices. While Cayetana struggles with the split between her middle-class upbringing and her current job, Zulema must sur-vive the physical abuse of a man who has promised her the documents necessary to become a legal resident in Spain. After Cayetana learns of Zulema's plight, the two become friends. Zulema's status as an undocumented immigrant renders her more vulnerable to the whims of a sadistic client who continually promises to get her legal documents but who, instead, physically tortures her. She is also more vulnerable to the whims of clients who do not want to use condoms. In the end, Zulema never receives the promised documentation, and instead finds out that she is HIV-positive. She decides to return to her family in the Dominican Republic. Knowing of her plans to return to her homeland, Cayetana gifts Zulema the savings originally meant for her cosmetic surgery.

Princesas criticizes overtly racist stereotypes of "hypersexual" Dominican women and other racialized women by justifying the noble, maternal reasons behind a Dominican woman's need to work abroad, far from her child. In some ways, however, the film also perpetuates some of the same neoliberal emphasis on self-determination and freedom of choice in which people in dire circumstances must rely on individual acts of kindness. Added to this is the film's expulsion of Zulema from the Spanish national body, a rejection of the immigrant body, as I discuss below. Cayetana's kind gesture both signals Cayetana's transgression of the racist stereotypes that had previously prevented the possibility of this friendship and emphasizes the dichotomy of the helpless third world woman and the economically empowered first world woman. The dichotomy is subtle only because the two women are sex workers, but it is clear from the film's portrayal of Cayetana's middle-class background that their economic and cultural distance is considerable. As in "Novia," the socioeconomic and ethnic difference between the two women translates into their unequal access to the products of globalization and dictates how each woman negotiates her surroundings. For instance, while Cayetana wants to save money for elective cosmetic surgery, Zulema's income goes toward helping to support her family in the Dominican Republic.

Zulema leaves Spain not only because she misses her son, but also because she is HIV-positive. Though the narrative is entirely plausible, it is worth asking why the film must end in this way. Zulema's HIV-positive status and the desire to be with her son are the main determining factors in her decision to leave Spain. The narrative choice to push Zulema out of Spain intimates a need to expel the foreign, racialized, and contaminated body. Subtly, the film acts as a morality tale in which a foreign woman becomes infected with HIV, presumably in one of the many exploitative encounters with clients, and at least one Spanish man exposes himself to the virus by forcing Zulema to have sex with him without a condom. What kind of movie would *Princesas* be if it had been Cayetana who had been HIV-positive, if Zulema had gotten her legal resident status, brought her son to Spain, and stayed to help her Spanish friend? After all, Dominicans in Spain are more likely than any other non-E.U. migrants to stay in Spain and become naturalized.[95] The decision to close the narrative in this manner showcases both the film's actual ambivalence toward the kind of lasting and meaningful transnational/transethnic alliance at its center, as well as its sobering acknowledgement that the neoliberal parameters proscribing their possibilities cannot be eradicated through a strong friendship.

Unlike the alliance between the two sex workers, the patriarchal values espoused by a Dominican immigrant family blind them to the possibility of an alliance with Zulema based on a shared plight. In order to save money, Zulema shares an apartment with a Dominican family in shifts, with Zulema having access to it during the day. Though she tries to leave as soon as the family arrives, she takes a bit longer than usual to gather her things on one occasion. As she gets ready to leave, the couple complains about Zulema's presence in hushed tones, and the husband then confronts Zulema:

> Husband: My wife wants me to let you know to please change the bed sheets after you sleep on them.
> Zulema: Why doesn't she change them herself?
> Husband: Because she's not the one who fucks ten men each day. She also wants me to let you know to be out of the house before eight o'clock. It's because of our son, we don't want him to see you.[96]

While the wife had been most upset, it is the husband who communicates their request to Zulema by repeatedly mentioning that he was sent ("le manda decir") by his wife, conveying that he is only the messenger. In this manner, the proper Dominican wife and mother avoids contact with the indecent "fallen" woman. This exchange evinces what Carlos Decena, Michelle Shedlin, and Angela Martinez consider a "hierarchy of femininities that rewards sexual conservatism and that punishes sexual assertiveness and consumption."[97] The couple's primary concerns are to maintain the familial purity of the domestic space and prohibit their young son from exposure to what they deem to be the sex worker's immoral lifestyle.

The couple's chastisement shows that they consider Zulema's presence to be a form of contamination: both figuratively through her visibility in front of their son and materially through her body's "dirt" sullying the legitimate couple's sheets. The space inhabited part-time by a woman who so threatens patriarchal values must be purged of its contamination in order for the nuclear family to feel at home. Discussing women in the Latin American national imaginary, Mary Louise Pratt argues that "[i]n the face of their exclusion from the national fraternity [. . .] women's political and social engagement became heavily internationalist, and often antinationalist."[98] In the MODEMU book of sex worker testimonials, Roxana recalls defending a Colombian woman against the violence of a Dominican man. He threatens Roxana, arguing that because they were both Dominican, she had to be on his side. She refuted his logic, contending that her "family was everyone who was by her side, whether they be Dominican, Colombian or from whatever country, and if what he had done was wrong."[99] Similarly, the transnational alliance—however short-lived—between Zulema and Cayetana is more viable than one based on a shared national, ethnic, and class status between Zulema and the Dominican family.

Another Spanish film, *Flores de otro mundo*, explores intra-Caribbean and Caribbean-Spanish friendship between women both constrained and empowered by their socioeconomic circumstances and citizenship status. While this film portrays Spanish women's animosity toward nonwhite Caribbean women that precludes any transnational feminist solidarity, it also emphasizes the intra-Caribbean friendships among immigrant women that help them overcome strife. It centers on two women, Patricia, a nonwhite Dominican woman who travels from Madrid with her two young children, and Marirrosi, a professional and divorcée from Bilbao who "represents the new, prosperous Spain."[100] An ad placed by the town's single men looking for serious romantic relationships attracted the women to a small rural Spanish town. The film also develops the story of a third woman, Afro-Cuban Milady, who arrives in the village with her much older Spanish boyfriend, a native of the town. Beyond dealing with the culture shock of living in the Spanish country-side with a quiet, if smitten, man and a hateful mother-in-law, Patricia has the added pressure of fending off her abusive and violent Domini-can ex-husband, who blackmails her into giving him more money if she does not want her Spanish partner to learn of his existence. The two nonwhite Caribbean women seek legal resident status in Spain. Their arrival into this rural town prompts various reactions from the towns-folk, ranging from a hypersexualizing admiration from some of the men to outright indignation from some of the women, who do not treat the Spanish Marirrosi in the same way. Though these women's actions could not be described as sex work proper, the presence of Caribbean women, especially from the Dominican Republic and Cuba, conjures images of caretaking through sex or domesticity, or both. It is telling that Marir-rosi is a professional "career woman," while the two *caribeñas* are either hypersexualized (in the case of Cuban Milady) or domestic and mater-nal (in the case of Dominican Patricia).

Unlike the unfriendliness of the other Dominican immigrants in *Princesas*, *Flores de otro mundo* pauses on how Patricia's and Milady's survival in a hostile environment requires female friendship among Ca-ribbean women. Patricia helps a younger Milady, especially when the latter's Spanish boyfriend beats her. Furthermore, Patricia's Domini-can friends visit her from Madrid and they liven up Patricia's gener-ally dreary life. They also make Patricia realize that she does not need to accept her mother-in-law's likely racist rudeness. The last scene in *Flores de otro mundo* pans over the faces of the village's young children welcoming the following year's busload of single women. Among these faces are those of Patricia's children. This comprises a significant dif-ference from *Princesas*, in which the narrative ends with Zulema's de-parture from Spain. This difference, I argue, stems from the women's different places within a larger transnational economy of desire. While the Dominican Patricia in *Flores de otro mundo* is always hard at work in the field and caretaking her husband and children, Dominican Zulema in *Princesas* is first and foremost a sex worker. Despite her son's central-ity as the motivating factor behind Zulema's decision to migrate and to become a sex worker, the film does not develop this relationship on screen, prioritizing instead Zulema's travails in relation to her job.

The narrative in *Flores de otro mundo* may embrace Patricia, but it also banishes Cuban Milady. Her relationship with her partner had started when the latter traveled to Cuba, and the yawning gaps in age, as well as her disinterest in him as a sexual or romantic partner, points toward the possibility that he had gone to Cuba as a sex tourist. Unlike Patricia, whose maternal and caretaking abilities embed her in a local Spanish family and weave her into the fabric of the small community, Milady is a very young, stylish, and lively woman unhappy with the slow pace of life in the village. Her attention-grabbing and revealing outfits not only attract the village men's (racist) sexual attention and invite the ire of envious Spanish women but they are also a reminder of the extent to which she does not fit in to her new environment. In addition, she is shown to carry on a relationship with a Cuban boyfriend back home and to endure the physical abuse of her Spanish boyfriend. Milady cannot and does not become part of this Spanish community and in that sense her story resembles Zulema's in *Princesas*.

The differences between the situations of Cuban Milady and Dominican Patricia prompt uncomfortable questions about what comprises a "real" relationship that cannot be categorized within the realm of sex work. It is difficult to sift out what makes these kinds of relationships different from other relationships not ruled by passion, which is a recent phenomenon in the history of marriage.[101] As Kempadoo writes about the Caribbean, "Sexuality has multiple meanings in such contexts, not all of which have to do with a reciprocity of sexual desire or feelings of love. [. . .] Sex, love, and desire thus emerge in Caribbean accounts as variable in meanings and value, some of which coincide with and reproduce hegemonic heterosexual regimes, and others offering a counterhegemonic interpretation."[102] The wide gaps between Milady and her boyfriend, as well as her passionate investment in a Cuban boyfriend back home, point toward the probability that her relationship with her much older Spanish boyfriend is unrelated to "love" and is more a transaction between two people who have practical desires. However, it would be quite difficult to call Milady a sex worker in the same way that Zulema in *Princesas* conforms to the standard definition. In Patricia's case, the issue becomes grayer, for, while she and her boyfriend seem to be mutually attracted to each other and resemble each other in age and in other ways, we also know that this relationship is practical for Patricia.

Its practicality and advantages push her to work through the many negative aspects of her life in the countryside. She needs documents to legalize her and her children's status in Spain and to secure a better future for
all of them. In this manner, these two Spanish films ponder the possibility of folding Dominican women into the national fabric. Together, the
message they broadcast is that showcasing too obviously their emplacement along the continuum of a transnational economy of desire renders
them "surplus," to borrow from Roderick Ferguson, or inassimilable
to the national body.[103] Dominican (and nonwhite Caribbean women
more broadly) can be imagined within the Spanish national fabric only
through an embrace of respectable heterosexual coupling and a traditional family structure.

The Colonial Imaginary in a Dominican Film

In the summer of 2015, I attended the Maryland screening of the critically acclaimed film *Dólares de arena* (Sand Dollars), which opened
that year's American Film Institute Latin American Film Festival.
Directed by Dominican director Laura Amelia Guzmán and her husband, Mexican director Israel Cárdenas, the film loosely adapts French
writer Jean-Noël Pancrazi's novel *Les dollars des sables* (2007). By then,
the film had been chosen to represent the Dominican Republic for the
2016 Academy Awards. The film stars Geraldine Chaplin, daughter of
the iconic silent film star, and Yanet Céspedes, a young Afro-Dominican
woman with no previous acting experience. Chaplin plays Anne, a white
European woman in her sixties or seventies who falls in love with the
much younger Noelí, played by Céspedes. The film is set in Las Terrenas,
a touristic town with a long-term presence of European immigrants and
tourists. Though there are sex workers and sex tourists, the town cannot
be described as a "sexscape," as Brennan, borrowing from Appadurai,
describes Sosúa. During the Q&A with Guzmán after the film, the director recalled how she and Chaplin—who had enthusiastically joined the
cast as soon as she had heard of the project—found Céspedes. Auditions
had failed to produce someone who had the right chemistry with Chaplin. In Guzmán's recollection, she and Chaplin went to a local club and
spotted Céspedes on the dance floor. She remembers that something
about her dancing provoked the director and famed actress to approach

Céspedes to teach them how to dance *bachata*. They asked Céspedes if she could audition for the film the next day, ultimately leading to her casting. Céspedes's talent seems to belong to a more seasoned actress and I was as surprised as other audience members upon learning that this had been her first acting role.

A film such as *Dólares de arena* complicates several of the binaries evident in the transnational economies of desire developed in the other narratives I analyze in this chapter. At the most obvious level, the film portrays a same-sex relationship between two women. Nevertheless, the relationship between a wealthy, older white woman and a poor, younger black woman evinces some of the same inequalities in age, wealth, mobility, race, social milieu, and desire in other portrayals. If Noelí, the young woman, has any power, it rests entirely on the extent of Anne's attraction to her. While Noelí has the power to ignore Anne's phone calls, causing the latter great distress, Anne has the power to acquire a passport and a visa for Noelí. This passport and visa would give Noelí the geographic mobility and the *potential* to change her future, as well as the future of her unborn child. However, the film shows that life for Dominicans like Noelí and her boyfriend is governed more by precarity than by possibility. Unlike them, Anne's experience of mobility allows her to say to a fellow white guest at her hotel that she foresees that Noelí will be unhappy in France. At the end of the film, Noelí leaves Anne, stealing the latter's cash and credit card. However, we have seen enough in the film to know that Anne will be fine, at least financially. Unlike the overt political stakes of Schafer's photo essay (i.e., to support sex work legalization worldwide), Arias's implied critique (i.e., the inequality in access in globalization), and the two Spanish films' ambivalent political messages about the place of Dominican migrants in Spain, Sánchez outright rejects the idea that her film might contain a political message. Asked by an audience member about the film's potential message, Sánchez responded that she does not make films with a political agenda.[104] It is true that the film arguably does not judge Anne's and Noelí's relationship, either way. Nevertheless, it portrays the marked inequality in socioeconomic and geographic mobility between Anne and Noelí.

The film depicts both women's complex desires through its nuanced narrative and filmic choices. Despite her clear socioeconomic disadvantage and her limited geographic mobility, Noelí is stealthy, intelligent, and charming, all resources she uses constantly in her daily life and especially in her relationship with Anne. The film develops the two women's parallel, at times intersecting, desires. In an early scene, Anne surprises Noelí with a new phone. While Noelí plays with her new gadget, she deftly evades Anne's questions regarding Noelí's life outside of her time with Anne. She is especially curious about Noelí's latest reason for needing money: a fictional brother's motorcycle accident. The evasion evident in this scene parallels a later scene when Noelí asks Anne for an update on the visa and flight information. Like Noelí had done before, Anne evades Noelí's questions and requests. Perpetually heartbroken by Noelí's absences, Anne seems to enjoy the power she has in those moments. Moreover, despite what she calls her love of Noelí, Anne is unsure whether or not she actually wants to bring Noelí to Europe, a situation that mimics the hesitation of many sex tourists that Brennan and other scholars describe.

As is the case for many European tourists and so-called expatriates, Anne does not want to return to Europe. For her, the town of Las Terrenas represents paradise. Some of the social interactions that Anne has among her wealthy, white peers—members of a transnational cosmopolitan elite—take place at a luxury hotel. Called the Peninsula House, the hotel is "a two-story plantation house with Victorian gables and wraparound veranda."[105] (See Figure 5.1.) The dream project of a "French proprietor [. . .] and her American partner," it is decorated with "antiques

Figure 5.1. Promotional photograph of the Peninsula House from the hotel's website.

and artifacts from a lifetime's collecting by [the French owner]."[106] The plantation and Victorian styles evident in the house's architecture are rare in the Dominican Republic.[107] Like the economies of desire I have been describing throughout this chapter, the Peninsula House conforms to a colonialist imaginary that has little to do with Dominicanness. Rather, it conforms to a trope of the Caribbean as the site of idyllic plantations where nonwhite subjects serve the desires of a white clientele. The hotel instantiates the process of what Krista Thompson calls "tropicalization," which describes "the complex visual systems through which the islands were imaged for tourist consumption and [. . . which] delineates how certain ideals and expectations of the tropics informed the creation of place-images in some Anglophone Caribbean islands."[108] While she focuses on Jamaica and the Bahamas, the Peninsula House models itself precisely on this idea of the Caribbean and "the tropics." Indeed, the hotel's website evokes the language of tropicalization, promising potential guests the experience of "[c]asual elegance at home in the tropics . . ." The ellipses here evoke the Caribbean languor that guests can expect to enjoy. The word "tropics" adds to this allure and conforms to a plantation imaginary; Dominicans, even those in the elite, would have no need to use such a word. The word holds weight within a denationalized, ahistorical sense of a place where comfort and luxury involve fantasies of colonialism. This place could be anywhere in the Caribbean. Within this transnational, neocolonial imaginary, national specificity has little value. That is, the hotel provides a global demand for a colonial fantasy accommodated to the neoliberal era. This is not only a problem of so-called authenticity, but also, as Thompson argues after novelist Edgar Mittelholzer, that "[e]xplicit in tourists' insistent quests for tropicalisms, their unrelenting eye for the tropics [. . .] was a refusal to see the islands as intrinsically a part of the modern world."[109] We have been privy to the violence with which Western entities, from humanitarian initiatives to outright military occupations, respond in the face of what they consider premodern or antimodern.

The economic and other details of the Peninsula House and Anne's more modest, but still luxurious, oceanfront residence illustrate some of the colonial underpinnings of present-day inequalities I have been outlining throughout this chapter. The scenes at the two hotels portray plantation-style service, common at other high-end tourist sites across the island, in which dark-skinned servants and musical talent serve foreign tourists and a light-skinned Dominican elite. Moreover, at the Peninsula House rooms start at over US$550 per night (excluding 28 percent taxes) as of April 2017; staying for even a few days is unimaginably beyond reach for most of the world's population and certainly for most of the Dominicans and Haitians working in Las Terrenas.

Dólares de arena inadvertently asks which women have access to what things. As of this writing, Céspedes has played two roles and both of them are as women operating in domestic and caretaking economies.[110] With her dark brown skin and Afro hairstyle, there is little room for Céspedes within mainstream Dominican television and media, which continues to prefer white Dominican beauty. Unlike these spaces, darker skinned women donning their natural curls have dominated high-fashion runways outside of the Dominican Republic in the last decade, some of them reaching international fame. A brown-skinned, curly haired Dominican woman, Denny Méndez, won Miss Italy almost two decades before Yaritza Reyes, another Afro-Dominican woman wearing her hair in its natural curls, won Miss Dominican Republic in 2013. These examples show the differences in how Dominican women's bodies are valued in a national space versus an international space.[111] That is, conservative Dominican nationalist paradigms remain invested in whiteness while foreign economic markets, including in the creative fashion and film industries, expect and pay for "Caribbean" blackness. Even more striking within the context of this book is the extent to which *Dólares de arena* bridges the distance between earlier examples of Dominican cultural texts and a foreign colonial imaginary that did not apply to the Dominican context. Though the film adapted a French novel that featured the same-sex relationship between an older white foreign man and a Dominican man, the film maintains its grounding in a colonial imaginary. That is, it is a Dominican text that bears all the traces of a global neoliberal paradigm rooted in colonial desires. Like the Peninsula House, the film could be based in any languorous tropical space.

Women Create at the Border

Lorena Duran's short documentary *Fronterizas* (Borderwomen, 2015) is an apt way to close a chapter about working-class women's enterprising

labor in the neoliberal era. The film portrays the activism and entrepreneurship of the Dominican and Haitian Border Network of Women
Artisans.[112] These artisans overcome mutual stereotypes to create and
benefit from a transnational collaborative effort that subverts the notion
that "citizens of Haiti and the Dominican Republic are consumed with
animosity toward their island neighbor."[113] Unable to cross the border
to meet in each other's towns, the women meet at the staircase of the
customs house at the border. Through the sale of their artisan products,
which "recycle and take advantage of the resources provided to them by
nature and their environment," and the mutual aid society it hosts, the
women secure a form of self-sufficiency.[114]

While the title describes directly the women's residence in several
towns of the northern region on both sides of the border, the title has two
subtler meanings. It conveys the women's border/marginal/peripheral
status as nonwhite, working-class women living far from centers of
national and international economies and power. And, it also signals that
as "border" subjects who had to create an expressive and entrepreneurial
space beyond nation-state and global economies, these artisans comprise
an avant garde—a frontier—of supranational belonging, cultural expression, and entrepreneurship among nonwhite women of this island.

Durán's documentary celebrates the Network as an entity that subverts
ideological, practical, and political impediments to the artisans' and other
border subjects' community formation and socioeconomic subsistence
and success.[115] However, as with some of the other acts of self-subsistence
and entrepreneurship explored in this chapter, I am left with the sense that
the need for the Network signals the depth of the failure of neoliberal policies. Within this world order of things, conscientious consumer-citizens
can purchase items produced by artisans in the Network—while avoiding
goods from free-trade-zone companies—and believe that all is right in
the world. But of what use is the current order in which the neoliberal
nation-state both seeks to survey all of its citizens with a totalizing gaze
but cannot provide the basic resources (e.g., housing, schooling, medical
care, and so on) necessary for their thriving within it?

* * *

In this chapter, I enumerated the limits of nonwhite Dominican wom-
en's engagements with, and manipulations of, an uneven transnational

economy. I question the optimism behind individual and business phi-lanthropy that takes for granted the larger world order, assuming equal access to global citizenship acquired and consolidated through con-sumer choices. I analyzed the contours of a transnational economy of desire—a slice of what Ehrenreich and Hochschild term the "caretak-ing" economy—from the perspective of the consumer-citizen and the caretaking laborer as evident in various cultural texts. Analyses of these texts, produced in the Dominican Republic, the U.S., and Spain, unearth the deep colonial roots of purportedly modern global paradigms. As I argued in earlier chapters, autonomous, anonymous black and mixed-race Dominican subjectivity developed both alongside and outside the Plantation. It was the Plantation—as a system and logic—that shaped much of what we consider to be coterminous with a dominant gene-alogy of colonialism. This monte reality, and nationalists' attempts to erase it, emerges in the ghosts that populate the very heart of Domini-can nationalism. Despite the determining influence of el monte, which renders the Dominican case unique among other former colonies in the Americas, my analyses in this chapter showed that the consolida-tion of the Dominican nation-state, U.S. imperialism, and transnational neoliberal policies have absorbed Dominican subjects into a dominant genealogy of colonialism rooted in the Plantation.

Conclusion

Searching for Monte Refusals

The population of Puerto Plata is variously estimated at from two to three thousand inhabitants, mostly "people of colour"; which may mean jet-black African, mulatto, or not pure white. This name, however, is never bestowed on a Dominican if possible, as they are very "touchy" on this subject, all being equally citizens.
—Samuel Hazard, *Santo Domingo: Past and Present, with a Glance at Hayti* (1873)

Ghosts point to places where denied, erased, or unresolved state violence has occurred.
—Anne McClintock, "Imperial Ghosting and National Tragedy" (2014)

Colonial Phantoms argued that Dominican cultural texts evince the ghosted singularities of this territory's history and demographic composition.[1] As is common to the culture and literature of other former colonies, Dominican cultural expressions are full of spirits, specters, graveyards, ruins, and other signs of hauntings. I showed how the Dominican Republic, which so well evokes various rehearsals of nationalist, colonial, and imperial power in the hemisphere, would come to be almost entirely ignored, misunderstood, or outright silenced by a host of cultural producers and policymakers. What kind of national culture do you create when leaders of the world powers, on whose recognition you depend, rarely remember your nation's name or keep confusing you with Haiti, a nation they fear and hate?

Several chapters, especially chapters one and two, offered responses to this question by focusing on the consolidation of a nationalist literature

and culture in the late nineteenth and early twentieth century. Dominican lettered nationalists forestalled full confrontations with being denied a seat at the global table by mythologizing Columbus and the early
colonial past, as well as by consecrating the ideal of a white male patriot. These efforts, however, did not entirely erase this society's "strange"
demographic composition and history, as evident in the ambivalences
and contradictions with which Dominican nationalism is rife. Chapters
three, four, and five turned to cultural expressions by and about Dominicans who were excluded from these nationalist ideals. In what ways have
these marginalized Dominicans—the vast majority of the population—
expressed their own national, transnational, and supranational forms
of belonging? I explored not only Dominicans' attempts to belong to
various national and supranational communities but also their refusals
to adhere to categories and interpellations that they do not believe to be
accurate. In their attempts to resist various local, nationalist, and imperialist powers, they have also narrated new models of belonging. While
some of these sketches were recorded for posterity, most were ephemeral
and in other ways lost to time.

The colonial, imperial, and nationalist gaze has been central to this
book from its first lines. How do subjects with more power perceive and
then shape the world? I addressed this question especially in relation to
what constitutes blackness and whiteness (and, to a lesser extent, indigeneity) in the Dominican context. As I have shown, non-Dominicans
have often interpreted Dominican perspectives on race—elite and
nonelite—as peculiar. This marker of difference was as salient in late
nineteenth-century writings of U.S. subjects traveling to the country as
they are for diasporic Dominicans currently living in the U.S. We may
consider Samuel Hazard's descriptions of Dominicans' "touchiness"
at being described as people of color, as cited in the epigraph. I interpret nonwhite Dominicans' emphasis on their status as citizens, rather
than as nonwhite subjects, as loaded reactions to the gaze of a white
U.S. government representative. (Hazard was part of a commission organized by President Ulysses S. Grant to consider the annexation of the
Dominican Republic.) These responses are heavy with the weight of a
history of black citizenship and governance on an island that had been
surrounded by hostile slaveholding colonies for dozens of years. Hazard's gaze is neither innocent nor impartial, and the refusals it occasions

from these Dominicans must be interpreted with a full consideration of its power. Perhaps they are also aware that in the U.S., subjects "of color" were rarely considered full citizens. The issue of how Dominicans approach their or what is perceived to be their blackness persists in the present day. For instance, diasporic Dominicans who deny their blackness or who insist on mixed-race categories are often asked "would a cop consider you black?" Though more covertly in Hazard's case, in both examples the surveillance and policing of a white supremacist state determine blackness.

The level of surveillance (or hypervisibility) of Afro-descendent subjects shifts not only depending on the situational context but also on the historical and social context of a region or country. As I have argued throughout this book, the historical and social context of the Dominican Republic differs markedly not only from the U.S. but even from some of its Caribbean neighbors in that it had a majority free black and mixed-race population for centuries. Strategies of what Simone Browne calls "dark sousveillance" or "undersight," which "situate the tactics employed to render one's self out of sight, and strategies used in the flight to freedom from slavery as necessarily ones of undersight," also differ depending on the context.[2] Browne "plot[s] dark sousveillance as an imaginative place from which to mobilize a critique of racializing surveillance, a critique that takes form in antisurveillance, countersurveillance, and other freedom practices."[3] In her reading of Frantz Fanon, Sylvia Wynter proposes that the "experience of being black" is shaped fundamentally (even at the cognitive level) by being seen and recognized as an inferior Other. Wynter writes, "So total is this that he [Fanon; the black man] is compelled to see himself as he is seen by those 'white' eyes, which are the only 'real' eyes because they are the only 'normal' eyes.'"[4] Writing about black life under U.S. Plantation society, Browne contends that the "cumulative white gaze [. . .] functioned as a totalizing surveillance" and the "violence of this cumulative gaze continues in the postslavery era."[5] Browne continues that "[u]nder these conditions of terror and the violent regulation of blackness by way of surveillance, the inequities between those who were watched over and those who did the watching are revealed."[6] If we agree with Browne's contention that the totalizing white gaze of the U.S. Plantation endures today, then what do we make of Dominicans and Dominican society, in which the white gaze was severely curtailed by the colonial neglect and in which free black subjects lived, quite literally, beyond colonial (white) purview and sight?

Chapter five ended with the sobering realization that the U.S.-led restructuring of the hemispheric economy, which reached its height with the transnational and unequal neoliberal policies of the late twentieth- and early twenty-first centuries, left few spaces for subaltern subjects to escape or refuse quantification and surveillance. When I refer to subaltern subjects, I mean not only subjects excluded from the nation-state, but also those who have little to benefit from being legible by the state. Their racialized, nonideally gendered, queer, or in other ways nonnormative bodies and cultural practices render them vulnerable to the violence of—rather than safeguarded by—the set of institutions, laws, and ideals comprising the nation-state. When being legible to the nation-state is more dangerous than protective, what discursive and performative spaces of illegibility—of refusal—remain?

While this book has been concerned with how Dominican subjects have negotiated being ghosted from various Western imaginaries, I want to consider the power of *not* being legible and *not* being recorded for posterity. As I argued in the introduction, it was precisely monte subjects' anonymity and autonomy (away from the colonial centers of power) that worried colonial and national governments for centuries, arguably until the Trujillo dictatorship of 1930–1961. We must remain cognizant of the variants of being seen, legible, heard, and recorded. Being recognized as a full human and as a citizen-subject with full rights is not the same as, but is on a continuum with, being surveilled and quantified.

Let us consider two cultural texts that prompt the following questions. Who holds the power to evade (photographic and ethnographic) capture? Who evades this gaze because they are not ethnographically "interesting"—that is, they represent "normative" humanity as defined by Enlightenment thought—versus who tries to evade this gaze through what Simone Browne terms "dark sousveillance" or the "tactics employed to render one's self out of sight"?[7] And, finally, what are the crucial differences between rendering visible in order to empower otherwise subaltern subjects and rendering visible for personal pleasure, edification, or possession? Peter Schaefer's photographic portrayals of Dominican sex workers as discussed in chapter five, for instance, stand in stark contrast to MODEMU's book of sex worker testimonials. Ruling elites have been most able to record and disseminate their ideas of how to be in the world, but this is not the equivalent of subaltern subjects' appearing in official or elite records in ways that have little to do with their own agency. Subaltern subjects have often been recorded for posterity precisely at the moment of their punishment or subjugation in the pages of government documents as well as in "scientific," ethnographic, and travel accounts as imbricated with colonial and imperial projects. This is why those of us interested in understanding the lives of nonelite, nonwhite subjects from earlier centuries have to sift through this deeply unjust archive, hoping that we are reading "against the grain."

Yanet Mojica, one of the protagonists of *Sand Dollars* as discussed in chapter five, also stars in the short film *De Djess* as a beautiful, childlike maid in a mysterious hotel/nunnery.[8] Italian director Alice Rohrwacher created this surreal short film for designer clothing brand Miu Miu as part of an initiative called Women's Tales. This initiative allowed several world-renowned female directors to showcase their talents. Toward the end of *De Djess*, a Miu Miu dress magically runs away from its owner—a white diva character—and embraces Mojica's body, as if the sentient dress had refused the original (white) body to which it had been assigned. The dress enfolds Mojica, covering her bare breasts—the only moment of nudity in the film. Her blackness contrasts with the rest of the white cast, especially since the other women modeling the Miu Miu outfits don cartoonish platinum blond wigs. Wearing the lipstick she finds in the diva's dressing room, as well as the glittering gown that had enveloped her, Mojica's character greets a slew of paparazzi. However, their cameras lose battery power the moment she appears, preventing them from recording the moment. The film ends with the paparazzi's frustration and the maid's playful laughter at their defeat (see Figures C.1, C.2, and C.3). She laughs in part because the cameras cannot capture her misbehaving when she is supposed to be doing her job. Her transgression at playing "the princess" instead of continuing her cleaning chores has not been recorded for posterity. In a sense, this small transgression is an inadvertent metaphor for how ephemeral acts of resistance frequently go unrecorded. Her joy reminds us that being accounted for and recorded have often meant being controlled and punished.

Figures C.1, C.2, and C.3: Film stills from *De Djess*.

Just as the ghosts of el monte appear in nationalist Dominican narratives, subaltern subjects' acts of refusal emerge even in imperial government archives. These acts are not necessarily as obvious as they might be in a court transcript that describes a subject's criminal recalcitrance. At times, they become evident only because their "strangeness" prompts a second look. A photograph in the Hanna-McCormick Family Papers at the Library of Congress occasioned one of these pauses (see Figure C.4). Its caption—"The girl who chased me at Cotuí (also double exposure)"—confirms that the photographer purposefully rendered it strange through a "double exposure" technique in which two separate images are superimposed to create a ghostly effect. The shadowiness of the palm fronds records the moment as phantasmagorical, preventing the image from seeming "tropical" and therefore safe, containable, wholly possessed by the gazer.[9]

Why was this girl chasing the photographer/captioner? Did she want her picture taken? Was she simply curious about these foreign travelers?

Figure C.4. "The girl who chased me at Cotuí (also double exposure),"
Hanna-McCormick Family Papers, ca. 1904–1905. (Courtesy of the Library
of Congress, LC-11208.)

Did the travelers insult or deny her in some way that required her chasing them? More important, why did the photographer render phantasmagorical this moment of confrontation? Was the photographer's intention to blur for posterity the young woman's defiant gaze and body? After all, she chased him/her. Is the technique of double exposure also a technique of ghosting? Perhaps, like Amasa Delano in "Benito Cereno", this U.S. photographer needs to render "strange" the encounter in order for it to fit within his or her vision of the world order. The girl seems recalcitrant, unwieldy, even defiant. On the other hand, she could simply be squinting against a blaring midday sun. Leaving us with more questions than answers, this photograph is nonetheless a rare instance in which an ephemeral act of refusal or recalcitrance by a nonelite subject was recorded for posterity.

Like many of the other cultural texts I discussed throughout this book, this image and its caption remain ambivalent. The open-endedness of the photograph, determined by the girl's demeanor and act of chasing, refuses the "power of the [tourist] gaze to define [her] being."[10] Moreover, this irresolution unmasks the scene as a "contact zone," which Mary Louise Pratt defines as a "social spac[e] where disparate cultures meet, clash, and grapple with each other, often in highly asymmetrical relations of domination and subordination."[11] In this case, the photographer did not record "a young woman from Cotuí" as an ahistorical, ethnographic type and an unspeaking Other as predetermined by centuries of Western convention in travel writing, painting, and photography. Instead, the photographer recorded a young woman who unmasked a scene of "grappling" and in some way refused her role as acquiescing Other.

ACKNOWLEDGMENTS

Many events and circumstances could have prevented my finishing this book if not for the people who had faith in me, even when I had none in myself.

I think of my grade school teachers in Santo Domingo who forced me to skip grades even though, as a terrifically shy little girl, I hated being surrounded by strange and older students. I think of my school teachers in New York City who took extra time and effort to help me learn English. I think of Mr. Jeremiah, the computer teacher at C.E.S. 145 in the Bronx, who nominated me for the Albert G. Oliver Program. From Brown University's Comparative Literature Department, Meera Viswanathan, who nominated me to be a Mellon Minority Undergraduate Fellow (now the Mellon Mays Undergraduate Fellowship Program or MMUF), and Michel-Andre Bossy were my two biggest supporters. Joyce Foster, then Dean and Director of MMUF at Brown University, became an important mentor. I think of my graduate advisor, Sara Johnson, who gave me a box full of precious out-of-print books that had belonged to her recently deceased mentor, Vèvè Clark. Sara did not know that I had walked into that office to tell her that I was quitting graduate school and academia. The financial downturn and the general crisis in academia did not guarantee that I would find a tenure-track job, but her gift buoyed me so much that I decided to give this profession another chance.

The list of those who had a direct hand in the creation of this book, from comments on early drafts to copyediting in later drafts, is long. At UC San Diego, Sara Johnson, Fatima El-Tayeb, Milos (Misha) Kokotovic, Lauren (Robin) Derby, and Nancy Postero will recognize mere smatterings of the version they read, but their influence on my scholarship is foundational. Thanks also to Winnifred Woodhull's and Lisa Lowe's mentorship. Thank you to the UC San Diego friends who read drafts of my work, including Allison Winston, Margarita Levantovskaya, Chase Smith, Joel Dodge, Diego Ubiera, and Brendan Thornton.

Those who encouraged me at various writing and professional MMUF retreats have my endless gratitude. Among them are Rosa Andújar, Miguel de Baca, Kimberly Juanita Brown, Lucía Cantero, Todne Thomas Chipumuro, Kaysha Corinealdi, Maggie Gover, Z'étoile Imma, Jacqueline Lazú, Uri McMillan, Shana Redmond, Gabriela Spears-Rico, Cally Waite, Michelle M. Wright, and pretty much everyone at Mellon. I thank the folks at the African American Studies Program at Princeton University, who awarded me with a yearlong postdoc. From my time there, special thanks to Nimisha Barton, Wallace Best, Daphne Brooks, Aaron Carico, Arcadio Díaz-Quiñónez, Rachel Price, Jennifer Rodríguez, and Alexandra Vázquez. While at Princeton, I had the opportunity to receive input on an early draft of my book from Sibylle Fischer and Silvio Torres-Saillant, for whom I have the utmost gratitude.

At Yale University, I am fortunate to be part of the American Studies Program, the Ethnicity, Race, and Migration Program, and, most recently, the Women, Gender, and Sexuality Studies Program and the Spanish and Portuguese Department. I thank those who had a direct impact on my manuscript, including Hazel Carby, Anne Eller, Aníbal González, Matt Jacobson, Stephen Pitti, Alicia Schmidt-Camacho, and Laura Wexler. I am particularly grateful for the mentorship of Alicia, Stephen, Hazel, Matt, Kathryn Dudley, Kathryn Lofton, Mary Lui, and Joanne Meyerowitz. Yale would be a scary place without their kind guidance and support. Yale librarians David Gary and Jana Krentz, thank you! Special thanks to Jean Cherniavsky, Tatjana Cisija, and Susan Shand, without whom my two home departments would surely fall apart.

Those who helped shape this book at writing groups, conferences, and conversations include Leticia Alvarado, Laura Barraclough, Denise Brennan, Ginetta Candelario, Genevieve Carpio, Raj Chetty, Carlos Decena, Shane Dillingham, Zaire Dinzey-Flores, Daylet Domínguez, Crystal Feimster, Juan Flores, Jorge Giovannetti Torres, Winston Groman, Maja Horn, Karen Jaime, Miriam Jiménez Román, Demetra Kasimis, Albert Laguna, Antonio López, Eva Lucks, Sharina Maillo-Pozo, Oscar Márquez, Monica Martínez, Rita de Maessener, Elizabeth Manley, Yolanda Martínez San Miguel, April Mayes, Viviana McManus, Marisel Moreno, Daniel Nemser, Ricardo Ortiz, Jennifer Ponce de León, Rachel Purvis, Rachel Afi Quinn, Petra Rivera-Rideau, Nicole Rizzuto, Josie Saldaña, David Sartorius, Médar Serrata, Devyn Spence Benson, Maritza

Stanchich, Elizabeth Steeby, Chelsea Stieber, Tashima Thomas, Gary Tomlinson, Elena Valdez, Deb Vargas, Cheryl Wall, Adam Warren, Kyla Wazana Tompkins, Fan Yang, and April Yoder. Particular thanks are due to the rock stars in my various writing groups: Albert, Leticia, Monica, Chelsea, Viviana, and Fan. Maja Horn and Anne Eller, thank you for being two of my most important interlocutors in the last few years. The heartiest of thanks to Alicia Schmidt Camacho, Aníbal González, José David Saldívar, and Anne McClintock for their energetic reflections and the contagious excitement they expressed at my Book Colloquium, hosted by Yale's American Studies, in 2016.

So many organizations and institutions have funded this project along the way, including the MMUF; the Social Science and Research Council; the Woodrow Wilson National Fellowship Foundation; the Center for Iberian and Latin American Studies at UCSD; and, from Yale's coffers, the A. Whitney Griswold Faculty Research Fund; the Morse Fellowship; the Deputy Dean for Diversity and Faculty Development; the Race, Indigeneity, and Transnational Migration Center Faculty Fellowship; the Ethnicity, Race, and Migration Program; the American Studies Program; the Frederick W. Hilles Publication Fund; and the Provost's Office. Thanks to the people at CCNY's Dominican Studies Institute and Library—especially Ramona Hernández, Sarah Aponte, and Anthony Stevens-Acevedo—and the Archivo General de la Nación in Santo Domingo—especially Alejandro Paulino and Ingrid Suriel—for guiding me to all those precious documents. I have great appreciation for the writers and scholars based in the Dominican Republic and the U.S. who took the time to meet with me, including José Alcántara Almánzar, Chiqui Vicioso, Aurora Arias, Avelino Stanley, Lusitania Martínez, and Junot Díaz.

I would like to express deep gratitude to my grandfather, Julio Santana, who has always been an incredible storyteller and, as such, a frequent source of inspiration for my scholarship. And the most special and heartfelt thanks to my stepfather, Darío Tejeda, who has been there all along, offering me his deep knowledge of Dominican history, literature, and culture, as well as for sharing his contacts and references with me.

Thanks to Eric Zinner, Alicia Nadkarni, John Raymond, the anonymous readers, and everyone else at NYU Press for helping me make my dream come true. Thanks also to Cecelia Cancellaro for polishing my words, Camille Owens for help with the bibliography, and Julia Alvarez and Miguel D. Mena for pointing me toward Salomé Ureña's daguerreotype. Much gratitude to Vanessa Pérez Rosario for introducing me to Firelei Báez's work.

One of my favorite games as a little girl was "pretend teacher," when I imagined that my stuffed animal/students were absorbing my lessons. Since the fall of 2005, my human students have—thankfully—been a much less silent, often recalcitrant, and unwieldy presence in my life. They have influenced my research and worldview deeply. My students at Yale have especially been a dream. Having the luxury of teaching my favorite books and topics to some of the most brilliant people I have ever met has given me moments of undiluted joy. Abrazos to the students of La Casa Cultural Julia de Burgos, especially to the members of the Dominican Student Association (Quisqueyalies). You came to my job talk wearing your Quisqueyalies sweatshirts and we reminded each other that people like us belonged at Yale.

Gratitude, appreciation, and love are what I feel for my close friends. From Trinity School, Elizabeth Raji, Carolina Ventura, Vanessa Martínez, Christina Rumpf, Kate Barth, Hanna Callaway, and Julia Kiechel. My beloveds Rachel Katzman, Angelika Daskalopoulous, and Becky Birnbaum from Brown University and Eva Lucks from study abroad in Japan: Where would I be without you four women? You have sustained me over and over again. From UC San Diego, Caralyn Bialo, Sean Dinces, Maggie Levantovskaya, Viviana McManus, Annie Mendoza, Isa Murdock-Hinrichs, Yumi Pak, Chase Smith, and Allison Winston: so many inside jokes, so many death glares across seminar rooms, so much despair over Kant. Laura Stevens, bottom line: San Diego would have been unbearable without you. Aventura! To my newest Yale-years friends—Sandra Caridad, Anne Eller, Greta LaFleur, Briallen Hopper, Ben Glaser, Leslie Harkema, Marina Niessner, Joanna Radin, and Dillon Vrana—thank you for your friendship and for making me laugh. Special love and recognition goes to Lev Weitz, a calming presence during years of turmoil, a tireless supporter of my work, and a patient celebrant of my colorful modes of self-expression.

This book exists because reading sustained me as a child as much as food and water. The people in my family encouraged this love more than anyone else. A heartfelt thank you to my aunts, Yuly Santana D'Oleo,

Arisleida Santana D'Oleo, and Ramonita Ramírez Valdez; my grandparents, Deidamia D'Oleo and Julio Santana; and my parents, Dixa D'Oleo-Tejeda and José Ramírez Valdez. Together, they taught me to read before I stepped foot inside any classroom. To my little brother José Antonio/Josian/Jo: I'm so happy to be your big sis' and to give you the best nicknames. Pa, thank you for sharing Tony Seval's story with me. Ma, thank you for all you've given me. Last, but definitely not least, hugs and kisses to my feline family Osiris (RIP), Motzi, and Grey Phillip, whom I like more than most people most of the time.

NOTES

INTRODUCTION

1 Melville, "Benito Cereno," 145–146.

    Harris was an African American activist searching for a more hospitable country for his brethren either in the Dominican Republic or in Haiti. See Harris, *A Summer on the Borders of the Caribbean Sea*, 27.

    Gordon, *Ghostly Matters*, 183.

2 Melville, "Benito Cereno," 161.

3 Melville, "Benito Cereno," 163.

4 Melville, "Benito Cereno," 163.

5 See Sundquist, *To Wake the Nations*, and Grandin, *The Empire of Necessity*.

6 This ghosting is so pervasive that it is beyond the scope of this book to include all the examples in which Santo Domingo/the Dominican Republic should have been studied but was not. However, we may consider scholarship within the burgeoning field of Afro-Latin America, which rarely includes the Dominican case. Several tomes dedicated to the study of black Latin America neither mention this first site of African slavery in the hemisphere nor seek to explore how ideas of blackness or whiteness developed there. For instance, the two-volume *Blackness in Latin America and the Caribbean*, ed. Whitten and Torres, which includes thirty-six articles by many different authors, does not contain a single essay on the Dominican Republic.

7 Anne McClintock, "Imperial Ghosting and National Tragedy," 820. Thanks to Anne McClintock for introducing me to the term "ghosting" and the literature around it.

    Raphael Dalleo also opens his book with the words: "U.S. Imperialism is built on amnesia" (*American Imperialism's Undead*).

8 These two economies were intertwined. As Anne Eller writes: "At Saint-Domingue's height, colonists relied heavily on the Santo Domingo cattle trade" ("'All Would Be Equal in the Effort,'" 127n93). See also Soler, *Santo Domingo Tierra de Frontera 1750–1800*.

    I borrow Antonio Benítez-Rojo's capitalization of the word "Plantation" to differentiate between a single plantation and a "society dominated by plantation economy" (*The Repeating Island*, 317n8). Juan José Ponce-Vázquez calls Santo Domingo a "post-plantation" society ("Unequal Partners in Crime," 3).

9 In *Tropics of Haiti*, Marlene Daut also argues for complicating calcified narratives of what it meant to be revolutionary during the Haitian Revolution.

10 Melville, "Benito Cereno," 146.
11 McClintock, "Imperial Ghosting and National Tragedy," 827.
12 Gordon, *Ghostly Matters*, 178–179, emphasis mine.
13 See, for instance, the controversial *Miami Herald* article "Black Denial" by Frances Robles, which held that Dominicans' preference for straightened hair was irrefutable proof that the entire citizenry denied their blackness. See also "Black in the Dominican Republic," *HuffPost Live*, and Gates, "Haiti and the Dominican Republic."
14 Chetty, "'La calle es libre,'" 41.
15 Berlin, *Many Thousands Gone*. See also Knight, *The Caribbean*.
16 There are many works about the Plantation system and its effects in modern-day societies across the Americas. See, for instance, Kutzinski, *Sugar's Secrets*; Hartman, *Scenes of Subjection*; and White, *Ar'n't I a Woman*. For an analysis of how white supremacist violence also defined urban slavery, including in Santo Domingo, see Ponce-Vázquez, "Unequal Partners in Crime," and Fuentes, *Dispossessed Lives*.
17 Here I include the varied scholarship of Raj Chetty, Lorgia García-Peña, Angela Hernández, Maja Horn, Danny Méndez, Néstor Rodríguez, Doris Sommer, Silvio Torres-Saillant, and Sherezada (Chiqui) Vicioso.
18 For an elaboration of displacement as both migration and exile in relation to Hispanophone Caribbean writers, see Pérez Rosario, "Introduction: Historical Context of Caribbean Latino Literature," in *Hispanic Caribbean Literature of Migration*, 1–20.
19 See Trouillot, *Silencing the Past*; Bergland, *The National Uncanny*; Gordon, *Ghostly Matters*; and McClintock, *Unquiet Ghosts of the Forever War*.
20 Walcott, *The Antilles*.
21 Walcott, *The Antilles*.
22 Taylor, *The Archive and The Repertoire*, 142. For more on repetition and state violence, see Fischer, *Modernity Disavowed*; Guidotti-Hernández, *Unspeakable Violence*; and García-Peña, *The Borders of Dominicanidad*.
23 Bergland, *The National Uncanny*, 5.
24 Gordon, *Ghostly Matters*, xvi.
25 McClintock, "Imperial Ghosting and National Tragedy," 827.
26 With Haitian governance in 1822 came the final abolition of slavery in this former Spanish colony, rendering the island the sole example of a black-led nation-state in the midst of a sea of slaveholding colonies. That is, throughout the nineteenth century and, arguably, beyond, Dominicans—alongside Haitians—had to contend with the contempt of a world that was not ready for black freedom and autonomy. See Eller, *We Dream Together*, which "recounts the immense opposition to self-rule directed toward the island" (1).
27 In 2000, Chris Dixon writes that "Haiti had changed little since the 1820s [to the 1850s]" (Dixon, *African America and Haiti*, 97). But there *was* an important change during these 30 years; in the 1820s, Haiti was the entire island, while in the

1850s, the western third of the island was Haiti and the other two-thirds were the Dominican Republic. That is, an entirely new nation had been founded during these years. In 2014, Greg Grandin repeats the misnamings that had been prevalent for two centuries. Referencing Herman Melville's novella "Benito Cereno," Grandin writes: "Melville settled on calling the ship San Dominick, identifying it with Haiti's old French colonial name, Santo Domingo" (Grandin, *The Empire of Necessity*, 197). This is, of course, not Haiti's old French colonial name and is, instead, the Dominican Republic's old Spanish name. This book then cites an 1855 New York City lecture by Charles Wyllys Elliott, which invokes a 1521 slave revolt on the plantation of Columbus's son. Grandin then notes that Elliot had "reminded his audience that Haiti used to be called Santo Domingo" (Grandin, *The Empire of Necessity*, 199). In a fascinating replication of mistakes, Grandin fails to mention that this plantation was in what had already, by 1855, become the Dominican Republic.

What concerns me about these inaccuracies in otherwise rigorous and necessary scholarship is that they have the unmistakable handprint of U.S.-centricity. Sean X. Goudie offers a sobering critique of "how scholars and critics, in treating Caribbean presences in works authored by U.S. authors, turn to the Caribbean according to a North-South trajectory to spy out influence without ever relocating themselves according to a South-North directionality, a reality that reflects their and their field's institutional location, hierarchies of assumption, and investments" (Goudie, "The Caribbean Turn in C19 American Literary Studies," 135).

28 See Torres-Saillant, "The Tribulations of Blackness," 127.

29 When I use the terms "first world" and "third world" instead of terms such as "center" and "periphery," "global north" and "global south," or "West" and "rest," I do so purposefully. Unlike these other terms, first world and third world have been uncritically used from developmentalist perspectives. The reader should assume that my usage of these terms always includes scare quotes though I cease to include them after the first mention in each chapter.

30 See Franck, "The Land of Bullet Holes," 260–264; Moscoso Puello, "From Paris to Santo Domingo," 195–200; and Lugo, "El estado dominicano ante el derecho público."

Coincidentally, as Matthew Jacobson asserts, "[s]cientists and politicians freely cited the first-hand accounts of white travelers in order to assert this or that truth about Africa or Asia, and yet those accounts—like the travelers' experiences—had already been structured by technologies, modes of seeing, a set of social relations, and an epistemology entwined in the project of Euro-American exploration and imperial expansion" (Jacobson, *Whiteness of a Different Color*, 11). It becomes clear that travel writing and scientific racism built on each other.

31 See, for instance, Bell, preface in *Black Separatism in the Caribbean*. He clarifies for the potentially confused reader the variety of spellings and names used

by the two authors in the anthology. Sundquist and Eller also note the variety of spellings referring to one or both sides of the island. See Sundquist, *To Wake the Nations*, 140n; and Eller, "'Awful Pirates' and 'Hordes of Jackals,'" 90n50.

32 Consider, for instance, that the 1806 Spanish version of a French book translated the title *La vie de Jean-Jacques Dessalines, chef des noirs révoltés de Saint-Domingue* (1804) into *La Vida de J.J. Dessalines, gefe de los negros de Santo Domingo*. The Spanish edition mistakenly translated Saint Domingue (future Haiti) into Santo Domingo (future Dominican Republic). See Dubroca, *Vida de J.J. Dessalines, gefe de los negros de Santo Domingo*.

33 According to the U.S. census of 2010, the Dominican population was 1.5 million. See Motel and Patten, "Hispanics of Dominican Origin in the United States, 2010."

34 Trouillot, *Silencing the Past*, 99.

35 McClintock, "Imperial Ghosting and National Tragedy."

36 "centro de ensayo colonial español en América" (Batista, *Mujer y esclavitud en Santo Domingo*, 23).

37 Lowe, *The Intimacies of Four Continents*, 58.

38 Hall, "Cultural Identity and Diaspora," 224, italics in original.

I borrow Ginetta Candelario's definition of identity based on "the relationship between institutions and individuals, and between official discourse and every-day life practices." She continues: "In particular, I am influenced by the nets of symbolic interactionism in which the self is produced through interactions with others, groups and institutions and that are enacted through multiple role identities. Thus, particular identities of a given individual will be more or less salient in different circumstances and contexts" (*Black behind the Ears*, 6–7).

39 Candelario, "La ciguapa y el ciguapeo," 101.

40 Candelario, "La ciguapa y el ciguapeo," 103.

41 Morrison, *Beloved*.

42 Gordon, *Ghostly Matters*, 140.

43 Gordon, *Ghostly Matters*, 139.

44 Trouillot, *Silencing the Past*, 97.

45 See Trouillot, *Silencing the Past*; Fischer, *Modernity Disavowed*; Johnson, *The Fear of French Negroes*; Dubois, *Haiti*; and Ferrer, *Freedom's Mirror*.

Julia Gaffield, however, argues against the notion of Haiti's diplomatic and commercial isolation after the Revolution. See *Haitian Connections in the Atlantic World*.

46 Ulysse, "Why Representations of Haiti Matter Now More Than Ever," 39.

47 Goudie, "The Caribbean Turn in C19 American Literary Studies," 132.

48 See Fischer, "Appendix A: Imperial Constitution of Haiti, 1805," in *Modernity Disavowed*, 275–281.

49 Sundquist, *To Wake the Nations*, 32.

If we consider how the rights of Haitian migrants and their Dominican descendants have been under attack throughout the twentieth century in the Dominican Republic—and, in the late twentieth-century U.S., the refusal to grant Haitians refugee status unlike their Cuban counterparts—the legacy of white supremacist reactions to black Haitian self-determination endures still.

50 C. L. R. James's influential *The Black Jacobins* ([1938] 1963) remains one of the most canonical accounts of the Haitian Revolution. See also Scott, "The Common Wind"; Fick, *The Making of Haiti*; Scott, *Conscripts of Modernity*; and Dubois, *Avengers of the New World*.

51 Fanning, *Caribbean Crossing*, 55.

52 To learn more about these subjects, see Michel, *La Revolución Haitiana y Santo Domingo*; Franco, *Blacks, Mulattos, and the Dominican Nation*; Lora, "El sonido de la libertad"; Johnson, *The Fear of French Negroes*; Ferrer, *Freedom's Mirror*; Nessler, *An Islandwide Struggle for Freedom*; and Eller, "'All Would Be Equal in the Effort'" and *We Dream Together*.

53 See Candelario, *Black behind the Ears*.

54 See, for instance, the work of Sherezada (Chiqui) Vicioso, Angela Hernández, Pedro L. San Miguel, Pedro Mella, Quisqueya Lora, Silvio Torres Saillant, Ginetta Candelario, Lauren (Robin) Derby, April Mayes, Lorgia García-Peña, Néstor Rodríguez, Micah Wright, Danny Méndez, Anne Eller, Graham Nessler, Edward Paulino, Raj Chetty, and Maja Horn. I am particularly inspired by these scholars' refusals of conservative Dominican nationalists' outright fabrications on which rest their ideologies, often anti-Haitianist, antipoor, and misogynist.

55 Grant, "Making the Case for U.S. Annexation," in Roorda, Derby, and González, eds., *The Dominican Republic Reader*, 159.

56 Guitar, "Boiling It Down," 42. See also Moya Pons, *La otra historia dominicana*, 77–81.

The Spanish brought the first African slaves to the Americas in 1502, but they soon fled and took "refuge with the native people" (Gibson, *Empire's Crossroads*, 43). For more information on the hemisphere's first sugar mills, see Benítez-Rojo, *The Repeating Island*.

57 According to Guitar, Spaniards brought with them enslaved subjects of African, indigenous, and mixed descent to settle other parts of the Americas. See Guitar, "Boiling It Down," 43.

58 Sagás and Inoa, eds., *The Dominican People*, 1.

59 Ponce-Vázquez, "Unequal Partners in Crime," 5. See also the introduction to Roorda, Derby, and González, eds., *The Dominican Republic Reader*, 1–8, and González, *De esclavos a campesinos*.

The main reason for the impoverishment of the territory is that the Spanish became distracted by the wealth to be plundered from the Aztec, Incan, Mayan, and other indigenous societies located especially on the continent. According to historians Eric Paul Roorda, Lauren Derby, and Raymundo González, "a full two years could pass without Spanish ships stopping at local ports" at the height of the colony's impoverishment (*The Dominican Republic Reader*, 88).

60 See, for instance, Howard, *Coloring the Nation*; Sagás, *Race and Politics in the Dominican Republic*; Stinchcomb, *The Development of Literary Blackness in the*

Dominican Republic; Fischer, *Modernity Disavowed*; Martínez Vergne, *Nation and Citizen in the Dominican Republic*; Robles, "Black Denial"; and Gates, "Haiti and the Dominican Republic."

61 Roorda, Derby, and González, eds., *The Dominican Republic Reader*, 93.

62 Harry Hoetink warns that "[t]he scanty data on the number of inhabitants in the course of the nineteenth century must, of course, be used with the greatest caution. But, at the least, the general tendencies that they reflect are probable" (*The Dominican People*, 19).

63 Knight, *The Caribbean*, 366–367.

64 "Etat general de la partie de l'est de Saint Domingue, a l'epoque de premiere janvier 1808."

65 Fischer, *Modernity Disavowed*, 145.

66 Cuba became independent from both Spain and the U.S. in 1902 and slavery was abolished in 1886.

67 Cited in Fischer, *Modernity Disavowed*, 145. Dixon Porter would go on to fight in the U.S.-Mexico War of 1848 and the U.S. Civil War. See Candelario, *Black behind the Ears*, 46–49.

68 "A diferencia de otras sociedades caribeñas, en la República Dominicana [. . .] no existió una economía de plantación que impidiese el surgimiento y la existencia del campesinado" (San Miguel, *El pasado relegado*, 129).

69 The 1681 census data is taken from Ponce-Vázquez, "Unequal Partners in Crime," 13.

70 A prime example of a large-scale slave rebellion during the colonial era took place in 1796 at the largest sugar plantation on the colony, the Boca Nigua sugar plantation near Santo Domingo. Since it occurred during the Haitian Revolution, slave-owners and colonial administrators had much reason to panic. Indeed, the timing and the overall plan of enslaved subjects destroying other plantations in the colony proves that what is now known as the Haitian Revolution was a series of rebellions that took place *all over the island*, not only in what is now Haiti. See Geggus, "The Boca Nigua Revolt," in Roorda, Derby, and González, eds., *The Dominican Republic Reader*, 109–114.

71 Ponce-Vázquez, "Unequal Partners in Crime," 14.

72 Ponce-Vázquez, "Unequal Partners in Crime," 14.

73 Ernesto Sagás and Orlando Inoa describe and translate the legal document on the case in *The Dominican People*, 46–47.

74 Scott, "The Common Wind," 8.

75 For more on the arrival of the advanced sugar plantation in the Dominican Republic, see del Castillo, "The Formation of the Dominican Sugar Industry."

76 See Mayes, *The Mulatto Republic*.

77 "La plantación es el sistema agrícola dominante en la República Dominicana" (Moya Pons, *La otra historia dominicana*, 212).

78 "su aparición no estuvo ligada al proceso inicial de formación nacional independiente del pueblo dominicano" (Moya Pons, *La otra historia dominicana*, 212).

79 Burnard and Garrigus, *The Plantation Machine*, 2. See also Torres-Saillant, "The Tribulations of Blackness," 135, and Turits, *Foundations of Despotism*, 49–50.

80 Raymundo González, "Ideología del progreso y campesinado en el siglo XIX," 30. Hazard, *Santo Domingo*, 181.

81 Roorda, Derby, and González, eds., *The Dominican Republic Reader*, 4. For more on "masterless" men, see Scott, "The Common Wind." For more on Caribbean buccaneering, see Bosch, *De Cristóbal Colón a Fidel Castro*, and Moya Pons, *History of the Caribbean*.

82 Quoted in González, *De esclavos a campesinos*, 16–17.

83 Cited in Turits, *Foundations of Despotism*, 36.

Complaints about nonwhite Dominicans' disinterest in cultivating the land for profit frustrated elite locals and foreigners in the colonial and national periods. For instance, García also complains of these freepeoples' preference for subsistence living: "There are an infinite number of blacks and mulattos who live in dispersed huts throughout the countryside, without more patrimony than that which they or their ancestors brought from Guinea. And they are happy and at ease simply because they are free. They never work, except when they are hungry" (cited in Turits, *Foundations of Despotism*, 36). Around this time, Martinican visitor M. L. E. Moreau de Saint Méry also complained about the inability, or refusal, of subjects living in Santo Domingo to be productive in the way French colonists found appropriate, blaming Spanish indolence. Frederick Douglass repeats similar observations to Ulysses S. Grant when he visits the country a century later in the 1870s as part of an official U.S. delegation, though, instead of indolence, he believes that Dominicans do not wish to cultivate beyond subsistence because "amid constantly recurring revolutions, it is very uncertain who may reap the crop; besides, there is no market now for surplus produce" (Frederick Douglass, "Dominican Support for Annexation," in Roorda, Derby, and González, eds., *The Dominican Republic Reader*, 168).

84 For more on the Black Code of 1784, see González, *De esclavos a campesinos*.

85 Franco, *Blacks, Mulattos, and the Dominican Nation*, 59, bracketed comment in the original.

86 See Turits, *Foundations of Despotism*, 38.

87 Moreau de Saint-Méry, *A Topographical and Political Description of the Spanish Part of Santo Domingo*, 56.

88 Moreau de Saint-Méry, *A Topographical and Political Description of the Spanish Part of Santo Domingo*, 56.

89 Moreau de Saint-Méry, *A Topographical and Political Description of the Spanish Part of Santo Domingo*, 57.

90 González, "The 'People-Eater,'" 103. For more on el monte and *monteros*, see Bonó, *El Montero*. For more on *montería* during the colonial era and into the twentieth century, see Silié, "El hato y el conuco"; San Miguel, *El pasado relegado*; Raymundo González, "Ideología del progreso y campesinado en el siglo XIX" and *De esclavos a campesinos*; and Davis, "La Montería." For more on the *terrenos*

comuneros (shared lands) in the nineteenth century, see Moya Pons, "The Land Question in Haiti and Santo Domingo," and Turits, *Foundations of Despotism*.

91 See Davis, "La Montería," in Roorda, Derby, and González, eds., *The Dominican Republic Reader*, 446.

92 "mujeres pobres que iban a la iglesia y mantenían sus familias con su trabajo de sirvientas, costureras, vendedoras de conmida, fabricantes de dulces, prostitutas o concubinas" (Moya Pons, *La otra historia dominicana*, 104).

93 "[C]ette littérature féminine a un contenu social que dépasse le propos apparemment anecdotique de tel ou tel écrivain. Elle se situe au coeur des préoccupations de l'ensemble de la société" (Condé, *La parole des femmes*, 39).

94 See Batista, *Mujer y esclavitud en Santo Domingo*; Bush, *Slave Women in Caribbean Society*; Shepherd, Brereton, and Bailey, eds., *Engendering History*; Sharpe, *Ghosts of Slavery*.

It should not be surprising that traces of black and other nonwhite women would be difficult to find across the written archives of the Western world. Scholars of gender and race in the Americas have had to cobble together fragments using various established methods or create new methodologies wholesale, including M. Jacqui Alexander, Saidiya Hartman, Jenny Sharpe, Barbara Bush, Celsa Albert Batista, Sara Johnson, and Marisa J. Fuentes, to name just a few.

95 Citing Larrazábal Blanco's *La esclavitud del negro en Santo Domingo*: "la mujer africana como 'mecanismo de contra insurgencia'" (Batista, *Mujer y esclavitud en Santo Domingo*, 20).

96 I have not found any source that specifies Hazard as a white man, but the exclusion of this descriptor in the nineteenth-century U.S. context usually means that the person is white. For more on Harris, see Bell, preface in *Black Separatism in the Caribbean*. For more on Hazard, see Candelario, *Black behind the Ears*, 53–57.

97 Cited in García-Peña, *The Borders of Dominicanidad*, 9.

98 Hazard, *Santo Domingo*, 184.

For more on Dominican women in the archive, see Lora, "Las mujeres anónimas de inicios del siglo XIX dominicano."

99 Hazard, *Santo Domingo*, 184.

100 Harris, *A Summer on the Borders of the Caribbean Sea*, 43.

101 García-Peña, *The Borders of Dominicanidad*, 52.

102 García-Peña, *The Borders of Dominicanidad*, 52.

103 See González, *De esclavos a campesinos*.

104 "Desde la fundación de la República, en 1844, el campesinado había constituido un sector social de difícil control por los organismos estatales. Por tal razón, desde fines del siglo XIX, los esfuerzos estatales se encaminaron, en buena medida a 'domesticar' al campesinado" (San Miguel, *El pasado relegado*, 139). See also González, *De esclavos a campesinos*, 142.

105 Martínez Vergne, *Nation and Citizen in the Dominican Republic*, 8. See also Zeller, *Discursos y espacios femeninos en República Dominicana*.

106 Pedro Francisco Bonó, letter to Gregorio Luperón (1887), quoted in Hoetink, *The Dominican People*, 188.

107 "La inmensa mayoría de la población residía en el campo, donde no había instituciones educativas de ningún tipo. Pero incluso en las escasas y pequeñas ciudades, la generalidad de la población permanecía en el analfabetismo" (Cassá, *Salomé Ureña*, 13).

Around this time, the few women fortunate enough to receive any education were unable to advance beyond basic literacy. In 1860 the magazine *Quincenal Dominicana* conducted a census on primary schools in Santo Domingo, which totaled 35 schools with 335 girls and 329 boys. The total estimated population at the time was 12,000 residents (Castro Ventura, *Salomé Ureña*, 22). By 1887, the number of schools around the country had increased to 300 with about 10,000 students (Alvarez Leal, *La República Dominicana*, 29).

108 "el presupuesto para dicho propósito era sólo un 3 por ciento de los gastos totales del gobierno" (Zeller, *Discursos y espacios femeninos*, 19).

109 "las mayorías analfabetas, indígenas o afrodescendientes" (Mella, *Los espejos de Duarte*, 39). Here, Mella refers to Rama's writings directly. That is, he is not suggesting that the "real city" in the Dominican Republic includes "indigenous" people.

110 "sirviendo también como sinécdoques que pretenden representar discursivamente a la República Dominicana como un todo" (Mella, *Los espejos de Duarte*, 39).

111 In the late seventeenth century, for instance, the archbishop of the colony complains to the Spanish crown about rumors that in just a few years the whole government will be controlled by blacks and "mulattos" and that there is already a town governed by two "mulattos." See Ugarte, *Estampas coloniales*, vol. 2, 132–133.

112 See Silié, "El hato y el conuco"; González, "Ideología del progreso y campesinado en el siglo XIX"; Eller, *We Dream Together*; Torres-Saillant, "The Tribulations of Blackness."

113 For more on these political factions, see Moya Pons, *The Dominican Republic*.

114 For more on the U.S. occupation of the Dominican Republic (1916–1924), see Calder, *The Impact of the Intervention*; Tillman, *Dollar Diplomacy by Force*; and García-Peña, *The Borders of Dominicanidad*.

115 "Durante más de 400 años y, particularmente durante los siglos XVIII y XIX, la vida dominicana estuvo dominanada por formas campesinas" (Moya Pons, *La otra historia dominicana*, 111).

116 Moya Pons cites these numbers from the 1920 national census (*La otra historia dominicana*, 355).

117 Mejía, "RD tiene población de 9.4 millones."

118 Motel and Patten, "Hispanics of Dominican Origin in the United States, 2010."

119 Among these we can include the following monographs: Moya Pons, ed., *La migración dominicana a los Estados Unidos*; Grasmuck and Pessar, *Between Two Islands*; Duany, *Quisqueya on the Hudson*; Torres-Saillant and Hernández, *The*

Dominican Americans; Torres-Saillant, *El retorno de las yolas*; Martínez-San Miguel, *Caribe Two Ways*; Sagás and Molina, *Dominican Migration*; Suárez, *The Tears of Hispaniola*; Candelario, *Black behind the Ears*; Soy, *Dominican Women across Three Generations*; Hoffnung-Garskof, *A Tale of Two*; Flores, *The Diaspora Strikes Back*; Heredia, *Transnational Latina Narratives in the Twenty-First Century*; Pérez Rosario, *Hispanic Caribbean Literature of Migration*; Decena, *Tacit Subjects*; Méndez, *Narratives of Migration and Displacement in Dominican Literature*; Roth, *Race Migrations*; Graziano, *Undocumented Dominican Migration*; and García-Peña, *The Borders of Dominicanidad*.

120 According to Torres-Saillant, "nuestra emigración es una expatriación" ("our emigration is an expatriation") ("El retorno de las yolas," in *El retorno de las yolas*, 18).

121 Consider, for instance, Haitians' attempts to seek asylum in the U.S. in the 1990s, only to be sent back to a politically unstable homeland—unstable, in great part, due to U.S. intervention.

122 This is evident in interviews with contemporary Caribbean writers such as Antiguan Jamaica Kincaid, Guadeloupian Maryse Condé, Haitian Dany Laferrière, among many others, who often explain that their geographic displacement has nourished their literary and scholarly output. This is also the case of deceased intellectuals and writers like Martinicans Aimé Césaire and Frantz Fanon and Haitian Marie Chauvet, whose work either centralizes or, in the case of Chauvet, necessitated exile. We may also consider José Martí and Eugenio María de Hostos, nineteenth-century national heroes in their respective Cuba and Puerto Rico, whose bodies of work are unthinkable without their extensive experiences living in exile throughout the Americas.

123 Torres-Saillant, *Caribbean Poetics*, 25.

124 Kanellos, "A Schematic Approach to Understanding Latino Transnational Literary Texts," 39.

125 Maja Horn's *Masculinity after Trujillo* provides a wonderful analysis of some of the literary efforts produced in the latter half of the twentieth century. See also Ricourt, "From Mamá Tingó to Globalization," and García-Peña, *The Borders of Dominicanidad*.

126 I wrote an op-ed about this issue for the Dominican press. See Ramírez, "Por un patriotismo que no se base en el odio ni en la exclusión." See also Torres-Saillant, "El retorno de las yolas," 31–33.

127 For more on how rural Dominicans influenced or challenged the culture of Dominican cities, see Martínez Vergne, *Nation and Citizen in the Dominican Republic*, and Hoffnung-Garskof, *A Tale of Two Cities*.

128 Rohter, "In the Language of Romance, Romeo Santos Is a True Superstar."

129 Wright, *Physics of Blackness*, 49.

130 Ortíz, "A Future Yet to Be Unfolded," 12.

131 Báez, "Firelei Báez," 26.

132 Báez, "Firelei Báez," 26.
133 Báez, "Firelei Báez," 25.

CHAPTER 1. UNTANGLING DOMINICAN PATRIOTISM

1 Coronado, *A World Not to Come*, 69.
   I presented an early version of this chapter at the American Studies Association meeting in Los Angeles in 2014 ("'Gozamos, sufrimos, amamos': Charting the Reading Practices and Politics of Late Nineteenth-Century Dominican Exiles.")
2 "elegantemente adornad[a]"; "flores, cuadros, luces"; "azafates con dulces y licores" (Justo, "Ovación al genio," 44 and 46).
3 "rendir el tributo de estimación y de justicia a la Avellaneda dominicana" (Justo, "Ovación al genio," 44).
4 "magníficos tercetos de óperas y con deliciosos valses nacionales" (Justo, "Ovación al genio," 45).
5 "Penson nos regaló un extenso, muy extenso, demasiado extenso trabajo literario" (Justo, "Ovación al genio," 46).
6 "se dió la lectura a una *Oda a la Patria* de la eminente poetisa Ureña (Justo, "Ovación al genio," 46).
7 "la legitimación de la irrupción de las mujeres de las clases medias y altas en el trabajo y en la esfera pública" (Brea and Duarte, *Entre la calle y la casa*, 19).
8 For more on how gender roles were legally enforced in Santo Domingo toward the end of Salomé Ureña's life and the early twentieth century, see Martínez-Vergne, *Nation and Citizen in the Democratic Republic*; Zeller, *Discursos y espacios femeninos en República Dominicana*; and Mayes, *The Mulatto Republic*.
9 Borrowing from Robin Bernstein, I consider "a script as theater directors do: a script is a dynamic substance that deeply influences but does not entirely determine live performances, which vary according to agential individuals' visions, impulses, resistances, revisions, and management of unexpected disruptions" (Bernstein, *Racial Innocence*, 71).
10 Patriotic women writers had preexisted Ureña. For instance, Emilio Rodríguez Demorizi attributes some of the popularity of General Pedro Santana as a politician to Manuela Aybar o Rodríguez's verses (Rodríguez Demorizi, *Poesía popular dominicana*, 206–7). Aybar o Rodríguez, known as La Deana (1790–1850), printed her own verses at home "in pamphlets that she herself disseminated and that had great demand" ("repartidos por ella misma, en volantes que tenían grandísima demanda" (Rodríguez Demorizi, *Poesía popular dominicana*, 206). However, her poetry never reached the level of national adulation as Ureña, perhaps in part because it was partisan. Though Ureña and her family were Liberals, Ureña's works were often read as "pure" evocations of patriotism that transcended political party.
11 The instances are numerous. For just one example, see F. A. de Meriño's "Fiat Lux!" in which he calls Ureña "la musa de Quisqueya" (the muse of Quisqueya) (in Emilio Rodríguez Demorizi, ed., *Salomé Ureña y el Instituto de Señoritas*, 84).

12 Anne McClintock's writing on gendered symbols in nationalist literature was influential to my thinking on this issue. See "'No Longer in a Future Heaven.'" See also Sommer, *One Master for Another* and *Foundational Fictions*; and Vallejo, *Las madres de la patria y las bellas mentiras*.

13 For more on Ureña's legacy, see Silveria R. de Rodríguez Demorizi, *Salomé Ureña de Henríquez*; Emilio Rodríguez Demorizi, ed., *Salomé Ureña y el Instituto de Señoritas*; Paravisini-Gebert, "Salomé Ureña de Henríquez (1850–1897)"; Vicioso and Ureña de Henríquez, *Salomé Ureña de Henríquez (1850–1897)*; Castro Ventura, *Salomé Ureña*; Ureña de Henríquez et al., *100 años de poesía*; Cassá, *Salomé Ureña*; Zeller, *Discursos y espacios femeninos en República Dominicana*; and Mayes, *The Mulatto Republic*.

14 "Pero Pedro y yo no nos conformábamos de ser noveles hacedores de colecciones de versos, tomándolos de los periódicos: quisimos tener periódicos propios. Yo lancé a la circulación en el hogar una hojilla manuscrita semanal [. . .]. Le puse por nombre: *La Tarde*. Naturalmente, se editaba un solo ejemplar, que circulaba por la casa de mano en mano. [. . .] Pedro echó a la circulación otra hojita, también hebdomadaria, que bautizó: *La Patria*, y en ella aparecieron reproducciones de nuestros poetas, con comentarios suyos, que acaso fueron la primera manifestación de sus futuras dotes de crítico y ensayista" (Henríquez Ureña, *Hermano y maestro*, 21).

15 The family would later move to a larger, two-story house in the same neighborhood (Henríquez Ureña, *Hermano y maestro*, 18).

16 See Vicioso, *Salomé Ureña de Henríquez (1850–1897)*, 26.

17 Martínez Vergne, *Nation and Citizen in the Dominican Republic*, 1.

18 Martínez Vergne, *Nation and Citizen in the Dominican Republic*, 1.

19 Baud, "'Constitutionally White,'" 123.

20 For interpretations of these texts, see Sommer's *One Master for Another* and Fischer's *Modernity Disavowed*.

21 For more on the mythical past and future that made for a positivist nationalism, see Vallejo, *Las madres de la patria y las bellas mentiras*, 26.

22 Fischer, *Modernity Disavowed*, 163.

23 Sommer, *Foundational Fictions*, 21–22.

24 Fischer, *Modernity Disavowed*, 168.

    Fischer's thesis comes to stand in for all of Dominican Studies in *Haiti and the Americas*, eds., Carla Calargé, Raphael Dalleo, Luis Duno-Gottberg, and Clevis Headley (Jackson: University Press of Mississippi, 2013), 8. In an earlier publication, I also suggested that Galván's novel has an ultimately anti-Haitianist aim. Without entirely contradicting that earlier stance, I now consider the issue to be much more complicated. See Ramírez, "Forced Intimacies and Murky Genealogies," 211.

25 García-Peña, *The Borders of Dominicanidad*, 39. See also Martínez Vergne, *Nation and Citizen in the Dominican Republic*, 101–102.

26 Fumagalli, *On the Edge*, 350.

27 See Geggus, "The Naming of Haiti."

28 Eller, "Let's Show The World We Are Brothers," 420n53.

Karin Weyland also contextualizes Dominican *indigenismo* with other Latin American counterparts. See "Producción de conocimiento y el discurso colonial a través de la fotografía en el Caribe Hispánico, 1898–1940," 761–762.

29 See Incháustegui and Malagón, eds., *Familia Henríquez Ureña*, vol. I.

30 Bernstein defines a "scriptive thing" as "an item of material culture that prompts meaningful bodily behaviors" (Bernstein, *Racial Innocence*, 71).

31 Justo, a society columnist, estimates that there were 80 women and 70 men present at the event. See Justo, "Ovación al genio," 44.

32 Castellanos, ed., *Lira de Quisqueya*.

Emilio Rodríguez Demorizi writes that her poems "were generally published in newspapers in Santo Domingo [. . .] and sometimes, by exception, appeared for the first time in Cuba" ("se publicaban generalmente en periódicos de Santo Domingo [. . .] y a veces, por excepción, aparecían por primera vez en Cuba"). See Emilio Rodríguez Demorizi, preface to *Salomé Ureña y el Instituto de Señoritas*, 16. According to Silveria R. de Rodríguez Demorizi, Ureña was even plagiarized in Honduras (Rodríguez Demorizi, *Salomé Ureña de Henríquez*, 18n10).

33 Ureña de Henríquez, *Poesías completas*, 23. Unless otherwise indicated, all translations throughout this book are my own.

34 Ureña de Henríquez, *Poesías completas*, 19.

35 Ureña de Henríquez, *Poesías completas*, 20.

36 Ureña de Henríquez, *Poesías completas*, 21.

37 Ureña de Henríquez, *Poesías completas*, 60.

38 "Fue ella la primera que tuvo en Santo Domingo el sentimiento de la gran poesía, de la única verdaderamente grande, porque lejos de recluirse en la intimidad de quien escribe, para recoger solo el eco de sus propias miserias, se levanta para dominar el espectáculo entero de la vida y tiende a hacerse intérprete de zonas más amplias y a la vez más fecundas de la sensibilidad humana" (Balaguer, *Letras dominicanas*, 289).

39 Palmer, "Salomé Ureña," 112.

40 Fiol-Matta, *A Queer Mother for the Nation*, xxii.

41 The word *varonil* connotes not only manliness but also energy. See Incháustegui and Malagón, eds., *Familia Henríquez Ureña: Epistolario*, vol. I, 149.

42 S. Rodríguez Demorizi, *Salomé Ureña de Henríquez*, 32.

43 See Fiol-Matta, *Queer Mother for the Nation*, and Reyes-Santos, *Our Caribbean Kin*.

44 "más parece poeta, que poetisa" (Nicolás Heredia, "Salomé Ureña," in Emilio Rodríguez Demorizi, ed., *Salomé Ureña y el Instituto de Señoritas*, 33).

45 "No busquéis en él la ternura del sentimiento femenil más *blando* mientras más se acerca a la poesía, no" (Nicolás Heredia, "Salomé Ureña," in Emilio Rodríguez Demorizi, ed., *Salomé Ureña y el Instituto de Señoritas*, 35, emphasis mine).

46 "En esta época inmediata post-Independencia, el concepto 'patria' se personifica con frecuencia en el concepto 'mujer. [. . .] Generalmente [. . .] la personificación de la patria recae en la madre" (Vallejo, *Las madres de la patria y las bellas mentiras*, 93).

47 "La Patria es siempre concepto abstracto" (Vallejo, *Las madres de la patria y las bellas mentiras*, 94).

48 See Federico Henríquez y Carvajal, "Salomé Ureña: Eminente poetisa dominicana," in Emilio Rodríguez Demorizi, ed., *Salomé Ureña y el Instituto de Señoritas*, 56–72.

49 Federico Benigno Pérez, "Salomé Ureña de Henríquez," in Emilio Rodríguez Demorizi, ed., *Salomé Ureña y el Instituto de Señoritas*, 110–115, and Rafael Deligne, "Salomé Ureña de Henríquez," in Emilio Rodríguez Demorizi, ed., *Salomé Ureña y el Instituto de Señoritas*, 116–120.

50 "Pero la cuerda que más vibra en la lira de oro de la señora Ureña de Henríquez, es indudablemente la del patriotismo" (Federico García Godoy, "Salomé Ureña de Henríquez," in Emilio Rodríguez Demorizi, ed., *Salomé Ureña y el Instituto de Señoritas*, 100–101).

51 "Su musa no desciende a ciertas *trivialidades*, ni se deja llevar por las corrientes que arrastran siempre a los talentos mediocres. *Viril* y llena de grandeza es su poesía, como elaborada al calor de las grandes ideas de regeneración y de progreso que el espíritu moderno propaga continuamente por todos los ámbitos del globo" (Federico García Godoy, "Salomé Ureña de Henríquez," in Emilio Rodríguez Demorizi, ed., *Salomé Ureña y el Instituto de Señoritas*, 99, emphasis mine).

52 "Salomé Ureña era poeta de nervio; en su pecho de mujer jamás tuvo cabida esa sensiblería que hace en ciertas ocasiones algo repugnante el canto de algunas poetisas" (Luis A. Bermúdez, "Da. S. Ureña de Henríquez," in Emilio Rodríguez Demorizi, ed., *Salomé Ureña y el Instituto de Señoritas*, 264).

53 See José Lamarche, "Salomé Ureña de Henríquez," in Emilio Rodríguez Demorizi, ed., *Salomé Ureña y el Instituto de Señoritas*, 77, and Luis A. Bermúdez, "Da. S. Ureña de Henríquez," in Emilio Rodríguez Demorizi, ed., *Salomé Ureña y el Instituto de Señoritas*, 266.

54 "El 10 de Junio del año que acaba de pasar, en una sesion literaria que nuestra sociedad 'Amigos del País' celebró con el nombre de Conferencia, tuve la dicha de ver á U. [. . .]. Yo no la conocía á u. personalmente, pero por sus obras sí, en las cuales siempre la hube admirado, como la admiré en la que en aquella noche dió á conocer á los que estaban á su alrededor. Las simpatías que ya me había inspirado [. . .] me dominaban, me positaron en el caso de acercarme á U., y, casi imprudentemente, de dirijirle algunas palabras, sin duda anhelando por saber, si en el acento de sus labios habia la misma dulzura que en el de su poesía (Incháustegui and Malagón, eds., *Familia Henríquez Ureña*, vol. I, 5–6).

55 "Las leyes generales de la naturaleza segun las cuales en los cuerpos se operan fenómenos que modifican su propiedades, ó alteran su íntima composicion, no

es ménos indispensable conocer" (Incháustegui and Malagón, eds., *Familia Henríquez Ureña*, vol. I, 7).

56 "Inpírense los políticos en esas composiciones, que el genio de nuestra joven poetisa nos brinda. Ahí tiene lecciones todos los hijos de la Patria, lecciones llenas de una moralidad admirable, de una virtud fecunda en bienes. A los que se miran en la cumbre de la sociedad, ella les recuerda sus deberes con una voz que no revela temor ninguno; a los que son la esperanza del país, los alienta, les infunde valor, les traza un sendero [. . .] (Francisco Henríquez y Carvajal, "Salomé Ureña en 1878," in Emilio Rodríguez Demorizi, ed., *Salomé Ureña y el Instituto de Señoritas*, 42).

57 "Ruborícense los que inútilmente pasan el tiempo, pudiendo descollar en el estudio," (Francisco Henríquez y Carvajal, "Salomé Ureña en 1878," in Emilio Rodríguez Demorizi, ed., *Salomé Ureña y el Instituto de Señoritas*, 43).

58 "Pero sepan todos que para escribir en tono tan alto como ella, es necesario vigorizar el pensamiento con el cultivo de las ciencias, y una profunda erudición literaria" (Francisco Henríquez y Carvajal, "Salomé Ureña en 1878," in Emilio Rodríguez Demorizi, ed., *Salomé Ureña y el Instituto de Señoritas*, 43).

59 "los jóvenes de ambos sexos" and "restaurar la Patria en todos sus males" (Francisco Henríquez y Carvajal, "Salomé Ureña en 1878," in Emilio Rodríguez Demorizi, ed., *Salomé Ureña y el Instituto de Señoritas*, 43).

60 "Sí, la Señorita Ureña estudia sin cesar, y sigue con ardor el estudio de la ciencia. De ese modo vemos cómo se va elevando de punto en punto a la cumbre desde el cual mañana, en voz más alta aún, hablará a todos los pueblos, y por todos será oída" (Francisco Henríquez y Carvajal, "Salomé Ureña en 1878," in Emilio Rodríguez Demorizi, ed., *Salomé Ureña y el Instituto de Señoritas*, 43).

61 "Con cuánto entusiasmo he leido y releido estos dias los cantos que ha producido tu musa patriótica! La ausencia de la Patria y el constante pensar en ella; en su porvenir, en su Gloria como en sus presentes desgracias, á veces ponen en suspenso mi espíritu y me producen profundas conmociones. *No pudiendo dar en esos momentos forma á mis ideas, ni salida á mi sensibilidad exaltada, acudo á tí y veo en tus pensamientos retratados los mios, y vuelvo á llenarme de ese mismo entusiasmo con que en los años de mi mas tierna juventud te admiraba y me acercaba á tí*" (Incháustegui and Malagón, eds., *Familia Henríquez Ureña*, vol. I, 23, emphasis mine).

62 "Cualquier cosa que escribes ya sabes cuánto me entusiasmaría. Cualquier recuerdo en esa forma me sería de gran aliento" (Incháustegui and Malagón, eds., *Familia Henríquez Ureña*, vol. I, 36).

63 "La figura del hombre sensible que no se avergüenza de llorar o hacer visibles sus emociones ocupa un espacio importante en los textos de [several Latin American writers]. El fluir de lágrimas masculinas en textos casi canónicos da cuenta de que en el siglo XIX el hombre femineizado no era incompatible con los proyectos civilizatorios y que los paradigmas de la masculinidad dan un salto cuantitativo

en lo que va de un siglo a otro" (Peluffo and Sánchez Prado, introduction to *Entre hombres*, 12, emphasis mine).

64 See González Stephan, "Narrativas duras en tiempos blandos."

65 Balaguer, *Letras dominicanas*, 77–78.

66 "distinguida poetisa, gloria de las letras dominicanas" (Machado, "Salomé Ureña de Henríquez.")

67 Machado uses the first person plural to refer to himself.

68 "Leímos los versos; los volvimos á leer y no sabemos cuantas veces recorrieron nuestros ojos esas líneas que despertaban en nuestra memoria tantos recuerdos y decian á nuestra alma tantas cosas!

Su lectura produjo en nosotros un *sentimiento raro*, una mezcla indefinible de *alegría y de tristeza*, una de esas impresiones que no se pueden trasladar al papel, ni pueden nuestros labios repetir.

Quedámonos largo tiempo pensativos y se levantó ante nuestra mente la imagen de la patria con todos sus encantos y atractivos.

Fué aquello un verdadero *éxtasis* en que nos sentimos envueltos en la tibia y embalsamada atmósfera de sus brisas y aspiramos al olor de sus flores y escuchamos *sobrecogídos* los misteriosos rumores que pueblan sus selvas. Sentímonos transportados á Santo Domingo, á esa ciudad querida donde se abrieron nuestros ojos á la luz y corrieron tranquilos y felices nos años de nuestra infancia; donde se eleva la casa de nuestros padres que solitarios hoy lloran la ausencia de sus hijos y donde nuestros abuelos duermen el sueño de la tumba. [. . .]

Y [donde] *gozamos, sufrimos y amamos.*

Todo eso produjo en nosotros la lectura de esos versos!

Ah! cuánto se *goza* y *sufre* cuando á través de los tiempos y la ausencia contemplabamos la imagen de lo que nos es querido, embellecida por la luz de los recuerdos!" (Machado, "Salomé Ureña de Henríquez," emphasis mine)

69 "Recordamos haber suspendido más de una vez la lectura para prorrumpir en exclamaciones de admiración y entusiasmo, y que también ¿porqué no descirlo? más de una furtiva lágrima nos humedeció los ojos" (Machado, "Salomé Ureña de Henríquez").

70 Vicioso notes that "during the 47 years of Salomé Ureña's life, the country had thirty-one governments, several of them of the same person" ("durante los 47 años que vivió Salomé Ureña, el país tuvo treinta y un gobiernos, entre ellos varios de la misma persona"). See Vicioso and Ureña de Henríquez, *Salomé Ureña de Henríquez*, 14.

71 "[s]oy un desterrado de la vida" (Incháustegui and Malagón, eds., *Familia Henríquez Ureña*, 274).

72 "parece que el destierro presta vuelo al sentimiento poético" (Incháustegui and Malagón, eds., *Familia Henríquez Ureña*, 113).

73 "Vivo en París sin haberlo visitado nunca. A pesar de todo, no tengo muchos deseos de ir; deseo que tú vengas, pero no ir yo. Solo en caso de suma necesidad iria

yo á tu encuentro" (Incháustegui and Malagón, eds., *Familia Henríquez Ureña*, vol. I, 189).

74 Ureña de Henríquez, *Poesías completas*, 13.

75 Ureña de Henríquez, *Poesías completas*, 14.

76 Ureña de Henríquez, *Poesías completas*, 20, emphasis mine.

77 Ureña de Henríquez, *Poesías completas*, 21.

78 Ureña de Henríquez, *Poesías completas*, 21.

79 For more on working-class immigrants arriving to the Dominican Republic during this time, see Mayes, *The Mulatto Republic*. On rural to urban migration, see Martínez Vergne, *Nation and Citizen in the Dominican Republic*, and Hoffnung-Garskof, *A Tale of Two Cities*.

80 "es en su poesía 'doméstica' donde Salomé escapa las limitaciones de su educación clásica y los valores de su tiempo para expresarse como lo que era: una mujer con sus angustias, sus inseguridades, sus miedos, su necesidad de apoyo y compañía, su nostalgia, sus alegrías, sus amores. Como un ser humano" (Vicioso and Ureña de Henríquez, *Salomé Ureña de Henríquez*, 21).

See also Paravisini-Gebert, "Salomé Ureña de Henríquez (1850–1897)."

81 "Tú no te acuerdas, mamá? / El sol ¡qué bonito era / cuando estaba aquí papá!" (Ureña de Henríquez, *Poemas y biografía de Salomé Ureña*, 60.)

82 "Ya sabia yo que á tu lado [Francisco] no me echaria de menos. [. . .] El te quiere á ti mas que á mí; estoy convencida de ello. Ya ves que ni el sol le parecía bello porque le faltabas tú" (Incháustegui and Malagón, eds., *Familia Henríquez Ureña: Epistolario*, vol. I, 167).

83 "Yo no quiero títulos, yo no quiero nada que no seas tú. Por grandes que fueran las dichas y las pompas que me aguardan yo las diera todas por no haber sufrido, por no haberme separado nunca del esposo de mi alma, del padre amorosísimo de mis pobres hijos. ¿Recuerdas cuando me decias que mis aspiraciones eran muy mezquinas? Yo deseaba un hogar pequeño, un hogar sin lujo donde vivir contigo y mis hijos sin cuidarme del mundo, con tu cariño y la virtud por toda riqueza. Comparo esa vida con la presente, y veo que yo tenia razon y que el errado eras tú" (Incháustegui and Malagón, eds., *Familia Henríquez Ureña*, vol. I, 195).

84 "¿Qué es esto? Dios mío! ¿qué es esto? Yo no puedo mas, yo no tengo fuerzas para esperar seis meses mas; me siento morir cuando es necesario que viva para mis hijos, ¡Qué desgracia tan inmensa la que me abruma! Nuestro Franc tenia razón: qué pálido es ahora el sol! Qué triste todo lo que me rodea! Quisiera huir de mí misma; quisiera huir lejos, muy lejos á donde no se me siguiera el pensamiento; quisiera no pensar porque esto me mata. Y no tengo á quien confiar mi amargura, porque nadie me comprende. Tú solo me comprenderías; tú solo que has sufrido, que sufres lo que yo sufro.

Y á tí no puedo decirlo tampoco, porque sería matarte" (Incháustegui and Malagón, eds., *Familia Henríquez Ureña: Epistolario*, vol. I, 196–197).

85 "Yo quisiera decirte cuánto sufro; yo quisiera decirte que no puedo esperarte con animo tranquilo, porque ya mi espíritu no tiene fuerzas para prolongar su

martirio. Soñaba con la esperanza de verte dentro de tres ó cuatro meses, y me matas diciéndome que el dia de vernos está tan lejano que es imposible fijarlo. Pero, Dios mio! Si yo no puedo vivir asi por mas tiempo; si vivo aterrada, si tengo miedo de la vida, si tengo miedo de esta soledad del espíritu!" (Incháustegui and Malagón, eds., *Familia Henríquez Ureña*, vol. I, 194).

86 "En cuanto á lo de jíbaro, yo te aseguro que así hombron y todo, cuando llegaste á París no parecias el que eres hoy [. . .]. De seguro que, sin pensarlo tú, tenias aire de asombrado y distraido. Y tú querias que el pobre muchachito, arrancado al calor de su madre para lanzarlo a una navegacion de mas de veinte dias, experimentando sacudidas violentas á la vista de un mundo desconocido para él, permaneciera inalterable como un viajero consumado que todo lo ha visto y que con nada nuevo se impresiona. [. . .] *No te estes figurando que aquí era un idiota y que ha despertado ahora en Paris*" (Incháustegui and Malagón, eds., *Familia Henríquez Ureña*, vol. I, 184–185, emphasis mine).

87 José Martí's influential essay "Our America" urges Latin American intellectuals and politicians to turn away from Europe as the guiding light of their nation's culture and to look toward their own people for inspiration.

88 "Respecto a mi viaje te diré que es una idea muy halagadora, pero de muy difícil realizacion. El imposible es el Instituto. Imposible, imposible, ésto sin mí se desplomaria, y nuestra obra es obra de porvenir" (Incháustegui and Malagón, eds., *Familia Henríquez Ureña*, vol. I, 164).

89 "algunas veces has avanzado la idea de escojer otra patria para tu familia, si las circunstancias lo exijieren. Pero no creo que suceda nunca; el porvenir nos espera y tenemos que llevar a cabo algunas obras de bien en provecho del pais" (Incháustegui and Malagón, eds., *Familia Henríquez Ureña*, vol. I, 181).

90 "No seas bobo queriendo presentarte como una notabilidad en ciencias naturales" (Incháustegui and Malagón, eds., *Familia Henríquez Ureña*, vol. I, 50).

91 José Dubeau (1857–1925) was an educator and sometime politician who opened normal schools in Puerto Plata (see Brugal, "El Maestro Dubeau"). Emilio Prud'Homme (1856–1932) was an influential educator, politician, and poet. His greatest claim to fame, however, was that he wrote the lyrics to the Dominican national anthem (Balaguer, *Historia de la literatura dominicana*, 237–241).

92 "Tú creiste siempre que con mi trabajo y el tuyo viviriamos más holgados; y Dubeau y Prud'homme nos han demostrado que cuando la mujer laboriosa se consagra á la direccion de su hogar se vive mejor, porque se economiza mas y se hace mas productivo el trabajo del esposo" (Incháustegui and Malagón, eds., *Familia Henríquez Ureña*, vol. I, 206). Though some of her values, such as the universal education of women, as well as her lifestyle, could be considered feminist, she never used the word herself, unlike some of her contemporaries in the country, the Caribbean, and Latin America. However, I have not found a document where she denies being a feminist.

93 "El deseo! Ya no tengo otro que el de regresar. Regresaría con gusto, aunque fuera abandonado la carrera médica. Pero ahí es donde vienen las reflexiones. [. . .] Así

harían los espíritus débiles, incapaces de una obra magna, impropios para soportar la fatiga moral, *variables en sus deseos* y en sus intenciones" (Incháustegui and Malagón, eds., *Familia Henríquez Ureña*, vol. I, 73, emphasis mine).

94 "Y sin embargo, podrías enorgullecerte [. . .] de tener un esposo tan fiel como yo, que hasta ahora permanece in Paris aislado por complete del contacto de las mugeres.

Esto no obstante, es contra la naturaleza, y en vez de agradarte, debe desagradarte. Creer en la fidelidad de los hombres es una falsa creencia: no pueden ser fieles, porque la naturaleza no se lo permite. Como yo no sé mentir, hablo así.

Ahora bien, cómo se explica entónces mi conducta en ésta? Muy sencillamente: todas las potencias de mi espíritu están consagradas á solo fin invariable. El resto de la naturaleza está como adormida por ahora. En algunas treguas siento conmoverme; pero entónces surgen en mi mente ideas indecibles, sueños indescriptibles, deseos inconcebibles, músicas lejanas, voces interiors, esperanzas lisonjeras, en fin, lo que se ha designado muy bien con la palabra francesa *revêrie*" (Incháustegui and Malagón, eds., *Familia Henríquez Ureña*, vol. I, 79–80).

95 Incháustegui and Malagón, eds., *Familia Henríquez Ureña*, vol. I, 79.

96 Incháustegui and Malagón, eds., *Familia Henríquez Ureña*, vol. I, 80.

97 The only reference to Henríquez y Carvajal's infidelity in the two-volume published family epistolary emerges in a November 1934 letter that he writes to his sons Pedro and Max. He writes, "my daughter Mercedes died in Paris on the 29th of last October" ("mi hija Mercedes murió en París el 29 del pasado mes de octubre"), confirming that he'd had an illegitimate half-French daughter. See Incháustegui and Malagón, eds., *Familia Henríquez Ureña*, vol. II, 288.

98 "Veo con suma satisfaccion los progresos de Pibin [Pedro], pero desearía que al mismo tiempo se me marcaran los de Fran. [. . .]

Me darás una idea el grado de ella [la instrucción] en Fran, apuntándome en cada ramo hasta donde alcanza. Me explicarás que género de ideas llaman mas su atencion y si se debilita ó aumenta su cualidad de observador" (Incháustegui and Malagón, eds., *Familia Henríquez Ureña*, vol. I, 19).

99 "ciencias, derecho, letras medicinas" and "Camila quizás pueda también hacer un doctorado en letras ó filosofía" (Incháustegui and Malagón, eds., *Familia Henríquez Ureña*, vol. I, 270–271).

100 "toda la energía moral" and "avanzarán serenos a la adquisición de la victoria" (Incháustegui and Malagón, eds., *Familia Henríquez Ureña*, vol. I, 271).

101 "A pesar de lo mucho que te he aconsejado que salgas y que lleves á pasear á los niños, no lo haces. Es preciso que lo hagas y que procures distraerte. No hay cosa peor que encerrarse entre cuatro paredes, porque así la reflexion continua acaba por enfermar el ánimo" (Incháustegui and Malagón, eds., *Familia Henríquez Ureña*, vol. I, 33).

102 Incháustegui and Malagón, eds., *Familia Henríquez Ureña*, vol. I, 71.

103 Ureña de Henríquez, *Poesías completas*, 104.

104 Ureña de Henríquez, *Poesías completas*, 106.

105 "se equivalen las posiciones de amada y esposa [y] presenta un sujeto amante que incluye las dos categorías" (Vallejo, *Las madres de la patria y las bellas mentiras*, 174).

106 Suárez Findlay, *Imposing Decency*, 72.

107 "Como soltera, es un problema; como casada, un efecto; como viuda, una tentación; como hija, un premio; como hermana, una causa; como madre, un ángel; como amante, un lujo; como suegra, un demonio, [*sic*] como madrastra, un infierno" (cited in Vallejo, *Las madres de la patria y las bellas mentiras*, 236).

108 "Para que la mujer sea bella, debe tener: / Tres cosas blancas: la piel, los dientes y las manos; / tres cosas negras: los ojos, las cejas y las pestañas; / tres cosas largas: el talle, los cabellos y las manos" (cited in Vallejo, *Las madres de la patria y las bellas mentiras*, 237).

109 Because of the increasingly important role of motherhood within the national body, the poems that emphasized Ureña's maternal love—including "El ave y el nido"—became as canonical as her patriotic poetry. As Paravisini-Gebert writes, "It is not surprising [. . .] that the poems set aside as the best of the [intimate poem] group are those on the subject of motherhood" ("Salomé Ureña de Henríquez (1850–1897)," 527). Ureña's other intimate poems, which reveal her anxieties over her husband's absence and her sexual desire for him, attain secondary status.

110 Dillon, *The Gender of Freedom*, 15.

111 For some examples of these letters, see Emilio Rodríguez Demorizi, ed., *Salomé Ureña y el Instituto de Señoritas*.

112 "fueron pioneras en explorar una esfera que no siempre quedaba restringida al devenir de la unidad familiar" (Zeller, *Discursos y espacios femeninos*, 38).

April Mayes also discusses the influence of this education on women vis-à-vis the public sphere in the *Mulatto Republic*, especially in chapter 6, "Gender and *Hispanidad* in the New Era."

CHAPTER 2. RACE, GENDER, AND PROPRIETY IN DOMINICAN COMMEMORATION

1 Suárez Findlay, *Imposing Decency*, 25.

"Las letras nacionales están de duelo" ("In memoriam," *El Eco de la Opinion*, March 13, 1897. As seen in Incháustegui and Malagón, eds., *Familia Henríquez Ureña*, vol. I, 275).

A portion of this chapter was published for a special issue on "Dominican Race" in *The Black Scholar*. See Ramírez, "Salomé Ureña's Blurred Edges."

2 For details about the funeral procession and burial, including several of the speeches and panegyrics, see Emilio Rodríguez Demorizi, ed., *Salomé Ureña y el Instituto de Señoritas*.

3 See Candelario, *Black behind the Ears*.

4 "aquellos que pretendían esconder su originen racial hacían uso de 'las introducidas pelucas', tras las cuales ocultaban 'los pelos naturales que testificaban de dónde por calidad venían los hombres'" (Ugarte, *Estampas coloniales*, vol. 2, 203).

5 For examples of colonial laws preventing nonwhites from wearing certain materials, see Bautista, *Mujer y esclavitud en Santo Domingo*, 79–80, and Ugarte, *Estampas coloniales*, vol. 2.

6 When I refer to the rise of institutionalized antiblackness, I refer to the post-1822 years after the final abolition of slavery with the Haitian unification of the island. Before then, institutional antiblackness helped support slavery and vice versa.

7 Brickhouse, *Transamerican Literary Relations and the Nineteenth-Century Public Sphere*, 258.

8 "revisi[ones] radical[es] de las *bases conceptuales* del estudio literario, y un examen de los postulados teóricos sobre la lectura y escritura, los cuales han estado basados en las experiencias literarias masculinas [. . .]" (Vicioso and Ureña de Henríquez, *Salomé Ureña de Henríquez*, 22).

9 See Alvarez, "A White Woman of Color," and Vicioso, "Dominicanyorkness."

10 Eller, *We Dream Together*, 19.

11 See Balaguer, *El Cristo de la libertad*.

12 Debates about whether or not Duarte is the nation's "true" founding father continue to this day. See Jimenes Grullón, *El mito de los Padres de la Patria*, and Mella, *Los espejos de Duarte*.

13 Eller, *We Dream Together*, 14.

14 To learn more about the fascinating Burgos, see Pérez Rosario, *Becoming Julia de Burgos*.

15 "nunca se hubiera imaginado que su biografía saldría publicada en un libro sobre mujeres afrocaribeñas o afrodominicanas" (Valerio-Holguín, "Salomé Ureña de Henríquez," 520).

16 *Black behind the Ears*, 100–101. See also Roth, *Race Migrations*.

17 Balaguer, *La isla al revés*.

   As I discuss further in chapter three, Balaguer, along with other canonical scholars, argued that the mountains surrounding the region protected it from Haitian incursion and, thus, racial "degeneracy."

18 Smith, "'Looking at One's Self through the Eyes of Others,'" 275.

19 Smith, "'Looking at One's Self through the Eyes of Others,'" 286, emphasis mine.

20 Smith, "'Looking at One's Self through the Eyes of Others,'" 287.

21 Quoted in Hobbs, *A Chosen Exile*, 309.

22 Hobbs, *A Chosen Exile*, 45.

23 Simmons, *Reconstructing Racial Identity and the African Past in the Dominican Republic*, 4.

24 Hughes, "Playboys," 2.

25 Consider the triumphalist, future-driven photo essays that present racially ambiguous subjects as evidence of what U.S. subjects "will all look like in a few decades." See, for instance, Funderburg, "The Changing Face of America."

Regarding how diasporic Dominicans affect racial discourse on the island, see Candelario, *Black behind the Ears*; Flores, *The Diaspora Strikes Back*; and Roth, *Race Migrations*.

26 Roth, *Race Migrations*, 48–50.
27 This is not to suggest that Dominican conservative ideology has not enforced a Latin American version of white supremacy.
28 See Miller, *Historia de la pintura dominicana*.
29 "requería del minucioso retoque para conseguir la belleza del sujeto retratado" (De los Santos, *Raíces e impulso nacional*, 248).
30 Emilio Rodríguez Demorizi as quoted in De los Santos, *Raíces e impulso nacional*, 249 and 247.
31 See Emilio Rodríguez Demorizi, ed., *Salomé Ureña y el Instituto de Señoritas*, 263n.
32 See De los Santos, *Raíces e impulso nacional*, 351.
33 We may consider, for example, the case of Olivorio (Papá Liborio) Mateo, a folk healer turned messianic leader assassinated by U.S. occupation officials in 1922. His armed followers, most of them poor, black, and living in the mountains near the southern border, comprised a serious threat to the authority of the foreign occupiers and of the Dominican ruling classes. Mateo and his followers certainly represented el monte.
34 See Derby, *The Dictator's Seduction*.
35 For critiques of Trujillo-era and post-Trujillo-era nationalism, see San Miguel, *The Imagined Island*; Rodríguez, *La isla y su envés*; Torres-Saillant, *El retorno de las yolas*; Martínez, "Not a Cockfight"; and Baud, "Manuel Arturo Peña Batlle y Joaquín Balaguer y la identidad nacional dominicana."
36 Johnson, *The Fear of French Negroes*, 53.
37 Writings about Ureña published during the Trujillo era include Silveria R. de Rodríguez Demorizi, *Salomé Ureña de Henríquez*; Balaguer, *Letras dominicanas* and *Historia de la literatura dominicana*; and the prologue in Ureña de Henríquez, *Poesías completas*, 12–29; Herrera, *La poesía de Salomé Ureña en su función social y patriótica*; Emilio Rodríguez Demorizi, ed., *Salomé Ureña y el Instituto de Señoritas*.
38 See De los Santos, *Impulso y desarrollo moderno*, 176 and 145.
39 See García Romero, *Ruinas*.
40 "En la mañana parece otra mujer, cuando el pelo todavía no está recogido en un rodete y la cabellera cae oscura, con algunas hebras de plata, frondosa y crespa" (García Romero, "Salomé, madre y maestra ejemplar").
41 "Foto descrita en el texto y que resume la imagen de la madre, la poetisa y la maestra Salomé Ureña."
42 "Al educar apreciemos el legado de Salomé Ureña, a través de su mejor obra: la dedicación y constancia en la educación de sus hijos."
43 In reference to Ureña, César A. Herrera writes: "No hay en América más alto ejemplo de abnegación femenina" (*La poesía de Salomé Ureña en su function social y patriótica*, 30).

44 "La crítica ha sido eco de referencias estereotipadas, apocantes y hasta caricatur-
escas en el enjuiciamiento de las creaciones femininas" (Hernández, "De críticos y
creadoras," 431).

45 "feísima" and "solterona" (Hernández, "De críticos y creadoras," 431).

46 "mujercita flaquita, hasta medio feita" (Ureña de Henríquez, et al., *100 Años de
Poesía*, 28).

47 Cocco de Filippis, "Indias y Trigueñas No Longer," 145.

48 Sheller, "Work That Body," 352.

49 Incháustegui and Malagón, eds., *Familia Henríquez Ureña*, vol. I, 230 and 264.

50 Mayes, "Why Dominican Feminism Moved to the Right," 354.

51 Ureña sought funding from the city council to make the Institute available to
girls of all classes (Salomé Ureña de Henríquez, "Al Sr. Presidente del Ayunta-
miento de Santo Domingo," in Emilio Rodríguez Demorizi, ed., *Salomé Ureña
y el Instituto de Señoritas*, 125–126). See also Zeller, *Discursos y espacios femeninos*, 32.

52 Silveria R. de Rodríguez Demorizi, *Salomé Ureña de Henríquez*.

53 "notas manuscritas del Dr. Pedro Henríquez Ureña, así como noticias verbales
que nos comunicó en Cambridge, Massachusetts, en 1941" (Silveria R. de Rodríguez
Demorizi, *Salomé Ureña de Henríquez*, 5n1).

54 Silveria R. de Rodríguez Demorizi, *Salomé Ureña de Henríquez*, 9.

55 Antecedentes, Nacimiento y Sacerdocio, Vocación Poética, Patriotismo, Salomé
en el Hogar, Femineidad, En la Escuela, La Muerte.

56 "Salomé no descuidó sus deberes de madre por los del magisterio" (Silveria R. de
Rodríguez Demorizi, *Salomé Ureña de Henríquez*, 25).

57 Silveria R. de Rodríguez Demorizi, *Salomé Ureña de Henríquez*, 22–23.

58 Incháustegui and Malagón, eds., *Familia Henríquez Ureña*, vol. I, 109.

59 "Salomé Ureña no alcanzó a liquidar el 'ángel del hogar', pero en ocasiones logró
burlarlo" (Hernández, "De críticos y creadoras," 428).

60 Incháustegui and Malagón, eds., *Familia Henríquez Ureña*, vol. I, 72.

61 "Salomé Ureña fué extremadamente femenina" (Silveria R. de Rodríguez Demorizi, *Salomé Ureña de Henríquez*, 31).

62 It would not be surprising if Silveria R. de Rodríguez Demorizi was aware of
Gabriela Mistral's reputation as a "rara"/queer poet and educator, for Mistral was
well known throughout Latin America (Fiol-Matta, *A Queer Mother for the Nation*, xxvii). Moreover, Mistral and Pedro Henríquez Ureña shared a close friend
and confidante in Mexican intellectual Alfonso Reyes and moved in the same intellectual circles in this country. Pedro and Mistral also met while they were both
in Mexico (Henríquez Ureña de Hlito, *Pedro Henríquez Ureña*, 91). Consciously
or subconsciously thinking of Mistral, perhaps Pedro communicated Ureña's
unmistakable femininity to her biographer.

63 "no se refiere a odiosos rezumos varolines, a manifestaciones de bastarda masculinidad en sus versos, sino a la majestad de su inspiración; hombre también en la
grandeza de la acción, pero femenina siempre en su actitud. Nunca fué hombre

en la actitud esta mujer, de tan extrema femineidad" (Silveria R. de Rodríguez Demorizi, *Salomé Ureña de Henríquez*, 32).

64 "algún sentimiento delicado, alguna recóndita sonrisa de complacencia, algún noble estímulo para la vida" (Silveria R. de Rodríguez Demorizi, *Salomé Ureña de Henríquez*, 31).

65 "De no ser así [femenina], ella habría sido digna de aplauso en un sentido, pero no en el más sagrado, porque ni aun la gloria más alta vale en la mujer el sacrificio de su femineidad" (Silveria R. de Rodríguez Demorizi, *Salomé Ureña de Henríquez*, 31).

66 Brea and Duarte, *Entre la calle y la casa*, 20. For more on Trujillo's policies regarding motherhood, see Madera, *"Never Forget Syphilis"*, and Mayes, "Why Dominican Feminism Moved to the Right."

67 Vicioso, *Salomé U.*

68 I have been unable to locate the manuscript form of Germana Quintana's play *Y no todo era amor* (And Not Everything Was Love).

69 "Lo más importante es subrayar que el hilo conductor de este monólogo es la ausencia de un ser querido, mirada y sentida a través de la óptica de dos mujeres escritoras, separadas por un siglo" ("La obra," in *Salomé U.*, 8).

70 "Esta revalorización de la poesía 'doméstica' de la mujer, y por lo tanto de su obra como un todo, como siempre ha sido analizada la obra masculina, se convertiría, casi un siglo después del nacimiento de Salomé Ureña, en uno de los temas centrales de la crítica literaria feminina" (Vicioso and Ureña de Henríquez, *Salomé Ureña de Henríquez*, 21).

71 Vicioso, *Salomé U.*, 41.

72 "En esta escena la escritora internaliza el sentido del poema de Salomé y se realiza la transferencia, es decir, ya el poema pasa a ser SU poema, y a tener consecuencias inicialmente devastadoras" (Vicioso, *Salomé U.*, 42).

73 Alvarez, *In the Name of Salomé*.

74 Wright, *Becoming Black*, 171.

75 Maja Horn has a similar dialogical reading of Dominican women's writings about Trujillo. See Horn, *Masculinity after Trujillo*.

76 Ureña de Henríquez, *Poesías completas*, 159.

77 I use first names when referring to the characters in the play.

78 In general, feminist scholarship has demonstrated that the feminized domestic sphere and the masculinized political sphere are intertwined. Elizabeth Dillon argues that "[p]rivacy [. . .] is constructed and articulated in the public sphere. The privacy of women is the product not of women's seclusion within their homes, but of a public articulation and valuation of women's domestic position" (Dillon, *The Gender of Freedom*, 4). Amy Kaplan's work on the nineteenth-century U.S. also applies in that it "demonstrat[es] that the private feminized space of the home both infused and bolstered the public male arena of the market and the sentimental values attached to maternal influence were used to sanction women's entry into the wider civic realm from which those same values theo-

retically excluded them" (Kaplan, "Manifest Domesticity," 111). Finally, a similar impetus drives work on the role of sexual politics in colonialism by Eileen Suárez Findlay, who writes: "I resolved to try to break down the conceptual wall between the grand, public arenas and the rather mysterious and seemingly unimportant 'private' spheres of peoples' lives where sexual and racial identities loomed large" (Suárez Findlay, *Imposing Decency*, 3).

79 "la considerada inferioridad de la mujer, su confinamiento al ámbito de lo privado y lo doméstico, la exaltación de la maternidad, el control del cuerpo de la mujer a través de una exaltación como objeto de reproducción de la especie humana, o como objeto de placer." Brea and Duarte, *Entre la calle y la casa*, 14.

80 "Una de las estrategias de la crítica feminist latinoamericana [. . .] consistió en demonstrar que la construcción del sujeto femenino republicano como privado, hogareño y sentimental era un discurso más deseado que real" (Peluffo and Sánchez Prado, introduction to *Entre hombres*, 10).

81 Some of Vicioso's work demonstrates that she does not share this character's anti-Haitian bias. See Durán-Almarza's essay about Vicioso's *Nuyor/Islas*, "*Ciguapas* in New York," 152.

82 "Cuando era chiquita pensaba que la patria debía ser una mujer muy hermosa para que papá—por ella—se arriesgara tanto y nos abandonara. / Ya más grandecita percibí que no era sólo papá./ En el Este, la patria tenía loco a Santana. / En el Sur, en un ir y venir, a Báez. / En el Cibao, persistente y firme, a Luperón. / Todos peleándose unos con otros en nombre de la patria" (Vicioso, *Salomé U.*, 29–30, emphasis mine).

83 "The Great Silence from which These Two Women Emerge" is taken from the acknowledgments section in Alvarez, *In the Name of Salomé*, 357.

84 Her family, which had long-standing ties to the U.S., fled during the Trujillo dictatorship.

85 I use first names to distinguish the fictional characters in the novel from the historical figures.

86 Alvarez, *In the Name of Salomé*, 2.

87 Alvarez, *In the Name of Salomé*, 138.

88 Alvarez, *In the Name of Salomé*, 177.

89 Alvarez, *In the Name of Salomé*, 177.

90 Alvarez, *In the Name of Salomé*, 177.

91 Alvarez, *In the Name of Salomé*, 174–175.

92 Alvarez, *In the Name of Salomé*, 134.

93 Alvarez, *In the Name of Salomé*, 144.

94 Sommer, *One Master for Another*, 61.

95 The novel suggests that Ureña knew about the affair, but I found no evidence of this in the family's correspondence.

96 Odile Ferly's study of Caribbean women writers also adopts the metaphor of echo as a weapon against their texts' silencing: "In fact, pan-Caribbeanism has been crucial to the elaboration of sense of collective identity. Throughout the region,

the female tradition has faced exclusion, which has resulted in its near silencing. By recuperating the pan-Caribbean legacy, this study is able to engage in a comparative approach that allows the female voices to resonate strongly, amplified by mutual echoing" (Ferly, *A Poetics of Relation*, 2).

97 Alvarez, *In the Name of Salomé*, 356.

98 Bhabha, "Are You a Man or a Mouse?," 59.

99 Imbert Brugal, "The Manly Intellectual Woman," 170.

100 Because I did not have a recorder with me at this time, I am paraphrasing her statement, made in Spanish, from memory.

101 Alvarez, *In the Name of Salomé*, 94.

102 Alvarez, *In the Name of Salomé*, 280–281.

103 See Pedro Henríquez Ureña, *Memorias, diario, notas de viaje*, 29–30.

CHAPTER 3. FOLLOWING THE ADMIRAL

1 Hughes, "Columbia."
   McClintock, "Imperial Ghosting and National Tragedy," 824.
   An early version of a section in this chapter was published as "Great Men's Magic." I also presented portions of this chapter at the 2010 Comparative Literature Association Meeting in New Orleans ("Discourses of the Trujillo Dictatorship from a Present-Day Exile"), the 2014 Latin American Studies Association Congress in Chicago ("The Columbus Lighthouse as Symbol of Dominican Intellectual Masculinism"), and at the 2015 Coloquio Internacional del Programa de Estudios sobre Latinos en los Estados Unidos at Casa de Las Américas in Havana ("Dominicanos de 'pura cepa': El patriotismo, el transnacionalismo, y la esfera pública").
   The *dembow* musical genre speeds up the beat of *reggaetón* and adds repetitive lyrics.

2 Guzmán, "Ministerio Público apresó a 'El Alfa' por offender a padres de la Patria."

3 "expresó que los padres de la de la Patria y el emblemático lugar merecen respeto" (Guzmán, "'El Alfa' se disculpa por palabras obscenas que dijo contra los padres de la Patria.")

4 See Enecia, "El 'Alfa' tendrá que limpiar la Plaza de la Bandera y cantar el Himno Nacional" and "'El Alfa' cumple segunda día de sanction limpieza Plaza de la Bandera."

5 "Pido disculpa a mi público y al pueblo dominicano porque ellos son La Patria, nunca fue mi intención ofenderlos, ni a los heroes mártires de mi país [. . .]. Dije eso a raíz de que las malas lenguas estaban especulando que yo me quedé en Estados Unidos para hacer papeles, cuando en realidad estaba trabajando. Estaba contento de estar en mi tierra e hice ese video aclarándole a muchos que no es verdad lo que se dice" (quoted in Guzmán, "'El Alfa' se disculpa por palabras obscenas que dijo contra los padres de la Patria.")

6 "Yo me siento totalmente bien con la decisión que se tomó [. . .]" ("'El Alfa' cumple segunda día de sanction limpieza Plaza de la Bandera").

7 A "transmigrant" is a subject who lives part-time in both the homeland and a "host" nation (Grasmuck and Pessar, *Between Two Islands*). "El Alfa," who mentions that he lived in the United States for a few months for employment, is a good example of this kind of mobility. Rather than cause for celebration, this status emblematizes the limited economic opportunities for transmigrants in both places. Silvio Torres-Saillant cautions against uncritical celebrations of this kind of transnational life: "The wisest thing at this juncture would be to contain the compulsion to celebrate. The transnational condition is not an idyl [*sic*]. Though hailed by journalists and scholars, it is often tragic. [. . .] Only the well-off can achieve multilocality without sorrow" (Torres-Saillant, *Diasporic Disquisitions*, 35).

   For more on Dominican migration, trans- or uni-directional, see also Hernández, *The Mobility of Workers under Advanced Capitalism*; Pessar, *A Visa for a Dream*; Sagás and Molina, eds., *Dominican Migration*; Martínez-San Miguel, *Caribe Two Ways*; and Hoffnung-Garskof, *A Tale of Two Cities*.

8 See Torres-Saillant, *Diasporic Disquisitions*.

9 To my knowledge, no one has written critically about *La Soga*. In contrast, scholarly analyses of *Oscar Wao* abound, though few of them engage with the Dominican history and culture on which the novel is based. This chapter builds on some of these conversations, especially those that revolve around questions of masculinity and imperialism. See Mahler, "The Writer as Superhero"; Hanna, "'Reassembling the Fragments'"; Horn, *Masculinity after Trujillo*; Machado Sáez, "Dictating Desire, Dictating Diaspora"; Mermann-Jozwiak, "Beyond Multiculturalism"; Harford Vargas, "Dictating a Zafa"; González, *Reading Junot Díaz*; Hanna, Harford Vargas, and Saldívar, eds., *Junot Díaz and the Decolonial Imagination*; Ostman, *The Fiction of Junot Díaz*; and Saldívar, *Junot Díaz*.

10 "Este monumento será como la luz de una terrible estrella fugaz con ambición milenaria, astro que ya desaparecido aún billa extrañamente en el bajo cielo nocturno del mar Caribe" (Rodríguez Juliá, *Caribeños*, 95).

   Director of the Dominican Permanent Commission for the Celebration of the Fifth Centennial, referring to the criticisms of the construction of the Columbus Lighthouse. Quoted in French, "For Columbus Lighthouse, a Fete That Fizzled."

11 *Columbus Memorial*, n.p., emphasis mine.

12 Schmidt-Nowara, *The Conquest of History*, 58.

13 Trouillot, *Silencing the Past*, 123 and 133–134.

14 Trouillot, *Silencing the Past*, 133.

15 Adorno writes: "Thanks in large measure to Irving's success, the feats of Columbus were identified with early North American history and the account of Columbus' deeds with the foundation of its letters" (Adorno, "Americanist Visions," 19).

16 For more on whiteness and citizenship in the U.S. in the late nineteenth and early twentieth centuries, see Jacobson, *Whiteness of a Different Color*.

17 Ober writes a long report on his travels to the West Indies for the World's Fair called *In the Wake of Columbus*. A few years later he published another account of his travels through the Caribbean, which included this account about Heureaux. See Ober, *Our West Indian Neighbors*.

18 Ober, *Our West Indian Neighbors*, 195.

19 Ober, *Our West Indian Neighbors*, 195.

20 Ober, *Our West Indian Neighbors*, 195–196.

21 Ober, *Our West Indian Neighbors*, 191.

22 Coincidentally, Jean du Sable, born in what is now Haiti, founded the settlement that is now Chicago. See "Jean du Sable, Explorer Who Founded Chicago."

23 Ureña de Henríquez, "A la Patria," in *Poemas y biografía de Salomé Ureña*, 14.

24 See Magee, *The Hegel Dictionary*.

25 See Cestero, *Colón*, 55, and González, *Designing Pan-America*, xvii.

26 "Efemérides de la Sociedad 'Amigos del País: desde su instalación hasta el día."

27 González, *Designing Pan-America*, 108. For more on Columbus's remains, see Moya Pons, *Los restos de Colón*.

28 González, *Designing Pan-America*, 108.

29 Earlier that century, the Monroe Doctrine established the U.S. government's paternalist stance toward the Caribbean, Latin America, and other formerly European colonies.

30 In response, Latin American intellectuals and politicians turned to a variety of Eurocentric discourses to invoke the irremediable cultural and spiritual differences between a *Latin* America and the Anglo-Saxon, Protestant, and capitalist North America. For influential examples of this Latin American anxiety vis-à-vis U.S. imperial designs, see Cuban José Martí's "Our America" (1891), Uruguayan José Enrique Rodó's *Ariel* (1900), and Nicaraguan Rubén Darío's "A Roosevelt" (1904). For examples of U.S. media perspectives on Latin America, see Johnson, *Latin America in Caricature*.

31 Rodríguez Juliá, *Caribeños*, 77.

32 González, *Designing Pan-America*, 106. The Pan-American Union Building in Washington, DC, and the Columbus Lighthouse Memorial "were supposed to have been a pair" in "the name of U.S.-defined Pan-Americanism" (González, *Designing Pan-America*, 106).

33 González, *Designing Pan-America*, 107.

34 "The Columbus Lighthouse."

35 Rodríguez Juliá, *Caribeños*, 77.

36 Candelario, *Black behind the Ears*, 280, and Rodríguez Juliá, *Caribeños*, 79.

37 Cited in González, *Designing Pan-America*, 138.

38 González, *Designing Pan-America*, 144.

39 "masivo, opresivamente monumental" (Rodríguez Juliá, *Caribeños*, 93).

40 "apreciar su posadura nada grácil" (Rodríguez Juliá, *Caribeños*, 93 and 109).

41 Reid-Dove, "Waiting for Columbus," 72.

42 Rosenfeld, "Goodbye Columbus," 231.

43 Ferbel, "The Politics of Taino Indian Heritage in the Post-Quincentennial Dominican Republic," 142.

44 Hulme, "Quincentenary Perspectives," 230.

45 For more on some of the debates surrounding the quincentennial celebrations of Columbus's arrival to this hemisphere, see Wynter, "1492."

46 Ferbel, "The Politics of Taino Indian Heritage," 144.

47 Reid-Dove, "Waiting for Columbus," 71; Ferbel, "The Politics of Taino Indian Heritage," 142.

48 Ferbel, "The Politics of Taino Indian Heritage," 143–144.

49 Krohn-Hansen, *Political Authoritarianism in the Dominican Republic*, 4. See also René Fortunato's documentary about Balaguer, *La violencia del poder*.

50 Ferbel, "The Politics of Taino Indian Heritage," 142.

51 Derby, *The Dictator's Seduction*, 221.

52 "una especie de chiste macabro, de oscura maldición merenguera. [. . .] El fucú sigue" (Rodríguez Juliá, *Caribeños*, 117–118).

53 French, "For Columbus Lighthouse, a Fete That Fizzled."

54 Rodríguez Juliá, *Caribeños*, 107.

55 According to Rodríguez Juliá, three of them crashed, while Robert Alexander González cites only one plane crash. Rodríguez Juliá, *Caribeños*, 107; González, *Designing Pan-America*, 140.

56 Rodríguez Juliá, *Caribeños*, 107.

57 Reid-Dove, "Waiting for Columbus," 72.

58 See French, "For Columbus Lighthouse, a Fete That Fizzled"; González, "Costly Columbus Lighthouse Inaugurated; Students, Labor Groups to Protest"; and Farah, "Curse of Columbus?" See also Robert Alexander González, *Designing Pan-America*, 103.

59 "Yo creo que a Trujillo [. . .] hay que volverlo a matar en el imaginario de poder del pueblo dominicano. Hay que volverlo a matar, y cómo se mata a Trujillo de nuevo, bueno, habilitando una democracia que no lo justifique" (Soto Jimenéz, "Estima Que a Trujillo 'Hay Que Volverlo a Matar"). Soto Jiménez is a historian and former secretary of the Armed Forces.
        Gordon, *Ghostly Matters*, 5.

60 See Schmidt-Nowara, *Conquest of History*.

61 "por entender que podría interpretarse como una afirmación de legitimidad" (de la Cruz Hermosilla, "Los restos de Colón en Santo Domingo," 10).

62 González, *Designing Pan-America*, 106.

63 "La historia de la literatura dominicana se inicia con el nombre de Colón que nos dejó, en su diario maritime y en sus cartas, las primeras descripciones sobre la naturaleza de la isla y que supo sentir y expresar como nadie los encantos del paisaje nacional y aún transmitirnos sobre él una visión poética y a veces sobremanera literaria" (Balaguer, *Historia de la literatura dominicana*, 11).

64 Trouillot, *Silencing the Past*, 45.

65 Díaz, *Oscar Wao*, 275.

66 Díaz, *Oscar Wao*, 296.
67 Díaz, *Oscar Wao*, 1.
68 Díaz, *Oscar Wao*, 1.
69 Derby, *The Dictator's Seduction*, 217.
70 Jiménez, *Savia dominicana*, 66.
71 Olliz Boyd, *Latin American Identity and the African Diaspora*, 3–4.
72 Olliz Boyd, *Latin American Identity*, 5.
73 Díaz, *Oscar Wao*, 3.
74 Díaz, *Oscar Wao*, 213.
75 Díaz, *Oscar Wao*, 214.
76 Díaz, *Oscar Wao*, 248–250.
77 Díaz, *Oscar Wao*, 251.
78 Díaz, *Oscar Wao*, 251–258.
79 Díaz, *Oscar Wao*, 243.
80 Díaz, *Oscar Wao*, 226.
81 See Derby, "In the Shadow of the State."
82 Nanita, "Biography of a Great Leader," 304.
83 "Al honorable presidente de la República Dominicana, Gral. Don Rafael Leonidas Trujillo Molina, propulsor del Faro Conmemorativo de Colón" (Cestero, *Colón*, n.p.).
84 "Dedicado al Generalísimo Doctor Rafael Leonidas Trujillo Molina, / Benefactor de la Patria y Padre de la Patria Nueva. / Este libro no es sino un reflejo muy incomplete de las grandes obras realizadas por él, y de la incomparable belleza hospitalaria de República Dominicana" (Stopelman, *Quisqueya*, n.p.).
85 Derby, "In the Shadow of the State," 329.
86 The epigraph opens Bernard Diederich's *Trujillo*, a journalistic work chronicling the events surrounding the dictator's assassination. This is also an epigraph in *Oscar Wao*, inclusive of the ellipses. Because both epigraphs share the same exclusions signaled by the ellipses, I deduce that Díaz is citing the Diederich rather than the original in *La Nación* (Díaz, *Oscar Wao*, 204). This newspaper played a key role in the smooth functioning of the Trujillo machinery.
87 Examples of Trujillo's inescapable power abound. For instance, in 1956 Trujillo had the Basque exile and Columbia University doctoral candidate Jesús de Galíndez kidnapped from New York City, flown secretly to Santo Domingo, and likely killed. Galíndez had written an unflattering dissertation about Trujillo and his regime, after having gathered firsthand evidence during his asylum in the Dominican Republic from 1939 to 1946 and in his role within Trujillo's inner circles.
88 To learn more about the events leading up to and following the assassination, refer to Balcácer, *Trujillo*, and Diederich, *Trujillo*.
89 For instance, Dominican ethnographer Carlos Esteban Deive writes: "The world of malevolent magic is the world of uncontrolled and ungovernable desire. The great sorceresses in classic literature are women dominated by an erotic passion. Their determination to win back a lover or to gain the affections of a man eloquently

illustrates the tragedy and impotence of those beings trapped in the web of an ardent and unhealthy sexuality" (Deive, *Vodú y magia en Santo Domingo*, 267). Other scholars have written about the feminization of magico-religious practices in non-Dominican contexts. For example, in the Mexican context, Jean Franco has written about seventeenth-century mystical nuns in *Plotting Women*, while Luisa Campuzano and Catharina Vallejo included inquisitional accounts of women accused of sorcery in colonial Mexico in *Yo con mi viveza*.

90 Moya Pons, *The Dominican Republic*, 116.

91 De Pree's *Beware of the Baca!* is a collection of folktales about magico-religious practices, many of which focus on men. Deive's *Vodú y magia* and Davis's *La otra ciencia* provide scholarly context to similar stories and practices. When women are associated with sorcery in literature, they tend to be racialized as black. See Vicioso, "Indias and Trigueñas No Longer."

92 Díaz, *Oscar Wao*, 2–3.

93 I include the Greek satyr in this tradition. The title of Mario Vargas Llosa's bestselling novel *The Feast of the Goat* (2001; *La fiesta del chivo* [2000])—which is about the Trujillo dictatorship—is also a well-known example based on this sobriquet already introduced to a non-Dominican audience many years earlier by journalist Bernard Diederich's *Trujillo*. The main Spanish editions of Vargas Llosa's novel use a section of the fourteenth-century fresco *Allegory of Bad Government* by Siena painter Ambrogio Lorenzetti, which depicts Tyranny as a two-horned devil.

94 Derby, *The Dictator's Seduction*, 216. The word *baká* is also spelled *bacá*. See also Derby's "Beyond Fugitive Speech."

95 Deive, *Vodú y magia*, 257.

96 Deive, *Vodú y magia*, 257.

97 De Pree, *Beware of the Baca!*, 8–9.

98 Derby, "Male Heroism, Demonic Pigs, and Memories of Violence in the Haitian-Dominican Borderlands," 3.

99 Deive, *Vodú y magia*, 258.

100 Díaz, *Oscar Wao*, 149.

101 Díaz, *Oscar Wao*, 149, italics in original.

102 For more on bakás as evocations of trauma around the loss of rural, agricultural life, see Derby, "Male Heroism."

103 The word "mongoose" is capitalized in the novel when it refers to the other-worldly creature that resembles the animal.

104 Caruth, *Unclaimed Experience*, 4.

105 Díaz, *Oscar Wao*, 301.

106 Citing Rosario Espinal, Maja Horn argues that "[t]his Manichean view of society is [. . .] part and parcel of the 'hegemonic political discourse' of the Trujillato, which 'for three decades had been structured around two antagonistic poles, one divine (of order, peace, and progress) and the other malicious (of disorder, war, and misery)'" (Horn, *Masculinity after Trujillo*, 140).

107 For a more thorough review of this idea, as well as a fascinating study of the Puerto Rican *chupacabra* (goat-sucker), refer to Lauren Derby's "Imperial Secrets."

108 Danticat, *Create Dangerously*, 70.

109 Derby, *The Dictator's Seduction*, 174 and 185.

110 Cited in Roorda, *The Dictator Next Door*, 164.

111 Roorda, *The Dictator Next Door*, 164.

112 Derby, *The Dictator's Seduction*, 174 and 175.

113 Butler, *Gender Trouble*, 185.

　　Another reminder is that "it is important to separate maleness from masculinity, distinguishing that masculinity encompasses aggression and acts of violence primarily associated with men but predicated not on biology or gender but on power differentials" (Domino Rudolph, *Embodying Latino Masculinities*, 2.)

114 Derby, *The Dictator's Seduction*, 188.

115 For more on nonwhite privateers, Johnson, *The Fear of French Negroes*.

116 Johnson, *The Fear of French Negroes*, 93.

117 See Decena, *Tacit Subjects*, 15.

118 Another aspect that renders him unique in the pantheon of dictators is the national and international fascination with the regime. Testimonial narratives, reports, biographies, fictional narratives, and films describing the regime and its violent excesses abound. In 2013, Vargas Llosa's Trujillo-based *The Feast of the Goat* was chosen as the "novel of the century" in a poll organized by Spanish newspaper *ABC* ("'La fiesta del Chivo', novela del siglo," *ABC*, May 19, 2013, http://www.abc.es). Two years later, the *BBC* named *Oscar Wao* the most important novel of the twenty-first century (Flood, "*The Brief Wondrous Life of Oscar Wao* Declared 2st Century's Best Novel So Far"). That two major non-Dominican outlets voted these two works about the Trujillo regime as the best of the century signals the hold that his regime has in a global imaginary.

119 Decena also discusses the tíguere in relation to race: "Although neither Krohn-Hansen nor Collado name it as such, the close relation that class marginality has to racial subordination points to a body that, apart from being poor, is predominantly dark skinned" (Decena, *Tacit Subjects*, 131).

120 Derby, *The Dictator's Seduction*, 190.

121 "[d]ecir 'un Tíguere' daba por descontado que no era un blanquito 'de los de allá por adentro.'" The phrase "de los de allá por adentro' means literally 'from over there from the inside," alluding to the access to traditional forms of power that these men have (Collado, *El Tíguere dominicano*, 112).

122 Francisco Comarazamy in Collado, *El tíguere dominicano*, 2nd ed., 6.

123 Krohn-Hansen, "Masculinity and the Political among Dominicans," 108.

124 An exemplary instance of this idealization of masculine beauty was, perhaps, the crowning of the Hombre Más Feo/Ugliest Man by the literary and cultural magazine *Eros*. Starting in 1924, readers could submit names for the contest and, for months, the magazine published their names along with the number of votes.

By the sixth round in the July issue, Julio González Herrera was in the lead with 1,300 votes.

125 Díaz, *Oscar Wao*, 294.

126 Díaz, *Oscar Wao*, 296.

127 Díaz, *Oscar Wao*, 115.

128 For more on the exploits of these glamorous, rich, and famous Dominicans in relation to Trujillo's regime, see Lauren Derby's *The Dictator's Seduction*, Flor de Oro Trujillo's "My Tormented Life as Trujillo's Daughter," and Porfirio Rubirosa's *Mi vida como Playboy*.

129 Paravisini-Gebert and Woods Peiró, "Porfirio Rubirosa," 131.

130 Díaz, *Oscar Wao*, 19.

131 "carente de condiciones mínimas para salir exitosamente de cualquier situación problemática. El parigüayo es un individuo que siempre lleva la de perder y que constantemente se lamenta" (Collado, *El Tíguere dominicano*, 4th ed., 8–9).

132 Díaz, *Oscar Wao*, 11.

133 Díaz, *Oscar Wao*, 24.

134 For more on drug dealers, see Warmund, "Removing Drug Lords and Street Pushers," and Domino Rudolph, *Embodying Latino Masculinities*. See also films centered on migrant Dominican baseball players such as *Sugar*, directed by Anna Boden and Ryan Fleck, and *Ballplayer: Pelotero*, directed by Ross Finkel, Trevor Martin, and Jonathan Paley.

135 For more on how diasporas are not necessarily subversive spaces, see Gopinath, *Impossible Desires*.

136 Díaz, *Oscar Wao*, 54.

137 Díaz, *Oscar Wao*, 22n.

138 Decena, *Tacit Subjects*, 15. After Christian Krohn-Hansen, Antonio E. De Moya contends that "this [masculinity as a totalitarian and contradictory political discourse] is produced, reproduced and modified by ordinary people in everyday life in the Dominican Republic. [. . .] Verbal categories mainly based on sexual orientation, and labels used by Dominican men for classifying and evaluating each other as men [. . .] structure masculinity as a dominant discourse." See De Moya, "Power Games and Totalitarian Masculinity in the Dominican Republic," 70.

139 "Mi'jo tu ere' un muchacho muy sensible. Y nosotro' no podemo' darno' el lujo de ser sensible todo el tiempo."

140 The only morally unblemished character in the film is Luis's love interest, Jenny, played by Denise Quiñonez. They had grown up alongside each other, but Jenny and her family migrated to the U.S. when she was still a child. When Jenny returns to Santiago to live in her childhood home, she and Luis start a courtship. The film does not develop her character, but her whiteness, education, and other details place her securely within an appropriate Dominican middle class despite her status as a returning migrant.

Indeed, her portrayal stands in stark contrast with the dominant negative Dominican perception of returning women migrants. Anthropologist Steven

Gregory's study of Boca Chica and Andrés, two contiguous, predominantly working-class towns that have become tourist spots, includes an incident at a community meeting that highlights the tension caused by clashing expectations. At this meeting, a local man is angered by a returning migrant woman's opinion that Mother's Day gifts at the town festivities should be handed out to all the women—even nonmothers—who were active in community affairs, thereby challenging the assumption that adult women without children have no communal value. Gregory records the man's response as: "When women go over there [i.e. abroad], they change [. . .]. They become feminists. And when they return here, they want everything to change. Everything" (Gregory, *The Devil behind the Mirror*, 78, first ellipses in original). See also Flores, *The Diaspora Strikes Back*, 91.

Both Gregory and Flores provide examples of Dominicans who believe that women who spend time abroad absorb foreign behaviors, beliefs, and values antithetical to Dominican identity.

141 Hoffnung-Garskof, "The Prehistory of the *Cadenú*," 31. For more on the criminalization of the Dominicanyork and the fear of his or her return, see Torres-Saillant, "El retorno de las yolas," in *El retorno de las yolas*.

142 Adding power to this discourse is its transnationality. Torres-Saillant describes a front-page *New York Times* article that ascribed "typical Dominican immigrant" status to two men "awaiting trials on drug charges." As in the Dominican Republic, the article "equates the growth of illegitimate financial dealings" to these racialized Dominican migrants (Torres-Saillant, *Diasporic Disquisitions*, 16–17).

143 I use the word "interpellate" here in the Althusserian fashion.

144 García-Peña, *The Borders of Dominicanidad*, 72.

145 "Fellito Polanco es un hombre buscado. Mató un agente del FBI en Nueba Yol. E' un maldito delincuente, tecato, y vende-droga. Y no solo que vende droga, vende droga' aquí en Santiago."

146 "A pesar de que para muchos el campesino, sobre todo el campesino blanco, llegó a convertirse en el prototio del habitante de las Antillas hispanoparlantes, las obras sobre su evolución histórica son relativamente escasas" (San Miguel, *El pasado relegado*, 49).

147 Jiménez, *Al amor del bohío*.

148 Johnson, *The Fear of French Negroes*, 86.

149 "el negro [. . .] deja de ser criollo y aún más su cultura, volviendo ambos a ser considerados como africanos" (Silié, "El hato y el conuco," 162).

150 See Wynter, "1492," and Martínez, "The Black Blood of New Spain."

151 See Hernández, *Racial Subordination in Latin America*.

152 See, respectively, *Tango Negro: The African Roots of Tango*, directed by Dom Pedro; Reyes-Santos, *Our Caribbean Kin*; and Fuentes, *La muerte de Artemio Cruz*.

153 "Hablar como dominican-york presupone el reconocimiento de una marginalidad intrínsica. Implica reconocerce como voz de alteridad" (Torres-Saillant, "El retorno de las yolas," in *El retorno de las yolas*, 20).

154 Counihan, "Desiring Diaspora," 51–52.

155 Díaz, *Oscar Wao*, 276, italics in original.

156 Díaz, *Oscar Wao*, 295.

157 Díaz, *Oscar Wao*, 110.

158 Díaz, *Oscar Wao*, 119.

159 Díaz, *Oscar Wao*, 121.

160 Díaz, *Oscar Wao*, 138.

161 Díaz, *Oscar Wao*, 147. This beating in the cane fields recalls also the three Mirabal sisters' fate. In 1960, three sisters who had been involved in a failed coup d'etat in June 1959 were beaten to death. For many, the murder of three women from a respected family from the town of Salcedo signaled that R. Trujillo and his henchmen, especially the head of the Military Intelligence Service, Johnny Abbes, had finally gone too far. The UN chose November 25, the date of the killings, as the International Day for the Elimination of Violence against Women.

162 Díaz, *Oscar Wao*, 294.

163 Díaz, *Oscar Wao*, 295.

164 Díaz, *Oscar Wao*, 295.

165 See Martínez-San Miguel, *Caribe Two Ways*, for examples of literature and songs that evoke the hardships of the Dominican migrant and his or her nostalgia for the idealized tropical homeland.

166 From what Junot Díaz recalls, his father had worked in the same police precinct years before Seval's arrest. This is just another example of the "smallness" of Dominican society.

167 For a history of Seval and the band, see Peña Pastor, "Memoria Artística a Tony Seval."

168 See also Julián, *El cantante y sus asesinos*.

169 On the several versions of Seval's death, see Cabrera, "La muerte de Tony Seval."

170 See Junior Trinidad's report for the news television program *Objetivo 5*, "Viuda de Tony Seval rompe silencio tras 28 años de su muerte."

171 "Yo fui a buscar una muchacha que yo tengo amores con ella. Tú sabes como son estas muchachas con los artistas."

172 Camarena's asides about her expectations from Seval as a husband and father are also telling, for they reveal the common expectation that as long as a man provides for his family financially and in other ways, his wife should accept dalliances and even more serious affairs. See Baud, "Patrons, Peasants, and Tobacco."

173 "No en esa vida artística tuya yo no me meto porque yo no me metía en la vida de él. Porque él cumplía como esposo y como padre. Usted vé? Y como hijo también [. . .] Entonces él me dijo que el entró a la casa del señor Cuervo Gómez y estaban desmontando un furgón. El entró a esa casa fue a buscar a la muchacha y un guardia, que notó la presencia de él, le dijo al señor Cuervo Gómez que quién era ese hombre que estaba ahí. Y cuando el señor Cuervo Gómez cogió para allá le dijo él quién era él. Entonces la mamá de la joven le dijo que ese era el prometido de su hija y en ese momento ahí vino el problema. Bueno cuando yo veo

un carro [. . .] y se desmontan cinco hombres, uno con un bate, otro se desmonta con algo como [. . .] de lo que le dan a los caballos [. . .] y los otros tiene armas."

174 "A ti no te conviene, que te salga un muerto, porque to voy a asustar, porque te voy a empujar, porque to voy a jalar, porque te voy a arañar."

175 I found Cathy Caruth's elucidation of how literature describes and explores individual and collective trauma particularly useful. After Freud, she defines trauma as "not locatable in the simple violent or original event in an individual's past, but rather in the way that its very unassimilated nature—the way it was precisely not known in the first instance—returns to haunt the survivor later on" (Caruth, *Unclaimed Experience*, 4). She writes further that "[i]f Freud turns to literature to describe traumatic experience, it is because literature, like psychoanalysis, is interested in the complex relation between knowing and not knowing" (Caruth, *Unclaimed Experience*, 3).

176 Gordon, *Ghostly Matters*, 4.

CHAPTER 4. DOMINICAN WOMEN'S REFRACTED AFRICAN DIASPORAS

1 "Black in the Dominican Republic: Denying Blackness."
    I presented portions of this chapter at the 2007 Beyond Visibility: Rethinking the African Diaspora in Latin America Conference at UC Berkeley ("Diaspora, Homeland and Blackness in Contemporary Dominican Anti-Nationalist Literature") and at the 2014 Latino Studies Conference in Chicago ("Las Tígueras: Dominican-American Female Performers Maluca Mala and Amara La Negra").

2 Raj Chetty and Lorgia García-Peña model methodological modes of registering Dominican blackness. See Chetty, "'La calle es libre,'" and García-Peña, *The Borders of Dominicanidad*. See also *Cimarrón Spirit*, directed by Rubén Durán.

3 For an introduction to African diaspora as a field of study, imaginary, and reality, see Patterson and Kelley, "Unfinished Migrations."

4 Hall, "Cultural Identity and Diaspora," 222.

5 Hall, "Cultural Identity and Diaspora," 224.

6 Pinto, *Difficult Diasporas*, 7.

7 Glissant, *Poetics of Relation*, 11.

8 Chetty, "'La calle es libre,'" 42.

9 For more on cultural expressions of Latino antiblackness in Miami, see Hernández-Reguant and Arroyo, "The Brownface of Latinidad in Cuban Miami."

10 By this I mean that her appropriation of tigueraje does not, then, become "female masculinity." See Halberstam, *Female Masculinity*.

11 Michelle Wright adopts the term "multiverse" to describe this way of approaching blackness. See *Physics of Blackness*.

12 Wright, *Physics of Blackness*.

13 Stephens, "What Is This Black in the Black Diaspora?," 32.
    Vicioso's three-page essay was first published in the anthology *Caribbean Creolization* in 1998 and, two years later, in *Callaloo*'s issue on Dominican

literature with some minor differences in the translation. I cite from the first instantiation: "Dominicanyorkness: A Metropolitan Discovery of the Triangle," in *Caribbean Creolization.*

14 San Miguel, *La guerra silenciosa*, 106.

15 From Paulino, *Dividing Hispaniola*, 157.

16 For a review of some of this scholarship, see Candelario, *Black behind the Ears*, 19.

17 See Howard, *Coloring the Nation*, and Paulino, *Dividing Hispaniola*.

18 Roth, *Race Migrations*, 20.

19 See Simmons, *Reconstructing Racial Identity and the African Past in the Dominican Republic.* See also Celsa Albert Batista's chart on "contemporary terminology" during the 1980s and 1990s in which "mulato + negro = indio oscuro [dark indian]" (Batista, *Mujer y esclavitud en Santo Domingo*, 69).

20 See Candelario, *Black behind the Ears*, 38.

21 Roach, *Cities of the Dead*, 5.

22 See Yarbrough, *Race and the Cherokee Nation*; Coleman, *That the Blood Stay Pure*; Krauthamer, *Black Slaves, Indian Masters*; Chang, *The Color of the Land*; and the anthology *Crossing Waters, Cross Worlds*, edited by Sharon Patricia Holland and Tiya Miles.

23 Vicioso, "Dominicanyorkness," 64 and 65.

    A similar rhetorical move occurs in performance artist and poet Josefina Báez's long poem *Dominicanish.* Emilia María Durán-Almarza argues that Báez's statement, "'Con afro black is beautiful. Black is a color. Black is my color' [. . .] points both to her solidarity with black peoples in the US and to a process of transracialization as she is defining her identity outside the hegemonic racial discourses in the communities she inhabits" (Durán-Almarza, "*Ciguapas* in New York," 150).

24 Vicioso, "Dominicanyorkness," 63–64.

25 For more on Dominican women's domesticity and political involvement in the late twentieth century, see Brea and Duarte, *Entre la calle y la casa.*

26 Vicioso, "Dominicanyorkness," 63.

27 This imposed domesticity is evident even to outsiders. Samuel Guy Inman, a Protestant church leader from the United States who was sent to the Dominican Republic and Haiti during the United States occupation of both countries in 1919, observed: "The average [Dominican] girl has nothing with which to occupy her time. She is very closely chaperoned, is not allowed out alone, and can only sit in her parents' home and rock to and fro as she sees her brothers go out at night in pursuit of social enjoyment" (Inman, *Through Santo Domingo and Haiti*, 35). This observation ignores the ways in which girls were also policed in U.S. spaces.

28 Higginbotham, *Righteous Discontent*, 190.

29 Higginbotham, *Righteous Discontent*, 191.

30 Edmondson, "Public Spectacles," 5.

31 Cocco de Filippis, "Indias y Trigueñas No Longer," 156.

32 Vicioso, "Dominicanyorkness," 65.

33 García-Peña, *The Borders of Dominicanidad*, 191.

34 Vicioso, "Dominicanyorkness," 65.

35 Horn, *Masculinity after Trujillo*, 138.

36 Gopinath, *Impossible Desires*, 6.

37 The work of Evelyn Brooks Higginbotham for African American women, Natasha Barnes for Anglophone Caribbean women, Eileen Suárez Findlay for Puerto Rican women, and Rosa Linda Fregoso for Chicanas have all been influential to my thinking on respectability and various nationalisms.

38 Sheller, "Work That Body," 353.

39 See also Rosamond S. King on what she terms "sexual agency," which "describe[s] the activity of women voicing, advocating for, and/or pursuing control of their own sexuality or erotic pleasure on their own terms. [. . .] And while women's sexual pleasure is itself not necessarily culturally proscribed, the public expression of female desire is prohibited by heteropatriarchy in the Caribbean and elsewhere" (King, *Island Bodies*, 124).

40 Barnes, "Body Talk," 95.

41 For more on the limits of finding "resistance," see Guidotti-Hernández, *Unspeakable Violence*.

42 Pinto, *Difficult Diasporas*, 46.

43 *Black and Latino*, mun2.tv, NBC Universo, www.nbcuniverso.com.

44 Ana M. Lara also writes about how her U.S. passport gives her the freedom of mobility to, for instance, shave her head and "butch up" (Lara, "Uncovering Mirrors," 298).

45 The "natural hair movement" in the U.S. and other black diaspora spots around the world has reached the Dominican Republic. As of 2014, many more women around Santo Domingo sported their natural, nonstraightened hair—without being harassed—than before. Billboards that include nonwhite models, even those with unstraightened hair, dotted the urban landscape. On December 30, 2015, the *New York Times* published a piece documenting this shift and highlighting one of the foremost natural hair activists in the country, a woman who opened a salon in Santo Domingo after spending her life as a diasporic Dominican. See García, "At a Santo Domingo Hair Salon, Rethinking an Ideal Look."

46 "desafortunadamente [. . .] tienen el concepto que, para una negra, porque yo soy negra, para una negra ser bonita tiene que tener el pelo lacio. Tiene que tener el pelo por las rodillas. ¡Es mentira! Nosotros de naturaleza no somos así."

47 For more on antiblack discrimination based on hair in the Dominican context, see Batista, *Mujer y esclavitud en Santo Domingo*, 106.

48 "'nueva moda' es de tigueras, y locas" (Miss Rizos Facebook post, July 9, 2016, at 9 a.m.). Cited also in Moreno, "Miss Rizos Stands Up for Teen Shamed by School for Rocking Natural Hair."

49 Black school children in the U.S. have also been sent home for wearing natural hairstyles. In 2014, the U.S. military was also severely critiqued for its ban on natural black hairstyles.

50 Brooks, *Bodies in Dissent*, 7.

51 Maluca Mala, "Mala."

52 "Maluca Wepasode #2." S.O.B.'s, which stands for Sounds of Brazil, opened in 1982 "with the purpose of exposing the musical wealth and heritage of the Afro-Latino Diaspora" ("About SOBs").

53 For more on Maluca and other tígueras in Dominican music, see Hutchinson, *Tigers of a Different Stripe*.

54 Shamz, "Large Up Exclusive."

55 "What Is a Lola?"

56 Rivera-Rideau, *Remixing Reggaetón*, 22.

57 *Latinidad* translates generally into "Latinoness." What being Latinx even means is quite fraught but most people take it to refer to subjects with Spanish-speaking Latin American ancestry. This tends to exclude Brazilians but include indigenous, non-Spanish-speaking subjects. Black and Asian subjects of Latin American descent can also challenge dominant ideas about *latinidad*.

58 Vargas (following Roderick Ferguson), "Ruminations on *Lo Sucio*," 715.

59 Vargas, "Ruminations on *Lo Sucio*," 716.

60 Examples abound of when whiteness has been the main ingredient in rendering a previous "surplus" and *sucio* act acceptable—that is, marketable or respectable, or both. We may consider, for instance, hugely popular performers such as Carmen Miranda in relation to Afro-Brazil, Elvis Presley in relation to U.S. African America, Madonna in relation to queer of color communities, and so on.

61 See Gilroy, *There Ain't No Black in the Union Jack*; *From Mambo to Hip Hop*, directed by Henry Chalfant; and *24 Hour Party People*, directed by Michael Winterbottom.

62 Ulysse, "Uptown Ladies and Downtown Women," 151.

63 For instance, as a young Dominican immigrant in the Bronx I had to learn not only standard English but also the myriad ethnic terms that my classmates used to describe themselves and me in both English and Spanish. I learned that "Boricua" was the same as Puerto Rican, "Spanish" was "Hispanic" (no one ever used the word "Latino"), and "Jewish" meant white American.

64 Shamz, "Large Up Exclusive."

65 Maluca Mala, "El Tigeraso."

66 For more on the hair salon, see Vázquez, "Salon Philosophers."

67 Candelario, "Hair Race-Ing," 135.

68 Candelario, "Hair Race-Ing," 147.

69 See Muñoz, *Disidentifications*.

70 See, for instance, the controversial *Miami Herald* article "Black Denial," which held that Dominicans' preference for straightened hair was irrefutable proof that the entire citizenry denied their blackness. See Robles, "Black Denial."

71 García, "Heritage in All Its Rich Hues."

72 See "Rolos & Icons Posters."

73 See, for instance, Schmidt-Camacho's "Ciudadana X."

74 Tallaj, "'A Country That Ain't Really Belong to Me,'" 18.
75 "Maluca Wepasode #2."

CHAPTER 5. WORKING WOMEN AND THE NEOLIBERAL GAZE

1 "Annette Castellano Is My Nemesis."
  Holden, "Review: 'Sand Dollars,' Unrequited Love in the Dominican Republic."
  See my notes in the introduction on my choice to use "first world" and "third world" over other terms. The stereotypes and clichés I discuss throughout this chapter emerge from developmentalist perspectives, which, as I show, emerge from racist colonial paradigms.
2 Ehrenreich and Hochschild, *Global Woman*, 2.
  For my working definitions of sex work and sex workers, see McClintock, "Sex Workers and Sex Work."
3 Gregorio Gil discusses this issue in *Migración femenina*, 140–141. On the prevalence of women in Dominican migrations to Spain, see Oso Casas, "Dominican Women, Heads of Households in Spain."
4 See Cabezas, *Economies of Desire*.
5 For more on the "mulatto" woman as archetype and stereotype in colonial and nationalist imaginaries, see Dayan, *Haiti, History, and the Gods*; Kutzinski, *Sugar's Secrets*; Pratt, *Imperial Eyes*; Daut, *Tropics of Haiti*.
6 Kaplan, *The Anarchy of Empire*, 20.
7 Quijano, "Coloniality of Power, Eurocentrism, and Latin America," 536.
8 For more on the history of these stereotypes, see Bush, *Slave Women in Caribbean Society*, especially chapter 2, "'The Eye of the Beholder': Contemporary European Images of Black Women." See also the work of bell hooks, Saidiya Hartman, and Sandra Gunning for the hypersexualization of black women in the U.S.
9 For more on consumption in connection with globalization, neoliberalism, and citizenship, see García Canclini, *Consumers and Citizens*, and Appadurai, *Modernity at Large*.
10 I focus on cultural texts that explore European and North American—usually white—subjects' desire for Dominican women. However, these transnational economies of desire also operate when Dominican women represent light-skinned *latinidad* in other Caribbean countries, for instance, or for African American sex tourists. Though different, these configurations do not contradict my main conclusions regarding foreigners' association of the Dominican Republic with sex. For more on the desires driving these sex tourists and sex consumers, see Kempadoo's *Sexing the Caribbean* and O'Connell Davidson and Sánchez Taylor, "Fantasy Islands."
11 For an analysis of and cultural manifestations of what Aníbal Quijano calls the "coloniality of power" in the Americas, see Saldívar, *Trans-Americanity*.
12 "El poder gubernamental no toma carta en crear una nueva fuente de empleo que favorezca a la mujer rural, ni crean leyes que protejan la dignidad de la mujer y que dominen el machismo" (*Rien mis labios . . . llora mi alma*, 14).
  Freeman, *High Tech and High Heels in the Global Economy*, 26–27.

13 Freeman, *High Tech and High Heels*, 27.

14 Batista writes, for instance, about the shortage of white European women in the colony of Santo Domingo and how this affected enslaved black women (*Mujer y esclavitud en Santo Domingo*, 54–55).

15 World Bank, "Dominican Republic."

16 World Bank, "Dominican Republic."

17 See Ostry, Loungani, and Furceri, "Neoliberalism."

18 "CAFTA-DR (Dominican Republic–Central America FTA)," Office of the United States Trade Representative.

19 Sassen, *Globalization and Its Discontents*, 6.

20 Sassen, *Globalization and Its Discontents*, 6.

21 See Sassen, *Guests and Aliens*, and Schmidt Camacho, *Migrant Imaginaries*.

22 Lowe, *The Intimacies of Four Continents*, 3.

23 Sassen, *Globalization and Its Discontents*, 111.

24 For the case of Dominican women immigrants in Spain, see Gregorio Gil, *Migración femenina*. She cites a Dominican survey that shows that, in the late twentieth century, the vast majority of Dominican immigrants in Spain were women (54). In Madrid, almost all of them (93.6 percent) worked as domestic workers (72).

25 See Silvera, *Silenced*, and *Rien mis labios . . . llora mi alma*.

26 See Ehrenreich and Hochschild, *Global Woman*.

27 For more on male sex workers and other men working within a transnational economy of desire, see O'Connell Davidson and Sánchez Taylor, "Fantasy Islands"; Brennan, *What's Love Got to Do with It*; and Padilla, *Caribbean Pleasure Industry*.

 The term "sex worker" remains murky even for those who accept the descriptor. Researching both Cuban and Dominican transnational "economies of desire," Cabezas "realized that the unified object of my research, the 'sex worker,' did not exist, was ambiguous, or at the very least was quite an unstable subject. [. . .] Instead, [she] found many elusive travel romances and intimate encounters that did not fit the standard academic categories of 'prostitute' or 'sex worker.' For example, in spite of living off remittances and gifts from their transnational boyfriends, many women did not identify themselves as sex workers or consider their romantic liaisons with tourists a form of prostitution. Rather, their situations presented the interstices of transnational linkages but did not confirm an easy fitting with the category of sex worker" (Cabezas, *Economies of Desire*, 8).

28 For many sex workers, the ultimate goal is to marry a foreigner from a wealthier country, usually North American or European, who can then provide the documentation necessary for geographic and socioeconomic mobility. Achieving this goal requires labor above and beyond the timed sexual encounter that often constitutes "sex work." For more on the kinds of foreigners with capital that are attracted to either visit or move to the Dominican Republic, see Brennan, *What's Love Got to Do with It?*; Cabezas, *Economies of Desire*; Gregory, *The Devil*

behind the Mirror; and O'Connell Davidson and Sánchez Taylor, "Fantasy Islands." Generally speaking, the foreign men who hire sex workers tend to be white men whose capital is greater than most local Dominicans, but who are not necessarily wealthy in their home countries. In the last few years, several scholars and I have noted the rise in African American and Dominican American men as sex tourists. In a conversation we had in 2015, Brennan mentioned that white and black sex tourists, at least in Sosúa, were now younger, better economically situated, and more educated than they were during the years of her research.

29 See Gregory, *The Devil behind the Mirror*, 137–139. See also Schmidt Camacho, "Ciudadana X" and *Migrant Imaginaries*.

30 For more on the connection between agriculture, employment, and migration (both within the Dominican Republic and to other countries), see Ferrán and Pessar, *Dominican Agriculture and the Effect of International Migration*, and Hoffnung-Garskof, *A Tale of Two Cities*. For more on these issues in connection with male sex workers, see Padilla, *Caribbean Pleasure Industry*.

31 Sassen, *Globalization and Its Discontents*, 130.

32 Sassen, *Globalization and Its Discontents*, 114.

33 Sassen, *Globalization and Its Discontents*, 114.

34 Pratt, "Women, Literature, and National Brotherhood," 51.

35 For more on the first world demand for third world women's caretaking labor, see Ehrenreich and Hochschild, *Global Woman*.

36 For more on men as partners of sex workers, see Brea and Duarte, *Entre la calle y la casa*.

37 Brennan, *What's Love Got to Do with It?*, 86–87.

Writing about Mexican women working in factories near the U.S. border, Schmidt Camacho elucidates the correlation within Mexican patriarchal nationalism between women's wage labor (that is, paid labor outside the home) and prostitution, easing these women's vulnerability in the face of patriarchal rage and violence:

The feminization of labor—devalued and detached from any concept of labor power—is just one expression of a project of governance that generated new modes of spaces for income generation through the commodification of poor women's bodies and delimited citizenship. Images of women used to sell tourism, merchandise, labor, and sex saturate the border cities in ways that deliberately eroticize the exercise of dominance. The moral discourse linking *obreras* (women workers) and prostitutes both masks the state's interest in sexualizing female labor and legitimates subaltern women's exclusion from the protected sphere of citizenship (Schmidt Camacho, "Ciudadana X," 266).

38 Here, I acknowledge the important strides made by sex workers and other activists. For instance, organizations such as MODEMU (Movimiento de Mujeres Unidas) have been crucial to educating the general public about sex work and promoting sex workers' rights.

Sex work or prostitution is legal in the Dominican Republic, but, as Brennan notes is the case in Sosúa and Gregory shows for Boca Chica, tourism police often demand bribes from sex workers to keep them out of jail. See Brennan, *What's Love Got to Do with It?*, 233n3, and Gregory, *The Devil behind the Mirror*, 141–143.

39 Quijano, "Coloniality of Power, Eurocentrism, and Latin America," 539.

40 We may consider, for instance, the Clinton Foundation, whose "commit[ment] to Haiti's long-term recovery [through] economic development and job creation" has profited from the U.S. government's fight to maintain well-below poverty wages in Haiti during Hillary Clinton's time as U.S. secretary of state ("Clinton Foundation in Haiti"). See also Johnson, "Wikileaks," and Coughlin and Ives, "WikiLeaks Haiti."

41 Lowe, *The Intimacies of Four Continents*, 3.

42 Gordon, *Ghostly Matters*, 4.

43 Schafer, "Diary of a Sex Tourist."

44 Schafer, "Diary of a Sex Tourist."

45 Schafer, "Collection Photographer Interview."

46 Sheller, "Work That Body," 346.

47 See Schafer, "Collection Photographer Interview" and "Diary of a Sex Tourist."

48 Schafer, "Diary of a Sex Tourist."

49 For more on the connections between colonialism, travel, and fields of knowledge such as ethnography, see Pratt, *Imperial Eyes* and "Fieldwork in Common Places."

50 Schafer, "Diary of a Sex Tourist."

51 Schafer, "Diary of a Sex Tourist."

52 Schafer, "Diary of a Sex Tourist."

53 Schafer, "Diary of a Sex Tourist."

54 Lowe, *The Intimacies of Four Continents*, 52.

55 Schafer, "Collection Photographer Interview."

56 Schafer, "Collection Photographer Interview."

57 See Mulvey, "Visual Pleasure and Narrative Cinema."

58 Schafer, *Whores and Madonnas*.

59 Schafer, *Whores and Madonnas*.

60 See Alloula, *The Colonial Harem*; Wexler, *Tender Violence*; and Schneider, "Louis Agassiz and the American School of Ethnoeroticism."

61 Alloula, *The Colonial Harem*, 7, italics in original.

62 For more on Dominican sex worker's hypervisibility on the Internet, see Brennan, *What's Love Got to Do with It?*, 198–200, and Gregory, *The Devil behind the Mirror*, 139–141.

63 *Rien mis labios . . . llora mi alma*, 29.

64 "Pero, el trabajo sexual es nosotras, vendiendo nuestro cariño, nuestra imagen, dentro y afuera del negocio" (*Rien mis labios . . . llora mi alma*, 11).

65 "Entendemos que todo el que cambia sexo por dinero u objeto es una trabajadora sexual y las mujeres que están teniendo relaciones gratis, con más de una pareja,

también son trabajadoras sexuales porque eso alimenta el machismo, nos daña a nosotras y a los hombres también" (*Rien mis labios . . . llora mi alma*, 10).

66 "Muchas personas creen que el trabajo sexual solamente es una mujer que esté dentro de un bar o de un cabaret y no se dan cuenta de que ellos también son parte de una red. Por ejemplo, acostarte con el profesor para que te pase la material o acostarte con un viejo para que te pague la Universidad, eso es prostitución. Otras que están en empresas, se están prostituyendo a cambio de sus empleos" (*Rien mis labios . . . llora mi alma*, 10).

67 "Otra cosa es que a nuestra país viene mucho turismo y lo primero que le presentan es a la mujer en la playa, muy sensual, en tanga. En nuestro país, para vender cualquier artículo, se pone una mujer en tanga, no sabiendo que se está promoviendo la prostitución. Entonces, aquí el turista desde que llega sabe que hay playas donde hay chicas muy bonitas" (*Rien mis labios . . . llora mi alma*, 11).

68 See "República Dominicana vendida como destino sexual."

69 "Al revisar la página resulta chocante la forma en que se presenta al país. Asiendo enfasis en que en República Dominicana no está penada la prostitución y que este tipo de vacaciones son completamente legales."

70 Piera and the government representatives refer unfailingly to *trabajadores sexuales* (sex workers) and do not criticize them. I attribute this tone to the activism of Dominican sex worker organizations such as MODEMU.

71 "Muchos extranjeros que visitan Republica Dominicana a veces se crean unas expectativas con respecto a la mujer caribeña de que es una mujer fácil, de que es una mujer realmente, incluso más fogosa que muchas europeas y eso hace que muchas veces puede también se sienta la atracción por visitar algunos prostíbulos o algunos lugares donde puedan encontrar fácilmente [. . .] ese tipo de contacto."

72 O'Connell Davidson and Sánchez Taylor, "Fantasy Islands," 43.

73 In *Globalization and Its Discontents*, Sassen argues that globalization has been understood primarily through its wonders: the speed of information and increased access to it, the democratization of cultural creation, and other changes in the global economy and imagination seemingly removed from actual places and spaces. The goal is then to localize globalization, by highlighting the labor that leads to site-less (that is, physically inexistent) informational and financial changes at the global level, for it is in emphasizing this "hidden" element that one can evidence the complexity of globalization. In Sassen's words, "even the most advanced formation industries have a work process—that is, a complex of workers, machines, and buildings that are more place-bound than the imagery of the information economy suggests" (xxii).

74 "[e]s solo una prostituta. Un cuero" (Arias, *Emoticons*, 126).

75 "Jennifer, novia del Atlántico, víctima del subdesarrollo, quiero ser tu héroe, yo, James Gatto, ciudadano del Primer Mundo, te salvaré. Gatto tocas sus senos" (Arias, *Emoticons*, 126).

76 Fregoso, *MeXicana Encounters*, 15.

77 Brennan, *What's Love Got to Do with It?*, 47.

78 García Canclini, *Consumers and Citizens*, 26.

79 "dinero, decadencia, frustración sexual e impunidad de un lado; juventud, miseria, hambre del otro" (Arias, *Emoticons*, 119).

80 "'Diablo, papi, tú si tá bueno, buen perro!' [. . .] Un solo grito a plena voz y sin miedo, consciente de su poder" (Arias, *Emoticons*, 114).

81 Appadurai, *Modernity at Large*, 53.

82 Appadurai, *Modernity at Large*, 53.

83 "sentada en el bar, fuma, bebe, y canta, mirando llorosa una telenovela en la TV colocada detrás de las bartenders" (Arias, *Emoticons*, 119).

84 "se enamoran y se llevan a algunas de estas infelices a vivir con ellos para sus países" (Arias, *Emoticons*, 117).

85 In these narratives, the national romance of Latin American literature is "replaced (in reality, devoured) by stories of the brothel, where love and marriage are forbidden and where social projects disintegrate into detritus, degenerating the proposed social contract, displaying its grotesque exclusions" ("dislocadas (en realidad, devoradas) por los relatos de prostíbulo, donde están prohibidos el amor y el matrimonio y donde los proyectos sociales se descomponen hasta el detritus, degenerando los contratos sociales propuestos, mostrando sus groseras exclusiones") (Cánovas, *Sexualidad y cultura en la novela hispanoamericana*, 15). Hence, the brothel is a narrative space that allows the writer to portray the failures of modernity. For the most part, however, this canon of "brothel literature" is centered on a masculine narrator or protagonist whose quests and disappointments are, variously, resolved, challenged, upheld, or validated at or through the brothel. In Dominican literature, novels like Marcio Veloz Maggiolo's *De abril en adelante* (1975) and Andres L. Mateo's *La balada de Alfonsina Bairán* (1998), despite their political subversions and textual innovations, center on the lives of a male protagonist/narrator whose performance of masculinity at the brothel weaves itself into the narrative precisely through its invisibility and normalcy. The brothel then emerges both as a metaphorically rich space as well as a normalized, quotidian space for Dominican men. Women in these novels tend to be symbols or props to the development of the main male character. Sex workers in these narratives tend to function as contrasts to the proper woman worthy of marriage.

86 "dominicanita con cara de analfabeta desnutrida con mi pene en la boca y los ojos vacíos de tanto meter perico, qué bonita es y cómo disfruta de lo que hace. Búsquenla, es fácil de encontrar en la red, miren su cara, la suya; no la mía, que borré para no ser reconocido, por si la chica es menor" (Arias, *Emoticons*, 117–8).

87 Arias, *Emoticons*, 117.

88 Lilón and Lantigua, "Dominican Transmigrants in Spain," 141. For an in-depth study of Dominican immigrants in Spain, see Gregorio Gil, *Migración femenina*.

89 García Domínguez and Paiewonsky, *Gender, Remittances, and Development*, 35.

90 See Gregorio Gil, *Migración femenina*, 54.

91 Lilón and Lantigua, "Dominican Transmigrants in Spain," 143.

92 Lilón and Lantigua, "Dominican Transmigrants in Spain," 142. This element of domestic, and other kinds of underpaid, work has been difficult to unionize.

93 Lilón and Lantigua, "Dominican Transmigrants in Spain,"142.

94 Lilón and Lantigua, "Dominican Transmigrants in Spain," 142.

95 More specifically: "In addition to legalization and naturalization processes, the relatively long history of the Dominican community in Spain has created the conditions for the establishment of family ties with Spaniards, other EU citizens and naturalized Spanish citizens. This has led to a higher percentage of Dominicans who hold EU residence permits at 33.4% (of which 60% are women), compared to 12.9% of all migrants from non-EU countries. On the other hand, the Dominican community has the largest number of births in Spain compared to its Latin American counterparts" (García Domínguez and Paiewonsky, *Gender, Remittances, and Development*, 34).

96 "Husband: 'Mi mujer le manda decirle si hace el favor de cambiar las sábanas de la cama después de que duerma en ella.' / Zulema: '¿Por qué no las cambia ella?' / Husband: 'Porque no es ella quien se coge diez machos cada día. También me manda decirle que esté fuera de la casa antes de las ocho. Es por nuestro hijo, no queremos que la vea.'"

97 Decena, Shedlin, and Martinez, "Los hombres no mandan aqui," 51.

98 Pratt, "Women, Literature, and National Brotherhood," 52.

99 "familia era todo el que estaba al lado mío, ya fueran dominicanas, colombianas o del país que fueran y si lo que él había hecho estaba mal" (*Rien mis labios . . . llora mi alma*, 29).

100 Martín-Cabrera, "Postcolonial Memories and Racial Violence in *Flores de otro mundo*," 46.

101 For more on the murkiness of these transnational economies of desire, see Kempadoo, *Sexing the Caribbean*, and Brennan, *What's Love Got to Do with It?*

102 Kempadoo, *Sexing the Caribbean*, 43–44.

103 See Ferguson, *Aberrations in Black*.

104 I paraphrase this exchange from memory.

105 Keown, "Love at First Sight."

106 Harper, "The Peninsula House, Dominican Republic," and Keown, "Love at First Sight," 56.

107 One of the few places in the country that has several examples of Victorian-style architecture is the northern city of Puerto Plata, which is quite far from Las Terrenas.

108 Thompson, *An Eye for the Tropics*, 5.

109 Thompson, *An Eye for the Tropics*, 23.

110 She appears also in another Guzmán film, *Noelí en los países* (2016), which follows her *Sand Dollars* character to Europe. There, she stars in an Italian commercial and reunites with her mother, a housekeeper in Spain. As of this writing, the film has yet to be widely released. See Dale, "IFF Panama/Cannes." She also appears in *De Djess*, directed by Alice Rohrwacher.

111 See a discussion of this issue in Perdomo, "Yo amo mi pajón."

112 *Fronterizas*, directed by Lorena Durán.

113 Martínez, "Not a Cockfight," 80.

114 *Fronterizas*.

115 For more on intraisland communal efforts and activism, see Reyes-Santos, *Our Caribbean Kin*.

CONCLUSION

1 Hazard, *Santo Domingo*, 180.

McClintock, "Imperial Ghosting and National Tragedy," 821.

I presented portions of this epilogue at the 2016 Caribbean Studies Association Meeting in Haiti ("'The Girl Who Chased Me at Cotuí': Returning the Imperial Gaze in the Early Twentieth-Century Dominican Republic") and at the 2016 Tepoztlán Institute Conference ("Illegible Blackness; or, Dominicans Return, Reject, and Elide the Imperial Gaze").

2 Browne, *Dark Matters*, 21.

3 Browne, *Dark Matters*, 21.

4 Wynter, "Towards the Sociogenic Principle," 42.

5 Browne, *Dark Matters*, 21.

6 Browne, *Dark Matters*, 21.

7 Browne, *Dark Matters*, 21.

8 *De Djess*.

9 For more on palm trees and tropicalization, see Thompson, *An Eye for the Tropics*.

10 Sheller, *Citizenship from Below*, 219.

11 Pratt, *Imperial Eyes*, 7.

BIBLIOGRAPHY

24 Hour Party People. Directed by Michael Winterbottom. 2002. MGM, 2003. DVD.

"About SOBs." www.sobs.com. Accessed April 12, 2017.

Adorno, Rolena. "Americanist Visions: Stanley T. Williams, Washington Irving, and Christopher Columbus." *Yale Review* 99, no. 2 (2011): 1–25.

Alcántara Almánzar, José. Personal interview by author. August 24, 2006.

Alloula, Malek. *The Colonial Harem*. Translated by Myrna Godzich and Wlad Godzich. Minneapolis: University of Minnesota Press, 1986.

Alvarez, Julia. *In the Name of Salomé*. Chapel Hill: Algonquin Books, 2000.

———. "Re: Question from a Dominican PhD Student." E-mail message to the author. December 14, 2009.

———. "A White Woman of Color." In *Purpose and Process: A Reader for Writers*. 5th ed. Upper Saddle River, NJ: Pearson Education, 2003.

Alvarez Leal, Francisco. *La República Dominicana 1888: Territorio, clima, agricultura, industria, comercio, inmigración y anuario estadístico*. Santo Domingo: Editora Búho, (1888) 2014.

"Annette Castellano Is My Nemesis." *The Mindy Project*, season 2, episode 3. 20th Century Fox. Streamed through *Hulu*. www.hulu.com.

Appadurai, Arjun. *Modernity at Large: Cultural Dimensions of Globalization*. Minneapolis: University of Minnesota Press, 1996.

Arias, Aurora. *Emoticons*. San Juan: Terranova, 2007.

———. Personal interview by author. December 18, 2007.

———. Personal interview by author. August 28, 2006.

Báez, Firelei. "Firelei Báez: In Conversation with Naima J. Keith." In *Firelei Báez: Bloodlines*. Miami: Pérez Art Museum Miami, 2015.

Balaguer, Joaquín. *El Cristo de la libertad: Vida de Juan Pablo Duarte*. 4th ed. Santo Domingo: J. D. Postigo, 1968.

———. *Historia de la literatura dominicana*. 5th ed. Buenos Aires: Gráfica Guadalupe, 1972.

———. *La isla al revés: Haití y el destino dominicano*. 11th ed. Santo Domingo: Editora Corripio, 2002.

———. *Letras dominicanas*. 3rd ed. Santo Domingo: Editora Corripio, 1990.

Balcácer, Juan Daniel. *Trujillo: El tiranicidio de 1961*. 3rd ed. Santo Domingo: Taurus, Grupo Santillana, 2008.

Ballplayer: Pelotero. Directed by Ross Finkel, Trevor Martin, and Jonathan Paley. 2011. Strand Releasing Home Video, 2012. DVD.

Barnes, Natasha. "Body Talk: Notes on Women and Spectacle in Contemporary Trinidad Carnival." *Small Axe* 7 (2000): 93–105.

Bautista, Celsa Albert. *Mujer y esclavitud en Santo Domingo*. Santo Domingo: Ediciones CEDEE, 1990.

Baud, Michiel. "'Constitutionally White': The Forging of a National Identity in the Dominican Republic." Chapter 7 in *Ethnicity in the Caribbean: Essays in Honor of Harry Hoetink*, edited by Gert Oostindie. London: Macmillan Caribbean, 1996.

———. "Manuel Arturo Peña Batlle y Joaquín Balaguer y la identidad nacional dominicana." In *Política, identidad y pensamiento social en la República Dominicana (Siglos XIX y XX)*, edited by Raymundo González, Michiel Baud, Pedro L. San Miguel, and Roberto Cassá, 153–179. Santo Domingo: Ediciones Doce Calles, 1999.

———. "Patrons, Peasants, and Tobacco." In *The Dominican Republic Reader*, edited by Eric Paul Roorda, Lauren H. Derby, and Raymundo González, 217–224. Durham: Duke University Press, 2014.

Bell, Howard H., ed. *Black Separatism in the Caribbean, 1860*. Ann Arbor: University of Michigan Press, 1970.

Belliard, Basilio. Personal interview by author. August 26, 2006.

Benítez-Rojo, Antonio. *The Repeating Island: The Caribbean and the Postmodern Perspective*. 2nd ed. Translated by James Maraniss. Durham: Duke University Press, 1996.

Bergland, Renée. *The National Uncanny: Indian Ghosts and American Subjects*. Hanover, NH: Dartmouth College, University Press of New England, 2000.

Berlin, Ira. *Many Thousands Gone: The First Two Centuries of Slavery in North America*. Cambridge: Harvard University Press, 1998.

Bermúdez, Luis A. "Da. S. Ureña de Henríquez." In *Salomé Ureña y el Instituto de Señoritas: Para la historia de la espiritualidad dominicana*, edited by Emilio Rodríguez Demorizi. Ciudad Trujillo: Impresora Dominicana, 1960.

Bernstein, Robin. *Racial Innocence: Performing American Childhood from Slavery to Civil Rights*. New York: New York University Press, 2011.

Bhabha, Homi K. "Are You a Man or a Mouse?" Chapter 8 in *Constructing Masculinity*, edited by Maurice Berger, Brian Wallis, and Simon Watson, 57–65. New York: Routledge, 1995.

Black and Latino. mun2.tv, NBC Universo. www.nbcuniverso.com.

"Black in the Dominican Republic: Denying Blackness." *HuffPost Live*, June 10, 2014. http://live.huffingtonpost.com.

Bonó, Pedro Francisco. *El Montero: Novela de constumbres*. San Francisco de Macorís: Comisión Organizadora Permanente de la Feria Nacional del Libro, (1856) 1989.

———. *El Montero, Epistolario*. Santo Domingo: Ediciones de la Fundación Corripio, 2000.

Bosch, Juan. "Contrabandistas, bucaneros y filibusteros." Chapter 8 in *De Cristóbal Colón a Fidel Castro: El Caribe, frontera imperial*. Madrid: Alfaguara, 1970.

———. *De Cristóbal Colón a Fidel Castro: El Caribe, la frontera imperial*. Santo Domingo: Ediciones Fundación Juan Bosch, 2012.

Brea, Ramonina, and Isis Duarte. *Entre la calle y la casa: Las mujeres dominicanas y la cultura política a finales del siglo XX*. Santo Domingo: Editora Búho, 1999.

Brennan, Denise. *What's Love Got to Do with It? Transnational Desires and Sex Tourism in the Dominican Republic*. Durham: Duke University Press, 2004.

Brickhouse, Anna. *Transamerican Literary Relations and the Nineteenth-Century Public Sphere*. Cambridge: Cambridge University Press, 2004.

Brooks, Daphne. *Bodies in Dissent: Spectacular Performances of Race and Freedom, 1850–1910*. Durham: Duke University Press, 2006.

Browne, Simone. *Dark Matters: On the Surveillance of Blackness*. Durham: Duke University Press, 2015.

Brugal, Rafael A. "El Maestro Dubeau: Cronología, semblanza y pensamiento pedagógico." *eme eme* 8, no. 43 (1979): 3–33.

Burnard, Trevor G., and John Garrigus. *The Plantation Machine: Atlantic Capitalism in French Saint-Domingue and British Jamaica*. Philadelphia: University of Pennsylvania Press, 2016.

Bush, Barbara. *Slave Women in Caribbean Society, 1650–1838*. Kingston: Heinemann Publishers, 1990.

Butler, Judith. *Gender Trouble: Feminism and the Subversion of Identity*. New York: Routledge Classics, (1990) 2007.

Cabezas, Amalia L. *Economies of Desire: Sex and Tourism in Cuba and the Dominican Republic*. Philadelphia: Temple University Press, 2009.

Cabrera, Carlos. "La muerte de Tony Seval: Entre mitos, dudas y recuerdos." *EntreMiras*, November 5, 2010. http://robertalmonte.blogspot.com.

"CAFTA-DR (Dominican Republic–Central America FTA)." Office of the United States Trade Representative. https://ustr.gov.

Calder, Bruce J. *The Impact of the Intervention: The Dominican Republic during the U.S. Occupation of 1916–1924*. Austin: University of Texas Press, 1984.

Campuzano, Luisa, and Catharina Vallejo. *Yo con mi viveza: Textos de conquistadoras, monjas, brujas, poetas y otras mujeres de la colonia*. Havana: Fondo Editorial Casa de las Américas, 2003.

Candelario, Ginetta E. B. *Black behind the Ears: Dominican Racial Identity from Museums to Beauty Shops*. Durham: Duke University Press, 2007.

———. "Hair Race-Ing: Dominican Beauty Culture and Identity Production." *Meridians* 1, no. 1 (Fall 2000): 128–156. www.jstor.org/stable/40338439.

———. "La ciguapa y el ciguapeo: Dominican Myth, Metaphor, and Method." *Small Axe* 20, no. 51 (2016): 100–112. doi:10.1215/07990537-3726890.

Cánovas, Rodrigo. *Sexualidad y cultura en la novela hispanoamericana: La alegoría del prostíbulo*. Santiago, Dominican Republic: LOM Ediciones, 2003.

Caruth, Cathy. *Unclaimed Experience: Trauma, Narrative, and History*. Baltimore: Johns Hopkins University Press, 1996.

Cassá, Roberto. *Salomé Ureña: Mujer total*. Santo Domingo: Tobogán, 2000.

Castellanos, José, ed. *Lira de Quisqueya*. Santo Domingo: García Hermanos, 1874.

Castro Ventura, Santiago. *Salomé Ureña: Jornada fecunda*. Santo Domingo: Editora de Colores, 1998.

Cestero, Tulio. *Colón (Su nacionalidad, el predescubrimiento de América, su tumba y el faro conmemorativo)*. Buenos Aires: Libreria Cervantes de J. Suarez, 1933.

Chang, David. *The Color of the Land: Race, Nation, and the Politics of Landownership in Oklahoma, 1832–1929*. Chapel Hill: University of North Carolina Press, 2010.

Chetty, Raj. "'La calle es libre': Race, Recognition, and Dominican Street Theater." *Afro-Hispanic Review* 32, no. 2 (Fall 2013): 41–58. www.jstor.org/stable/24585142.

Cimarrón Spirit. Directed by Rubén Durán, with Donna Pinnick, Michael Brims, and Rachel Afi Quinn. Cab 95 Films and Cosmic Light Productions. 2015.

"Clinton Foundation in Haiti." Clinton Foundation. www.clintonfoundation.org.

Cocco de Filippis, Daisy, ed. *Antología de cuentos escritos por mujeres dominicanas*. Santo Domingo: Editora Taller, 1992.

———. "Indias y Trigueñas No Longer: Contemporary Dominican Women Poets Speak." In *Documents of Dissidence: Selected Writings by Dominican Women*, edited by Daisy Cocco de Filippis. New York: CUNY Dominican Studies Institute, 2000.

Coleman, Arica L. *That the Blood Stay Pure: African Americans, Native Americans, and the Predicament of Race and Identity in Virginia*. Bloomington: Indiana University Press, 2013.

Collado, Lipe. *El tíguere dominicano*. 2nd ed. Santo Domingo: Editora Collado, 1992.

———. *El tíguere dominicano*. 4th ed. Santo Domingo: Editora Collado, 2004.

"The Columbus Lighthouse." *New York Times*, January 3, 1928, 24. ProQuest Historical Newspapers, New York Times (1851–2006).

Columbus Memorial: Progress, Achievement. Chicago: John W. Iliff & Co. Publishers, 1893.

Condé, Maryse. *La parole des femmes: Essai sur des romancières des Antilles de langue française*. Paris: l'Harmattan, 1997.

Coronado, Raul. *A World Not to Come: A History of Latino Writing and Print Culture*. Cambridge: Harvard University Press, 2013.

Coughlin, Dan, and Kim Ives. "WikiLeaks Haiti: Let Them Live on $3 a Day." *Nation*, June 1, 2011. www.thenation.com.

Counihan, Clare. "Desiring Diaspora: 'Testing' the Boundaries of National Identity in Edwidge Danticat's *Breath, Eyes, Memory*." *Small Axe* 16, no. 1 (2012): 36–52. doi:10.1215/07990537–1548110.

Dale, Martin. "IFF Panama/Cannes: 'Noeli en Los Paises' Tops 2nd Primera Mirada, Heads to Cannes." *Variety*, April 13, 2016. http://variety.com.

Dalleo, Raphael. *American Imperialism's Undead: The Occupation of Haiti and the Rise of Caribbean Anticolonialism*. Charlottesville: University of Virginia Press, 2016.

Danticat, Edwidge. *Create Dangerously: The Immigrant Artist at Work*. Princeton: Princeton University Press, 2010.

Daut, Marlene. *Tropics of Haiti: Race and the Literary History of the Haitian Revolution in the Atlantic World, 1789–1865*. Liverpool: Liverpool University Press, 2015.

Davis, Martha Ellen. "La Montería: The Hunt for Wild Pigs and Goats." Translated by Alex Huezo and Martha Ellen Davis. In *The Dominican Republic Reader*, edited by Eric Paul Roorda, Lauren H. Derby, and Raymundo González, 446–449. Durham: Duke University Press, 2014.

———. *La otra ciencia: El vodú dominicano como religión y medicina populares*. Santo Domingo: Editora Universitaria, UASD, 1987.

Dayan, Joan. *Haiti, History, and the Gods*. Berkeley: University of California Press, 1995.

Decena, Carlos. *Tacit Subjects: Belonging and Same-Sex Desire among Dominican Immigrant Men*. Durham: Duke University Press, 2011.

Decena, Carlos, Michele G. Shedlin, and Angela Martinez. "Los hombres no mandan aqui: Narrating Immigrant Genders and Sexualities in New York." *Social Text* 24, no. 3 (2006): 35–54. doi:10.1215/01642472-2006-003.

De Djess. "Miu Miu: Women's Tales #9." Directed by Alice Rohrwacher. YouTube video, 14.33. Posted by Miu Miu, February 18, 2015. https://www.youtube.com/watch?v=Z MEByBDPPJM.

Deive, Carlos Esteban. *Vodú y magia en Santo Domingo*. Santo Domingo: Museo del Hombre Dominicano, 1975.

de la Cruz Hermosilla, Emilio. "Los restos de Colón en Santo Domingo." *Organo de la Academia Dominicana de la Historia* 53, no. 141 (1984): 7–30.

del Castillo, José. "The Formation of the Dominican Sugar Industry: From Competition to Monopoly, from National Semiproletariat to Foreign Proletariat." In *Between Slavery and Free Labor: The Spanish-Speaking Caribbean in the Nineteenth Century*, edited by Manuel Moreno Fraginals, Frank Moya Pons, and Stanley L. Engerman, 215–235. Baltimore: Johns Hopkins University Press, 1985.

De los Santos, Danilo. *Impulso y desarrollo moderno, 1920–1950*. Vol. 2, *Memoria de la pintura dominicana*. Santo Domingo: Grupo León Jimenes, 2003.

———. *Raíces e impulso nacional, 2000 A.C.-1924*. Vol. 1, *Memoria de la pintura dominicana*. Santo Domingo: Grupo León Jimenes, 2003.

De Moya, Antonio E. "Power Games and Totalitarian Masculinity in the Dominican Republic." In *Interrogating Caribbean Masculinities: Theoretical and Empirical Analyses*, edited by Rhoda E Reddock. Kingston: University of the West Indies Press, 2004.

De Pree, Ken. *Beware of the Baca! Folklore of Dominican Republic*. N.p.: Ken De Pree, 1989.

Derby, Lauren. "Beyond Fugitive Speech: Rumor and Affect in Caribbean History." *Small Axe* 44, no. 2 (2014): 123–140. doi:10.1215/07990537-2739893.

———. *The Dictator's Seduction: Politics and the Popular Imagination in the Era of Trujillo*. Durham: Duke University Press, 2009.

———. "Imperial Secrets: Vampires and Nationhood in Puerto Rico." *Past & Present* 199, no. 3 (2008): 290–312. https://doi.org/10.1093/pastj/gtm069.

———. "In the Shadow of the State: The Politics of Denunciation and Panegyric during the Trujillo Regime in the Dominican Republic, 1940–1958." *Hispanic American Historical Review* 83, no. 2 (2003): 295–344.

———. "Male Heroism, Demonic Pigs, and Memories of Violence in the Haitian-Dominican Borderlands." *Center for the Study of Women Update Newsletter*, May 10, 2010. http://escholarship.org.

Díaz, Junot. *The Brief Wondrous Life of Oscar Wao.* New York: Riverhead Books, 2007.
———. Personal interview by author. October 16, 2009.
Diederich, Bernard. *Trujillo: The Death of the Goat.* Boston: Little, Brown, 1978.
Dillon, Elizabeth Maddock. *The Gender of Freedom: Fictions of Liberalism and the Literary Public Sphere.* Stanford: Stanford University Press, 2004.
Dixon, Chris. *African America and Haiti: Emigration and Black Nationalism in the Nineteenth Century.* Westport, CT: Greenwood Press, 2000.
"Dominican Republic: Overview." World Bank. Updated April 10, 2017. Accessed November 24, 2016. http://www.worldbank.org.
Domino Rudolph, Jennifer. *Embodying Latino Masculinities: Producing Masculatinidad.* New York: Palgrave Macmillan, 2012.
Douglass, Frederick. "Dominican Support for Annexation: US Commission of Inquiry to Santo Domingo." 1871. In *The Dominican Republic Reader,* edited by Eric Paul Roorda, Lauren H. Derby, and Raymundo González. Durham: Duke University Press, 2014.
Duany, Jorge. *Quisqueya on the Hudson: The Transnational Identity of Dominicans in Washington Heights.* New York: CUNY Dominican Studies Institute, 1994.
Dubois, Laurent. *Avengers of the New World: The Story of the Haitian Revolution.* Cambridge: Harvard University Press, 2009.
———. *Haiti: The Aftershocks of History.* New York: Metropolitan Books, 2012.
Dubroca. *Vida de J.J. Dessalines, gefe de los negros de Santo Domingo; con notas my circunstanciadas sobre el origen, carácter y atrocidades de los principals gefes de aquellos rebeldes desde el principio de la insurreccion en 1791.* Mexico: En la oficina de D. Mariano de Zúñiga y Ontiveros, 1806. https://archive.org.
Durán-Almarza, Emilia María. "*Ciguapas* in New York." *Journal of American Studies* 46, no. 1 (2012): 139–153. doi:10.1017/S0021875811001332.
Edmondson, Belinda. "Public Spectacles: Caribbean Women and the Politics of Public Performance." *Small Axe* 1, no. 7 (2003): 1–16. https://search.proquest.com.
"Efemérides de la Sociedad 'Amigos del País': desde su instalación hasta el día." *El Lápiz,* May 18, 1891.
Ehrenreich, Barbara, and Arlie R. Hochschild, eds. *Global Woman: Nannies, Maids, and Sex Workers in the New Economy.* New York: Metropolitan Books, 2003.
"'El Alfa' cumple segunda día de sanction limpieza Plaza de la Bandera." *Enfoque matinal.* YouTube video, 3:38. May 7, 2015. https://www.youtube.com/watch?v=ljFOM_AiGps.
Eller, Anne. "'All Would Be Equal in the Effort': Santo Domingo's 'Italian Revolution,' Independence, and Haiti, 1809–1822." *Journal of Early American History* 1, no. 2 (2011): 105–141. doi:10.1163/187707011X577432.
———. "'Awful Pirates' and 'Hordes of Jackals': Santo Domingo/the Dominican Republic in Nineteenth-Century Historiography." *Small Axe* 18, no. 2 (Summer 2014): 80–94. doi:10.1215/07990537-2739866.
———. "Let's Show the World We Are Brothers: The Dominican *Guerra de Restauración* and the Nineteenth-Century Caribbean." PhD diss., New York University, 2011.

——. *We Dream Together: Dominican Independence, Haiti, and the Fight for Caribbean Freedom*. Durham: Duke University Press, 2016.

Enecia, Hogla. "El 'Alfa' tendrá que limpiar la Plaza de la Bandera y cantar el Himno Nacional." *El Caribe*, May 5, 2015. elcaribe.com.do.

"Etat general de la partie de l'est de Saint Domingue, a l'epoque de premiere janvier 1808." Colonies CC/9a/45. Paris: Centre d'Acceuil et de Recherche des Archives Nationales (CARAN).

Fanning, Sara. *Caribbean Crossing: African Americans and the Haitian Emigration Movement*. New York: New York University Press, 2015.

Farah, Douglas. "Curse of Columbus?" *Washington Post*, October 7, 1992. washingtonpost.com.

Ferbel, Peter J. "The Politics of Taino Indian Heritage in the Post-Quincentennial Dominican Republic: When a Canoe Means More Than a Water Trough." PhD diss., University of Minnesota, 1995.

Ferguson, Roderick. *Aberrations in Black: Toward a Queer of Color Critique*. Minneapolis: University of Minnesota Press, 2004.

Ferly, Odile. *A Poetics of Relation: Caribbean Women Writing at the Millennium*. New York: Palgrave Macmillan, 2012.

Ferrán, Fernando I., and Patricia R. Pessar. *Dominican Agriculture and the Effect of International Migration*. Washington, DC: Commission for the Study of International Migration and Cooperative Economic Development, 1990.

Ferrer, Ada. *Freedom's Mirror: Cuba and Haiti in the Age of Revolution*. New York: Cambridge University Press, 2014.

Fick, Carolyn E. *The Making of Haiti: The Saint Domingue Revolution from Below*. Knoxville: University of Tennessee Press, 1990.

Fiol-Matta, Licia. *A Queer Mother for the Nation: The State and Gabriela Mistral*. Minneapolis: University of Minnesota Press, 2002.

Fischer, Sibylle. *Modernity Disavowed: Haiti and the Cultures of Slavery in the Age of Revolution*. Durham: Duke University Press, 2004.

Flood, Alison. "*The Brief Wondrous Life of Oscar Wao* Declared 21st Century's Best Novel So Far." *Guardian*, January 20, 2015. http://www.theguardian.com.

Flores, Juan. *The Diaspora Strikes Back: Caribeño Tales of Learning and Turning*. New York: Routledge, 2009.

Franck, Harry. "The Land of Bullet Holes." In *The Dominican Republic Reader: History, Culture, Politics*, edited by Eric Paul Roorda, Lauren Derby, and Raymundo González, 260–264. Durham: Duke University Press, 2014.

Franco, Franklin J. *Blacks, Mulattos, and the Dominican Nation*. Translated by Patricia Mason. New York: Routledge, 2015.

Franco, Jean. *Plotting Women: Gender and Representation in Mexico*. New York: Columbia University Press, 1989.

Freeman, Carla. *High Tech and High Heels in the Global Economy: Women, Work, and Pink-Collar Identities in the Caribbean*. Durham: Duke University Press, 2000.

Fregoso, Rosa Linda. *MeXicana Encounters: The Making of Social Identities on the Borderlands*. Berkeley: University of California Press, 2003.

French, Howard W. "For Columbus Lighthouse, a Fete That Fizzled." *New York Times*, September 25, 1992, A4.

From Mambo to Hip Hop: A South Bronx Tale. Directed by Henry Chalfant. 2006.

Fronterizas. Directed by Lorena Durán. 2015. Vimeo. Uploaded July 2, 2014. Accessed December 1, 2016. https://vimeo.com.

Fuentes, Carlos. *La muerte de Artemio Cruz*. México, DF: Fondo de Cultura Económica, 1962.

Fuentes, Marisa J. *Dispossessed Lives: Enslaved Women, Violence, and the Archive*. Philadelphia: University of Pennsylvania Press, 2016.

Fumagalli, Maria Cristina. *On the Edge: Writing the Border between Haiti and the Dominican Republic*. Liverpool: University of Liverpool Press, 2015.

Funderburg, Lise. "The Changing Face of America." *National Geographic*, October 2013. ngm.nationalgeographic.com.

Gaffield, Julia. *Haitian Connections in the Atlantic World: Recognition after Revolution*. Chapel Hill: University of North Carolina Press, 2015.

García, Sandra E. "At a Santo Domingo Hair Salon, Rethinking an Ideal Look." *New York Times*, December 30, 2015.

———. "Heritage in All Its Rich Hues: M. Tony Peralta Explores His Dominican Roots." *New York Times*, January 2, 2014.

García Canclini, Néstor. *Consumers and Citizens: Globalization and Multicultural Conflicts*. Translated by George Yúdice. Minneapolis: University of Minnesota Press, 2001.

García Domínguez, Mar, and Denise Paiewonsky. *Gender, Remittances, and Development: The Case of Women Migrants from Vicente Noble, Dominican Republic*. Santo Domingo: United Nations International Research and Training Institute for the Advancement of Women (UN-INSTRAW), 2006.

García-Peña, Lorgia. *The Borders of Dominicanidad: Race, Nation, and Archives of Contradiction*. Durham: Duke University Press, 2016.

García Romero, Raphael. *Ruinas*. Santo Domingo: Ediciones CEDIBIL, 2005.

———. "Salomé, madre y maestra ejemplar." *Listín Diario*, August 22, 2011. www.listindiario.com.

Gates, Henry Louis, Jr. "Haiti and the Dominican Republic: An Island Divided." *Black in Latin America*. Film series, PBS, 2011.

Geggus, David P. "The Boca Nigua Revolt." In *The Dominican Republic Reader*, edited by Eric Paul Roorda, Lauren H. Derby, and Raymundo González. Durham: Duke University Press, 2014.

———. "The Naming of Haiti." *New West Indian Guide* 71, nos. 1–2 (1997): 43–68. http://www.jstor.org/stable/41849817.

Gibson, Carrie. *Empire's Crossroads: A History of the Caribbean from Columbus to the Present Day*. New York: Grove Press, 2015.

Gilroy, Paul. *There Ain't No Black in the Union Jack: The Cultural Politics of Race and Nation*. Chicago: University of Chicago Press, 1991.

Glissant, Edouard. *Poetics of Relation*. Translated by Betsy Wing. Ann Arbor: University of Michigan Press, 1997.

González, Christopher. *Reading Junot Díaz*. Pittsburgh: University of Pittsburgh Press, 2015.

González, Raymundo. *De esclavos a campesinos: Vida rural en Santo Domingo colonial*. Santo Domingo: Archivo General de la Nación, 2011.

———. "Ideología del progreso y campesinado en el siglo XIX." *Ecos* 1, no. 2 (1993): 25–43.

———. "The 'People-Eater.'" In *The Dominican Republic Reader*, edited by Eric Paul Roorda, Lauren H. Derby, and Raymundo González. Durham: Duke University Press, 2014.

González, Robert Alexander. *Designing Pan-America: U.S. Architectural Visions for the Western Hemisphere*. Austin: University of Texas Press, 2011.

González, Ruddy. "Costly Columbus Lighthouse Inaugurated; Students, Labor Groups to Protest." *Associated Press*, October 6, 1992. apnewsarchive.com.

González Stephan, Beatriz. "Narrativas duras en tiempos blandos: Sensibilidades amenazadas de los hombres de letras." *Revista de Crítica Literaria Latinoamericana* 26, no. 52 (2000): 107–134.

Gopinath, Gayatri. *Impossible Desires: Queer Diasporas and South Asian Public Cultures*. Durham: Duke University Press, 2005.

Gordon, Avery. *Ghostly Matters: Haunting and the Sociological Imagination*. Minneapolis: University of Minnesota Press, 2008.

Goudie, Sean X. "The Caribbean Turn in C19 American Literary Studies." In *Turns of Events: Nineteenth-Century American Literary Studies in Motion*, edited by Hester Blum, 127–150. Philadelphia: University of Pennsylvania Press, 2016.

Grandin, Greg. *The Empire of Necessity: The Untold Story of a Slave Rebellion in the Age of Liberty*. New York: Oneworld Publications, 2014.

Grant, Ulysses S. "Making the Case for U.S. Annexation." 1869. In *The Dominican Republic Reader*, edited by Eric Paul Roorda, Lauren H. Derby and Raymundo González. Durham: Duke University Press, 2014.

Grasmuck, Sherrie, and Patricia R. Pessar. *Between Two Islands: Dominican International Migration*. Berkeley: University of California Press, 1991.

Graziano, Frank. *Undocumented Dominican Migration*. Austin: University of Texas Press, 2013.

Gregorio Gil, Carmen. *Migración femenina: Su impacto en las relaciones de género*. Madrid: Narcea, S.A. de Ediciones, 1998.

Gregory, Steven. *The Devil behind the Mirror: Globalization and Politics in the Dominican Republic*. Berkeley: University of California Press, 2007.

Guidotti-Hernández, Nicole. *Unspeakable Violence: Remapping U.S. and Mexican National Imaginaries*. Durham: Duke University Press, 2011.

Guitar, Lynne. "Boiling It Down: Slavery on the First Commercial Sugarcane Ingenios in the Americas (Hispaniola, 1530–45)." In *Slaves, Subjects, and Subversives: Blacks in Colonial Latin America*, edited by Jane G. Landers and Barry M. Robinson. Albuquerque: University of New Mexico Press, 2006.

Guzmán, Sandra. "'El Alfa' se disculpa por palabras obscenas que dijo contra los padres de la Patria." *El Caribe*, April 30, 2015. www.elcaribe.com.do.

———. "Ministerio Público apresó a 'El Alfa' por offender a padres de la Patria." *El Caribe*, May 1, 2015. www.elcaribe.com.do.

Halberstam, Jack. *Female Masculinity*. Durham: Duke University Press, 1998.

Hall, Stuart. "Cultural Identity and Diaspora." In *Identity: Community, Culture, Difference*, edited by Jonathan Rutherford, 222–237. London: Lawrence and Wishart, 1990.

Hanna, Monica. "'Reassembling the Fragments': Battling Historiographies, Caribbean Diction, and Nerd Genres in Junot Díaz's *The Brief Wondrous Life of Oscar Wao*." *Callaloo* 33, no. 2 (Spring 2010): 498–520. http://www.jstor.org/stable/40732888.

Hanna, Monica, Jennifer Harford Vargas, and José David Saldívar, eds. *Junot Díaz and the Decolonial Imagination*. Durham: Duke University Press, 2016.

Harford Vargas, Jennifer. "Dictating a Zafa: The Power of Narrative Form in Junot Díaz's *The Brief Wondrous Life of Oscar Wao*." *MELUS* 39, no. 3 (2014): 8–30. doi:10.1093/melus/mlu034.

Harper, Andrew. "Gallery: The Peninsula House, Dominican Republic." May 16, 2013. www.andrewharper.com.

Harris, J. Dennis. *A Summer on the Borders of the Caribbean Sea*. Middletown, DE: Reprint from the Collections of the University of California Libraries, 2015.

Hartman, Saidiya. *Scenes of Subjection: Terror, Slavery, and Self-Making in Nineteenth-Century America*. New York: Oxford University Press, 1997.

Hazard, Samuel. *Santo Domingo: Past and Present, With a Glance at Hayti*. London: Sampson Low, Marston, Low, & Searle, 1873.

Henríquez Ureña, Max. *Hermano y maestro*. Ciudad Trujillo: Libería Dominicana, 1950.

Henríquez Ureña, Pedro. *Memorias, diario, notas de viaje*. 2nd ed. México, DF: Fondo de Cultura Económica, 2000.

Henríquez Ureña de Hlito, Sonia. *Pedro Henríquez Ureña: Apuntes para una biografía*. México, DF: Siglo Veintiuno, 1993.

Heredia, Juanita. *Transnational Latina Narratives in the Twenty-First Century: The Politics of Gender, Race, and Migrations*. New York: Palgrave Macmillan, 2009.

Hernández, Angela. "De críticos y creadoras." In *Antología de cuentos escritos por mujeres dominicanas*, edited by Daisy Cocco de Filippis. Santo Domingo: Editora Taller, 1992.

Hernández, Ramona. *The Mobility of Workers under Advanced Capitalism*. New York: Columbia University Press, 2002.

Hernández, Tanya K. *Racial Subordination in Latin America: The Role of the State, Customary Law, and the New Civil Rights Response*. Cambridge: Cambridge University Press, 2013.

Hernández-Reguant, Ariana, and Jossianna Arroyo. "The Brownface of Latinidad in Cuban Miami." *Cuba Counterpoints*, July 13, 2015. https://cubacounterpoints.com.

Herrera, César A. *La poesía de Salomé Ureña en su función social y patriótica*. Ciudad Trujillo: Impresora Dominicana, 1951.

Higginbotham, Evelyn Brooks. *Righteous Discontent: The Women's Movement in the Black Baptist Church, 1880–1920*. Cambridge: Harvard University Press, 1993.

Hobbs, Allyson. *A Chosen Exile: A History of Racial Passing in American Life*. Cambridge: Harvard University Press, 2014.

Hoetink, Harry. *The Dominican People, 1850–1900: Notes for a Historical Sociology*. Baltimore: Johns Hopkins University Press, 1982.

Hoffnung-Garskof, Jesse. "The Prehistory of the *Cadenú*: Dominican Identity, Social Class, and the Problem of Mobility, 1965–1978." In *Immigrant Life in the US: Multi-Disciplinary Perspectives*, edited by Donna R. Gabaccia and Colin Wayne Leach, 31–50. New York: Routledge, 2004.

———. *A Tale of Two Cities: Santo Domingo and New York after 1950*. Princeton: Princeton University Press, 2008.

Holden, Stephen. "Review: 'Sand Dollars,' Unrequited Love in the Dominican Republic." *New York Times*, November 5, 2015. www.nytimes.com.

Holland, Sharon Patricia, and Tiya Miles, eds. *Crossing Waters, Cross Worlds: The African Diaspora in Indian Country*. Durham: Duke University Press, 2006.

Horn, Maja. *Masculinity after Trujillo: The Politics of Gender in Dominican Literature*. Gainesville: University Press of Florida, 2014.

Howard, David. *Coloring the Nation: Race and Ethnicity in the Dominican Republic*. Oxford: Signal Books, 2001.

Hughes, Langston. "Columbia." In *The Collected Poems of Langston Hughes*, edited by Arnold Rampersad and David Roessel, 168–169. New York: Alfred A. Knopf, 1995.

———. "Playboys." *New York Post Magazine*, July 9, 1965.

Hulme, Peter. "Quincentenary Perspectives." *History Workshop* 36 (1993): 228–231.

Hutchinson, Sydney. *Tigers of a Different Stripe: Performing Gender in Dominican Music*. Chicago: University of Chicago Press, 2016.

Imbert Brugal, Carmen. "The Manly Intellectual Woman." In *Documents of Dissidence: Selected Writings by Dominican Women*, edited and translated by Daisy Cocco De Filippis, 169–170. New York: CUNY Dominican Studies Institute, 2000.

Incháustegui, Arístedes, and Blanca Delgada Malagón, eds. *Familia Henríquez Ureña: Epistolario*. 2 vols. Santo Domingo: Secretaría de Estado de Educación, Bellas Artes y Cultos, 1996.

Inman, Samuel Guy. *Through Santo Domingo and Haiti: A Cruise with the Marines*. Charleston, SC: BiblioLife Reprint, (1919) 2009.

Jacobson, Matthew Frye. *Whiteness of a Different Color: European Immigrants and the Alchemy of Race*. Cambridge: Harvard University Press, 1998.

James, C. L. R. *The Black Jacobins: Toussaint Louverture and the San Domingo Revolution*. New York: Vintage Books, (1938) 1989.

Jaramillo, María Mercedes, and Lucía Ortiz, eds. *Hijas del Muntu: Biografías críticas de mujeres afrodescendientes de América Latina*. Bogotá: Panamericana Editoria, 2011.

"Jean du Sable, Explorer Who Founded Chicago." African American Registry. Accessed December 15, 2016. www.aaregistry.org.

Jimenes Grullón, Juan Isidro. *El mito de los Padres de la Patria: Debate histórico.* 3rd ed. Santo Domingo: Archivo General de la Nación, 2014.

Jiménez, Ramón Emilio. *Al amor del bohío (tradiciones y costumbres dominicanas).* Santo Domingo: V. Montalvo, 1927–1929.

———. *Savia dominicana.* Santiago: Editorial El Diario, 1947.

Johnson, John J. *Latin America in Caricature.* 2nd ed. Austin: University of Texas, 1997.

Johnson, Robert. "Wikileaks: U.S. Fought to Lower Minimum Wage in Haiti So Hanes and Levi's Would Stay Cheap." *Business Insider*, June 3, 2011. www.businessinsider .com.

Johnson, Sara. *The Fear of French Negroes: Transcolonial Collaboration in the Revolutionary Americas.* Berkeley: University of California Press, 2012.

Julián, Alquíles. *El cantante y sus asesinos.* Santo Domingo: Editora Libros de Regalo, 2013. http://issuu.com.

Justo. "Ovación al genio: Solemne conferencia literaria." In *Salomé Ureña y el Instituto de Señoritas: Para la historia de la espiritualidad dominicana,* edited by Emilio Rodríguez Demorizi. Ciudad Trujillo: Impresora Dominicana, 1960.

Kanellos, Nicolás. "A Schematic Approach to Understanding Latino Transnational Literary Texts." In *Imagined Transnationalism: U.S. Latino/a Literature, Culture, and Identity,* edited by Kevin Concannon, Francisco A. Lomelí, and Marc Priewe. New York: Palgrave Macmillan, 2009.

Kaplan, Amy. *The Anarchy of Empire in the Making of U.S. Culture.* Cambridge: Harvard University Press, 2005.

———. "Manifest Domesticity." In *The Futures of American Studies,* edited by Donald E. Pease and Robin Wiegman, 111–134. Durham: Duke University Press, 2002.

Kempadoo, Kamala. *Sexing the Caribbean: Gender, Race, and Sexual Labor.* New York: Routledge, 2004.

Keown, Ian. "Love at First Sight." *Caribbean Travel & Life* (August–September 2009): 48–57. http://thepeninsulahouse.com.

King, Rosamond S. *Island Bodies: Transgressive Sexualities in the Caribbean Imagination.* Gainesville: University Press of Florida, 2014.

Knight, Franklin W. *The Caribbean: The Genesis of a Fragmented Nationalism.* New York: Oxford University Press, 1978.

Krauthamer, Barbara. *Black Slaves, Indian Masters: Slavery, Emancipation, and Citizenship in the Native American South.* Chapel Hill: University of North Carolina Press, 2013.

Krohn-Hansen, Christian. "Masculinity and the Political among Dominicans: 'The Dominican Tiger.'" In *Machos, Mistresses, Madonnas: Contesting the Power of Latin American Gender Imagery,* edited by Marit Melhuus and Kristi Anne Stølen. London: Verso, 1996.

———. *Political Authoritarianism in the Dominican Republic.* New York: Palgrave Macmillan, 2009.

Kutzinski, Vera M. *Sugar's Secrets: Race and the Erotics of Cuban Nationalism.* Charlottesville: University of Virginia Press, 1993.

"'La fiesta del Chivo,' novela del siglo." *ABC*, May 19, 2013. http://www.abc.es.

Lamarche, José. "Salomé Ureña de Henríquez." In *Salomé Ureña y el Instituto de Señoritas: Para la historia de la espiritualidad dominicana*, edited by Emilio Rodríguez Demorizi. Ciudad Trujillo: Impresora Dominicana, 1960.

Lara, Ana M. "Uncovering Mirrors: Afro-Latina Lesbian Subjects." In *The Afro-Latin@ Reader: History and Culture in the United States*, edited by Miriam Jiménez Román and Juan Flores, 298–313. Durham: Duke University Press, 2010.

La Soga. Directed by Josh Crook. 2009. New York: Screen Media Films, 2011. DVD.

La violencia del poder. Directed by René Fortunato. Santo Domingo: Videocine Palau, 2004. VHS.

Lilón, Domingo, and Juleyka J. Lantigua. "Dominican Transmigrants in Spain." Chapter 6 in *Dominican Migration: Transnational Perspectives*, edited by Ernesto Sagás and Sintia E. Molina. Gainesville: University Press of Florida, 2004.

Lora, Quisqueya. "El sonido de la libertad: 30 años de agitaciones y conspiraciones en Santo Domingo (1791–1821)." *Clío* 182 (2011): 109–140.

———. "Las mujeres anónimas de inicios del siglo XIX dominicano." *Clío* 176 (2008): 81–122.

Lowe, Lisa. *The Intimacies of Four Continents*. Durham: Duke University Press, 2015.

Lugo, Américo. "El estado dominicano ante el derecho público: Para el doctorado sustentada por Américo Lugo." PhD diss., Universidad Central de Santo Domingo, 1916.

Machado, Francisco J. "Salomé Ureña de Henríquez." *El Lápiz*, April 21, 1891.

Machado Sáez, Elena. "Dictating Desire, Dictating Diaspora: Junot Díaz's *The Brief Wondrous Life of Oscar Wao* as Foundational Romance." *Contemporary Literature* 52, no. 3 (2011): 522–555. doi:10.1353/cli.2011.0029.

Madera, Melissa. *"Never Forget Syphilis": Public Health, Modernity and Gender in the Discourse of Prevision Social during the Trujillato*. New York: CUNY Dominican Studies Institute, 2008.

Magee, Glenn Alexander. *The Hegel Dictionary*. New York: Continuum International Publishing, 2010.

Mahler, Anne Garland. "The Writer as Superhero: Fighting the Colonial Curse in Junot Díaz's *The Brief Wondrous Life of Oscar Wao*." *Journal of Latin American Cultural Studies* 19, no. 2 (August 2010): 119–140. doi:10.1080/13569325.2010.494928.

Maluca Mala. "El Tigeraso." Directed by Lazlo. YouTube video, 2:51. Posted by Mad Decent, December 2, 2009. www.youtube.com/watch?v=T1bHlWkwyqM.

———. "Mala." Soundcloud audio, 2:43. 2016. https://soundcloud.com/maluca-mala.

———. "Maluca Wepasode #2: Dominican Independence Day Special!!!" Directed by Bijoux Altamirano. YouTube video, 4:38. Posted by MalucaWepa, April 27, 2011. www.youtube.com/watch?v=g-6D1eT-buI.

Martí, José. "Our America." In *José Martí: Selected Writings*, edited and translated by Esther Allen. New York: Penguin Books, (1892) 2002.

Martín-Cabrera, Luis. "Postcolonial Memories and Racial Violence in Flores de otro mundo." *Journal of Spanish Cultural Studies* 3, no. 1 (2002): 43–55. doi:10.1080/1463620020127013.

Martínez, Lusitania. Personal interview by author. July 31, 2009.

Martínez, María Elena. "The Black Blood of New Spain: Limpieza de Sangre, Racial Violence, and Gendered Power in Early Colonial Mexico." *William and Mary Quarterly* 61, no. 3 (2004): 479–520. www.jstor.org/stable/3491806.

Martínez, Samuel. "Not a Cockfight: Rethinking Haitian-Dominican Relations." *Latin American Perspectives* 30, no. 3 (May 2003): 80–101. www.jstor.org/stable/3185037.

Martínez-San Miguel, Yolanda. *Caribe Two Ways: Cultura de la migración en el Caribe insular hispánico*. San Juan: Ediciones Callejón, 2003.

Martínez Vergne, Teresita. *Nation and Citizen in the Dominican Republic, 1880–1916*. Chapel Hill: University of North Carolina Press, 2005.

Mayes, April. *The Mulatto Republic: Class, Race, and Dominican National Identity*. Gainesville: University Press of Florida, 2014.

———. "Why Dominican Feminism Moved to the Right: Class, Colour and Women's Activism in the Dominican Republic, 1880s–1940s." *Gender & History* 20, no. 2 (2008): 349–371. doi:10.1111/j.1468-0424.2008.00525.

McClintock, Anne. "Imperial Ghosting and National Tragedy: Revenants from Hiroshima and Indian Country in the War on Terror." *PMLA* 129, no. 4 (October 2014): 819–829. doi:10.1632/pmla.2014.129.4.819.

———. "'No Longer in a Future Heaven': Gender, Race, and Nationalism." In *Dangerous Liaisons: Gender, Nation, and Postcolonial Perspectives*, edited by Anne McClintock, Ella Shohat, and Aamir R. Mufti, 89–112. Minneapolis: University of Minnesota Press, 1998.

———. "Sex Workers and Sex Work: Introduction." *Social Text*, no. 37 (1993): 1–10.

———. *Unquiet Ghosts of the Forever War: Militarization and Environmental Crises*. Durham: Duke University Press, forthcoming.

Mejía, Mariela. "RD tiene población de 9.4 millones; el 74.3% vive en zonas urbanas." *Diario Libre*, May 25, 2012. Accessed November 24, 2016. www.diariolibre.com.

Mella, Pablo. *Los espejos de Duarte*. Santo Domingo: Amigo del Hogar, 2013.

Melville, Herman. "Benito Cereno." In *Billy Budd, Sailor and Other Stories*, 145–232. New York: Bantam Dell, 2006.

Mena, Miguel D. "Re: Pregunta acerca de Salomé." E-mail message to the author. December 8, 2009.

Méndez, Danny. *Narratives of Migration and Displacement in Dominican Literature*. New York: Routledge, 2012.

Mercado, Juan Carlos. Personal interview by author. October 23, 2009.

Mermann-Jozwiak, Elizabeth Maria. "Beyond Multiculturalism: Ethnic Studies, Transnationalism, and Junot Díaz's Oscar Wao." *Ariel: A Review of International English Literature* 43, no. 2 (2013): 1–24.

Michel, Emilio Cordero. *La Revolución Haitiana y Santo Domingo*. Santo Domingo: Editora Nacional, 1968.

Miller, Jeannette. *Historia de la pintura dominicana*. 2nd ed. Santo Domingo: Amigo del Hogar, 1979.

Miss Rizos. Facebook post. July 9, 2016. https://www.facebook.com.

Moreau de Saint-Méry, M. L. E. *A Topographical and Political Description of the Spanish Part of Santo Domingo.* Vol. 1. Translated by William Cobbett. Philadelphia, 1798.

Moreno, Carolina. "Miss Rizos Stands Up for Teen Shamed by School for Rocking Natural Hair." *Huffington Post,* July 13, 2016. www.huffingtonpost.com/.

Morrison, Toni. *Beloved.* New York: Vintage International, (1987) 2004.

Moscoso Puello, Francisco. "From Paris to Santo Domingo." In *The Dominican Republic Reader: History, Culture, Politics,* edited by Eric Paul Roorda, Lauren Derby, and Raymundo González, 195–200. Durham: Duke University Press, 2014.

Motel, Seth, and Eileen Patten. "Hispanics of Dominican Origin in the United States, 2010: Statistical Profile." *Pew Research Center, Hispanic Trends,* June 27, 2012. www.pewhispanic.org.

Moya Pons, Frank. *The Dominican Republic: A National History.* Princeton: Markus Wiener Publishers, 1998.

———. *History of the Caribbean: Plantations, Trade, and War in the Atlantic World.* Princeton: Markus Wiener Publishers, 2007.

———, ed. *La migración dominicana a los Estados Unidos.* Santo Domingo: Forum, 1988.

———. "The Land Question in Haiti and Santo Domingo." In *Between Slavery and Free Labor: The Spanish-Speaking Caribbean in the Nineteenth Century,* edited by Manuel Moreno Fraginals, Frank Moya Pons, and Stanley L. Engerman, 181–214. Baltimore: Johns Hopkins University Press, 1985.

———. *La otra historia dominicana.* Santo Domingo: Librería La Trinitaria, 2008.

———. *Los restos de Colón: Bibliografía.* Santo Domingo: Academia Dominicana de la Historia, 2006.

Mulvey, Laura. "Visual Pleasure and Narrative Cinema." *Screen* 16, no. 3 (1975): 6–18. doi:10.1093/screen/16.3.6.

Muñoz, José. *Disidentifications: Queers of Color and the Performance of Politics.* Minneapolis: University of Minnesota Press, 1999.

Nanita, Abelardo. "Biography of a Great Leader." In *The Dominican Republic Reader: History, Culture, Politics,* edited by Eric Paul Roorda, Lauren Derby, and Raymundo González. Durham: Duke University Press, 2014.

Nessler, Graham T. *An Islandwide Struggle for Freedom: Revolution, Emancipation, and Reenslavement in Hispaniola (1789–1809).* Chapel Hill: University of North Carolina Press, 2016.

Ober, Frederick A. *In the Wake of Columbus; Adventures of the Special Commissioner Sent by the World's Columbian Exposition to the West Indies.* Boston: D. Lothrop Company, 1893.

———. *Our West Indian Neighbors: The Islands of the Caribbean Sea [. . .].* New York: J. Pott & Co., 1904.

O'Connell Davidson, Julia O'Connell, and Jacqueline Sánchez Taylor. "Fantasy Islands: Exploring the Demand for Sex Tourism." In *Sun, Sex, and Gold: Tourism and Sex*

Work in the Caribbean, edited by Kamala Kempadoo, 37–54. Lanham, MD: Rowman and Littlefield, 1999.

Olliz Boyd, Antonio. *Latin American Identity and the African Diaspora: Ethnogenesis in Context*. Amherst, NY: Cambria Press, 2010.

Ortíz, María Elena. "A Future Yet to Be Unfolded." In *Firelei Báez: Bloodlines*. Miami: Pérez Art Museum Miami, 2015.

Oso Casas, Laura. "Dominican Women, Heads of Households in Spain." In *Caribbean Migration to Western Europe and the United States: Essays on Incorporation, Identity, and Citizenship*, edited by Margarita Cervantes-Rodríguez, Ramón Grosfoguel, and Eric Mielants, 208–231. Philadelphia: Temple University Press, 2009.

Ostman, Heather. *The Fiction of Junot Díaz: Reframing the Lens*. Lanham, MD: Rowman and Littlefield, 2017.

Ostry, Jonathan D., Prakash Loungani, and Davide Furceri. "Neoliberalism: Oversold?" In *Finance and Development* 53, no. 2 (June 2016). Accessed November 24, 2016. www.imf.org.

Padilla, Mark. *Caribbean Pleasure Industry: Tourism, Sexuality and AIDS in the Dominican Republic*. Chicago: University of Chicago Press, 2007.

Palmer, Mariano Riera. "Salomé Ureña." *La cuna de América* 1, no. 14 (1903): 112.

Paravisini-Gebert, Lizabeth. "Salomé Ureña de Henríquez (1850–1897): Dominican Republic." In *Spanish American Women Writers: A Bio-Bibliographical Source Book*, edited by Diane E. Marting, 522–553. New York: Greenwood Press, 1990.

Paravisini-Gebert, Lizabeth, and Eva Woods Peiró. "Porfirio Rubirosa: Masculinity, Race, and the Jet-Setting Latin Male." In *Latin American Icons: Fame across Borders*, edited by Dianna C. Niebylski and Patrick O'Connor. Nashville: Vanderbilt University Press, 2014.

Patterson, Tiffany R., and Robin D. G. Kelley. "Unfinished Migrations: Reflections on the African Diaspora and the Making of the Modern World." *African Studies Review* 43, no. 1 (2000): 11–45. www.jstor.org/stable/524719.

Paulino, Edward. *Dividing Hispaniola: The Dominican Republic's Border Campaign against Haiti, 1930–1961*. Pittsburgh: University of Pittsburg Press, 2016.

Peluffo, Ana, and Ignacio M. Sánchez Prado, eds. *Entre hombres: Masculinidades del siglo XIX en América Latina*. Madrid: Iberoamericana, 2010.

Peña Pastor, Freddy. "Memoria Artística a Tony Seval." YouTube video, 7:21. May 29, 2013. www.youtube.com/watch?v=EQgq7SO2kjs.

Perdomo, Virginia. "Yo amo mi pajón." *Acento*, January 29, 2016. http://acento.com.do.

Pérez Rosario, Vanessa. *Becoming Julia de Burgos: The Making of a Puerto Rican Icon*. Urbana: University of Illinois Press, 2014.

———, ed. *Hispanic Caribbean Literature of Migration: Narratives of Displacement*. New York: Palgrave Macmillan, 2010.

Pessar, Patricia R. *A Visa for a Dream: Dominicans in the United States*. Boston: Allyn and Bacon, 1995.

Pinto, Samantha. *Difficult Diasporas: The Transnational Feminist Aesthetic of the Black Atlantic*. New York: New York University Press, 2013.

Ponce-Vázquez, Juan José. "Unequal Partners in Crime: Masters, Slaves and Free People of Color in Santo Domingo, c. 1600–1650." *Slavery & Abolition* 37, no. 4 (2016): 704–723. doi:10.1080/0144039X.2016.1174451.

Pratt, Mary Louise. "Fieldwork in Common Places." In *Writing Culture: The Poetics and Politics of Ethnography*, edited by James Clifford and George E. Marcus, 27–50. Berkeley: University of California Press, 1986.

———. *Imperial Eyes: Travel Writing and Transculturation*. New York: Routledge, 1992.

———. "Women, Literature, and National Brotherhood." In *Women, Culture, and Politics in Latin America*, compiled by the Seminar on Feminism and Culture in Latin America. Berkeley: University of California Press, 1990.

Quijano, Aníbal. "Coloniality of Power, Eurocentrism, and Latin America." *Nepantla: Views from South* 1, no. 3 (2000): 533–580.

Ramírez, Dixa. "Forced Intimacies and Murky Genealogies: Émile Ollivier's Mère-Solitude and Marisela Rizik's El tiempo del olvido." *Comparative Literature* 67, no. 2 (2015): 207–227. doi:10.1215/00104124-2890977.

———. "Great Men's Magic: Charting Hyper-Masculinity and Supernatural Discourses of Power in Junot Díaz's *The Brief Wondrous Life of Oscar Wao*." *Atlantic Studies Journal* 10, no. 3 (2013): 384–405.

———. "Por un patriotismo que no se base en el odio ni en la exclusion." *Acento*, December 14, 2013. www.acento.com.do.

———. "Salomé Ureña's Blurred Edges: Race, Gender, and Commemoration in the Dominican Republic." *Black Scholar: Journal of Black Studies and Research* 45, no. 2 (2015): 45–56. doi:10.1080/00064246.2015.1012998.

Reid-Dove, Alastair. "Waiting for Columbus." *New Yorker*, February 24, 1992, 57–75.

"República Dominicana vendida como destino sexual." YouTube video, 5:09. Posted by Cachica.com, July 24, 2011. https://www.youtube.com/watch?v=8IofmfbhnOQ.

Reyes-Santos, Alaí. *Our Caribbean Kin: Race and Nation in the Neoliberal Antilles*. New Brunswick, NJ: Rutgers University Press, 2015.

Ricourt, Milagros. "From Mamá Tingó to Globalization: Dominican Peasant Women." *Women's Studies Review*. Lehman College, CUNY, 2003.

Rien mis labios . . . llora mi alma. Santo Domingo: Movimiento de Mujeres Unidas (MODEMU), 2013.

Rivera-Rideau, Petra. *Remixing Reggaetón: The Cultural Politics of Race in Puerto Rico*. Durham: Duke University Press, 2015.

Roach, Joseph. *Cities of the Dead: Circum-Atlantic Performance*. New York: Columbia University Press, 1996.

Robles, Frances. "Black Denial." *Miami Herald*, June 13, 2007. http://media.miamiherald.com.

Rodríguez, Néstor. *La isla y su envés: Representaciones de lo nacional en el ensayo dominicano contemporáneo*. San Juan: Editorial Instituto de Cultura Puertoriqueña, 2003.

Rodríguez Demorizi, Emilio. *Poesía popular dominicana*. [Santo Domingo]: Editorial "La Nación," 1938.

——, ed. *Salomé Ureña y el Instituto de Señoritas: Para la historia de la espiritualidad dominicana*. Ciudad Trujillo: Impresora Dominicana, 1960.

Rodríguez Demorizi, Silveria R. de. *Salomé Ureña de Henríquez*. Buenos Aires: Imprenta López, 1944.

Rodríguez Juliá, Edgardo. *Caribeños*. San Juan: Editorial del Instituto de Cultura Puertorriqueña, 2002.

Rohter, Larry. "In the Language of Romance, Romeo Santos Is a True Superstar." *New York Times*, July 10, 2014. www.nytimes.com.

"Rolos & Icons Posters." www.peraltaproject.com. Accessed April 1, 2017.

Roorda, Eric Paul. *The Dictator Next Door: The Good Neighbor Policy and the Trujillo Regime in the Dominican Republic, 1930–1945*. Durham: Duke University Press, 1998.

Roorda, Eric Paul, Lauren Derby, and Raymundo González, eds. *The Dominican Republic Reader*. Durham: Duke University Press, 2014.

Rosenfeld, Michael J. "Goodbye Columbus: Dominicans and the 'Wall of Shame.'" *Nation*, February 24, 1992, 231–235.

Roth, Wendy D. *Race Migrations: Latinos and the Cultural Transformation of Race*. Stanford: Stanford University Press, 2012.

Rubirosa, Porfirio. *Mi vida como Playboy*. Santo Domingo: Letra Gráfica, 2008.

Sagás, Ernesto. *Race and Politics in the Dominican Republic*. Gainesville: University Press of Florida, 2002.

Sagás, Ernesto, and Orlando Inoa, eds. *The Dominican People: A Documentary History*. Princeton: Markus Weiner Publishers, 2003.

Sagás, Ernesto, and Sintia Molina. *Dominican Migration: Transnational Perspectives*. Gainesville: University Press of Florida, 2004.

Saldívar, José David. *Junot Díaz: On the Half-Life of Love*. Durham: Duke University Press, forthcoming.

——. *Trans-Americanity: Subaltern Modernities, Global Coloniality, and the Cultures of Greater Mexico*. Durham: Duke University Press, 2011.

San Miguel, Pedro L. *El pasado relegado: Estudios sobre la historia agraria dominicana*. Santo Domingo: Editorial Libreria La Trinitaria, FLACSO, 1999.

——. *The Imagined Island: History, Identity, and Utopia in Hispaniola*. Chapel Hill: University of North Carolina Press, 2005.

——. *La guerra silenciosa: Las luchas sociales en la ruralía dominicana*. México, DF: Instituto de Investigaciones Dr José María Luis Mora, 2004.

Sassen, Saskia. *Globalization and Its Discontents*. New York: New Press, 1998.

——. *Guests and Aliens*. New York: New Press, 2000.

Schafer, Peter Brian. "Collection Photographer Interview: Peter Brian Schafer." World Photography Organisation. Feb. 21, 2014. www.worldphoto.org.

——. "Diary of a Sex Tourist." *Vantage*, August 4, 2015. https://medium.com.

——. *Whores and Madonnas*. https://www.lensculture.com.

Schmidt Camacho, Alicia. "Ciudadana X: Gender Violence and the Denationalization of Women's Rights in Ciudad Juárez, Mexico." *CR: The New Centennial Review* 5, no. 1 (2005): 255–292. doi:10.1353/ncr.2005.0030.

———. *Migrant Imaginaries: Latino Cultural Politics in the U.S.-Mexico Borderlands.* New York: New York University Press, 2008.

Schmidt-Nowara, Christopher. *The Conquest of History: Spanish Colonialism and National Histories in the Nineteenth Century.* Pittsburgh: University of Pittsburgh Press, 2006.

Schneider, Suzanne. "Louis Agassiz and the American School of Ethnoeroticism: Polygenesis, Pornography, and Other 'Perfidious Influences.'" In *Pictures and Progress: Early Photography and the Making of African American Identity,* edited by Maurice O. Wallace and Shawn Michelle Smith, 211–243. Durham: Duke University Press, 2012.

Scott, David J. *Conscripts of Modernity: The Tragedy of Colonial Enlightenment.* Durham: Duke University Press, 2004.

Scott, Julius Sherrard. "The Common Wind: Currents of Afro-American Communication in the Era of the Haitian Revolution." PhD diss., University of Michigan, 1986.

Shamz. "Large Up Exclusive: Now Things—Maluca Mala." Accessed April 1, 2017. www.okayplayer.com.

Sharpe, Jenny. *Ghosts of Slavery: A Literary Archaeology of Black Women's Lives.* Minneapolis: University of Minnesota Press, 2003.

Sheller, Mimi. *Citizenship from Below: Erotic Agency and Caribbean Freedom.* Durham: Duke University Press, 2012.

———. "Work That Body: Sexual Citizenship and Embodied Freedom," Chapter 14 in *Constructing Vernacular Culture in the Trans-Caribbean,* edited by Holger Henke and Karl-Heinz Magister. Lanham, MD: Lexington Books, 2008.

Shepherd, Verene, Bridget Brereton, and Barbara Bailey, eds. *Engendering History: Caribbean Women in Historical Perspective.* New York: St. Martin's Press, 1995.

Silié, Rubén. "El hato y el conuco: Contexto para el surgimiento de la cultura criolla." In *Ensayos sobre cultura dominicana,* edited by Bernardo Vega, Carlos Dobal, Carlos Esteban Deive, Rubén Silié, José del Castillo, and Frank Moya Pons, 145–168. Santo Domingo: Fundación Cultural Dominicana, 1988.

Silvera, Makeda. *Silenced: Talks with Working Class Caribbean Women about Their Lives and Struggles as Domestic Workers in Canada.* Toronto: Sister Vision Press, 1989.

Simmons, Kimberly Eisen. *Reconstructing Racial Identity and the African Past in the Dominican Republic.* Gainesville: University Press of Florida, 2011.

Smith, Shawn Michelle. "'Looking at One's Self through the Eyes of Others.'" In *Pictures and Progress: Early Photography and the Making of African American Identity,* edited by Maurice O. Wallace and Shawn Michelle Smith, 274–298. Durham: Duke University Press, 2012.

Soler, Sevilla. *Santo Domingo Tierra de Frontera 1750–1800.* Seville: Escuela de Estudios Hispano-Americanos, 1980.

Sommer, Doris. *Foundational Fictions: The National Romances of Latin America.* Berkeley: University of California Press, 1993.

———. *One Master for Another: Populism as Patriarchal Rhetoric in Dominican Novels.* Lanham, MD: University Press of America, 1983.

Soto Jiménez, José Miguel. "Estima Que a Trujillo 'Hay Que Volverlo a Matar.'" *almomento*, May 27, 2011. http://almomento.net.

Soy, Rosie M. *Dominican Women across Three Generations: Educational Dreams, Goals, and Hopes*. New York: CUNY Dominican Studies Institute, 2008.

Stanley, Avelino. Personal interview by author. August 25, 2006.

Stephens, Michelle. "What Is This Black in the Black Diaspora?" *Small Axe* 29 (June 2009): 26–38. doi:10.1215/02705346-2009-004.

Stevens-Acevedo, Anthony. Personal interview by author. October 23, 2009.

Stinchcomb, Dawn. *The Development of Literary Blackness in the Dominican Republic*. Gainesville: University Press of Florida, 2004.

Stopelman, Francis. *Quisqueya: Umbral de América/Threshold of the Americas*. Bergen op Zoom: Nederlandsche Rotogravure Maatschappij.

Suárez, Lucía M. *The Tears of Hispaniola: Haitian and Dominican Diaspora Memory*. Gainesville: University Press of Florida, 2006.

Suárez Findlay, Eileen J. *Imposing Decency: The Politics of Sexuality and Race in Puerto Rico, 1870–1920*. Durham: Duke University Press, 2000.

Sugar. Directed by Anna Boden and Ryan Fleck. 2008. Sony Pictures Home Entertainment, 2009. DVD.

Sundquist, Eric J. *To Wake the Nations: Race in the Making of American Literature*. Cambridge: Harvard University Press, 1993.

Tallaj, Angelina. "'A Country That Ain't Really Belong to Me': Dominicanyorks, Identity and Popular Music." *phoebe* 18, no. 2 (2006): 17–30.

Tango Negro: The African Roots of Tango. Directed by Dom Pedro. 2013.

Taylor, Diana. *The Archive and the Repertoire: Performing Cultural Memory in the Americas*. Durham: Duke University Press, 2003.

Tejeda, Darío. Personal interview by author. August 30, 2006.

Thompson, Krista A. *An Eye for the Tropics: Tourism, Photography, and Framing the Caribbean Picturesque*. Durham: Duke University Press, 2007.

Tillman, Ellen D. *Dollar Diplomacy by Force: Nation-Building and Resistance in the Dominican Republic*. Chapel Hill: University of North Carolina Press, 2016.

Torres-Saillant, Silvio. *Caribbean Poetics: Toward an Aesthetic of West Indian Literature*. Cambridge: Cambridge University Press, 1997.

———. *Diasporic Disquisitions: Dominicanists, Transnationalism, and the Community*. New York: CUNY Dominican Studies Institute, 2000.

———. *El retorno de las yolas: Ensayos sobre diáspora, democracia y dominicanidad*. Santo Domingo: Editora Manatí, 1999.

———. "The Tribulations of Blackness: Stages in Dominican Racial Identity." *Callaloo* 23, no. 3 (Summer 2000): 1086–1111. http://www.jstor.org/stable/3299726.

Torres-Saillant, Silvio, and Ramona Hernández. *The Dominican Americans*. Westport, CT: Greenwood Press, 1998.

Trinidad, Junior. "Viuda de Tony Seval rompe silencio tras 28 años de su muerte." *Objetivo 5*. YouTube video, 6:14. Posted by Cachica.com, October 28, 2013. www.youtube.com/watch?v=19FpuGZeE00.

Trouillot, Michel-Rolph. *Silencing the Past: Power and the Production of History.* Boston: Beacon Press, 1995.

Trujillo, Flor de Oro. "My Tormented Life as Trujillo's Daughter." 1965. In *Trujillo en la intimidad según su hija Flor,* translated by Paula Vega Guerra, edited by Bernardo Vega. Santo Domingo: Fundación Cultural Dominicana, 2009.

Turits, Richard Lee. *Foundations of Despotism: Peasants, the Trujillo Regime, and Modernity in Dominican History.* Stanford: Stanford University Press, 2003.

Ugarte, María. *Estampas coloniales: Siglos XVII-XVIII-XIX.* Vol. 2. Santo Domingo: Comisión Permanente de la Feria Nacional del Libro, 1998.

Ulysse, Gina. "Uptown Ladies and Downtown Women: Female Representations of Class and Color in Jamaica." In *Representations of Blackness and the Performance of Identities,* edited by Jean Muteba Rahier, 147–172. Westport, CT: Bergin and Garvey, 1999.

———. "Why Representations of Haiti Matter Now More Than Ever." *NACLA Report on the Americas* 43, no. 4 (July–August 2010): 37–43. https://search.proquest.com.

Ureña de Henríquez, Salomé. *Poemas y biografía de Salomé Ureña.* Edited by Castro Burdiez. Santo Domingo: Fundación para la Educación y el Arte, 2006.

———. *Poesías completas.* 9th ed. Santo Domingo: Editora de Colores, 1997.

Ureña de Henríquez, Salomé, et al. *100 Años de Poesía: Homenaje a Salomé Ureña.* Santo Domingo: Universidad Autónoma de Santo Domingo, 1999.

Valerio-Holguín, Fernando. "Salomé Ureña de Henríquez (1850–1897)." In *Hijas del Muntu: Biografías críticas de mujeres afrodescendientes de América Latina,* edited by María Mercedes Jaramillo and Lucía Ortiz, 520–529. Bogotá: Panamericana Editorial, 2011.

Vallejo, Catharina. *Las madres de la patria y las bellas mentiras: Imágenes de la mujer en el discurso literario nacional de la República Dominicana, 1844–1899.* Miami: Ediciones Universal, 1999.

Vargas, Deborah R. "Ruminations on *Lo Sucio* as a Latino Queer Analytic." *American Quarterly* 66, no. 3 (September 2014): 715–726. doi:10.1353/aq.2014.0046.

Vargas Llosa, Mario. *The Feast of the Goat.* New York: Farrar, Straus and Giroux, 2001.

Vázquez, Alexandra T. "Salon Philosophers: Ivy Queen and Surprise Guests Take Reggaetón Aside." In *Reggaeton,* edited by Raquel Z. Rivera, Wayne Marshall, and Deborah Pacini Hernández, 300–311. Durham: Duke University Press, 2009.

Vicioso, Sherezada (Chiqui). "Dominicanyorkness: A Metropolitan Discovery of the Triangle." In *Caribbean Creolization: Reflections on the Cultural Dynamics of Language, Literature, and Identity,* translated by Maria Cristina Canales, edited by Kathleen M. Balutansky and Marie-Agnès Sourieau, 62–66. Gainesville: University Press of Florida, 1998.

———. "Indias and Trigueñas No Longer: Contemporary Women Poets Speak." In *Documents of Dissidence: Selected Writings by Dominican Women,* edited by Daisy Cocco De Filippis, 142–161. New York: CUNY Dominican Studies Institute, 2000.

———. Personal interview by author. July 10, 2009.

———. "Re: Entrevista." E-mail message to author. October 4, 2006.

——. "Re: Pregunta acerca de Salomé." E-mail message to author. December 7, 2009.

——. *Salomé U.: Cartas a una ausencia*. Santo Domingo: Editora Búho, 2001.

Vicioso, Sherezada, and Salomé Ureña de Henríquez. *Salomé Ureña de Henríquez (1850–1897): A cien años de un magisterio*. Santo Domingo: Comisión Permanente de la Feria Nacional del Libro, 1997.

Walcott, Derek. *The Antilles: Fragments of Epic Memory*. New York: Farrar, Straus and Giroux, 1992.

Warmund, Joshua H. "Removing Drug Lords and Street Pushers: The Extradition of Nationals in Colombia and the Dominican Republic." *Fordham International Law Journal* 22, no. 5 (1998). http://ir.lawnet.fordham.edu.

Wexler, Laura. *Tender Violence: Domestic Visions in an Age of U.S. Imperialism*. Chapel Hill: University of North Carolina Press, 2000.

Weyland, Karin. "Producción de conocimiento y el discurso colonial a través de la fotografía en el Caribe Hispánico, 1898–1940." *Ciencia y Sociedad* 29, no. 4 (2004): 754–778.

"What Is a Lola?" YouTube video, 2:37. Posted by MalucaWepa, August 30, 2011. www.youtube.com/watch?v=NUXb7H3265U.

White, Deborah Gray. *Ar'n't I a Woman? Female Slaves in the Plantation South*. New York: W. W. Norton, 1999.

Whitten, Norman E., Jr., and Arlene Torres, eds. *Blackness in Latin America and the Caribbean*. 2 vols. Bloomington: Indiana University Press, 1998.

World Bank. "Dominican Republic: Overview." Updated April 10, 2017. First accessed November 24, 2016. www.worldbank.org.

Wright, Michelle M. *Becoming Black: Creating Identity in the African Diaspora*. Durham: Duke University Press, 2004.

——. *Physics of Blackness: Beyond the Middle Passage Epistemology*. Minneapolis: University of Minnesota Press, 2015.

Wynter, Sylvia. "1492: A New World View." In *Race, Discourse, and the Origin of the Americas: A New World View*, edited by Vera Lawrence Hyatt and Rex Nettleford, 5–57. Washington, DC: Smithsonian Institution Press, 1995.

——. "Towards the Sociogenic Principle: Fanon, Identity, and the Puzzle of Conscious Experience, and What It Is Like to Be 'Black.'" Chapter 2 in *National Identities and Sociopolitical Changes in Latin America*, edited by Mercedes F. Durán-Cogan and Antonio Gómez-Moriana, 30–66. New York: Routledge, 2001.

Yarbrough, Fay A. *Race and the Cherokee Nation: Sovereignty in the Nineteenth Century*. Philadelphia: University of Pennsylvania Press, 2008.

Zeller, Neici. *Discursos y espacios femeninos en República Dominicana, 1880–1961*. Santo Domingo: Editorial Letra Gráfica, 2012.

INDEX

Abbes García, Johnny, 145

Adams, John Quincy, 12

Adorno, Rolena, 116

aesthetics, 155; aesthetic labor, 78; of black Atlantic hip-hop, 174; romanticist aesthetics, 85

African diaspora, 4–5, 94. *See also* women of African diaspora

afrolatinidad, 35, 154, 168, 169, 176

Alloula, Malek, 195

Alvarez, Julia, 9, 26, 33, 79–80, 99; biography by, 102–8; critique by, 104; as ethnic minority, 102; nationalist imagery by, 109; Vicioso thanked by, 105

Amara la Negra, 34, 155–56, *166*, *168*; Dominicanness of, 168–69, 180; hair and, 169–70; women of African diaspora and, 165–71

ambivalent presence of ghosts, 3

Amigos del País, 36–37, 51

Al amor del bohío (Jiménez), 142–43

"Amor y anhelo" (Ureña), 69–71, 95

"Anacaona" (Ureña), 41, 44

Andrades, Tony, 169

Angulo Guridi, Francisco Javier, 10

antiblackness, 135; Balaguer and, 33; institutional, 78, 253n6; Trujillo and, 33

antisurveillance, 221

Appadurai, Arjun, 203, 211

archives, 19; for El Alfa, 113; cultural, 168; first written, 20; silencing in, 11; subaltern subjects and, 223, 225; for Ureña, 50, 76, 97; women in, 240n94; World Sex, 203–4

Arias, Aurora, 34, 200–204, 206, 212

Aybar o Rodríguez, Manuela, 93, 243n10

bachata, 9, 27, 212

Báez, Firelei, 28–29, *30*, 31, *31*

Báez, Josefina, 269n23

baká, 131, 132

Balaguer, Joaquín, 46–47, 55, 83–84, 88, 142–43; as antiblack, 33; Columbus Lighthouse Memorial and, 117–18, 120–22; government of, 24, 151; henchmen of, 135; magic and, 130; presidencies of, 113; sadism of, 145; self-promotion of, 126; vision of, 125

Batista, Celsa Albert, 10, 20

Baud, Michiel, 40–41

Beck, R. H., *19*

Behn, Aphra, 193

Benigno Pérez, Federico, 49

Benítez Rojo, Antonio, 4

"Benito Cereno" (Melville), 1–2, 226, 235n27

Bergland, Renée, 6

Berlin, Ira, 4

Bermúdez, Luis A., 50

Bernstein, Robin, 43

Bhabha, Homi, 106

biography, 82; by Alvarez, 102–7; commemoration in, 78; of Ureña, 95–97, 102–7

Black and Latino, 174

black Atlantic hip-hop, 174

Black Code (Código Negro Carolino), 18

black consciousness, 135, 154, 156

black denial, 4, 82, 158; hair and, 176

ABOUT THE AUTHOR

Dixa Ramírez is Assistant Professor of American Studies and Ethnicity, Race, and Migration at Yale University.

CPSIA information can be obtained
at www.ICGtesting.com
Printed in the USA
JSHW041908090921
18587JS00001B/60

9 781479 867561